THE
BILL JAMES
GOLD MINE
2008

THE BILL JAMES GOLD MINE 2008

by Bill James

ACTA SPORTS

The Bill James Gold Mine 2008
by Bill James

Edited by John Dewan and Gregory F. Augustine Pierce
Cover Design by Tom A. Wright
Text Design and Typesetting by Patricia A. Lynch

Published by ACTA Sports, a division of ACTA Publications
5559 W. Howard Street, Skokie, IL 60077
800-397-2282 www.actasports.com info@actasports.com

Printed in the United States of America by Hess Print Solutions

ISBN: 978-0-87946-320-5
ISSN: 1940-7998
Year: 12 11 10 09 08
Printing: 5 4 3 2 First

CONTENTS

'Knowledgements / 7

I Dunno / 9

Arizona Diamondbacks / 11

Atlanta Braves / 19

Baltimore Orioles / 25

Comp List / 31

Boston Red Sox / 35

Three to Five Run Records / 41

Chicago Cubs / 45

Chicago White Sox / 53

Cincinnati Reds / 61

The Targeting Phenomenon / 67

Cigar Points / 73

Cleveland Indians / 79

Colorado Rockies / 85

Clutch Hitter of the Year / 93

Detroit Tigers / 97

Atypical Seasons / 103

Florida Marlins / 107

Houston Astros / 113

The Turk Farrell Award / 121

Kansas City Royals / 127

Los Angeles Angels / 133

The Nolan Ryan Award / 141

Los Angeles Dodgers / 145

Milwaukee Brewers / 151

Measuring Consistency / 159

Minnesota Twins / 171

New York Mets / 177

End Game / 183

New York Yankees / 187

Closer Fatigue / 193

Oakland Athletics / 197

Philadelphia Phillies / 203

Strength Up the Middle / 213

Pittsburgh Pirates / 219

St. Louis Cardinals / 223

Bullpens and Crunches / 229

San Diego Padres / 237

San Francisco Giants / 247

Hall of Famers Among Us / 253

Seattle Mariners / 265

Tampa Bay Rays / 271

Texas Rangers / 277

Herbie / 287

Toronto Blue Jays / 291

Washington Nationals / 299

Medley / 305

'Knowledgements

by Bill James

In the modern world the active participation of at least 200 companies is required to get your teeth brushed. This is not a comedic overstatement; it's actually, I am certain, a dramatic undercount. You've got your toothpaste, your toothbrush, and your teeth.

Your toothpaste, which you probably bought from the grocery store, Walgreens, Walmart, CVS or your local auto parts commissary, is the least complicated part. The toothpaste company bought their supplies from 25 or 225 other companies, which bought their supplies mostly from an Indian guy named Bharat, and then mixed them up and put them in little square boxes made by some other company and sold them to whoever sold them to the grocery store or whatever.

Your toothbrush, on the other hand...if you are like me you have finally yielded to the threats and insinuations or your dental practitioner/incisor warden/part-time tire salesman, and started using one of them electronic tooth machines that hums like a rusty amplifier and sends an e-mail to your mother if you stop brushing in less than 90 seconds per quadrant. God only knows how many companies were involved in producing that baby, and, if you are my age, even God doesn't have any idea where some of your teeth came from.

I couldn't begin to estimate how many small and large companies I work for and work with in this modern world, or how many people were directly or indirectly involved in producing this here Gold Mine. *The Bill James Gold Mine 2008* was the work essentially of eight people—myself, John Dewan, Greg Pierce, Tony Pellegrino, Pat Quinn, Patricia Lynch, Mat Olkin and Mike Webber.

"Myself" would be Bill James.

John Dewan is my partner in the Bill James Online (which is a company—Be Jolly, Inc., the name derived from BJOL). John was more or less the Producer of this book, the man who brought the elements together, not only in grand design but in patient detail, day by day, goal by goal.

> *This book consists of thousands of little pieces, sort of like your toothbrush, and there were more little pieces that we threw away than there were that we put into the book.*

Greg Pierce is John's partner in another company, ACTA Publications, or...wait a minute, is it ACTA Publications or ACTA Sports Publications? Or is ACTA Sports merely an imprint of ACTA Publications? You probably don't care, do you?

Greg was the publisher of this book...the Director of the movie, so to speak. He was a very active publisher and editor, reading every article, offering helpful suggestions and accepting gratuitous gruffness from the authors with such good humor that it almost ceased to be a challenge. He read all of the articles in the Bill James Online, a task I wouldn't wish on a demented divorce lawyer, and selected those that were suitable for the book, and handled every other task that came along and needed someone to look after it.

Pat Quinn works for John Dewan in...well, one of John's companies. I think he's theoretically an employee of Baseball Info Solutions. Anyway, this book consists of thousands of little pieces, sort of like your toothbrush, and there were more little pieces that we threw away than there were that we put into the book. Pat oversaw the process of keeping track of the pieces, keeping track of the schedules, keeping track of what we needed more of and what we needed less of, and also contributed his own thoughts and his own research to the book.

Tony Pellegrino is a programmer. He did the actual work of taking many of the "profiles" from the concept stage to the useful stage. He works for Be Jolly by way of BIS, Baseball Info Solutions, a company which has all of the raw information in the world about baseball.

Patricia Lynch is a book designer and page designer. Unless you is an author you can't really imagine what a vital function this is. Back when I was young and nasty, an essential step in the completion of every book that I wrote was the week when I would write a long, bloodcurdling memo to whatever hapless moron the publishing company had hired to design the Baseball Abstract for that season; you may think I'm exaggerating, but I assure you, I can call witnesses. We got through the design process for this book without a single confrontation, in part because I am older and calmer than I used to be, but in the main because Patricia Lynch is marvelous at her job, and actually takes seriously stuff like making the book look good, selecting the right type and the right border, making the spatial arrangements of a chart reflect the content of the chart, making the look of a two-paragraph note appropriate to the subject, and drawing the reader's eye into the text.

Mat Olkin did research for the book, helping John and I find what we called nuggets, which are little items of interest which are buried somewhere in the flint-hard mountains of data that is the Bill James Online. Mat was also extremely useful to us as a proofreader and fact checker...as, by the way, was Pat Quinn. And John Dewan. And Charles Fiore. And Greg Pierce. And Jon Vrecsics. When you make as many mistakes as I do, it takes a lot of people to catch them all.

Mike Webber also did research, mining nuggets from the mountains of Kansas, and offering his suggestions. Those eight of us were the core working group for the book, and, in all sincerity, I really can't tell you what a great joy it was to work with this group; this may not be the book that the old Abstracts were because I am not the writer that I was twenty-five years ago, but the pro-

cess of producing the book, compared to the draining, life-wrecking and infuriating madness of the Abstracts... or not even compared to that, but compared to more normal work experiences...I tell you honestly that it was just a delight. Which I guess means that it was hard on other people, rather than being hard on me, but from my standpoint, it was a wonderful thing.

There are a lot of other people here to be thanked. Steve Moyer, President of Baseball Info Solutions, for presiding over the assemblage of information that feeds the Bill James Online. Damon Lichtenwalner, programmer for BIS, who also designed many of the charts and calculated many of the decimal points that are in this book. Andrew Yankech and Charles Fiore, from the production/marketing arm of ACTA, who were good enough to care about this book. Tom Wright, who designed the cover. My wife and kids, for putting...oh, hell, everybody's got a wife and kids; if we get into that we'll be here forever. Retrosheet. Jim Swavely. Todd Radcliffe. Dan Casey. Dwight Schrute.

I thank you all for reading, and, since you were patient enough to actually read the Acknowledgements, I will tell you the secret of happiness. The secret of happiness is to build a circle of love around yourself. This book is a product of a circle, a wonderful circle of friends who enjoyed what we had to do and hope you get something out of reading it.

My wife and kids, for putting...oh, hell, everybody's got a wife and kids; if we get into that we'll be here forever.

I Dunno

by Bill James

Sometimes there is value in looking at data that you don't understand—or, if not, perhaps at least it is interesting. For the Bill James Online and this book we have generated a few elements of each team's batting and pitching record (a) in the games they won, and (b) in the games they lost. From this we learn, for example, that the Seattle Mariners were the only major league team to hit .250 in the games they lost (they hit .252), and that the Washington Nationals were the only major league team which failed to out-homer their opponents even in the games they won (they hit 75 homers and gave up 75). They OUT-SCORED their opponents in games they won, of course; that is true by definition. They outscored their opponents in games they won, 442-241—but didn't outhomer them at all. The Pittsburgh Pirates, in the games they won, had almost the same batting average, on-base percentage and slugging percentage as George Brett, whereas in the games they lost they had almost the same averages as Coco Laboy.

What does any of this mean? Frankly, we don't have a clue. Of course, many people are going to look at it like "that data is completely meaningless", because they don't know what it means. I look at it a little differently. I look at it like "Hey, this will be fun, trying to figure out why this data breaks the way it does." The fact that we don't understand the data, of course, does not really indicate that the data is useless. It merely indicates that it is yet to be deciphered.

As a starting point, take the major league norms for batting average, on-base percentage and slugging percentage. It appears that every team is above all of those norms in the games they win, and every team is below them in the games they lose. The Mariners had the highest batting average in losses (.252); the Padres had the lowest batting average in wins (.279). The Red Sox had the highest on-base percentage in losses (.313); the Padres, Diamondbacks and Blue Jays had the lowest on-base percentage in wins (.355). Milwaukee had the highest slugging percentage in losses (.384); the Giants had the lowest slugging percentage in wins (.454).

We've discovered the island of lost baseball statistics. Now we'll start working on a map.

The teams, then, sit astride the league averages like a man on a horse, with one leg on each side—always. You didn't know that ten minutes ago, did you? See; we're learning something from doing this.

One pattern is fairly apparent. The teams like the Padres and Blue Jays, which have suspect offenses but great pitching, have the least impressive batting records in games they win. That makes sense, because these teams are able to win even when they don't hit much. But many patterns, frankly, are anything but apparent. Why do the Brewers have a higher slugging percentage when they lose than the Yankees do? Can you explain that? The Yankees have phenomenal batting numbers when they win—easily the best in the majors—but averages that look exactly like everybody else's when they lose. Why is that?

One way of explaining some things is that teams excel, in losses, at whatever they specialize in. Whatever you're best at, that's what you do even when you lose. The Brewers aren't a particularly good team, but they've got power. The Red Sox specialize in getting people on base, so, even when they lose, they get people on base.

In three or four years, I think, we'll look at a lot of this data and say "Oh, yes, of course." But right now, it's head-scratching material. The Tampa Bay Devil Rays (yes, I know they are now merely the Rays, but at the time they were devilish) have almost exactly the same batting averages in games they win as do the Texas Rangers—Tampa Bay .313/.382/.523, and Texas .313/383/.522. But Tampa Bay's hitting numbers were far better when they lost—an OPS 51 points higher. Why?

I don't know. We'll figure it out, I guess. That's sort of the idea of the book: let's look at everything from a different angle, and figure out what we don't know, what we don't understand. We've discovered the island of lost baseball statistics. Now we'll start working on a map.

Arizona Diamondbacks

Arizona Diamondbacks – 2007
Team Overview

Description		Ranking
Won-Lost Record	90-72	
Place	1st of 5 in National League West	
Runs Scored	712	26th in the majors
Runs Allowed	732	10th in the majors
Home Runs	171	13th in the majors
Home Runs Allowed	169	19th in the majors
Batting Average	.250	29th in the majors
Batting Average Allowed	.262	9th in the majors
Walks Drawn	532	14th in the majors
Walks Given	546	18th in the majors
OPS For	.734	24th in the majors
OPS Against	.753	12th in the majors
Stolen Bases	109	10th in the majors
Stolen Bases Allowed	88	10th in the majors

Key Players

Pos	Player	G	AB	R	H	2B	3B	HR	RBI	SB	CS	BB	SO	Avg	OBP	Slg	OPS	WS
C	Chris Snyder	110	326	37	82	20	0	13	47	0	1	40	67	.252	.342	.433	.775	16
1B	Conor Jackson	130	415	56	118	29	1	15	60	2	2	53	50	.284	.368	.467	.836	13
2B	Orlando Hudson	139	517	69	152	28	9	10	63	10	2	70	87	.294	.376	.441	.817	21
3B	Mark Reynolds	111	366	62	102	20	4	17	62	0	1	37	129	.279	.349	.495	.843	14
SS	Stephen Drew	150	543	60	129	28	4	12	60	9	0	60	100	.238	.313	.370	.683	16
LF	Eric Byrnes	160	626	103	179	30	8	21	83	50	7	57	98	.286	.353	.460	.813	24
CF	Chris Young	148	569	85	135	29	3	32	68	27	6	43	141	.237	.295	.467	.763	14
RF	Carlos Quentin	81	229	29	49	16	0	5	31	2	2	18	54	.214	.298	.349	.647	5

Key Pitchers

Pos	Player	G	GS	W	L	Sv	IP	H	R	ER	BB	SO	BR/9	ERA	WS
SP	Brandon Webb	34	34	18	10	0	236.1	209	91	79	72	194	10.89	3.01	22
SP	Doug Davis	33	33	13	12	0	192.2	211	100	91	95	144	14.53	4.25	11
SP	Livan Hernandez	33	33	11	11	0	204.1	247	116	112	79	90	14.62	4.93	10
SP	Micah Owings	29	27	8	8	0	152.2	146	81	73	50	106	12.38	4.30	13
SP	Edgar Gonzalez	32	12	8	4	0	102.0	110	61	57	28	62	12.53	5.03	5
CL	Jose Valverde	65	0	1	4	47	64.1	46	21	19	26	78	10.49	2.66	14
RP	Brandon Lyon	73	0	6	4	2	74.0	70	25	22	22	40	11.31	2.68	11
RP	Tony Pena	75	0	5	4	2	85.1	63	36	31	31	63	10.44	3.27	11

Micah

As a freshman at Georgia Tech in 2003 Micah Owings led the team in home runs with 15—not bad when you consider that one of his teammates was Cubs' outfielder Matt Murton, who hit 13. Micah also went 9-3 on the mound, and, to prove it wasn't a fluke, went 9-3 again as a sophomore, belting another team-leading 15 home runs and driving in 64 runs, two behind the team leader. Those were good teams; the Ramblin' Wreck went 17-7 in the ACC in 2003, 18-5 in 2004. For some reason Owings transferred to Tulane in 2005, where he went 12-4 and also led the team in homers (18), RBI (63) and batting average (.355), lifting the team into the College World Series in Omaha.

Some people wanted to draft him as a hitter, some people wanted to draft him as a pitcher, and some people wanted to draft him to sell him to the Yankees to pay for a revival of "No, No, Nanette." The Diamondbacks drafted him and decided to put him on the mound. He's been pretty good, blowing through the minors with three losses—he was 10-0 in Triple-A—but it's still not clear whether they made the right decision, as, in the minors, he also hit .371.

As a rookie last year he hit only .333, but it was mostly power; 12 of his 20 hits were for extra bases. He drove in 15 runs, the most by a major league pitcher since 1983, with the sole exception of one year when Mike Hampton drove in 16, but Owings was able to do it without breaking or tearing anything in his body. His .683 slugging percentage was 49 points higher than the league leader.

Few pitchers have been able to sustain that kind of performance with the bat because

a) they don't get regular enough at bats, and
b) they're not really that good.

Is there a point at which the Diamondbacks would consider putting Owings in the lineup every day? Probably not; over the last two months he also made ten starts, striking out 45 hitters, walking 13 and posting a 3.02 ERA. He finished the season with a string of 15 shutout innings, although he was shelled, shellacked, pummeled and horsewhipped by the Rockies in his one post-season appearance. It's been a long time since a player tried to go both ways at the major league level; even the immortal Rick Ankiel could only handle one job at a time. Michah's future is probably on the mound. But if it doesn't work out for him…

Chris Young's 32 homers resulted in only 41 RBI. The two main reasons: 1) He batted leadoff for much of the season (which you can't blame him for); and 2) He was far less productive with men on base (which you can, but we won't).

Chris Young – 2007
RBI Analysis

Hits		RBI Hits		RBI Total		Drove In	
Home Runs:	32			RBI on Home Runs:	41	Emilio Bonifacio	1
Triples:	3	RBI Triples:	1	RBI on Triples:	2	Eric Byrnes	2
Doubles:	29	RBI Doubles:	7	RBI on Doubles:	9	Alberto Callaspo	2
Singles:	71	RBI Singles:	8	RBI on Singles:	9	Jeff Cirillo	2
				Sacrifice Flies:	5	Tony Clark	1
		Other RBI: Walks	0			Scott Hairston	3
		Other RBI: Ground Outs	0	Total Other:	2	Livan Hernandez	1
						Orlando Hudson	2
				Total RBI:	68	Conor Jackson	4
						Miguel Montero	2
						Micah Owings	1
						Yusmeiro Petit	1
						Carlos Quentin	3
						Mark Reynolds	5
						Jeff Salazar	2
						Chris Snyder	1
						Chad Tracy	2
						Justin Upton	1
						His Own Bad Self	32
						Total	68

Eric Byrnes in 2007, aged 31, doubled his previous career high in stolen bases, with 50. I was wondering whether anybody had ever done that before. Wally Moses, 1943; only guy since 1920, at least. Moses' previous career high in stolen bases was 16, but with the war on and the baseballs dead, Moses stole 56. There are a total of nine players since 1920 who have stolen 50 bases for the first time at age 30 or above, but they are mostly guys who had been regularly stealing 35 or 40. Moses is the only real parallel to Byrnes.

Eric Byrnes – 2002 - 2007
Baserunning Analysis

Year	1st to 3rd Adv	1st to 3rd Opp	2nd to Home Adv	2nd to Home Opp	1st to Home Adv	1st to Home Opp	DP Opp	GIDP	Bases Taken	BR Outs	BR Gain	SB Gain	Net Gain
2002	2	5	5	5	1	1	24	3	4	1	1	3	+4
2003	7	21	8	15	6	8	63	3	16	4	4	6	+10
2004	5	24	18	23	3	7	125	11	14	1	12	15	+27
2005	6	15	9	10	2	3	107	7	11	2	14	3	+17
2006	6	22	12	18	4	5	96	12	15	1	11	19	+30
2007	4	16	12	17	5	8	134	12	17	3	10	36	+46
Totals	30	103	64	88	21	32	549	48	77	12	52	82	+134
		29%		73%		66%		8%					

Look Quick

We couldn't catch Randy Johnson throwing a changeup last season. He threw 5% changes from 2003 to 2005, 1% in 2006, none at all—that we saw—in 2007.

Of course, what has happened to Randy isn't *essentially* that he's stopped throwing his change of pace. What's happened to him essentially is that he's gotten hurt, and also really old for a baseball player. And then, too, he's stopped throwing his change.

Randy Johnson – 2003
Pitch Type Analysis

Overall

Total Pitches	1809	
Fastball	901	50%
Curveball	1	0%
Changeup	89	5%
Slider	618	34%
Split Finger	21	1%
Not Charted	179	10%

	Vs. RHB		Vs. LHB	
Total Pitches	1530		279	
Outs Recorded	271		45	
Fastball	746	49%	155	56%
Curveball	1	0%	0	0%
Changeup	86	6%	3	1%
Slider	518	34%	100	36%
Split Finger	17	1%	4	1%
Not Charted	162	11%	17	6%

Randy Johnson – 2007
Pitch Type Analysis

Overall

Total Pitches	907	
Fastball	454	50%
Slider	324	36%
Split Finger	103	11%
Pitchout	2	0%
Not Charted	24	3%

	Vs. RHB		Vs. LHB	
Total Pitches	783		124	
Outs Recorded	142		28	
Fastball	383	49%	71	57%
Slider	277	35%	47	38%
Split Finger	98	13%	5	4%
Pitchout	2	0%	0	0%
Not Charted	23	3%	1	1%

If You Want It Done Right

Tony Clark drove himself in (with a home run) 17 times—three more times than he was driven in by all of his teammates combined.

Clark and Dave Ross were the only major leaguers in 2007 to account for over half of their runs scored by home runs (20 or more runs scored). Ryan Howard and Bengie Molina were at 50%.

The all-time percentage leader is Johnny Blanchard, 1963. Blanchard hit 16 homers—and scored 22 runs.

Tony Clark – 2007
Runs Scored Analysis

Reached on		Runs Scored After	
Home Runs	17		17
Triples	1	Scored after Triple	1
Doubles	5	Scored after Double	1
Singles	32	Scored after Single	6
Walk/HBP	21	Scored after Walk/HBP	5
Reached on Forceout	3	Vultured Runs	1
		Total Runs Scored	31

Brought in by		Driven in by	
Single	3	Himself	17
Double	7	Mark Reynolds	3
Triple	1	Stephen Drew	3
His own home run	17	Augie Ojeda	2
Sac Fly	1	Chris Snyder	1
Walk, Error, or Other	2	Chris Young	1
		Conor Jackson	1
		Eric Byrnes	1
		Scott Hairston	1
		No RBI	1

The Run Win Ratio

Arizona in 2007 scored only 136 runs in the games started by Brandon Webb—yet won 22 of those games. You can look at it this way: that's 16.2 wins per 100 runs that the pitcher had to work with.

That was the best ratio of wins per run (or wins per 100 runs of support, however you want to phrase it) in the major leagues. The top five:

1. Brandon Webb 16.2
2. John Lackey 15.8
3. Rich Hill 15.6
4. Miguel Batista 15.0
5. Erik Bedard 14.6

The least effective pitcher in the majors in this respect was Andy Sonnanstine of Tampa Bay—5.3 wins per 100 runs of support.

Arizona Diamondbacks – 2007
Performance by Starting Pitcher

Games Started By	G	RS	RA	Won	Lost
Webb, Brandon	34	136	111	22	12
Hernandez, Livan	33	144	172	16	17
Davis, Doug	33	140	145	20	13
Owings, Micah	27	138	138	14	13
Gonzalez, Edgar	12	50	51	6	6
Petit, Yusmeiro	10	34	42	4	6
Johnson, Randy	10	42	46	6	4
Kim, Byung-Hyun	2	15	20	1	1
Eveland, Dana	1	13	7	1	0
Team Totals	162	712	732	90	72

Half Brothers and Half Not

If you think about it, Livan Hernandez and his half-brother Orlando Hernandez are, in a sense, polar opposites. Livan is the ultimate innings eater—and there is great value in that. Livan takes the hill and piles up 200, 220 innings every year. He wins as many as he loses; he loses as many as he wins. Livan has made 203 starts since 2002, third-most in the majors behind Zito and Maddux, and his team is 98-105 in those 203 games. You'd like to have a staff of .600 pitchers, but very few teams do.

An average major league team gives 18 starts per season to pitchers with less than ten starts, and 48 starts per season to pitchers making 10 to 19 starts.

The overall team winning percentage for pitchers making less than 20 starts is .439; for pitchers making less than ten starts it is .411 (data covers 2002-2007). The great value in a Livan Hernandez is that he minimizes the games you have to give to those spot starters who are generally going to get you a loss.

Older brother Orlando, on the other hand, is anything *but* an innings-eater. He makes, 15, 20, 25 starts a year if you are lucky—but he wins them. Not all of them, of course, but 60% of them. Since 2002 he has made only 112 starts, but his team is 67-45 in those games.

Brandon Webb was second in the major leagues in 2007 in Ground Ball outs (309)—yet he was third on his own team in double play support! The Diamondbacks turned 20 double plays behind Webb, but 22 behind Livan Hernandez and 23 behind Doug Davis.

Why? Sometimes weird things just happen, but there are some contributing factors:

1. Davis and Hernandez walk more hitters than Webb and give up more hits, which puts more runners on base.

2. Davis and Hernandez don't get as many strikeouts as Webb, which means there are more balls in play with men on base.

3. Opposing managers fear the double play with Webb on the mound so much that they are more likely to try to run on him. There were 35 stolen base attempts against Webb last year, as opposed to 25 against Hernandez, 12 against Davis.

Brandon Webb – 2007
Batters Faced Analysis

Batters Faced	975
Reached Base	331
Retired	644
Reached Base by:	
Single	151
Double	42
Triple	4
Home Run	12
Walk	72
Hit Batsman	5
Error	12
Fielder's Choice - All Safe	3
(Fielder's Choice - Out Recorded)	(30)
Retired by:	
Strikeout	194
Ground Out	309
Line Out	27
Fly Out	101
Pop Out	13
Other	0

Doug Davis – 2007
Batters Faced Analysis

Batters Faced	862
Reached Base	341
Retired	521
Reached Base by:	
Single	146
Double	40
Triple	4
Home Run	21
Walk	95
Hit Batsman	5
Error	8
Fielder's Choice - All Safe	0
(Fielder's Choice - Out Recorded)	(22)
Retired by:	
Strikeout	143
Ground Out	194
Line Out	14
Fly Out	131
Pop Out	39
Other	0

Livan Hernandez – 2007
Batters Faced Analysis

Batters Faced	913
Reached Base	347
Retired	566
Reached Base by:	
Single	166
Double	42
Triple	5
Home Run	34
Walk	79
Hit Batsman	6
Error	3
Fielder's Choice - All Safe	0
(Fielder's Choice - Out Recorded)	(12)
Retired by:	
Strikeout	90
Ground Out	210
Line Out	14
Fly Out	203
Pop Out	49
Other	0

All 32 of Conor Jackson's career homers have gone to left field.

Conor Jackson – Career
Hitting Analysis

Batting Left-Handed							1B	2B	3B	HR
Ground Balls to Left	188	Outs	150	Hits	38	Average .202	Hit Type	30 - 8 - 0 - 0
Ground Balls to Center	101	Outs	74	Hits	27	Average .267	Hit Type	27 - 0 - 0 - 0
Ground Balls to Right	43	Outs	27	Hits	16	Average .372	Hit Type	16 - 0 - 0 - 0
Line Drives to Left	56	Outs	18	Hits	38	Average .679	Hit Type	20 - 16 - 0 - 2
Line Drives to Center	61	Outs	11	Hits	50	Average .820	Hit Type	41 - 9 - 0 - 0
Line Drives to Right	50	Outs	18	Hits	32	Average .640	Hit Type	23 - 9 - 0 - 0
Fly Balls to Left	101	Outs	62	Hits	39	Average .398	Hit Type	7 - 2 - 0 - 30
Fly Balls to Center	128	Outs	104	Hits	24	Average .197	Hit Type	11 - 12 - 1 - 0
Fly Balls to Right	134	Outs	122	Hits	12	Average .091	Hit Type	9 - 2 - 1 - 0
Total on Ground Balls	332	Outs	251	Hits	81	Average .244	Hit Type	73 - 8 - 0 - 0
Total on Line Drives	167	Outs	47	Hits	120	Average .719	Hit Type	84 - 34 - 0 - 2
Total on Fly Balls	363	Outs	288	Hits	75	Average .213	Hit Type	27 - 16 - 2 - 30
Total Hit to Left	345	Outs	230	Hits	115	Average .336	Hit Type	57 - 26 - 0 - 32
Total Hit to Center	290	Outs	189	Hits	101	Average .356	Hit Type	79 - 21 - 1 - 0
Total Hit to Right	227	Outs	167	Hits	60	Average .267	Hit Type	48 - 11 - 1 - 0
Bunts	3	Outs	3	Hits	0	Average .000	Hit Type	0 - 0 - 0 - 0
All Balls in Play	865	Outs	589	Hits	276	Average .324	Hit Type	184 - 58 - 2 - 32

Atlanta Braves

Atlanta Braves – 2007
Team Overview

Description		Ranking
Won-Lost Record	84-78	
Place	3rd of 5 in National League East	
Runs Scored	810	9th in the majors
Runs Allowed	733	11th in the majors
Home Runs	176	12th in the majors
Home Runs Allowed	172	20th in the majors
Batting Average	.275	9th in the majors
Batting Average Allowed	.259	6th in the majors
Walks Drawn	534	12th in the majors
Walks Given	537	17th in the majors
OPS For	.774	9th in the majors
OPS Against	.742	11th in the majors
Stolen Bases	64	26th in the majors
Stolen Bases Allowed	98	17th in the majors

Key Players

Pos	Player	G	AB	R	H	2B	3B	HR	RBI	SB	CS	BB	SO	Avg	OBP	Slg	OPS	WS
C	Brian McCann	139	504	51	136	38	0	18	92	0	1	35	74	.270	.320	.452	.772	15
1B	Scott Thorman	120	287	37	62	18	0	11	36	1	1	14	70	.216	.258	.394	.652	2
2B	Kelly Johnson	147	521	91	144	26	10	16	68	9	5	79	117	.276	.375	.457	.831	19
3B	Chipper Jones	134	513	108	173	42	4	29	102	5	1	82	75	.337	.425	.604	1.029	25
SS	Edgar Renteria	124	494	87	164	30	1	12	57	11	2	46	77	.332	.390	.470	.860	19
LF	Matt Diaz	135	358	44	121	21	0	12	45	4	0	16	63	.338	.368	.497	.865	11
CF	Andruw Jones	154	572	83	127	27	2	26	94	5	2	70	138	.222	.311	.413	.724	15
RF	Jeff Francoeur	162	642	84	188	40	0	19	105	5	2	42	129	.293	.338	.444	.782	20

Key Pitchers

Pos	Player	G	GS	W	L	Sv	IP	H	R	ER	BB	SO	BR/9	ERA	WS
SP	Tim Hudson	34	34	16	10	0	224.1	221	87	83	53	132	11.31	3.33	17
SP	John Smoltz	32	32	14	8	0	205.2	196	78	71	47	197	10.81	3.11	14
SP	Chuck James	30	30	11	10	0	161.1	164	77	76	58	116	12.44	4.24	8
SP	Buddy Carlyle	22	20	8	7	0	107.0	117	67	62	32	74	12.70	5.21	3
SP	Kyle Davies	17	17	4	8	0	86.0	92	61	55	44	59	14.44	5.76	1
CL	Bob Wickman	49	0	3	3	20	43.2	48	22	19	20	35	14.43	3.92	4
RP	Peter Moylan	80	0	5	3	1	90.0	65	27	18	31	63	10.30	1.80	9
RP	Tyler Yates	75	0	2	3	2	66.0	64	44	38	31	69	13.36	5.18	2

Last year the Braves out-homered their opponents by only four home runs, narrowly avoiding being out-homered for the first time in the Bobby Cox era. Over Cox's first 16 full seasons as the Braves' manager (1991-2006), the Braves out-homered their opponents 2872-2051, a margin of more than 51 per season. The last year in which they gave up more homers than they hit was 1988.

Atlanta Braves – 2007
Record by Home Runs

Home Runs	W – L
0 homers	20 - 38
1 homer	26 - 25
2 homers	26 - 11
3 or more homers	12 - 4

Mark Teixeira drove in 39 Braves other than himself. They were divided into equal thirds, Chipper Jones 13 times, Yunel Escobar 13 times, all other Braves 13 times.

Mark Teixeira – Tex-Atl – 2007
RBI Analysis

Hits		RBI Hits		RBI		Drove In	
HomeRuns:	30			RBI on Home Runs:	50	Matt Diaz	1
Triples:	2	RBI Triples:	1	RBI on Triples:	1	Victor Diaz	1
Doubles:	33	RBI Doubles:	16	RBI on Doubles:	20	Yunel Escobar	13
Singles:	86	RBI Singles:	25	RBI on Singles:	27	Jerry Hairston	3
				Sacrifice Flies:	2	Willie Harris	3
		Other RBI: Walks	2			Tim Hudson	1
		Other RBI: Ground Outs	1	Total Other:	5	Kelly Johnson	3
						Chipper Jones	13
				Total RBI:	105	Matt Kata	1
						Ian Kinsler	2
						Gerald Laird	1
						Kenny Lofton	12
						Kevin Mahar	2
						Desi Relaford	1
						Edgar Renteria	5
						Ramon Vazquez	3
						Brad Wilkerson	1
						Michael Young	9
						His Own Bad Self	30
						Total	105

Every player in the top ten in batting average in the major leagues in 2007 had at least two games with four or more hits, except Chipper Jones.

Chipper Jones – 2007
Games with X Hits

	G	AB	R	H	2B	3B	HR	RBI	Avg
0 Hits	26	83	10	0	0	0	0	1	.000
1 Hits	62	239	45	62	17	1	13	46	.259
2 Hits	27	105	26	54	12	1	9	26	.514
3 Hits	19	86	27	57	13	2	7	29	.663

Hole in His Game

Last year Edgar Renteria was the best major league shortstop at making plays up the middle (+18) but next-to-worst at going into the hole (-19). He showed exactly the same pattern the year before, ranking as the majors' second-best shortstop at going to his left but the second-worst at going to his right.

Edgar Renteria – 2005-2007
Fielding Bible Basic Data

Shortstop										
Year	Team	G	GS	Inn	PO	A	E	DP	Pct	Rng
2005	Bos	153	150	1293.0	227	398	30	90	.954	4.35
2006	Atl	146	146	1265.1	185	399	13	76	.978	4.15
2007	Atl	121	121	1019.1	147	322	11	71	.977	4.14
Total		420	417	3577.2	559	1119	54	237	.969	4.22

Edgar Renteria – 2005-2007
Fielding Bible Plus/Minus

Shortstop															
			GROUND DP				PLAYS				PLUS/MINUS				
			GIDP				Expected Outs		Outs Made		To His	Straight	To His				
Year	Team	Inn	Opps	GIDP	Pct	Rank	GB	Air	GB	Air	Right	On	Left	GB	Air	Total	Rank
2005	Bos	1293.0	154	82	.532	30	352	110	343	108	+3	-14	+2	-9	-2	-11	26
2006	Atl	1265.1	128	73	.570	25	363	78	364	83	-17	0	+18	+1	+5	+6	10
2007	Atl	1019.1	111	70	.631	9	293	69	291	70	-19	-1	+18	-2	+1	-1	20
Total		3577.2	393	225	.573	30	1008	257	998	261	-33	-15	+38	-10	+4	-6	20

Peter Moylan led the major leagues in intentional walks in 2007, with 12. Not a one of them came around to score.

Peter Moylan – 2007
Runs Allowed Analysis

Reached by Single:	48	Scored:	11	23%
Reached by Double:	9	Scored:	2	22%
Reached by Triple:	2	Scored:	2	100%
Reached by Homer:	6			
Reached by Walk:	31	Scored:	2	6%
Reached by HBP:	7	Scored:	0	0%
Reached by Error:	3	Scored:	1	33%
Reached by FC - All Safe:	3	Scored:	1	33%
Reached by FC - Out:	11	Scored:	0	0%
Total On Base	120	Scored:	31	26%
Stolen Bases Allowed:	9	Scored:	3	33%
Caught Stealing:	2	Scored:	0	0%
Steal Attempts:	11	Scored:	3	27%
Intentional Walks:	12	Scored:	0	0%

Since 2002, Ron Mahay's ERA against winning teams is nearly two full runs lower than it is against losing teams.

Ray Mahay – 2002-2007
Career Records Against Quality of Opposition

Opponent	G	IP	W	L	SO	BB	ERA
.600 teams	8	9.0	1	0	7	5	6.00
.500 - .599 teams	149	170.2	8	3	146	80	2.90
.400 - .499 teams	78	79.1	2	4	63	39	4.76
sub .400 teams	21	27.2	1	1	31	14	5.53

Hey Bill

Question: A couple of years ago the Atlanta Braves lost their pitching coach of many years, Leo Mazzone. Mazzone moved over to the Baltimore Orioles, taking the reins there as their pitching coach. It would appear that he hasn't made that much of an impact with the Orioles, but has Mazzone's loss hurt the Braves pitching and/or the team as a whole?

Asked by: John Dewan

Answer: The Army is built on the theory that nobody is irreplaceable. It has to be built that way, because people get killed and you have to carry on. But I always thought maybe a better theory to describe a baseball team is that everybody is irreplaceable. The Braves had a fantastic unit, the greatest pitching staffs in the history of baseball. There were several people who were critical to making that work—Smoltz, Glavine, Maddux, Bobby Cox, John Schuerholz, Mazzone, Andruw Jones. They're mostly gone now.

If you're asking do I know how much Mazzone was worth compared to Cox, compared to Glavine, or compared to, let's say, the strength-and-conditioning coach, the answer is "No, I don't have a clue." I don't know how to parse it out, one from another. My theory is that in a top-of-the-line organization, everybody is irreplaceable.

(Editor's note: *Hey Bill* is a feature of **Bill James Online** where subscribers can pose a question to Bill. Bill will do his best to answer questions, usually on a weekly basis. The questions and answers will be posted in the online.)

No Cheapies

Tim Hudson posted a quality start in all 16 of his victories. He was one of only five pitchers to win 10+ games without receiving credit for a single victory in a non-quality start.

Tim Hudson – 2007
Decision Analysis

Group	G	IP	W	L	Pct	H	R	SO	BB	ERA
Wins	16	113.0	16	0	1.000	95	18	77	21	1.43
Losses	10	62.1	0	10	.000	77	44	24	17	5.78
No Decisions	8	49.0	0	0	—	49	25	31	15	4.59
Quality Starts: 16 in Wins, 4 in Losses, 5 in no-decisions										

Baltimore Orioles

Baltimore Orioles – 2007
Team Overview

Description		Ranking
Won-Lost Record	69-93	
Place		4th of 5 in American League East
Runs Scored	756	16th in the majors
Runs Allowed	868	28th in the majors
Home Runs	142	23rd in the majors
Home Runs Allowed	161	12th in the majors
Batting Average	.272	12th in the majors
Batting Average Allowed	.268	15th in the majors
Walks Drawn	500	25th in the majors
Walks Given	696	30th in the majors
OPS For	.746	18th in the majors
OPS Against	.766	18th in the majors
Stolen Bases	144	2nd in the majors
Stolen Bases Allowed	109	25th in the majors

Key Players

Pos	Player	G	AB	R	H	2B	3B	HR	RBI	SB	CS	BB	SO	Avg	OBP	Slg	OPS	WS
C	Ram. Hernandez	106	364	40	94	18	0	9	62	1	3	36	59	.258	.333	.382	.714	11
1B	Kevin Millar	140	476	63	121	26	1	17	63	1	1	76	94	.254	.365	.420	.785	12
2B	Brian Roberts	156	621	103	180	42	5	12	57	50	7	89	99	.290	.377	.432	.808	22
3B	Melvin Mora	126	467	67	128	23	1	14	58	9	3	47	83	.274	.341	.418	.759	10
SS	Miguel Tejada	133	514	72	152	19	1	18	81	2	1	41	55	.296	.357	.442	.799	14
LF	Jay Payton	131	434	48	111	21	5	7	58	5	2	22	42	.256	.292	.376	.668	7
CF	Corey Patterson	132	461	65	124	26	2	8	45	37	9	21	65	.269	.304	.386	.690	8
RF	Nick Markakis	161	637	97	191	43	3	23	112	18	6	61	112	.300	.362	.485	.848	20
DH	Aubrey Huff	151	550	68	154	34	5	15	72	1	1	48	87	.280	.337	.442	.778	12

Key Pitchers

Pos	Player	G	GS	W	L	Sv	IP	H	R	ER	BB	SO	BR/9	ERA	WS
SP	Erik Bedard	28	28	13	5	0	182.0	141	66	64	57	221	10.04	3.16	17
SP	Jeremy Guthrie	32	26	7	5	0	175.1	165	78	72	47	123	11.09	3.70	12
SP	Daniel Cabrera	34	34	9	18	0	204.1	207	133	126	108	166	14.54	5.55	6
SP	Steve Trachsel	25	25	6	8	0	140.2	151	73	70	69	45	14.20	4.48	8
SP	Brian Burres	37	17	6	8	0	121.0	140	81	80	66	96	15.69	5.95	3
CL	Chris Ray	43	0	5	6	16	42.2	35	22	21	18	44	11.60	4.43	6
RP	Jamie Walker	81	0	3	2	7	61.1	57	25	22	17	41	11.15	3.23	8
RP	Chad Bradford	78	0	4	7	2	64.2	77	28	24	16	29	13.78	3.34	6

Two years ago, when Eric Bedard went 6-8 with a 4.00 ERA, he threw 16% curve balls.

Last year, when he struck out 221 hitters in 182 innings, he threw 998 curve balls, the most of any major league pitcher.

The curve ball has always been a big strikeout pitch for some pitchers. Nolan Ryan probably got more strikeouts on curve balls than he did fastballs, Sandy Koufax the same.

Erik Bedard – 2007
Pitch Type Analysis

Overall		
Total Pitches	2946	
Fastball	1690	57%
Curveball	998	34%
Changeup	143	5%
Cut Fastball	90	3%
Pitchout	1	0%
Not Charted	24	1%

	Vs. RHB		Vs. LHB	
Total Pitches	2278		668	
Outs Recorded	439		107	
Fastball	1246	55%	444	66%
Curveball	819	36%	179	27%
Changeup	135	6%	8	1%
Cut Fastball	55	2%	35	5%
Pitchout	1	0%	0	0%
Not Charted	22	1%	2	0%

Not Counting the 416 Home Runs He Pulled Foul

Since 2004 Kevin Millar has hit 59 homers, 57 of them to left field, two to center, and none to right. All 17 he hit in 2007 were to left.

Kevin Miller – 2007
Hitting Analysis

Batting Right-Handed									1B	2B	3B	HR
Ground Balls to Left	69	Outs	61	Hits	8	Average	.116	Hit Type	8 -	0 -	0 -	0
Ground Balls to Center	34	Outs	28	Hits	6	Average	.176	Hit Type	6 -	0 -	0 -	0
Ground Balls to Right	9	Outs	7	Hits	2	Average	.222	Hit Type	2 -	0 -	0 -	0
Line Drives to Left	47	Outs	10	Hits	37	Average	.787	Hit Type	26 -	11 -	0 -	0
Line Drives to Center	22	Outs	5	Hits	17	Average	.773	Hit Type	17 -	0 -	0 -	0
Line Drives to Right	6	Outs	2	Hits	4	Average	.667	Hit Type	4 -	0 -	0 -	0
Fly Balls to Left	85	Outs	52	Hits	33	Average	.393	Hit Type	5 -	11 -	0 -	17
Fly Balls to Center	59	Outs	52	Hits	7	Average	.121	Hit Type	6 -	1 -	0 -	0
Fly Balls to Right	53	Outs	46	Hits	7	Average	.132	Hit Type	3 -	3 -	1 -	0
Total on Ground Balls	112	Outs	96	Hits	16	Average	.143	Hit Type	16 -	0 -	0 -	0
Total on Line Drives	75	Outs	17	Hits	58	Average	.773	Hit Type	47 -	11 -	0 -	0
Total on Fly Balls	197	Outs	150	Hits	47	Average	.241	Hit Type	14 -	15 -	1 -	17
Total Hit to Left	201	Outs	123	Hits	78	Average	.390	Hit Type	39 -	22 -	0 -	17
Total Hit to Center	115	Outs	85	Hits	30	Average	.263	Hit Type	29 -	1 -	0 -	0
Total Hit to Right	68	Outs	55	Hits	13	Average	.191	Hit Type	9 -	3 -	1 -	0
All Balls in Play	384	Outs	263	Hits	121	Average	.317	Hit Type	77 -	26 -	1 -	17

Jay Payton – 2007
Pitch Analysis

Climbing the Ladder

Jay Payton was the highest (54%) of only three major league hitters (minimum 500 pitches seen) who swung at more than half of the high pitches (out of the zone) he was thrown in 2007. The other two were Justin Morneau (51%) and Jeff Francoeur (50%). Payton also led the majors by a comfortable margin in 2006.

Overall		
Pitches Seen	1494	
Taken	694	46%
Swung At	800	54%
Pitches Taken		
Taken for a Strike	212	31%
Called a ball	482	69%
Pitches Taken by Pitch Location		
In Strike Zone	212	31%
High	70	10%
Low	205	30%
Inside	98	14%
Outside	109	16%
Swung At		
Missed	107	13%
Fouled Off	290	36%
Put in Play	403	50%
Swung At by Pitch Location		
In Strike Zone	556	70%
High	83	10%
Low	85	11%
Inside	27	3%
Outside	49	6%

If Only This Had Happened Five Years Ago

Corey Patterson's percentage of swings-and-misses dropped by 18% in 2006, and his strikeout rate declined by 23%. Last year, his swings-and-misses fell by another 11%, and his strikeout rate went down another 31%.

Corey Patterson – 2002-2007
Multi-Year Pitch Analysis

Year	Pitches Seen	Pitches Taken	%	Swung At	%	Taken Strikes	%	Taken Balls	%	Swung & Missed	%	Fouled Off	%	Put in Play	%
2002	2109	955	.45	1154	.55	319	.33	636	.67	298	.26	397	.34	459	.40
2003	1143	502	.44	641	.56	136	.27	366	.73	175	.27	212	.33	254	.40
2004	2348	1112	.47	1236	.53	305	.27	807	.73	339	.27	428	.35	469	.38
2005	1613	678	.42	935	.58	178	.26	500	.74	248	.27	346	.37	341	.36
2006	1558	641	.41	917	.59	180	.28	461	.72	199	.22	339	.37	379	.41
2007	1582	695	.44	887	.56	205	.29	490	.71	171	.19	303	.34	413	.47
Total	10353	4583	.44	5770	.56	1323	.29	3260	.71	1430	.25	2025	.35	2315	.40

One of These Things Is Not Like the Other
One of These Things Just Doesn't Belong

Daniel Cabrera's Runs Allowed per Nine Innings when he got the first man out last year was 2.73.

When he did not get the first man out his Runs/9 Innings was 12.38.

Daniel Cabrera – 2007
Inning Analysis

Innings Pitched	204.1
Runs Allowed	133
Innings Started	212
Runs in Those Innings	150
Shutout Innings	134
One-Run Innings	43
Two-Run Innings	19
Three-Run Inning	9
Four-Run Innings	2
Five-Run Innings	3
Nine-Run Innings	1
Ten+ Run Innings	1
Got First Man Out	132
Runs Scored in Those Innings	40
Runs/9 Innings	2.73
First Man Reached	80
Runs Scored in Those Innings	110
Runs/9 Innings	12.38
1-2-3 Innings	68
10-pitch Innings (or less)	30
Long Innings (20 or more pitches)	64
Failed to Finish Inning	14

Baltimore was unable to win (they were 14-21) even with a good game by the starting pitcher (game score 50 to 59).

Baltimore Orioles – 2007
Performance by Quality of Start

Game Score	#	ERA	W	-	L
80 and above	2	0.00	2	-	0
70 to 79	15	1.57	11	-	4
60 to 69	29	2.63	19	-	10
50 to 59	35	4.21	14	-	21
40 to 49	28	5.12	13	-	15
30 to 39	24	7.04	8	-	16
20 to 29	20	9.82	2	-	18
Below 20	9	10.27	0	-	9

The Orioles last year were 3-22 (!!) in games in which they scored 4 runs. That's hard to do, isn't it? I'd have to think…you score 4 runs, you should have SOME chance to win the game.

Baltimore Orioles – 2007
Record by Runs Scored and Allowed

	Scored	Allowed
10 runs or more	7 - 1	0 - 19
9 runs	5 - 0	2 - 7
8 runs	9 - 2	1 - 10
7 runs	7 - 6	2 - 11
6 runs	18 - 9	5 - 10
5 runs	7 - 6	5 - 11
4 runs	3 - 22	9 - 9
3 runs	9 - 12	14 - 12
2 runs	3 - 18	14 - 4
1 run	1 - 13	8 - 0
0 runs	0 - 4	9 - 0
Total	69 - 93	69 - 93

Daniel, We Need to Talk

There were six major league pitchers in 2007 who started 20 or more games lost by their teams. All of those pitchers except one were working with well below-average offensive support. The one exception: Oriole starter Daniel Cabrera. The Orioles scored 172 runs in the 34 games started by Cabrera—yet finished 13-21 in those games.

Opponents scored 213 runs in games started by Cabrera—eighteen more than in the games started by any other major league pitcher.

Baltimore Orioles – 2007
Performance by Starting Pitcher

Games Started By	G	RS	RA	Won	Lost
Cabrera, Daniel	34	172	213	13	21
Bedard, Erik	28	130	98	19	9
Guthrie, Jeremy	26	115	109	10	16
Trachsel, Steve	25	117	147	9	16
Burres, Brian	17	77	94	6	11
Olson, Garrett	7	31	46	2	5
Loewen, Adam	6	27	27	3	3
Leicester, Jon	5	24	29	3	2
Liz, Radhames	4	23	42	2	2
Wright, Jaret	3	4	16	0	3
Santos, Victor	3	15	19	1	2
Zambrano, Victor	2	11	11	1	1
Birkins, Kurt	2	10	17	0	2
Team Totals	162	756	868	69	93

Chris Ray's opponent batting line last year was nearly identical to that of his rookie year—it was a perfect match in doubles, triples, homers, walks and batting average, and was extremely close in every other category except runs and RBI. The biggest difference between the two seasons came in a category not shown here: ERA. Last year it was 4.43, while in 2005 it was 2.66. Neither mark was indicative of the true quality of his work—last year's mark was about a run too high, and his rookie ERA was about a run lower than he deserved.

Chris Ray – Career
Record of Opposing Batters

Season	AB	R	H	2B	3B	HR	RBI	BB	SO	SB	CS	GIDP	Avg	OBP	Slg	OPS
2005	153	15	34	6	1	5	23	18	43	1	1	2	.222	.304	.373	.677
2006	233	22	45	5	1	10	29	27	51	0	2	3	.193	.277	.352	.629
2007	158	22	35	6	1	5	26	18	44	2	1	2	.222	.301	.367	.668

Worst ERA When Recording a Hold
(pitchers with 10 or more holds in 2007)

Hold On Loosely

Danys Baez had a 4.97 ERA in games in which he recorded a hold. As poor as that is, it only places him sixth in worst ERA among pitchers with 10 or more holds in 2007.

Name	ERA	Holds
Brocail, Doug, SD	7.87	10
Marte, Damaso, Pit	7.50	15
Camp, Shawn, TB	6.43	11
Hennessey, Brad, SF	6.35	13
Farnsworth, Kyle, NYY	5.40	15
Baez, Danys, Bal	4.97	14
Parrish, John, Sea	4.91	10
Embree, Alan, Oak	4.76	16
Taschner, Jack, SF	4.15	13
Wise, Matt, Mil	3.72	13

Comp List

by Bill James

Do you all remember Mike Greenwell? Used to play left field for the Red Sox, good hitter but not exactly Devon White in the field? The Baltimore Orioles would like to remember him a little more often.

Mike Greenwell in his career hit .303 with an on base percentage of .368, slugging percentage of .463. These were almost exactly the same figures, it turns out, that the 2007 Baltimore Orioles had, as a team—when they won. When they won, they were Mike Greenwell; when they lost, they were more like former Cubs and Astros catcher Scott Servais—.245/.305/.374. (Servais actually was .245/.306/.375.)

For those of you who are connoisseurs of truly useless information, I took the batting, on base and slugging percentages for each major league team in wins and in losses, and identified the player to whom this was most similar. I kept expecting that I would find somewhere an exact match on all three stats, but I never did; you always come close, but I never exactly hit it—unless you count Oakland's losses. The Oakland A's, in games they lost, hit .222 with a .300 on

For those of you who are connoisseurs of truly useless information....

base percentage, .333 slugging. As it happens, you can match that in 10 plate appearances—two-for-nine with a walk and a double—and so some players did, four of them, I think. But I didn't remember any of those players and they're not meaningful averages, so I didn't think that was useful.

Almost every team, it turns out, hits like some slugging outfielder when they win—usually like a Hall of Famer—and almost everybody hits like a backup catcher when they lose. You may not remember Bob Geren, Jimmie Coker, Darrell Miller, Jake Gibbs, Jerry McNertney, Norm Sherry and Phil Roof, but they're all backup catchers. The Tampa Bay Rays when they lost actually hit almost exactly like their own backup catcher, Raul Casanova, although I listed another one. Herewith the comps:

Team and Group	Avg.	OBP	Slg.	Most Similar Hitter
Arizona in Wins	.281	.355	.480	Dave Winfield
Arizona in Losses	.209	.274	.325	Dave Stegman

Team and Group	Avg.	OBP	Slg.	Most Similar Hitter
Atlanta in Wins	.312	.383	.480	Goose Goslin
Atlanta in Losses	.232	.286	.350	Bob Geren

Team and Group	Avg.	OBP	Slg.	Most Similar Hitter
Baltimore in Wins	.304	.369	.461	Mike Greenwell
Baltimore in Losses	.245	.305	.374	Scott Servais

Team and Group	Avg.	OBP	Slg.	Most Similar Hitter
Boston in Wins	.308	.393	.508	Indian Bob Johnson
Boston in Losses	.235	.313	.348	Al Luplow

Team and Group	Avg.	OBP	Slg.	Most Similar Hitter
White Sox in Wins	.291	.363	.500	Billy Williams
White Sox in Losses	.208	.278	.324	Dave Stegman

Team and Group	Avg.	OBP	Slg.	Most Similar Hitter
Cubs in Wins	.303	.363	.483	Pedro Guerrero
Cubs in Losses	.235	.297	.353	Jimmie Coker

Team and Group	Avg.	OBP	Slg.	Most Similar Hitter
Cincinnati in Wins	.302	.375	.502	Jim Bottomley
Cincinnati in Losses	.235	.301	.378	Dale Sveum

Team and Group	Avg.	OBP	Slg.	Most Similar Hitter
Cleveland in Wins	.291	.372	.478	Al Kaline
Cleveland in Losses	.234	.298	.352	Jimmie Coker

Team and Group	Avg.	OBP	Slg.	Most Similar Hitter
Colorado in Wins	.318	.389	.515	Goose Goslin
Colorado in Losses	.228	.306	.334	Jim Gosger

Team and Group	Avg.	OBP	Slg.	Most Similar Hitter
Detroit in Wins	.319	.383	.529	Babe Herman
Detroit in Losses	.246	.295	.369	Tom Brookens

Team and Group	Avg.	OBP	Slg.	Most Similar Hitter
Florida in Wins	.308	.380	.527	Chick Hafey
Florida in Losses	.233	.297	.383	Dale Sveum

Team and Group	Avg.	OBP	Slg.	Most Similar Hitter
Houston in Wins	.294	.370	.497	Gabby Hartnett
Houston in Losses	.231	.295	.342	Jim Hegan

Team and Group	Avg.	OBP	Slg.	Most Similar Hitter
Kansas City in Wins	.313	.376	.477	John Stone
Kansas City in Losses	.221	.278	318	Chuck Cottier

I remember all of these guys, by the way. John (Rocky) Stone was a 1930s outfielder, very similar to Mike Greenwell. Chuck Cottier was a 1960s middle infielder, about whom Shirley Povich used to tell this story. One time he was sitting on the Senators bench, getting near game time, and he said, "Well, I'd better get out of here or Gil Hodges will put me in the game."

"Don't worry about it," said Cottier. "I've been sitting there for weeks, and he hasn't put me in yet." The only player here that I actually don't remember is Andy Tomberlin.

Team and Group	Avg.	OBP	Slg.	Most Similar Hitter
Dodgers in Wins	.307	.371	.458	Bubbles Hargrave
Dodgers in Losses	.241	.299	.349	Darrell Miller

Darrell Miller, who I think was the first player drafted one year, was the older brother of basketball superstar Reggie Miller, and also of women's basketball star Cheryl Miller.

Almost every team, it turns out, hits like some slugging outfielder when they win—usually like a Hall of Famer—and almost everybody hits like a backup catcher when they lose.

Koufax, apparently, struggled for years because whenever he got in trouble he would just try to blow away hitters with his fastball.
Josh Beckett used to do that, too.

Team and Group	Avg.	OBP	Slg.	Most Similar Hitter
Angels in Wins	.315	.377	.471	John Stone
Angels in Losses	.239	.295	.339	Jerry McNertney

McNertney, you will recall, is a character in Bouton's classic, Ball Four. John Stone also appears in a song by The Beach Boys (Sheriff John Stone, why don't you leave me alone?)

Team and Group	Avg.	OBP	Slg.	Most Similar Hitter
Milwaukee in Wins	.298	.369	.521	Hal Trosky
Milwaukee in Losses	.221	.282	.384	Ron Karkovice

Hal Trosky would be in the Hall of Fame except for debilitating headaches that started when he was about 25. Karkovice, like Jim Hegan, hit like any other backup catcher but had such exceptional defensive skills that he was a regular.

Team and Group	Avg.	OBP	Slg.	Most Similar Hitter
Minnesota in Wins	.296	.370	.464	Rico Carty
Minnesota in Losses	.232	.288	.318	Jake Gibbs

Team and Group	Avg.	OBP	Slg.	Most Similar Hitter
Yankees in Wins	.330	.408	.543	Stan Musial
Yankees in Losses	.232	.302	.349	Jimmie Coker

Team and Group	Avg.	OBP	Slg.	Most Similar Hitter
Mets in Wins	.299	.372	.487	Gabby Hartnett
Mets in Losses	.246	.305	.366	Russ Morman

Team and Group	Avg.	OBP	Slg.	Most Similar Hitter
Oakland in Wins	.293	.376	.486	Al Kaline
Oakland in Losses	.222	.300	.333	Torey Lovullo

Team and Group	Avg.	OBP	Slg.	Most Similar Hitter
Philadelphia in Wins	.306	.388	.522	Mo Vaughn
Philadelphia in Losses	.232	.307	.376	Andy Tomberlin

Team and Group	Avg.	OBP	Slg.	Most Similar Hitter
Pittsburgh in Wins	.305	.368	.494	George Brett
Pittsburgh in Losses	.230	.289	.347	Coco Laboy

Team and Group	Avg.	OBP	Slg.	Most Similar Hitter
San Diego in Wins	.279	.355	.472	Bobby Bonilla
San Diego in Losses	.216	.279	.336	Norm Sherry

Norm Sherry used to be famous for the role that he played in turning around the career of Sandy Koufax. Koufax, apparently, struggled for years because whenever he got in trouble he would just try to blow away hitters with his fastball. Josh Beckett used to do that, too.

It brings up another side topic, which is "players who are famous for their influence on another player." Bobby Castillo, for example, used to be famous for teaching Fernando Valenzuela to throw a screwball.

Team and Group	Avg.	OBP	Slg.	Most Similar Hitter
San Francisco in Wins	.292	.363	.454	Bruce Campbell
San Francisco in Losses	.223	.287	.332	Kevin Bell

Team and Group	Avg.	OBP	Slg.	Most Similar Hitter
Seattle in Wins	.313	.363	.482	Babe Phelps
Seattle in Losses	.252	.304	.354	Joe McEwing

Babe Phelps was basically a backup catcher, too, albeit a backup catcher who could really hit. He was sort of a regular from '36 through '40, lost his job in '41 when the Dodgers trained in Havana. He had a phobia about traveling over water, and, although he tried to, he could not force himself to get on the boat. At least, that's the story as I remember it.

Team and Group	Avg.	OBP	Slg.	Most Similar Hitter
St. Louis in Wins	.318	.380	.450	Bill Dickey
St. Louis in Losses	.229	.294	.321	Cap Peterson

Every team in 2007 hit at least 57 points higher in wins than they did in losses, but no team was 100 points higher, although some (including the Cardinals) were close. I tried to generalize about the differences, something like "teams with bad pitching have a wider separation because they have to hit more to win". But that's not quite it…there is some pattern there, but I don't understand it yet.

Team and Group	Avg.	OBP	Slg.	Most Similar Hitter
Tampa Bay in Wins	.313	.382	.523	Chick Hafey
Tampa Bay in Losses	.235	.301	.367	Danny Goodwin

Chick Hafey was selected to the Hall of Fame, but shouldn't have been. Danny Goodwin was selected number one in the draft twice, but shouldn't have been, either. Everybody makes mistakes.

Team and Group	Avg.	OBP	Slg.	Most Similar Hitter
Texas in Wins	.313	.383	.522	Chick Hafey
Texas in Losses	.218	.277	.340	Kenny Williams

Team and Group	Avg.	OBP	Slg.	Most Similar Hitter
Toronto in Wins	.284	.355	.465	Dave Nilsson
Toronto in Losses	.232	.295	.371	Bob Tillman

Team and Group	Avg.	OBP	Slg.	Most Similar Hitter
Washington in Wins	.302	.370	.469	Rico Carty
Washington in Losses	.217	.284	.323	Phil Roof

Chick Hafey was selected to the Hall of Fame, but shouldn't have been. Danny Goodwin was selected number one in the draft twice, but shouldn't have been, either.

Boston Red Sox

Boston Red Sox – 2007
Team Overview

Description		Ranking
Won-Lost Record	96-66	
Place	1st of 5 in American League East	
Runs Scored	867	4th in the majors
Runs Allowed	657	1st in the majors
Home Runs	166	18th in the majors
Home Runs Allowed	151	8th in the majors
Batting Average	.279	6th in the majors
Batting Average Allowed	.247	2nd in the majors
Walks Drawn	689	1st in the majors
Walks Given	482	6th in the majors
OPS For	.806	3rd in the majors
OPS Against	.705	2nd in the majors
Stolen Bases	96	15th in the majors
Stolen Bases Allowed	107	23rd in the majors

Key Players

Pos	Player	G	AB	R	H	2B	3B	HR	RBI	SB	CS	BB	SO	Avg	OBP	Slg	OPS	WS
C	Jason Varitek	131	435	57	111	15	3	17	68	1	2	71	122	.255	.367	.421	.787	14
1B	Kevin Youkilis	145	528	85	152	35	2	16	83	4	2	77	105	.288	.390	.453	.843	20
2B	Dustin Pedroia	139	520	86	165	39	1	8	50	7	1	47	42	.317	.380	.442	.823	18
3B	Mike Lowell	154	589	79	191	37	2	21	120	3	2	53	71	.324	.378	.501	.879	23
SS	Julio Lugo	147	570	71	135	36	2	8	73	33	6	48	82	.237	.294	.349	.643	11
LF	Manny Ramirez	133	483	84	143	33	1	20	88	0	0	71	92	.296	.388	.493	.881	14
CF	Coco Crisp	145	526	85	141	28	7	6	60	28	6	50	84	.268	.330	.382	.712	16
RF	J.D. Drew	140	466	84	126	30	4	11	64	4	2	79	100	.270	.373	.423	.796	12
DH	David Ortiz	149	549	116	182	52	1	35	117	3	1	111	103	.332	.445	.621	1.066	27

Key Pitchers

Pos	Player	G	GS	W	L	Sv	IP	H	R	ER	BB	SO	BR/9	ERA	WS
SP	Josh Beckett	30	30	20	7	0	200.2	189	76	73	40	194	10.50	3.27	18
SP	Tim Wakefield	31	31	17	12	0	189.0	191	104	100	64	110	12.33	4.76	10
SP	Daisuke Matsuzaka	32	32	15	12	0	204.2	191	100	100	80	201	12.49	4.40	12
SP	Curt Schilling	24	24	9	8	0	151.0	165	68	65	23	101	11.32	3.87	10
SP	Julian Tavarez	34	23	7	11	0	134.2	151	89	77	51	77	13.97	5.15	4
CL	Jonathan Papelbon	59	0	1	3	37	58.1	30	12	12	15	84	7.56	1.85	15
RP	Hideki Okajima	66	0	3	2	5	69.0	50	17	17	17	63	8.87	2.22	11
RP	Javier Lopez	61	0	2	1	0	40.2	36	16	14	18	26	12.84	3.10	4

The Red Sox are the only playoff team with double-digit Win Shares at each of the nine positions (DH, C, 1B, 2B, etc.).

Is the overshift over for David Ortiz?

Ortiz was essentially as valuable in 2007, hitting 35 home runs, as he was in 2006, hitting 54 homers—in part because he hit .529 on ground balls to left field, and .313 on ground balls to center. While Ortiz' totals of ground balls, fly balls and line drives were essentially the same in '07 as they were in '06, and his totals of balls hit to left, center and right were essentially the same, Ortiz in 2007 had 17 more hits on ground balls, and 10 more hits on fly balls to left, as well as a big increase in doubles to right field.

Do you know the old joke about the Polock hunting for land mines? We have to take the Polish person out of it to be sensitive to the three Polish guys who are actually offended by Polock jokes, and it's a visual joke anyway...imagine a guy covering his ears with his hands and closing his eyes extra tight, then stretching out his leg and tapping the ground with his foot. To me, the shift against Ortiz is quite a bit like a...like a dumb guy hunting for land mines. The big damage that David Ortiz does is when he hits the ball 380 feet and more—off the wall, over the wall, into the gap into right field. If the bomb goes off, you can put them damned infielders wherever you want them, a lot of good it's going to do you.

Yes, Ortiz does hit some blistering ground balls into the hole on the right side, only to see an infielder field them in shallow right and turn them into outs. But the fact is, most ground balls are outs, anyway. It isn't his ground balls that make David Ortiz deadly. It's the line drives and fly balls. In an effort to change the percentage of David's ground balls that are outs from 75% to 80%, opposing managers are:

a) conceding singles on check-swing rollers the opposite way,

b) putting their infielders, a certain number of times every year, so deep that when they do get to the ball there is nothing they can do with it anyway and

c) making the third baseman the pivot man on a double play attempt.

Watching the Red Sox every day, we see some really interesting defenses against Ortiz...four infielders on the right side with a left fielder covering short, third basemen playing second, and sometimes, when the Sox play Tampa Bay, something that looks like a town hall meeting in right field. I don't know that it does any harm, but study the stats, and show me where it's doing anybody any good.

David Ortiz – 2006
Hitting Analysis

Batting Left-Handed									1B	2B	3B	HR
Ground Balls to Left	13	Outs	8	Hits	5	Average	.385	Hit Type	5 -	0 -	0 -	0
Ground Balls to Center	48	Outs	35	Hits	13	Average	.271	Hit Type	13 -	0 -	0 -	0
Ground Balls to Right	100	Outs	86	Hits	14	Average	.140	Hit Type	13 -	1 -	0 -	0
Line Drives to Left	24	Outs	5	Hits	19	Average	.826	Hit Type	10 -	9 -	0 -	0
Line Drives to Center	16	Outs	2	Hits	14	Average	.875	Hit Type	13 -	1 -	0 -	0
Line Drives to Right	34	Outs	10	Hits	24	Average	.706	Hit Type	14 -	7 -	1 -	2
Fly Balls to Left	65	Outs	54	Hits	11	Average	.172	Hit Type	3 -	4 -	0 -	4
Fly Balls to Center	76	Outs	51	Hits	25	Average	.338	Hit Type	1 -	4 -	1 -	19
Fly Balls to Right	66	Outs	34	Hits	32	Average	.492	Hit Type	0 -	3 -	0 -	29
Total on Ground Balls	161	Outs	129	Hits	32	Average	.199	Hit Type	31 -	1 -	0 -	0
Total on Line Drives	74	Outs	17	Hits	57	Average	.781	Hit Type	37 -	17 -	1 -	2
Total on Fly Balls	207	Outs	139	Hits	68	Average	.335	Hit Type	4 -	11 -	1 -	52
Total Hit to Left	102	Outs	67	Hits	35	Average	.350	Hit Type	18 -	13 -	0 -	4
Total Hit to Center	140	Outs	88	Hits	52	Average	.377	Hit Type	27 -	5 -	1 -	19
Total Hit to Right	200	Outs	130	Hits	70	Average	.352	Hit Type	27 -	11 -	1 -	31
Bunts	4	Outs	1	Hits	3	Average	.750	Hit Type	3 -	0 -	0 -	0
All Balls in Play	446	Outs	286	Hits	160	Average	.363	Hit Type	75 -	29 -	2 -	54

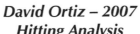

David Ortiz – 2007
Hitting Analysis

Batting Left-Handed								1B	2B	3B	HR
Ground Balls to Left	17	Outs	8	Hits	9	Average	.529	Hit Type	9 - 0	- 0	- 0
Ground Balls to Center	48	Outs	33	Hits	15	Average	.313	Hit Type	15 - 0	- 0	- 0
Ground Balls to Right	103	Outs	78	Hits	25	Average	.243	Hit Type	21 - 4	- 0	- 0
Line Drives to Left	19	Outs	3	Hits	16	Average	.842	Hit Type	8 - 8	- 0	- 0
Line Drives to Center	17	Outs	3	Hits	14	Average	.824	Hit Type	9 - 5	- 0	- 0
Line Drives to Right	41	Outs	17	Hits	24	Average	.585	Hit Type	18 - 6	- 0	- 0
Fly Balls to Left	72	Outs	51	Hits	21	Average	.300	Hit Type	7 - 10	- 0	- 4
Fly Balls to Center	61	Outs	36	Hits	25	Average	.417	Hit Type	7 - 12	- 1	- 5
Fly Balls to Right	70	Outs	37	Hits	33	Average	.471	Hit Type	0 - 7	- 0	- 26
Total on Ground Balls	168	Outs	119	Hits	49	Average	.292	Hit Type	45 - 4	- 0	- 0
Total on Line Drives	77	Outs	23	Hits	54	Average	.701	Hit Type	35 - 19	- 0	- 0
Total on Fly Balls	203	Outs	124	Hits	79	Average	.395	Hit Type	14 - 29	- 1	- 35
Total Hit to Left	108	Outs	62	Hits	46	Average	.434	Hit Type	24 - 18	- 0	- 4
Total Hit to Center	126	Outs	72	Hits	54	Average	.432	Hit Type	31 - 17	- 1	- 5
Total Hit to Right	214	Outs	132	Hits	82	Average	.383	Hit Type	39 - 17	- 0	- 26
Bunts	1	Outs	1	Hits	0	Average	.000	Hit Type	0 - 0	- 0	- 0
All Balls in Play	449	Outs	267	Hits	182	Average	.408	Hit Type	94 - 52	- 1	- 35

When David Ortiz led off for the Red Sox last year the Red Sox scored .78 runs per inning.

David Ortiz – 2007
Impact by Position in Inning

Position	Innings	Runs	Runs/Inning	Runs/RBI
Leading Off	106	83	.78	25/6
Batting Second	125	96	.77	22/7
Batting Third	269	204	.76	45/45
Batting Fourth	80	65	.81	12/22
Batting 5th or later	87	199	2.29	12/37

When Coco Crisp led off, they scored .54 runs per inning.

Coco Crisp – 2007
Impact by Position in Inning

Position	Innings	Runs	Runs/Inning	Runs/RBI
Leading Off	145	79	.54	26/1
Batting Second	138	64	.46	20/2
Batting Third	119	71	.60	12/6
Batting Fourth	87	73	.84	11/18
Batting 5th or later	102	261	2.56	14/33

The Red Sox in 2007 added two fairly costly free agents, J. D. Drew and Julio Lugo, both of whom struggled to get their bats started and had pretty ugly batting stats the first three months, although both finished the season playing well. Anyway, my thought was that Drew was perceived as having a bad season because he was expected to drive in runs and did poorly in that area, which overshadowed the fact that actually he was having an extremely good year in terms of scoring runs, while Lugo was expected to get on base, steal bases and score runs, and he had a poor year in those areas, which overshadowed the fact that he had a remarkably good year in terms of driving in runs (although Lugo was not driving in Drew…Lugo drove in Drew only five times).

Drew, battling some injuries and missing some playing time to being platooned, still scored 84 runs, in part because he walks and in part because he hit a lot of doubles leading off innings. Trot Nixon, the Red Sox' popular right fielder for the previous eight seasons, had only one year (2001) in which he scored more than 81 runs.

J.D. Drew – 2007
Runs Scored Analysis

Reached on		Runs Scored After	
Home Runs	11		11
Triples	4	Scored after Triple	4
Doubles	30	Scored after Double	17
Singles	81	Scored after Single	20
Walk/HBP	80	Scored after Walk/HBP	24
Reached on Error	6	Scored after ROE	1
Reached on Forceout	18	Vultured Runs	5
Inserted as Pinch Runner	2	Runs as pinch runner	2
		Total Runs Scored	84

Brought in by		Driven in by	
Single	26	Coco Crisp	15
Double	19	Mike Lowell	15
Triple	4	Jason Varitek	11
His own home run	11	Himself	11
Other home run	14	Julio Lugo	5
Sac Fly	3	Manny Ramirez	4
Walk, Error, or Other	7	Dustin Pedroia	4
		David Ortiz	4
		Kevin Youkilis	3
		No RBI	3
		Doug Mirabelli	2
		Alex Cora	2
		Eric Hinske	2
		Jacoby Ellsbury	1
		Bobby Kielty	1
		Kevin Cash	1

Trot Nixon – 2003
Runs Scored Analysis

Reached on		Runs Scored After	
Home Runs	28		28
Triples	6	Scored after Triple	2
Doubles	24	Scored after Double	10
Singles	77	Scored after Single	17
Walk/HBP	68	Scored after Walk/HBP	18
Reached on Error	3	Scored after ROE	2
Reached on Forceout	12	Vultured Runs	2
Inserted as Pinch Runner	1	Runs as pinch runner	1
Other	1	Other	1
		Total Runs Scored	81

Brought in by		Driven in by	
Single	18	Himself	28
Double	11	Jason Varitek	15
Triple	2	Johnny Damon	12
His own home run	28	Bill Mueller	6
Other home run	11	Todd Walker	6
Sac Fly	7	Shea Hillenbrand	5
Walk, Error, or Other	4	Gabe Kapler	2
		Jeremy Giambi	2
		No RBI	2
		Nomar Garciaparra	1
		Kevin Millar	1
		Doug Mirabelli	1

Opposing hitters have been remarkably consistent (and remarkably poor) against Josh Beckett, hitting no higher than .246 and no worse than .232 in any season of Beckett's six-year career.

Josh Beckett
Record of Opposing Batters

Season	AB	R	H	2B	3B	HR	RBI	BB	SO	SB	CS	GIDP	Avg	OBP	Slg	OPS
2002	401	56	93	14	5	13	52	44	113	12	5	4	.232	.308	.389	.697
2003	537	54	132	26	2	9	44	56	152	5	5	11	.246	.317	.352	.669
2004	582	72	137	32	5	16	67	54	152	5	5	15	.235	.300	.390	.690
2005	654	75	153	34	6	14	63	58	166	6	7	17	.234	.296	.369	.665
2006	780	120	191	44	4	36	109	74	158	15	1	20	.245	.310	.450	.760
2007	772	76	189	45	3	17	72	40	194	14	6	12	.245	.282	.377	.659

Southpaw Hideki Okajima's favorite pitches were his fastball, his changeup and his curveball, in that order. But when in a lefty-lefty matchup, he relied more on the curveball (25% of the time) than the changeup (19%). Against righties, the curveball was fairly rare (only 12% of his pitches).

Hideki Okajima – 2007
Pitch Type Analysis

Overall		
Total Pitches Thrown	1062	
Fastball	516	49%
Curveball	180	17%
Changeup	349	33%
Pitchout	5	0%
Not Charted	12	1%

	Vs. RHB		Vs. LHB	
Total Pitches Thrown	671		391	
Outs Recorded	136		71	
Fastball	302	45%	214	55%
Curveball	8	12%	97	25%
Changeup	276	41%	73	19%
Pitchout	4	1%	1	0%
Not Charted	6	1%	6	2%

The Red Sox opening-day starters accounted for 84% of their regular season starting lineups. No other team had more than 77%. The major league average is 70%.

Boston Red Sox – 2007
Games Played by Opening Day Starter at Each Position

Pos	Player	Starts
C	Varitek	121
1B	Youkili	136
2B	Pedroia	132
3B	Lowell	150
SS	Lugo	140
LF	Ramirez	131
CF	Crisp	137
RF	Drew	126
DH	Ortiz	147
Total		1220

When Baseball Info Solutions charts pitches, they chart them according to a fairly limited palette: Fastball, Slider, Curve, Change, Splitter, Cut Fastball and Knuckleball. There are a lot of other names used for pitches, and there are things that we could list as screwballs, sinkers, four-seam fastballs, palm balls, fork balls, etc. There's a straight change and a circle change, some people cut the fastball one way, some people cut it the other way. There is limitless variety.

But look at the Red Sox, and think about what this would do to the data. Okajima throws a kind of off-speed splitter used as a change which is called the Okie Dokie. Papelbon throws a cross between a slider and a cutter which he likes to call a slutter. Matsuzaka throws—or doesn't throw, depending on who you believe—a comic-book pitch called Gyro Ball; even if you don't count that one he throws like ten pitches.

First of all, we'd go crazy trying to keep track of all of these if we tried to chart everything by the pitcher's pet name for the pitch. We could deal with that, but it would ruin the data. We're trying to study stuff like "How does this hitter hit the slider, how does he deal with the change, etc.?" It would make the data a lot less useful if Okajima's changeup was in a different category from everybody else's changeup. We keep it simple to keep the data intelligible. The Okie Dokie is a change, the slutter is a slider and the Gyro Ball is a slider. They're not exactly the same pitch, but we don't want data for 208 pitches.

Three to Five Run Records

by Bill James

One of our new profiles in the Bill James Online is something called the "Record by Runs Scored and Allowed", which gives, for example, each team's won-lost record when they score six runs, when they allow six runs, when they score five, when they allow five, etc. For the 2007 season, we learned, for example, that:

- The Rangers were 2-6 when they scored six runs.
- The Angels were 10-7 when they allowed six runs.
- The Red Sox were 25-0 when they scored ten or more runs, and 2-5 when they allowed ten or more, both records being the best in the major leagues,
- Every team in baseball had a winning record when they scored 7 runs except the Reds (7-7) and Giants (2-4).
- Every team had a losing record when they allowed 7 runs except the Rockies (6-4).
- Every team without exception had a winning record when they scored 8 and a losing record when they allowed 8.
- The Blue Jays won twelve games in which they scored only two runs—more than the combined total of the Pirates, Phillies, Marlins, Diamondbacks, Yankees, Royals, White Sox, Brewers and Braves. All of those teams, taken together, won only eleven games in which they scored two runs.
- (Saving the best for last) Baltimore was a mind-boggling 3-22 when they scored four runs. A lot of teams were over .500 when they scored four...the Giants were 16-15, the Angels 13-5, the Indians 11-6. Three and twenty-two—given enough runs to win.

I was trying to sort out of this data some way to count "pitchers wins", "pitchers losses", "batting wins", "batting losses", "combined wins" and "combined losses". The idea is simple: if you win a game 2-1, that's a game that your pitching won for you; if you win 8-5, that's a game that your offense has won for you; if you lose 11-2, that's a combined loss; nobody did good.

Unfortunately there appears to be no way to make it work that is fair to both pitchers and hitters, so I'm moving on.

Unfortunately there appears to be no way to make it work that is fair to both pitchers and hitters, so I'm moving on. I was looking at "three to five records"—records when you score three to five runs, records when you allow three to five. The theory is that these games are indicative of something because those are games that the team had a chance to win. If you score one or two runs in a game, you're going to lose 90% of the time. If you give up six, seven, eight runs, you're going to lose the great majority of the time. If you keep it in the range of three to five, you have a chance to win that game. The Diamondbacks were 20-10 when they allowed four runs. The Padres were 9-11. Take those games out of it, and the Padres win the division in a walk.

A "three to five" game is any game in which a team *scores* three to five runs, or any game in which it *allows* three to five runs. The best teams at baseball at keeping the opposition at bay when they *scored* three to five runs were:

1. Angels	33-23	.589
2. Arizona	43-31	.581
3. Indians	33-24	.579
4. Mets	31-25	.554
5. Padres	36-34	.514

It's a pretty interesting list. The Angels, we are told often, are the best team in baseball at playing small ball. They don't score the most runs total, but that's not always what it's about; it's also about scoring runs when you need a run to win the game. This chart suggests that the Angels did in fact have that ability.

And the Diamondbacks...well, that, of course, was one of the defining stories of the season: the Diamond-

And the Diamondbacks...well, that, of course, was one of the defining stories of the season: the Diamondbacks finding just enough runs to survive.

backs finding just enough runs to survive. 43 times they scored three to five runs—but made it work.

On the other end of teams scoring three to five runs were:

1. Baltimore.......................................19-40   .322
2. Tampa Bay....................................19-39   .328
3. Reds 23-41   .359
4. Blue Jays.......................................23-40   .365
5. Marlins 25-43   .368

Fish and birds; don't want to be a fish or a bird in this category. The Blue Jays were fantastic at winning with two runs—did that twelve times—but stunk at holding on when they had three to five. Sometimes you just can't figure. It's not a .500 category, by the way. The overall winning percentage for teams which scored three to five runs was .450; for teams which allowed three to five runs, .550.

The best teams in baseball at winning when they *allowed* three to five runs were mostly the teams with the best offenses:

1. Seattle 35-18   .660
2. Cleveland 48-25   .658
3. Yankees...35-20   .636
4. Red Sox 36-21   .632
5. Marlins 42-25   .627
   Brewers (tie)..................................42-25   .627

The Indians had 73 games in which they allowed three to five runs—tying Toronto for the most in the majors—and won almost two-thirds of those games. On the other end of teams allowing three to five runs were:

1. Giants..30-39   .435
2. Nationals 32-37   .464
3. Astros..26-30   .464
4. Orioles...28-32   .467
5. Royals..32-35   .478

Except for the Cubs, it's a fairly safe generalization that if you can't find a way to win when your pitching allows only three to five runs, you can't win. The Cubs won the National League Central despite going 27-28 when they allowed three to five runs. The other seven teams that made the playoffs all had winning percentages of .585 or better in this group.

Combining scoring *and* allowing, the best teams in baseball in three-to-five games were:

1. Cleveland Native Americans...........81-49   .623
2. Los Angeles Winged Spirits 68-44   .607
3. Arizona Venom Squirters................81-55   .596
4. Seattle Seafarers.............................68-50   .576
5. New York Carpetbaggers.................55-43   .561

While the worst were:

1. Baltimore Small Colorful Birds........47-72   .395
2. Houston Space Cadets 54-72   .429
3. Toronto Squawkers 59-77   .434
4. San Francisco Pituitary Cases..........63-82   .434
5. Pittsburgh Bloodthirsty Cutthroats...56-72   .438

Those are not "true" won-lost records, by the way, because a team can both score and allow three to five runs in a game, so some games are double-counted. Also those are not the teams' true nicknames.

The overall winning percentage of teams in three-to-five games is .500; this is true by definition, since a game in which one team scores three to five is always a game in which the other team allows three to five, thus is both a win and a loss. There really were only a handful of teams in 2007 which had meaningful disparities between their three-to-five winning percentage and their overall winning percentage. Those included:

The Diamondbacks. Three-to-five games also *tend* to be close games; this is one of the reasons to pay a little attention to the category. The Diamondbacks won their division because they won the close games.

The Red Sox. The Red Sox were an appalling 23-32 in games in which they scored three to five runs, just missing the worst-in-baseball list, although they were pretty good when they allowed three to five. Their winning percentage was worse in three-to-five games than it was overall.

As a Red Sox observer, I know what many of those games were. They were what we called the Groundhog Day Games, because we kept playing the same game over and over. The team would be facing some pitcher of great promise but relatively modest accomplishment—Robinson Tejeda, or Andy Sonnanstine, or Ryan Feierabend—and would score a run or two in the first but leave the bases loaded, squander a scoring chance in the second, another in the third, ground into a double play in the fourth, fall into a 5-1 hole and rally late to lose 6-4. This went on for what seemed like months. The disparity between the Red Sox three-to-five winning percentage and overall winning percentage was easily the largest in baseball.

The White Sox. The White Sox were the opposite; they were really good in three-to-five games; they just couldn't compete when the game got ragged. The White Sox were 33-32 when they scored three to five runs, 35-29 when they allowed three to five, overall 68-61. Which would mean that they were 4-29 in other games, except, of course, that that's not exactly true because of that double-counting thing.

The Tigers. The Tigers were 57-60 in three-to-five games, but finished fourteen games over .500 overall.

The Blue Jays. The Jays poor performance in three-to-five games, perhaps related to the loss of their closer early in the season, essentially kept them from being competitive in the division. They were eighteen games under .500 in three-to-five games, twenty-two games over .500 otherwise, once more ignoring that double-counting problem.

The Blue Jays were fantastic at winning with two runs—did that twelve times—but stunk at holding on when they had three to five.

Chicago Cubs

Chicago Cubs – 2007
Team Overview

Description		Ranking
Won-Lost Record	85-77	
Place		1st of 6 in National League Central
Runs Scored	752	18th in the majors
Runs Allowed	690	3rd in the majors
Home Runs	151	21st in the majors
Home Runs Allowed	165	15th in the majors
Batting Average	.271	13th in the majors
Batting Average Allowed	.246	1st in the majors
Walks Drawn	500	25th in the majors
Walks Given	573	24th in the majors
OPS For	.754	15th in the majors
OPS Against	.721	4th in the majors
Stolen Bases	86	18th in the majors
Stolen Bases Allowed	116	27th in the majors

Key Players

Pos	Player	G	AB	R	H	2B	3B	HR	RBI	SB	CS	BB	SO	Avg	OBP	Slg	OPS	WS
C	Michael Barrett	57	211	23	54	9	0	9	29	2	2	17	36	.256	.307	.427	.734	2
1B	Derrek Lee	150	567	91	180	43	1	22	82	6	5	71	114	.317	.400	.513	.913	21
2B	Mark DeRosa	149	502	64	147	28	3	10	72	1	2	58	93	.293	.371	.420	.792	16
3B	Aramis Ramirez	132	506	72	157	35	4	26	101	0	0	43	66	.310	.366	.549	.915	21
SS	Ryan Theriot	148	537	80	143	30	2	3	45	28	4	49	50	.266	.326	.346	.672	11
LF	Alfonso Soriano	135	579	97	173	42	5	33	70	19	6	31	130	.299	.337	.560	.897	20
CF	Jacque Jones	135	453	52	129	33	2	5	66	6	3	34	70	.285	.335	.400	.735	14
RF	Cliff Floyd	108	282	40	80	10	1	9	45	0	0	35	47	.284	.373	.422	.795	8

Key Pitchers

Pos	Player	G	GS	W	L	Sv	IP	H	R	ER	BB	SO	BR/9	ERA	WS
SP	Ted Lilly	34	34	15	8	0	207.0	181	91	88	55	174	10.39	3.83	15
SP	Carlos Zambrano	34	34	18	13	0	216.1	187	100	95	101	177	12.56	3.95	16
SP	Jason Marquis	34	33	12	9	0	191.2	190	111	98	76	109	13.10	4.60	8
SP	Rich Hill	32	32	11	8	0	195.0	170	89	85	63	183	11.31	3.92	13
SP	Sean Marshall	21	19	7	8	0	103.1	107	52	45	35	67	12.45	3.92	6
CL	Ryan Dempster	66	0	2	7	28	66.2	59	36	35	30	55	12.15	4.73	8
RP	Bob Howry	78	0	6	7	8	81.1	76	31	30	19	72	10.73	3.32	11
RP	Mike Wuertz	73	0	2	3	0	72.1	64	30	28	35	79	12.32	3.48	6

Mays's Law

In the computer world there is something called Moore's Law. Moore's Law—doing some violence to a complicated discussion—states that the processing capacity of computers will double every eighteen months. Moore's Law was advanced in 1965, and holds true to today, probably will hold true for several more generations.

It used to be a noteworthy accomplishment when a player would hit 20 homers and steal 20 bases in a season. In the history of major league baseball through 1950 there were only seven players who hit 20 homers and stole 20 bases in the same season. If that number doubled every ten years, it would now be 364. It is now 320. It *is* leveling off, but here's the sequence since 1950:

1949		7 total
1950-59	11 more	18 total
1960-69	23 more	41 total
1970-79	47 more	88 total
1980-89	59 more	147 total
1990-99	99 more	246 total
2000-07	74 more	320 total

There are similar exponential patterns in the number of players hitting 25/25…that sequence, beginning in 1950, goes 1, 5, 9, 31, 62, 100, 129 through 2007…and players hitting 30/30 (1, 3, 5, 10, 17, 37, 51). Through 1955 only Ken Williams had hit 25 homers and stolen 25 bases in the same season, then Willie Mays did it four times, then Aaron did it twice, Bobby Bonds four times, and we took off from there. Five players did it in 2007. Three players in 2007 had 30/30—as many 30/30 players as there were in all of baseball history through 1962.

Mays's Law: the number of players hitting 20 homers and stealing 20 bases will double every ten years. To an astonishing extent, the Willie Mays profile has become the model of a modern outfielder—not that anybody else *is* Willie Mays, but everybody is sort of trying to be Willie Mays. Nobody is out there looking for a young Richie Asburn anymore, or, dating myself a little bit less, a young Tony Gwynn. The Willie Mays model has triumphed over the Ted Williams model, the Stan Musial model, the Joe DiMaggio, the Mickey Mantle model and the Ty Cobb model.

Alfonso Soriano is on the 30/30 list four times—2002, 2003, 2005 and 2006. Dan Quisenberry used to joke that he was a 30/30/30 man—30 saves, 30 strikeouts, 30 great plays by Frank White. Alfonso is a 30/30/30 man, too—30 homers, 30 steals, 30 walks. Last year he had only 19 stolen bases, but 33 homers, 31 walks. Naturally the Cubs signed him; they've been trying desperately since 1980 to come up with a player who had exactly the same number of stolen bases, home runs and walks.

In 1889 a player named Billy O'Brien had 9 homers, 9 walks and 10 stolen bases. These are the five players who came closest to matching numbers in all three areas (500 or more at plate appearances):

	HR	BB	SB
1. Billy O'Brien, 1888	9	9	10
2. Brian Jordan, 1995	22	22	24
3. Alfonso Soriano, 2003	38	38	35
4. Brandon Phillips, 2007	30	33	32
5. Joe Carter, 1986	29	32	29

After that it seems like it is mostly Cubs, or players that you associate with the Cubs although they may not have been Cubs yet—Shawon Dunston, 1986 (17/21/13), 1990 (17/15/25), 1991 (12/23/21), and 1995 (14/10/10), Andre Dawson, 1978 (25/30/28) and 1979 (25/27/35), Corey Patterson, 2002 (14/19/18), Sammy Sosa in 1993 (33/38/36), Soriano in 2005 (36/33/30), Billy Cowan in 1964 (19/18/12), Jacque Jones in 2003 (16/21/13) and Neifi Perez in 2005 (9/18/8). Joe Carter, originally a Cub but traded away early, appears on the list in '85, '86, '87 and '88.

I am running at what I am trying to say from an awkward angle here, armed with irrelevant lists. Alfonso Soriano is not Willie Mays. Willie Mays was a great defensive center fielder who walked as often as he struck out. Alfonso Soriano is to Willie Mays as Kerry Wood is to Roger Clemens.

Not being Willie Mays is not a crime; I'm not Charles Dickens, either. Alfonso's a good player. It's more the Neifi Perez, Corey Patterson and Jacque Jones tradition which has held the Cubs back. The Cubs had a very good year in 2007, a year that represents real progress. If you had enough Alfonso Sorianos you could probably win a pennant—but nobody could afford to win a pennant that way, even the Yankees. The future for the Cubs doesn't rest on getting more Alfonso Sorianos; it rests on getting development out of Felix Pie, Geovany Soto, Ryan Theriot, Rich Hill and Matt Murton.

The Cubs were ahead after the first inning an astonishing 53 times in 2007, best in the Natonal League.

Chicago Cubs – 2007
Innings Ahead/Behind/Tied

Inning	1	2	3	4	5	6	7	8	9	Extra	Final
Ahead	53	58	61	75	69	72	77	80	83	2	85
Behind	33	50	56	65	66	66	63	67	69	8	77
Tied	76	54	45	22	27	24	22	15	10	16	—

Last year Alfonso Soriano swung at 467 pitches that were outside the strike zone, third-most in the majors. It was only the second time since we began compiling the data in 2002 that he'd failed to lead the majors. Back in 2004, Vladimir Guerrero topped him by 33.

Three of the Cubs' opening-day starters started less than a third of the team's games, Michael Barrett, Cesar Izturis and Matt Murton. No other playoff team had more than two opening-day starters start less than 1/3 of their team's games.

Alfonso Soriano – 2007
Pitch Analysis

Overall		
Pitches Seen	2552	
Taken	939	42%
Swung At	1313	58%
Pitches Taken		
Taken for a Strike	239	25%
Called a ball	700	75%
Pitches Taken by Pitch Location		
In Strike Zone	239	25%
High	186	20%
Low	224	24%
Inside	111	12%
Outside	179	19%
Swung At		
Missed	335	26%
Fouled Off	526	40%
Put in Play	452	34%
Swung At by Pitch Location		
In Strike Zone	846	64%
High	54	4%
Low	204	16%
Inside	74	6%
Outside	135	10%

Chicago Cubs – 2007
Games Played by Opening Day Starter at Each Position

Pos	Player	Starts
C	Barrett	52
1B	Lee	147
2B	DeRosa	138
3B	Ramirez	129
SS	Izturis	48
LF	Murton	53
CF	Soriano	134
RF	Jones	113
Total		814

Chicago's opening-day starters accounted for 63% of their regular season starting lineup.

Can This Guy Throw, or What?

It doesn't look pretty but it gets the job done. Big time. That's what we can say about Alfonso Soriano's throwing arm in left field. He throws like the former second baseman that he is. It's that side-arm throw that all second baseman master to get their throws over to first base quickly. And that's what Soriano does in left field. That's part of the reason it's so successful; he gets rid of the ball quickly. There are two more reasons why he is so good: his great speed allows him to get to the ball quickly before making a throw, and he is incredibly dead-on accurate.

At the beginning of the 2006 season, Soriano was reluctant to move to left field after having played sec- ond base his entire career. He even refused to take the field in his first spring training game as a left fielder for the Nationals. But he finally agreed to play and he took to playing the outfield, particularly left field, like a duck to water. After a bit of an adjustment period, he became a very good outfielder. But it's his throwing that has really stood out.

How deadly has he been? In 2006, he had 15 baserunner kills (a direct throw to a base to "kill" a baserunner—no relay involved) in left field. The next-best left fielder had 10 (Craig Monroe). He got even better in 2007. He had 19 baserunner kills while the next-best left fielder had 7 (Jason Bay).

Alfonso Soriano – 2005-2007
Fielding Bible Plus/Minus

Left Field												
			THROWING					PLAYS			PLUS/MINUS	
Year	Team	Inn	Opps To Advance	Extra Bases	Kills	Pct	Rank	Expected Outs	Outs Made	Total	Enhanced	Rank
2006	Was	1373.2	157	65	15	.414	17	320	326	+6	+19	1
2007	ChC	1064.0	120	46	19	.383	10	247	245	-2	-2	17
	Total	2437.2	277	111	34	.401	15	567	571	+4	+17	6

Who Needs a Leadoff Man?

When the Cubs got their leadoff man on base four or more times in a game their record was 20-26 in 2007. When the leadoff man got on three times or less, they went 65-51. They are the only team in 2007 and only the second team in the last six years (180 team seasons) to have a winning record with three or less leadoff men getting on in a game and a losing record with four or more. The other team was the 2006 Arizona Diamondbacks. Go figure.

This is not a Cub team trend nor an Alfonso Soriano trend, by the way. In the five years prior to 2007, the Cubs were significantly better when they managed four or more leadoff men on base in a game. And nearly every previous Alfonso Soriano team has played significantly better with leadoff men getting on base.

Chicago Cubs – 2007
Record by Leadoff Hitter Reached

Leadoff Hitter Reached	W	-	L
6 times	4	-	4
5 times	8	-	5
4 times	8	-	17
3 times	31	-	13
2 times	24	-	17
1 times	10	-	17
0 times	0	-	4
Total, 4 or more LO men on	20	-	26
Total, 3 or less LO men on	65	-	51

The Cubs' most effective baserunner last year was not Alfonso Soriano (+11) or Ryan Theriot (+9), but rookie center fielder Felix Pie (+18), who made only 36 starts and batted less than 200 times. He aggressively took extra bases without ever being caught trying; he stole eight bases in nine attempts; and he didn't ground into a single double play at the major league level.

Felix Pie – Career
Baserunning Analysis

Year	1st to 3rd Adv	1st to 3rd Opp	2nd to Home Adv	2nd to Home Opp	1st to Home Adv	1st to Home Opp	DP Opp	GIDP	Bases Taken	BR Outs	BR Gain	SB Gain	Net Gain
2007	3	8	4	9	2	2	31	0	9	0	12	6	+18
		38%		44%		100%		0%					

Alfonso Soriano – 2002-2007
Baserunning Analysis

Year	1st to 3rd Adv	1st to 3rd Opp	2nd to Home Adv	2nd to Home Opp	1st to Home Adv	1st to Home Opp	DP Opp	GIDP	Bases Taken	BR Outs	BR Gain	SB Gain	Net Gain
2002	18	27	23	30	2	2	109	8	17	0	28	15	+43
2003	5	19	18	22	0	3	105	8	29	2	21	19	+40
2004	7	12	8	10	1	2	124	7	21	1	27	8	+35
2005	5	17	12	18	4	10	121	6	12	4	6	26	+32
2006	7	23	20	32	2	4	100	3	17	5	8	7	+15
2007	9	15	12	19	4	4	82	9	14	5	4	7	+11
Totals	51	113	93	131	13	25	641	41	110	17	94	82	+176
		45%		71%		52%		6%					

Ryan Theriot – Career
Baserunning Analysis

Year	1st to 3rd Adv	1st to 3rd Opp	2nd to Home Adv	2nd to Home Opp	1st to Home Adv	1st to Home Opp	DP Opp	GIDP	Bases Taken	BR Outs	BR Gain	SB Gain	Net Gain
2005	0	2	1	2	0	0	3	0	1	0	1	0	+1
2006	3	3	6	8	1	4	32	5	6	1	3	9	+12
2007	7	21	15	23	3	6	86	12	13	7	-11	20	+9
Totals	10	26	22	33	4	10	121	17	20	8	-7	29	+22
		38%		67%		40%		14%					

Chicago Cubs – 2007
Performance by Quality of Start

Game Score	#	ERA	W	-	L
80 and above	5	0.60	4	-	1
70 to 79	15	1.19	13	-	2
60 to 69	43	1.84	35	-	8
50 to 59	25	3.79	11	-	14
40 to 49	28	4.64	15	-	13
30 to 39	27	6.16	5	-	22
20 to 29	12	8.56	1	-	11
Below 20	7	9.74	1	-	6

The Cubs were 35-8 when their starting pitcher's Game Score was 60 to 69, but 11-14 when it was 50 to 59.

For Those of You Who STILL Insist That Baseball is 90% Pitching...

The Cubs last year had a better record with Jason Marquis on the mound than with Carlos Zambrano, Ted Lilly or any other starting pitcher.

Chicago Cubs– 2007
Performance by Starting Pitcher

Games Started By	G	RS	RA	Won	Lost
Zambrano, Carlos	34	157	129	18	16
Lilly, Ted	34	179	136	19	15
Marquis, Jason	33	180	152	20	13
Hill, Rich	32	109	130	17	15
Marshall, Sean	19	78	74	9	10
Trachsel, Steve	4	17	24	1	3
Guzman, Angel	3	16	20	1	2
Miller, Wade	3	16	25	0	3
Team Totals	162	752	690	85	77

Got a Gal in Every Port
Who's Suin' Me for Non-support

In 2007 the best-supported starting pitcher in the majors was Kyle Kendrick of Philadelphia, at 6.45 runs per start, but the best-supported starting pitcher relative to his team was Roy Halladay of Toronto, who received 29 runs more than expected given the Toronto offense (173 vs. 144 in 31 starts).

The worst-supported starting pitcher in the majors was Matt Cain of San Francisco, at 3.16 runs per start, but the worst-supported relative to his team was Rich Hill of the Cubs, 40 runs short of expected support.

Since 2002 the best-supported starting pitcher in a season has been Curt Schilling in 2004, at 7.00 runs per start, but the best-supported relative to his team was Cliff Lee in 2005 (+43 runs).

Since 2002 the worst-supported starting pitcher in a season is a tie between Cain last year and Nate Cornejo in 2003 (same data, 101 runs in 32 starts), but the worst-supported relative to his team was Kelvim Escobar in 2004 (-41 runs). Escobar was the only pitcher since 2002 to be shorted by his team worse than Rich Hill was.

In his career, Carlos Zambrano has performed best against the best teams, posting a 2.81 ERA against teams with a .600 winning percentage or better.

Carlos Zambrano – 2002-2007
Career Records Against Quality of Opposition

Opponent	G	IP	W	L	SO	BB	ERA
.600 teams	14	99.1	7	4	84	42	2.81
.500 - .599 teams	88	524.0	33	21	459	242	3.40
.400 - .499 teams	88	536.2	38	27	474	239	3.35
sub .400 teams	5	25.2	3	1	21	17	3.51

Chicago White Sox

Chicago White Sox – 2007
Team Overview

Description		Ranking
Won-Lost Record	72-90	
Place	4th of 5 in American League Central	
Runs Scored	693	28th in the majors
Runs Allowed	839	24th in the majors
Home Runs	190	6th in the majors
Home Runs Allowed	174	21st in the majors
Batting Average	.246	30th in the majors
Batting Average Allowed	.276	24th in the majors
Walks Drawn	532	14th in the majors
Walks Given	499	8th in the majors
OPS For	.722	26th in the majors
OPS Against	.773	21st in the majors
Stolen Bases	78	20th in the majors
Stolen Bases Allowed	98	17th in the majors

Key Players

Pos	Player	G	AB	R	H	2B	3B	HR	RBI	SB	CS	BB	SO	Avg	OBP	Slg	OPS	WS
C	A.J. Pierzynski	136	472	54	124	24	0	14	50	1	1	25	66	.263	.309	.403	.712	8
1B	Paul Konerko	151	549	71	142	34	0	31	90	0	1	78	102	.259	.351	.490	.841	16
2B	Tadahito Iguchi	90	327	45	82	17	4	6	31	8	1	44	65	.251	.340	.382	.723	10
3B	Josh Fields	100	373	54	91	17	1	23	67	1	1	35	125	.244	.308	.480	.788	12
SS	Juan Uribe	150	513	55	120	18	2	20	68	1	9	34	112	.234	.284	.394	.678	13
LF	Scott Podsednik	62	214	30	52	13	4	2	11	12	5	13	36	.243	.299	.369	.668	1
CF	Jerry Owens	93	356	44	95	9	2	1	17	32	8	27	63	.267	.324	.312	.636	6
RF	Jermaine Dye	138	508	68	129	34	0	28	78	2	1	45	107	.254	.317	.486	.804	11
DH	Jim Thome	130	432	79	119	19	0	35	96	0	1	95	134	.275	.410	.563	.973	21

Key Pitchers

Pos	Player	G	GS	W	L	Sv	IP	H	R	ER	BB	SO	BR/9	ERA	WS
SP	Javier Vazquez	32	32	15	8	0	216.2	197	95	90	50	213	10.55	3.74	18
SP	Mark Buehrle	30	30	10	9	0	201.0	208	86	81	45	115	11.55	3.63	17
SP	Jon Garland	32	32	10	13	0	208.1	219	114	98	57	98	12.10	4.23	13
SP	Jose Contreras	32	30	10	17	0	189.0	232	134	117	62	113	14.71	5.57	5
SP	John Danks	26	26	6	13	0	139.0	160	92	85	54	109	14.12	5.50	4
CL	Bobby Jenks	66	0	3	5	40	65.0	45	20	20	13	56	8.17	2.77	16
RP	Boone Logan	68	0	2	1	0	50.2	59	30	28	20	35	14.03	4.97	3
RP	Matt Thornton	68	0	4	4	2	56.1	59	31	30	26	55	13.90	4.79	4

Thome Poisoning

Does Jim Thome hit more opposite field home runs than any hitter ever?

I don't know the answer to that question, but if he doesn't, I can't imagine who did.

From 2002 to 2007, when Thome hit the ball on the ground he pulled it 63% of the time, hit to left only 10%.

When he hit a fly ball, he pulled it only 23%, and hit to the opposite field 42%.

For almost any power hitter that would be death, because most hitters have to get out in front of a pitch to drive it out of the park. Thome doesn't. Thome is so strong that he can swing late and leave the yard 10, 15 times every year on balls hit to the opposite field. Since 2002 he has hit 58 home runs to the opposite field, and 62 more to center.

A more typical case is Thome's teammate of the last two years, Juan Uribe. Uribe has good power, hits 20 homers a year. When he hits a fly ball to left, he hits .313 (over the last six years). But when he hits a fly ball to right, he hits .113.

The difference? Power. Uribe has hit 9 homers to right over the six years—but 79 to left.

Home Run Locations – 2002 thru 2007
Thome and Uribe

	Pull Field	Center Field	Opposite Field
Jim Thome	105	62	58
Juan Uribe	79	8	9

Where Have All the Line Drives Gone?

In 2003 Alex Cintron looked like the second coming of Tony Fernandez, hitting .317 with 70 runs scored in 117 games, playing shortstop for Arizona. Since then he has just melted gradually away like a snowman in March, spending 2007 as a backup infielder for the floundering White Sox.

What happened to him? He stopped hitting line drives. In 2003 26% of his balls in play were line drives. Since then he's hit line drives on 21% of his balls in play. Doesn't work out. You hit .700 on line drives, maybe .750. You hit .200, .250 on ground balls.

One is tempted to say it is Neifi Perez' disease. Cintron swings at a very high percentage of the pitches he sees, and, once the pitchers find out that you will expand the strike zone, it becomes harder and harder to center the bat on the ball. When he moved to a new league that gave him a new set of pitchers to work with, that revived him for a while, the same as it did for Corey Patterson.

OK, Smart Ass, so what happened to Brad Wilkerson?

Brad Wilkerson is one of the most selective hitters in baseball, the exact opposite of Alex Cintron—and yet essentially the same thing has happened to him. In 2004 and 2005, 23% of the balls he hit were line drives, which is enough to keep him above water, because some of his fly balls work out good, too. But since joining the Rangers the line drives have dropped to 15%, and his on-base percentage, which was the thing that made him useful, has dropped into the useless range.

It's called Ben Grieve's disease.

The truth is, baseball is a very, very difficult game, and there are many ways to fail.

Percentage of Balls in Play That Are Liners
Cintron and Wilkerson

	Early Career	Recently
Cintron	26%	21%
Wilkerson	23%	15%

The White Sox had the majors' worst winning percentage when held homerless (.228). Hardly surprising, since they had the most home-run-dependent offense of any team. They were sixth in the majors in home runs (190) but were dead last in doubles (249), batting average (.246) and on-base percentage (.318).

Chicago White Sox – 2007
Record by Home Runs

Home Runs	W – L
0 homers	13 - 44
1 homer	20 - 27
2 homers	19 - 14
3 or more homers	20 - 5

Worn Out His Welcome?

Despite an on-base percentage a bit lower than you'd like at the top of the order (.338 career on-base percentage), Scott Podsednik has proven quite effective as a leadoff man. Until last year. Every year prior to 2007 Pods' teams have scored significantly more runs when he led off an inning than when others have led off.

Scott Podsednik – 2003 - 2007
Leading Off an Inning

Year	Pods Leading Off		Others Leading Off		Gain
	Number	Team Runs/Inn	Number	Team Runs/Inn	Team Runs/Inn
2003	179	.70	1,293	.45	.25
2004	144	.48	1,170	.42	.06
2005	239	.73	1,231	.46	.27
2006	243	.80	1,215	.55	.25
2007	66	.47	1,393	.48	-.01

The Underachievers

In 2007 every White Sox batter with 150 or more at-bats except one (Rob Mackowiak) finished the season with an OPS below his previous career average. Even Mackowiak was below his career norm overall, but was above it with the White Sox before he was traded to San Diego. Ten different guys couldn't manage to reach their career-average OPS. That's major underachieving. In the last twenty years only three teams can compare. The 1998 expansion Tampa Bay Devil Rays and the 1988 Philadelphia Phillies had nine underachievers and no one bettering their previous career OPS. The 1990 New York Yankees suffered through nine players performing below his career average and only one above.

Chicago White Sox
(minimum 150 At Bats)

	2007 OPS	Career OPS	Difference
Joe Crede	.576	.763	-.187
Alex Cintron	.605	.727	-.122
Darin Erstad	.645	.756	-.111
Tadahito Iguchi	.723	.777	-.054
A.J. Pierzynski	.712	.765	-.053
Juan Uribe	.678	.730	-.052
Scott Podsednik	.668	.719	-.051
Jermaine Dye	.804	.825	-.021
Paul Konerko	.841	.849	-.008
Jim Thome	.973	.974	-.001
Rob Mackowiak	.772	.746	.026

The past three seasons the White Sox first five starting pitchers have made at least 150 starts each year.

Only two other clubs' first five starters have reached 150 starts in the same period, the 2005 A's and 2005 Cardinals.

Starts Made by First Five Starters

Team	Apr	May	June	July	Aug	Sept	Total
St. Louis 2005	22	29	27	26	28	28	160
Chicago 2006	24	26	27	25	29	28	159
Oakland 2005	24	24	24	26	28	30	156
Chicago 2005	24	26	23	25	27	27	152
Chicago 2007	23	25	28	27	26	21	150

Ozzie: "I'm Bringing in the Big Guy"

Bobby Jenks snapped up the closer job as a rookie in Chicago's 2005 World Championship season, finishing the year with six saves in eight tries, but more importantly, helping his teammates get their rings. He followed that up with a strong 2006 with 41 saves. But as good as those two seasons were, Jenks' Record of Opposing Batters shows how much better he was in 2007:

Bobby Jenks
Record of Opposing Batters

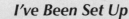

Season	AB	R	H	2B	3B	HR	RBI	BB	SO	SB	CS	GIDP	Avg	OBP	Slg	OPS
2005	151	15	34	10	0	3	17	15	50	7	0	1	.225	.295	.351	.646
2006	261	32	66	14	0	5	32	31	80	11	2	8	.253	.332	.364	.696
2007	227	20	45	5	0	2	23	13	56	5	0	4	.198	.242	.247	.488

I've Been Set Up

Jenks had a great season in 2007, but the rest of the White Sox bullpen struggled, floundered, gasped and choked. The Tampa Bay setup men in 2007 were, by our research (thanks to Retrosheet), the worst in the major leagues since 1974, posting a 6.33 ERA. But the White Sox still made the list:

The Worst Set-up Teams since 1974
(team relief ERA excluding the closer)

Team	Season	Wins	Losses	ERA
Tampa Bay Devil Rays	2007	19	30	6.33
Oakland Athletics	1980	2	10	6.19
Seattle Mariners	1999	16	25	6.11
Boston Red Sox	1994	12	17	6.08
Detroit Tigers	1996	21	29	6.05
Arizona Diamondbacks	2005	19	16	6.01
Seattle Mariners	1998	12	26	6.01
Chicago White Sox	2007	16	20	5.98
Minnesota Twins	1986	10	18	5.97
Baltimore Orioles	2007	19	29	5.86

The White Sox actually were seven games over .500 through the first four innings. Their plunge to the wrong side of the ledger took place entirely over the following three frames – they sunk to four games below .500 in the fifth, eight games under in the sixth, and 18 games under in the seventh, which is where their final won-lost record wound up.

Chicago White Sox – 2007
Innings Ahead/Behind/Tied

Inning	1	2	3	4	5	6	7	8	9	Extra	Final
Ahead	40	55	64	71	68	69	64	65	66	6	72
Behind	39	53	62	64	72	77	82	77	83	7	90
Tied	83	54	36	27	22	16	16	20	13	11	—

In 2007 Mark Buehrle was 9-5 with 6 no-decisions in his quality starts.
The prior two seasons he was 25-1 with 10 no decisions in his quality starts.

Mark Buehrle – 2005
Decision Analysis

Group	G	IP	W	L	Pct	H	R	SO	BB	ERA
Wins	16	122.0	16	0	1.000	97	24	86	8	1.48
Losses	8	53.2	0	8	.000	73	46	26	16	6.04
No Decisions	9	61.0	0	0	—	70	29	37	16	3.84
Quality Starts: 14 in Wins, 1 in Losses, 5 in no-decisions										

Mark Buehrle – 2006
Decision Analysis

Group	G	IP	W	L	Pct	H	R	SO	BB	ERA
Wins	12	87.1	12	0	1.000	82	26	42	17	1.85
Losses	13	75.0	0	13	.000	120	76	34	19	8.76
No Decisions	7	41.2	0	0	—	45	22	22	12	4.75
Quality Starts: 11 in Wins, 0 in Losses, 5 in no-decisions										

Mark Buehrle – 2007
Decision Analysis

Group	G	IP	W	L	Pct	H	R	SO	BB	ERA
Wins	10	75.1	10	0	1.000	69	16	42	16	1.79
Losses	9	58.1	0	9	.000	67	35	35	13	5.25
No Decisions	11	67.1	0	0	—	72	35	38	16	4.28
Quality Starts: 9 in Wins, 5 in Losses, 6 in no-decisions										

Move Over, Juan

The ChiSox acquired Orlando Cabrera in the offseason to take over the shortstop position from Juan Uribe. Our projections (from *The Bill James Handbook*) show Uribe with a projected OPS for 2008 better than Cabrera (.723 vs .709). Should the White Sox simply have stayed with Uribe? Based on their Skill Assessment comparisons, the answer is clearly "No Way".

Orlando Cabrera – 2007
Skills Assessment

Running:	96th percentile	95th percentile among shortstops
Plate Discipline:	65th percentile	68th percentile among shortstops
Hitting for Average:	59th percentile	58th percentile among shortstops
Hitting for Power:	18th percentile	37th percentile among shortstops

Juan Uribe – 2007
Skills Assessment

Hitting for Power:	48th percentile	82nd percentile among shortstops
Plate Discipline:	7th percentile	5th percentile among shortstops
Running:	6th percentile	5th percentile among shortstops
Hitting for Average:	5th percentile	3rd percentile among shortstops

Cincinnati Reds

Cincinnati Reds – 2007
Team Overview

Description		Ranking
Won-Lost Record	72-90	
Place		5th of 6 in National League Central
Runs Scored	783	14th in the majors
Runs Allowed	853	27th in the majors
Home Runs	204	3rd in the majors
Home Runs Allowed	198	27th in the majors
Batting Average	.267	17th in the majors
Batting Average Allowed	.282	27th in the majors
Walks Drawn	536	11th in the majors
Walks Given	482	6th in the majors
OPS For	.772	10th in the majors
OPS Against	.800	28th in the majors
Stolen Bases	97	14th in the majors
Stolen Bases Allowed	88	10th in the majors

Key Players

Pos	Player	G	AB	R	H	2B	3B	HR	RBI	SB	CS	BB	SO	Avg	OBP	Slg	OPS	WS
C	Dave Ross	112	311	32	63	10	0	17	39	0	0	30	92	.203	.271	.399	.670	7
1B	Scott Hatteberg	116	361	50	112	27	1	10	47	0	0	49	35	.310	.394	.474	.868	10
2B	Brandon Phillips	158	650	107	187	26	6	30	94	32	8	33	109	.288	.331	.485	.816	17
3B	Edwin Encarnacion	139	502	66	145	25	1	16	76	8	1	39	86	.289	.356	.438	.794	16
SS	Alex Gonzalez	110	393	55	107	27	1	16	55	0	1	24	75	.272	.325	.468	.793	10
LF	Adam Dunn	152	522	101	138	27	2	40	106	9	2	101	165	.264	.386	.554	.940	18
CF	Josh Hamilton	90	298	52	87	17	2	19	47	3	3	33	65	.292	.368	.554	.922	11
RF	Ken Griffey Jr.	144	528	78	146	24	1	30	93	6	1	85	99	.277	.372	.496	.869	14

Key Pitchers

Pos	Player	G	GS	W	L	Sv	IP	H	R	ER	BB	SO	BR/9	ERA	WS
SP	Aaron Harang	34	34	16	6	0	231.2	213	100	96	52	218	10.61	3.73	17
SP	Matt Belisle	30	30	8	9	0	177.2	212	111	105	43	125	13.27	5.32	5
SP	Bronson Arroyo	34	34	9	15	0	210.2	232	109	99	63	156	13.16	4.23	11
SP	Kyle Lohse	21	21	6	12	0	131.2	143	76	67	33	80	12.44	4.58	6
SP	Bobby Livingston	10	10	3	3	0	56.1	77	35	33	8	27	13.74	5.27	2
CL	David Weathers	70	0	2	6	33	77.2	67	33	31	27	48	11.47	3.59	13
RP	Jon Coutlangus	64	0	4	2	0	41.0	38	22	20	27	38	15.15	4.39	3
RP	Mike Stanton	69	0	1	3	0	57.2	75	39	38	18	40	15.29	5.93	1

In games Kyle Lohse started for the Reds in 2007 the Reds were 8-13.

In games he started for the Phillies they were 9-2.

Cincinnati Reds– 2007
Performance by Starting Pitcher

Games Started By	G	RS	RA	Won	Lost
Arroyo, Bronson	34	135	162	12	22
Harang, Aaron	34	180	140	24	10
Belisle, Matt	30	165	166	12	18
Lohse, Kyle	21	75	97	8	13
Livingston, Bobby	10	58	67	6	4
Bailey, Homer	9	49	54	5	4
Dumatrait, Phil	6	30	56	1	5
Milton, Eric	6	22	37	0	6
Shearn, Tom	6	35	26	3	3
Saarloos, Kirk	3	17	27	0	3
Ramirez, Elizardo	3	17	21	1	2
Team Totals	162	783	853	72	90

Red Menace

The Cincinnati Reds won 24 games started by Aaron Harang in 2007—the most by any major league pitcher.

In 2002 the Diamondbacks went 29-6 with Randy Johnson starting, and the Oakland A's went 28-7 with Barry Zito. Since 2002 the best record for any starting pitcher was 27-7, by the Twins with you-know-who in 2006.

One More Career Homer than the Easter Bunny

Norris Hopper had 335 plate appearances but pulled the ball in the air only seven times (zero line drives to left, seven fly balls to left).

Norris Hopper – 2007
Hitting Analysis

Batting Right-Handed									1B	2B	3B	HR
Ground Balls to Left	47	Outs	28	Hits	19	Average	.404	Hit Type	15 -	4 -	0 -	0
Ground Balls to Center	53	Outs	39	Hits	14	Average	.264	Hit Type	14 -	0 -	0 -	0
Ground Balls to Right	44	Outs	35	Hits	9	Average	.205	Hit Type	9 -	0 -	0 -	0
Line Drives to Center	25	Outs	9	Hits	16	Average	.640	Hit Type	15 -	1 -	0 -	0
Line Drives to Right	24	Outs	6	Hits	18	Average	.750	Hit Type	13 -	5 -	0 -	0
Fly Balls to Left	7	Outs	5	Hits	2	Average	.286	Hit Type	0 -	1 -	1 -	0
Fly Balls to Center	16	Outs	12	Hits	4	Average	.267	Hit Type	1 -	3 -	0 -	0
Fly Balls to Right	33	Outs	32	Hits	1	Average	.030	Hit Type	0 -	0 -	1 -	0
Total on Ground Balls	144	Outs	102	Hits	42	Average	.292	Hit Type	38 -	4 -	0 -	0
Total on Line Drives	49	Outs	15	Hits	34	Average	.694	Hit Type	28 -	6 -	0 -	0
Total on Fly Balls	56	Outs	49	Hits	7	Average	.127	Hit Type	1 -	4 -	2 -	0
Total Hit to Left	54	Outs	33	Hits	21	Average	.389	Hit Type	15 -	5 -	1 -	0
Total Hit to Center	94	Outs	60	Hits	34	Average	.366	Hit Type	30 -	4 -	0 -	0
Total Hit to Right	101	Outs	73	Hits	28	Average	.277	Hit Type	22 -	5 -	1 -	0
Bunts	32	Outs	14	Hits	18	Average	.692	Hit Type	18 -	0 -	0 -	0
All Balls in Play	281	Outs	180	Hits	101	Average	.369	Hit Type	85 -	14 -	2 -	0

Adam Dunn was the team RBI leader for the Reds in 2007, but only five of those ribbies came from his 27 doubles.

Adam Dunn – 2007
RBI Analysis

Hits		RBI Hits		RBI Total		Drove In	
Home Runs:	40			RBI on Home Runs:	66	Jorge Cantu	1
Triples:	2	RBI Triples:	1	RBI on Triples:	1	Jeff Conine	4
Doubles:	27	RBI Doubles:	5	RBI on Doubles:	5	Edwin Encarnacion	1
Singles:	69	RBI Singles:	21	RBI on Singles:	21	Ryan Freel	6
				Sacrifice Flies:	4	Alex Gonzalez	3
		Other RBI: Walks	4			Ken Griffey Jr.	13
		Other RBI: Ground Outs	2	Total Other:	9	Josh Hamilton	1
						Scott Hatteberg	10
				Total RBI:	106	Norris Hopper	3
						Jeff Keppinger	6
						Bobby Livingston	1
						Brandon Phillips	17
						His Own Bad Self	40
						Total	106

Bronson Arroyo and Aaron Harang made 34 starts each for the Reds in 2007. Arroyo had a better ERA in games that he won (2.43 to 3.14), a better ERA in games he lost (6.35 to 7.67) and a better ERA in no decisions (2.90 to 3.06)—but a worse ERA overall.

Bronson Arroyo – 2007
Decision Analysis

Group	G	IP	W	L	Pct	H	R	SO	BB	ERA
Wins	9	59.1	9	0	1.000	50	16	55	14	2.43
Losses	15	89.1	0	15	.000	123	71	60	30	6.35
No Decisions	10	62.0	0	0	—	59	22	41	19	2.90

Quality Starts: 7 in Wins, 7 in Losses, 8 in no-decisions

Aaron Harang – 2007
Decision Analysis

Group	G	IP	W	L	Pct	H	R	SO	BB	ERA
Wins	16	114.2	16	0	1.000	90	44	97	27	3.14
Losses	6	31.2	0	6	.000	47	27	37	5	7.67
No Decisions	12	85.1	0	0	—	76	29	84	20	3.06

Quality Starts: 11 in Wins, 0 in Losses, 9 in no-decisions

Aaron Harang has consistently pitched better against good teams than against weak teams.
Against teams with .600 or higher winning percentages, Harang has a career ERA of 3.92.
Against teams with .500 to .599 winning percentages, he has an ERA of 4.13.
Against teams with .400 to .499 winning percentages, he has an ERA of 4.18.
Against teams with sub-.400 winning percentages, his ERA is 4.34.

Aaron Harang
Career Records Against Quality of Opposition

Opponent	G	IP	W	L	SO	BB	ERA
.600 teams	6	39.0	2	4	26	11	3.92
.500 - .599 teams	82	488.2	26	26	406	152	4.13
.400 - .499 teams	67	428.1	32	18	361	98	4.18
sub .400 teams	7	37.1	3	1	35	15	4.34

Middle-Inning Stars

After the first inning the 2007 Cincinnati Reds were 15 games under .500—ahead 40 times, behind 55 times. For three innings after that they made steady progress, improving to 71-62 after four innings. Then they drifted away, winding up with only 72 wins.

What does it mean? We don't have a clue, but it is certainly very unusual. Most bad teams lose from the first inning on; most good teams win from the first inning on. Sometimes a team switches about the 6th inning, if they have a very good or a very bad bullpen. But for a team to switch directions twice…it's hard to explain.

Cincinnati Reds – 2007
Innings Ahead/Behind/Tied

Inning	1	2	3	4	5	6	7	8	9	Extra	Final
Ahead	40	54	62	71	75	72	65	63	62	10	72
Behind	55	61	60	62	67	68	73	82	82	8	90
Tied	67	47	40	29	20	22	24	17	18	20	—

Matt Belisle throws his changeup five times more often to left-handed batters than to right-handed batters.

Matt Belisle – 2007
Pitch Type Analysis

Overall

Total Pitches	2793	
Fastball	1718	62%
Curveball	364	13%
Changeup	174	6%
Slider	265	9%
Cut Fastball	210	8%
Pitchout	6	0%
Not Charted	56	2%

	Vs. RHB		Vs. LHB	
Total Pitches	1440		1353	
Outs Recorded	286		247	
Fastball	903	63%	815	60%
Curveball	214	15%	150	11%
Changeup	32	2%	142	10%
Slider	171	12%	94	7%
Cut Fastball	85	6%	125	9%
Pitchout	4	0%	2	0%
Not Charted	31	2%	25	2%

The Dave Kingman Award

Drum Roll, please.

Like our other stupid awards, the Dave Kingman Award has no actual history, no actual trophy, and is determined by a simple formula that obviates things like "thought", "judgment" and "discussion". It commemorates not excellence but a particularly limited type of accomplishment, a strong skill in one area that somehow doesn't quite carry to the bottom line.

The Dave Kingman Award is given to the hitter who best exemplifies the idea of hitting home runs without doing anything else positive as a hitter. The formula for the Dave Kingman Score is

$$\frac{\text{Home Runs}}{\text{Runs Created} + 10}$$

Runs Created plus ten, rather than simply Runs Created, because otherwise the winner in most years would just be some guy who hit one home run. Dave Kingman did not hit one home run a year; Dave Kingman was a guy you didn't necessarily want on your team even if he hit 40. Dave Kingman does not actually hold the all-time record for single-season Dave Kingman score (Tony Armas does), but Kingman led the majors in this area seven times, has five of the top eight scores of all time, and holds the career record.

And the 2007 winner is: Dave Ross of Cincinnati. Batting just 311 times, Ross struck out 92 times, dropped 17 bombs, but averaged just .203 with no triples or stolen bases, thus creating only 27 runs. The winners of the Dave Kingman Award over the last 30 years have been:

Dave Kingman Award Winners
(last 30 years)

1978—Lance Parrish	1988—Fred Lynn	1998—Jose Canseco
1979—Dave Kingman	1989—Matt Williams	1999—Sammy Sosa
1980—Bob Horner	1990—Steve Balboni	2000—Daryle Ward
1981—Gary Gray	1991—Sam Horn	2001—Mark McGwire
1982—Dave Kingman	1992—Juan Gonzalez	2002—Todd Greene
1983—Tony Armas	1993—Phil Plantier	2003—Jeromy Burnitz
1984—Ron Kittle	1994—Matt Williams	2004—Jose Valentin
1985—Ron Kittle	1995—Jay Buhner	2005—Andruw Jones
1986—Dave Kingman	1996—Sammy Sosa	2006—Ken Griffey Jr.
1987—Steve Balboni	1997—Mark McGwire	2007—Dave Ross

The Targeting Phenomenon

by Bill James

Let me ask you a question. Are there more pitchers, would you suppose, who win 15 games in a season, or 16? Are there more pitchers who win 7 games, or 8? Are there more pitchers who win 13 games, or 12?

Yes, of course; there are more pitchers who win 15 games in a season than 16, more who win 7 than 8, and more who win 12 than 13. The most common number of wins for a pitcher in a season is zero. The second most-common is one, the third most-common is two. Of course.

But then let me ask you another question. Are there more pitchers who win 19 games in a season, or 20?

Yes, of course; there are more pitchers who win 20 games than 19. You would know this by intuition; I am just pointing out to you the implications of what you already know. The number of pitchers with x wins in a season decreases constantly as x rises from zero to 26—except that there are more pitchers with 20 wins than 19. For an obvious reason. Twenty wins is a target. This actually is a count of all the pitchers with x wins in a season from 1900 through 2006:

I got to wondering what "targets" there are out there which disrupt the normal frequency curves.

In 2007 there were many 19-game winners, only one who hit 20. This research was done during the 2007 season, and I decided not to update the study to include the 2007 season, as it is a study of the underlying principle, rather than any specific player, and the underlying principle doesn't change quickly in time.

Anyway, I began by thinking about twenty-game winners and then I got to wondering what other "targets" there are out there which disrupt the normal frequency curves. Are there more .300 hitters, over time, than .299 hitters? There must be, but how many more?

I looked at this phenomenon in a general way. This is what I found:

Hits

There are 49 players in history who wound up the season with 200 hits, whereas there are only 27 players who wound up with 199 hits—another obvious example of targeting. (Counts for hitting stats, by the way, go back all the way to 1876.)

Other than that, I found no evidence of targeting any hit level. You don't have more players with 100 hits than with 99, for example, because 100 hits is not a standard of excellence, so it doesn't exert any "pull" on the players. Also, the distribution of hits actually goes *down* slightly from 135 to about 100. There are 1,887 players in history with 130-139 hits, but only 1,768 players with 100 to 109 hits. Again, for an obvious reason: the length of the schedule causes hit totals to cluster just under 150.

x =		x =		x =		x =	
41	1	29	5	19	216	9	1092
40	1	28	11	18	314	8	1158
37	1	27	27	17	353	7	1312
36	1	26	24	16	477	6	1439
35	1	25	44	15	592	5	1649
34	1	24	57	14	687	4	1961
33	4	23	83	13	750	3	2208
32	1	22	113	12	812	2	2748
31	7	21	167	11	913	1	3841
30	3	20	251	10	965	0	8110

There are 49 players in history who wound up the season with 200 hits, whereas there are only 27 players who wound up with 199 hits.

Home Runs

I found no evidence of successful "targeting" of any particular home run level. There are, for example, only five seasons in history of exactly 50 home runs, whereas there are twenty seasons of 49 home runs. There are more 39-homer seasons than 40s, more 29-homer seasons than 30s. It could be, perhaps, that when players try to force that last home run, they tend *not* to hit it.

Runs Scored and RBI

This one is puzzling. There is clear evidence of targeting in the RBI column. This is the distribution of RBI seasons between 105 and 95:

105 RBI— 69 seasons
104 RBI— 73 seasons
103 RBI— 78 seasons

102 RBI— 103 seasons
101 RBI— 93 seasons
100 RBI— 100 seasons

99 RBI— 79 seasons
98 RBI— 81 seasons
97 RBI— 88 seasons
96 RBI— 86 seasons
95 RBI— 109 seasons

Obviously, 100 RBI is a goal for many hitters, and hitters who are close to that level find a way to get there, causing a "bubble" in the data right above 100 RBI. The magnetic influence of magic number RBI is so strong, actually, that it appears to jog players all along the spectrum. There are more players with 90 RBI, for example, than with 89, more players with 70 RBI than with 69, more players with 60 RBI than with 59, etc. It doesn't hold at every level, but on balance, it appears that players who are on the verge of changing the first digit on their RBI count tend to push, in the last days of the season, to get over the hump. Maybe the guy who HAS 101 RBI takes the last day of the season off so that the guy with 89 RBI can bat cleanup and try to get to 90.

If this is true of RBI it must be true of runs scored, right? But no…there is no apparent evidence of "targeting" runs at any level. There is no bubble at 100 runs scored, not at all, no matter how you look at the data, and there is no evidence of targeting ten-levels. Either it is more difficult to manipulate the runs column, or it is less of a goal for players, or…something. You figure it out.

Stolen Bases

Since stolen bases involve stolen base *attempts*—that is to say, they involve the player's judgment or discretion—I would have guessed that stolen bases might be particularly vulnerable to manipulation by players attempting to reach goals. It is hard to say whether this is true or not, for two reasons. First, there really are no magic numbers in the stolen base arena, except perhaps 100 stolen bases, and that has been achieved so infrequently as to be useless for this type of study. Second, the downward slope of the stolen base line as it moves from zero to 100 is so severe that it masks aberrations in the data. In other words, if you compare 80 runs scored to 50 runs scored, there are 2,047 seasons in history with 80 to 89 runs scored, and 3,194 seasons with 50 to 59 runs scored. It's a *reasonably* flat line between them, which reveals bumps or irregularities.

But in stolen bases, there are 31 seasons in history with 80 to 89 stolen bases, and 234 seasons with 50 to 59—a seven-to-one ratio. The steep slope of the line tends to hide any little uptick along the way.

Anyway, it does appear that there is targeting of ten-levels. Despite the steep slope of the line there are eleven seasons in history of exactly 70 stolen bases, whereas there are only three seasons of 69 stolen bases. There are more seasons of 40 than 39, more of 30 than 29. On balance, it does appear there is some targeting in this category.

I remember a story about Rocky Colavito stealing a base. It was a nothing game, sort of getting out of hand, and Rocky took off for second, and they gave him a stolen base (the defensive indifference rule was virtually never applied in those days.) Asked about it after the game, Rocky joked that he liked to get into every category sometime during the year, and he had stolen bases taken care of now.

So you see, targeting *could* effect the distribution at any level. That's targeting, too. Rocky's target was one stolen base.

Batting Average

This is the big one. There are, in baseball history, 195 players who have finished the season hitting .300 (in 400 or more plate appearances), whereas there are only 107 players who have finished the season hitting .299—the largest "targeting" discrepancy that I found in this study. The ".300 lure" is strong enough that it affects all of the data points around .300:

.304	147
.303	123
.302	156
.301	157
.300	195
.299	107
.298	128
.297	138
.296	123

Altogether, there are 508 players who have finished the season hitting .300 to .302, as opposed to 373 players who have finished the season hitting .297 to .299.

Batting average, of course, is the Godfather of baseball stats, and there appears to be batting average targeting at other levels as well—.350 and .400, for example. But there the numbers are so small that you can't really be sure.

This data (on .300 hitters) was so dramatic that I asked myself whether this could be impacted by the fact that there is a simple combination—3 for 10—that figures up to exactly .300. In other words, could the number spike upward at .300 because the hitter has a chance every tenth at bat to land on exactly .300?

It could be, but...it isn't. You have a chance to land on exactly .300 every tenth at bat, but you have a chance to land on .286 every seventh at bat, as 2 for 7 is .286. If this caused a spike at .300, it should cause a larger spike at .286. But in fact there have been fewer .286 hitters in history than .285 hitters or .287 hitters. There is a second reason that I know that this isn't what's causing the spike in the data. I'll explain in a moment.

There is also a "ten-pull" in batting average. There are more players who hit .280 than .279, more players who hit .270 than .269, etc. Seems pretty clear.

Brooks Robinson used to tell this story on himself, don't know if he still does. He had a miserable year in 1963, and went into his last at bat of the season hitting exactly .250—147 for 588. If he made an out, he wound up the season hitting under .250—but he got a hit, and wound up at .251. He said it was the only hit he got all season in a pressure situation.

That's my point...players WANT to wind up the season hitting .250, rather than in the .240s. They tend to make it happen.

On Base and Slugging

I found no evidence whatsoever of "targeting" in the categories on-base percentage, slugging percentage and OPS.

On Base and Slugging only became focus statistics for players in the 1980s, late 1970s, and it may also be that these statistics are difficult to manipulate by deliberate actions. A player has limited options to manipulate his stats at season's end, and, to the extent that he can do that, he's going to tend to focus on batting average, rather than on-base percentage or slugging percentage.

The other way that we know that the spike in batting average at .300 isn't caused simply by players going 3 for each 10 is by looking at the .400 slugging percentage. If this phenomenon caused a spike in the data at this point, it would cause a huge spike in slugging percentage at .400, since a player has the opportunity to land on exactly .400 every FIVE at bats—twice as often as he can land on .300. Further, since the data around .400 is thinner, a "chance spike" of the same size would appear larger.

But in fact, there is no spike in slugging percentage whatsoever at .400. A player in 500 at bats has the opportunity to slug exactly .400, or .402, or .404, or .406. In 501 at bats, he can land on .399, or .401, or .403, or .405. So that effect completely washes out when a player has 400 or more plate appearances.

Pitchers

Other than wins, the only place where there seems pretty clear evidence of "targeting" in pitcher's stats is in strikeouts. There are seven pitchers (since 1900) who have finished the season with 300 to 304 strikeouts—as opposed to zero pitchers with 295 to 299 strikeouts.

There are also 38 pitchers who have finished the season with 200 to 202 strikeouts, as opposed to 27 pitchers with 197 to 199 strikeouts. This seems to indicate possible "targeting" in the strikeout columns.

Other than that, I was unable to see evidence of targeting in any pitchers' totals. I looked at innings pitched, and there could be some targeting there, but I can't really say. There are more pitchers with 200-219 innings pitched than with 180-199, but that very well could just be the way the data is. There are also more with 180-199 than with 160-179...the numbers flatten out in the 150 area.

I looked at ERAs, and again, there could be some targeting here, but I couldn't really say. There have been

The magnetic influence of magic number RBI is so strong, actually, that it appears to jog players all along the spectrum.

more pitchers with ERAs of 1.97 to 1.99 (that is, just under the 2.00 line) than with ERAs of 2.00 to 2.02 (33 to 27). There are more pitchers with ERAs of 2.97 to 2.99 than with ERAs of 3.00 to 3.02 (145 to 126). But there are no more pitchers with ERAs just under 4.00 than just over 4.00, and there are actually more pitchers with ERAs just over 5.00 than just under 5.00. There could be some "targeting" effects here, and I kind of think there are, but…you can't really tell.

Saves

I would have thought, because of the nature of the Save stat, that it would be a natural for this kind of manipulation. There is really no evidence of pitchers being pushed to meet threshold levels in Saves:

50 Saves—1 pitcher	49 Saves—1 pitcher
40 Saves—11 pitchers	39 Saves—11 pitchers
30 Saves—26 pitchers	29 Saves—29 pitchers
20 Saves—44 pitchers	19 Saves—42 pitchers

The Time Line

This study was actually done *after* the study on Cigar Points, which was written as a companion piece and appears next. This study naturally goes before that one in a logical sequence, but the work was done backward.

So I was telling John Dewan about the Cigar Points study, before I wrote it up, and I asked him to guess who had the most "Cigar Points" of any player in history. A cigar point is a point you get for ALMOST reaching a target, but not quite—close, but no cigar.

John guessed that whoever had the most cigar points would have to be a player who played a long time ago. *Why?* I asked, genuinely puzzled.

"Well," he said, "it seems like now, when a player gets close to those numbers, he's going to keep going until he gets there."

We weren't quite communicating. I was talking about magic numbers, and John thought that what I meant was things like 3,000 hits, 500 home runs, 300 wins—career cumulative totals. I also did consider those career milestones in the Cigar Points studies, but what I *mostly* had in mind was season standards like a .300 batting average, 100 RBI, 200 hits…the things we have discussed here.

That was just a misunderstanding based on my failure to communicate clearly, but then I got to thinking about the issue this raises. Is it true that there is more of this now than there was years ago? Are players *more* goal-oriented now than they were forty years ago?

When I got to that question, I almost immediately remembered lots of stories about players from my childhood making explicit efforts to meet statistical goals—like the Rocky Colavito and Brooks Robinson stories that I told earlier. Ron Santo talked publicly about his desire to hit .300 with 30 home runs, 100 RBI every year. Willie Stargell one year announced a goal of hitting .320 with 40 homers, 120 RBI.

In 1964 Tony Cloninger won his 19th game of the season with a couple of days left on the schedule. On the last day of the season the Braves led 6-0 after three innings. The manager, Bobby Bragan, asked Cloninger if he would like to go in and pitch a couple of innings to pick up his 20th win.

"No," said Cloninger. "When I win 20 games, I want to do it on my own." He did win twenty the next year—24, in fact. It's like the Ted Williams story on a small level—Williams being offered a chance to sit out the last day to keep his batting average at .400. Speaking of Ted Williams…Williams held the American League record for home runs by a rookie, 31, until 1950, when Walt Dropo hit 34. (Al Rosen in 1950 was not considered a rookie by the standards of the time.) In 1959 Bob Allison had 27 homers by the end of July, on pace for 40+, but hit only two in August and one in September, and missed the record. Again, his manager (Cookie Lavagetto) talked openly about how disappointed he was that Allison had failed to break the record. Allison, Callison. When Johnny Callison was at .301 with two days left in the season in 1962, his manager, Gene Mauch, gave him only one at bat over the last two days of the season so that he would stay at .300. He explained to the media that he wanted Callison, a young player, to go through the winter thinking of himself as a .300 hitter.

It seems to me, and this is just my intuition, but it seems to me that there was at least as much focus on players meeting statistical standards then as there is now. So then I got to thinking…has this really changed? And how could I measure that?

We can look at that by looking at the ratio of players who just meet a standard to those who just miss the standard. If the focus on meeting these records has increased, it should cause an increase in the ratio of those who just meet the standard to those who just miss, right? It seems to me that it should.

So I took the six (or seven) standards which most clearly are subject to targeting effects, which are

It's so rare that we pose a question like that and actually find the answer, but we have it here: clear, definitive evidence that the focus on magic numbers began about 1940.

200 hits
100 RBI
10-levels in stolen bases
a .300 average
20 wins
200 strikeouts and 300 strikeouts.

I looked at the number of players just meeting and just missing these targets in each decade, except that I continued to ignore pitcher's stats in the 19th century. (Twenty wins did not become a standard of excellence for a pitcher until about 1920.)

Anyway, in the 1800s there is no evidence that players had any interest whatsoever in meeting statistical magic numbers. Altogether, in the 1880s, 49 players just reached a magic number, while 55 players just missed one:

1880s	49 made	55 missed	.471 percentage
1890s	99 made	98 missed	.503 percentage

There is no data for the 1870s, since no player in the 1870s had 100 RBI, 200 hits, or 400 plate appearances.

In the first four decades of the twentieth century there is little evidence of motivation to meet these statistical standards:

1900s	97 made	90 missed	.519 percentage
1910s	95 made	77 missed	.552 percentage
1920s	98 made	118 missed	.454 percentage
1930s	99 made	92 missed	.518 percentage

Players throughout this era were essentially as likely to hit .299 as to hit .300, as likely to win 19 games as to win 20, which I take to be evidence that there was little focus on these magic numbers.

And then suddenly, in the 1940s, the ratios changed very dramatically:

1940s	76 made	52 missed	.594 percentage
1950s	101 made	63 missed	.616 percentage
1960s	96 made	73 missed	.568 percentage
1970s	176 made	114 missed	.607 percentage

Despite what people might assume, the focus on these magic numbers actually *decreased* somewhat once the free agent era began. I updated the "2000s" below to include 2007:

1980s	159 made	119 missed	.572 percentage
1990s	174 made	129 missed	.574 percentage
2000s	171 made	130 missed	.568 percentage

Isn't that cool? It's so rare that we pose a question like that and actually find the answer, but we have it here: clear, definitive evidence that the focus on magic numbers began about 1940.

Which makes sense when you think about it. In 1927,

For whatever it is worth, I am willing to believe that the emphasis on magic numbers has decreased since free agency.

when Ty Cobb got his 4,000th career hit, it was a matter of slight interest to the baseball public. In 1934 Sam Rice retired with 2,987 career hits.

But in 1938 the Washington Senators deliberately pushed Taffy Wright to the 100-game level, pinch-hitting him in the last week of the season so that (they believed) he would be eligible for the batting title—the first time that I know of such a thing being done. Over the next five years there would be several more controversies about batting titles and ERA titles. In 1941 there occurred the Ted Williams story—an oft-told tale in which Williams is portrayed as a hero for successfully meeting his personal statistical goal. The Joe DiMaggio 56-game hitting streak, also 1941, is also a story about a player performing purely personal statistical heroics.

In 1939 the Hall of Fame opened, and this certainly increased the focus on players' statistical accomplishments. Yes, players did have a demonstrated interest in personal statistics before 1940, but it certainly does seem that there was a ramping up of that interest right about that time—in fact, I think that I have written in the past somewhere that this occurred at about that time, without knowing what I now know, what I have learned while writing this article. The ratio of players with 200 hits to players with 199 hits, players hitting .300 to those hitting .299, players winning 20 games to those winning 19…those ratios are actually much MORE one-sided if you focus only on the years since 1940.

Obviously one cannot draw reliable inferences about the ethics of the game from a study of this nature. But for whatever it is worth, I am willing to believe that the emphasis on magic numbers has decreased since free agency. Free agency, in a sense, made selfishness less tolerated within the game—simply because it had to be that way.

There is a very healthy ethic within baseball today that "Yes, you can leave when the season is over. If you can make $40 million signing a contract to play for another team, good for you. But as long as you are a part of this team, you need to do what is best for this team." That team-first ethic hasn't gone away during the free agency era, and it may well have gotten stronger.

(My appreciation to Retrosheet for help with the details in re Brooks Robinson, Bob Allison, Johnny Callison and Tony Cloninger.)

Cigar Points

by Bill James

(This article is a companion piece to the article, "The Targeting Phenomenon". The other article is the first in the sequence; this is the second, although actually I did the research for this one first, then expanded it to the areas covered in that article.)

Who was the unluckiest player in baseball history, in terms of just missing the kind of arbitrary standards we use to define excellence? Magglio Ordonez in 2003 had 99 RBI, 29 homers, 95 runs scored, 192 hits. Gil Hodges in 1957 hit .299 with 98 RBI, 94 runs scored. Dusty Miller in 1898 hit .299 with 99 runs scored. Darrin Erstad in 1997 did exactly the same thing—.299, 99 runs scored. Terry Pendleton in 1992 had 98 runs scored, 199 hits. Donn Clendenon in 1966 hit .299 with 28 homers, 98 RBI. I always notice those things, and I always wonder who missed the most by the least, so to speak.

I always wonder who missed the most by the least, so to speak.

I set up a system to measure this. I guess I am required to explain the details of the system, but the details are as arbitrary as the standards. I gave a player 20 points for hitting .299, for example, 17 points for hitting .298, 14 points for hitting .297, but to get those points you had to have 400 plate appearances; if you hit .299 in less than 400 plate appearances the points were pro-rated per plate appearance. 90 RBI was one point, 91 RBI two points, 92 RBI three points...99 RBI was twenty points, same with 99 runs scored.

Altogether I gave points in the system for 39 types of near misses (or 38, since the MVP points are the same for hitters and pitchers.) The first twelve were for hitters in a season:

1) Just missing a .300 or .400 batting average.
2) Just missing 100 Runs Scored.
3) Just missing 100 RBI.
4) Doubles total ending in a "9" (three points if your doubles ended in a nine, no matter what the first digit was).
5) Triples total ending in a "9" (same).
6) Home Run total ending in a "9" (five points).
7) Just missing 100 walks (maximum of five points).
8) Slugging percentage ending with a 99, 98 or 97 (3 points maximum).
9) Just missing the batting title. (20 points for just missing the batting title by one point or less, fewer points for missing the batting title by slightly wider margins. I arbitrarily gave Nap Lajoie 30 points in 1910 for just missing a batting title that subsequent research showed that he had actually won.)
10) Just missing the league home run championship (with a total of 20 or more; I ignored the guys who hit six home runs when the league leader had seven; maximum of ten points).
11) Just missing the league RBI lead (maximum of ten points).
12) Just missing the MVP award (20 points for finishing within 10% of the winner in the MVP vote).

I gave points for CAREER batting "misses" in nine categories:

1) A career average of .290 to .299. (Up to 50 points for a career batting average of .299 in a substantial career.)
2) Just missing 3,000 career hits. (Sam Rice was given 96 points for retiring with 2,987 career hits—the largest point award in the system. Anything over 2700 hits earned a point in this category.)
3) Just missing 2,000 career hits (theoretical maximum of 50 points; Del Pratt got 49 points for having 1,996 career hits).

What I hadn't realized before is that Gee Walker is the Close-but-No-Cigar Guy that I was looking for—probably even more than Wally Pipp.

4) Career home run total ending 90 to 99 (maximum of 20 points).

5) Career doubles total ending 90 to 99 (maximum of 10 points).

6) Career triples total ending 90 to 99 (maximum of 10 points).

7) Career stolen base total ending 90 to 99 (maximum of 10 points).

8) 900 to 999 or 1900 to 1999 career runs scored (theoretical maximum of 50 points, although no one was actually over 39).

9) 900 to 999 or 1900 to 1999 career RBI (same…actual maximum was again 39).

Career points were not awarded to active players, for obvious reasons. The maximums for career totals were larger than for season totals, but those are one-time awards. If a player just misses 3,000 career hits, for example, I figure that's a really big miss. But 82% of the points awarded in the system were for season misses.

There were twelve "seasonal" standards for pitchers:

1) Just missing 20 wins or 30 wins (25 points for 19 or 29 wins, 5 points for 18 or 28 wins).

2) Just missing 10 wins (7 points for 9 wins).

3) Just missing 200 innings pitched (maximum of 10 points).

4) Just missing 200 or 300 strikeouts (maximum of 25 points for 199 or 299 strikeouts).

5) Saves ending in a "9" (6 points).

6) ERA just OVER a rung (maximum of 20 points for ending season with a 2.00 or 3.00 ERA, or any number such that getting out one or two more hitters would result in your ERA beginning with a different digit; full points for ERA required 150 innings pitched or 70 game appearances, and no points were awarded to pitchers with an ERA over 6.00).

7) Just missed leading the league in Wins (maximum of 15 points).

8) Just missed leading the league in Strikeouts (maximum of 10 points).

9) Just missed leading the league in ERA (maximum of 15 points).

10) Just missed leading the league in Saves (maximum of 10 points). These points, like "Just missed leading league in home runs", required a minimum of 20 saves. I didn't give anyone points for having two saves in a season when the league leader had three.

11) Just missed the MVP Award (same as for hitters).

12) Just missed the Cy Young Award (same again).

And there were six categories of awards to pitchers for just missing career totals:

1) Just missing 300 wins (theoretical maximum of 100, but the highest total actually awarded was 60, to Tommy John).

2) Just missing 200 wins (maximum of 40 points).

3) Just missing 100 wins (maximum of 10 points).

4) Career Saves total ending 90 to 99 (maximum of 10 points).

5) Career ERA ending .00 to .20 (maximum of 20 points).

6) Career strikeout total ending 900 to 999 (maximum of 20 points).

Altogether 145,853 points were awarded through 2007:

66,634 to hitters for just missing season targets
18,885 to hitters for just missing career targets
51,538 to pitchers for just missing season targets
8,796 to pitchers for just missing career targets.

And the Winner of No Cigar Is

Actually, on a certain level this study is kind of a dud. What I was looking for was the guys who just *missed* the numbers that mean glory in baseball. What I found was… well, I found those guys, too, but they're further down the list. At the top of the list of players who just miss the standards of excellence, it turns out, are players who also very regularly *hit* the standards of excellence and blow right past them. The pitchers who win 19 games most often are the pitchers for whom winning 19 games is no big whoop. Starting with:

1. Greg Maddux (336)

And it's a no-doubter. It's a successful study in a sense, I guess, because we learn something that (a) nobody knew until we did the study, and (b) is unquestionably true once you look at it. The arbitrariness of my system is not a problem with regard to the top spot, because Maddux is so far ahead that no matter how you set the standards, within reason, Maddux would win. Greg Maddux has:

Five seasons of 19 wins, plus two seasons if 18 wins, good for a total of 135 points.

One season of 199.1 innings pitched, good for 10 points, plus another of 198, good for 9 points.

Seasons of 199 strikeouts, 198 strikeouts, 197 strikeouts—in three consecutive years, no less—and another season of 190 strikeouts, good for a total of 76 points.

Seasons with ERAs of 3.00, 3.05 and 4.02, good for a total of 46 points.

Four seasons in which he missed leading the league in Wins by one, good for another 60 points.

Altogether, 336 points—by far the highest total in baseball history. He has no points for just missing Awards, and he has no points yet for career numbers, since he is still active. But, as fantastic as his career has been, he has only two 20-win seasons—but seven near misses in that category. Nobody in history can match that. No other pitcher is within 100 points of his near-miss total.

2. Frank Robinson (279)

Robby retired with 2,943 career hits and a .294 batting average, so he has a total of 106 points for career misses. That's the third-highest total ever for career misses—and he also has the second-highest total of season misses, 173 points worth.

Robinson had six seasons with home runs ending in a 9. He hit 49 homers, 39, 29 (twice), 19, and 9. He had a .290 average as a rookie in 1956 (1 point), and 97 runs scored, 197 hits, 29 doubles and 29 homers in his second season in 1957 (a total of 38 points—one of the highest ever). He hit .297 in 1960. He drove in 91 runs in '63, 96 runs in '64. He hit .296 in '65. He drove in 94 runs in '67, 99 runs in '71, and 97 runs in '73. Lots of players did some of this, but only one hitter—Henry Aaron—did more of it.

Robby's home run numbers can be summarized this way: he had four seasons in which he averaged more than 40 home runs—but he had only one season in which he actually hit 40 (49, 39, 38 and 37—an average of 40.75). He also had "only" six seasons in which he actually drove in 100 runs, but he had 15 seasons in which he averaged more than a hundred.

But while it is unquestionably true that Robinson did miss an unusual number of standards by an unusually thin margin, it is also true of Robinson, as it is of Maddux, that nobody much cared, because everybody knew he was a great player anyway. He doesn't really represent what I was trying to find.

3. Wally Pipp (228)

This is the guy I was trying to find. You all know what Wally Pipp is famous for, right? It fits perfectly, doesn't it? He's the guy on the *other* side of the story—the guy who got pushed aside, the guy who just missed the standards. He hit .300 a few times, but he hit .296, .295, .291—all of those in seasons of close to 600 at bats. He drove in 93 runs, 97 runs, 90 runs, 99 runs. He scored 96 runs, and, to prove it wasn't a fluke, did it again the next year. He hit ten or more homers only twice—but nine homers three times. He hit 9 triples—and 19 triples. He wound up his career with

996 RBI
974 runs scored
1941 hits
and 90 home runs.

4. Sam Rice (226)

A lot of that on his career hit total, 2,987 hits.

5. Randy Johnson (223)

Greg Maddux' rival for years as the number one pitcher in the National League—and the number two pitcher, behind Maddux, in terms of career near misses. Since he is still active at this writing, he gets no little units for career numbers. If he were to be forced into retirement just short of 300 career wins—which frankly seems likely—he might vault into second place all-time, ahead of Frank Robinson. But I don't think he could catch Maddux.

6. Gee Walker (210)

I wish I knew more about Gee Walker. I know that, as a rookie, the Tigers platooned him with his own brother, Hub Walker, making it pretty clear that one of them was going to win the job and the other was going back to the minors. I know that in 1934 he was benched for not hustling, and that by that he missed out on being a regular on the American League championship teams in '34 and '35. I know that he was very fast, of course—one of the fastest players of his time—and I know that he is always described in contemporary accounts as a "colorful" player, although I don't really have a clue why. I know that he was a huge fan favorite in Detroit, like Dixie Walker was in Brooklyn, but again, I don't really know why, and of course I know that he put up big numbers in '36 and

Barry Zito had no points through 2006, when I first did the research for this article, but picked up a few points in 2007 for pitching 196 innings, at a cost of roughly $100,000 an inning.

'37—.353 and .335 averages, 194 and 213 hits, 55 doubles in '36, and 18 homers and 113 RBI in '37.

But what I hadn't realized before is that Gee Walker is the Close-but-No-Cigar Guy that I was looking for—probably even more than Wally Pipp. He had a few markers in the season totals—96 RBI, 95 runs, .290+ averages, etc.—but look at those career numbers. He had

954 career runs scored
1991 career hits
399 doubles
997 RBI
and a .294 career batting average.

He also had 599 extra base hits, although I didn't give him any credit for that (600 extra base hits is not a recognized standard of excellence, I don't think). He made 4,998 career outs, although obviously I didn't give him any points for that.

If he'd played another week, he could have had 2,000 hits, 400 doubles, 1000 RBI. This really is the guy I was looking for.

7. Henry Aaron (208)

Had even more near-misses in season totals than Robby—a player to whom he was often compared while active.

8. Bert Blyleven (201)

Bert Blyleven is probably the best example of a player who missed the Hall of Fame—or anyway has missed it so far—by falling just short of the arbitrary numbers that people like to make a big deal out of.

9. Jake Beckley (201)

Cut loose by the Cardinals in 1907 with 2,930 career hits—a fact which probably nobody knew at the time, since at that time there was no organized system whatsoever for tracking player career totals.

10. Stan Musial (196)

11. Robin Roberts (196)

12. Al Kaline (195)

Al Kaline never hit 30 homers—but he hit 27 to 29 six times. He just missed the MVP Award in '55, just missed leading the league in RBI in '56, and was within ten points of the batting title in '63. In his career he had 498 doubles, 399 home runs—but, of course, he did hang in there to get his 3,000 career hits.

13. Phil Cavaretta (193)

Cavaretta is the third guy with nines-gone-wild in his career batting line, like Wally Pipp and Gee Walker. He is second behind Walker in career Cigar Points, with

990 runs scored
1977 hits
99 triples

95 homers
920 RBI
and a .293 career average
good for a total of 130 career cigar points, plus 63 for near misses in specific seasons.

14. Rogers Hornsby (193)

15. Mel Ott (193)

16. Harold Baines (192)

The Bert Blyleven of outfielders, he also could be left out of the Hall of Fame by his long string of near-misses, including

99 RBI in 1983
29 homers, 94 RBI in 1984
198 hits in 1985
a .296 average in 1986
a .293 average and 93 RBI in 1987
a .294 average in 1994
a .299 average in 1995
95 RBI in 1996.

17. Al Simmons (188)

18. Sam Crawford (186)

20. Ty Cobb (183)

21. Carl Furillo (181)

Furillo, of coursed, missed a career batting average of .300 by only one hit. This fact is well known, and I actually thought about calling these "Furillo points". He also had a bunch of seasons of hitting in the .290s (.295, .297, .295, .294, .290, .290) and driving in and scoring 90+ runs (95, 99, and 93 runs scored in consecutive years, with RBI counts including 91, 92, 96 and 95).

22. Ed Delahanty (180)

23. Mickey Mantle (178)

24. Dante Bichette (177)

I never could stand Dante Bichette, honestly. He hit .340 in 1995 with 40 homers, 128 RBI—but he had a strikeout/walk ratio of 96 to 22, and they're Rocky Mountain numbers. It used to drive me crazy to hear people talk about what a great player he was. But he did wind up with a .299 career average, .499 slugging, 934 runs, 1906 hits.

25. Babe Ruth (176)

Most Notable SEASONS for Cigar Points

Here again I don't much like my own answer, but my answer is Derek Jeter, 2006. Jeter gets

20 points for just missing the MVP Award
14 points for driving in 97 runs
11 points for just missing the batting title
and 3 points for hitting 39 doubles
a total of 48 points.

That's the number one season by the system I set up, but if I was just making an arbitrary choice, I might be more attracted to Carl Yastrzemski, 1963 (99 runs scored, 191 hits, 19 homers, 94 RBI and a .296 average), or Magglio Ordonez, 2003 (outlined in the opening), or Rod Carew, 1976 (97 runs, 9 homers, 90 RBI, 49 stolen bases, just missed the batting title on the last day of the season). I'll give you the top 25 near-miss batting seasons:

No other pitcher is within 100 points of Maddux's near-miss total.

Rank	Player	YEAR	
1	Derek Jeter	2006	
2	Carl Yastrzemski	1962	
3	Magglio Ordonez	2003	
4	Rod Carew	1976	
5	Gil Hodges	1957	
6	Lou Brock	1969	97 runs, 195 hits, .298 average.
7	Jim Bottomley	1926	.299 average, 98 runs scored.
8	Jim Ray Hart	1967	98 runs scored, 29 homers, 99 RBI.
9	Sal Bando	1973	97 runs cored, 29 homers, 98 RBI.
10	Keith Hernandez	1980	99 RBI, 39 doubles, 191 hits, Just missed the batting title.
11	Terry Pendleton	1992	
12	Dusty Miller	1898	
13	Barry Bonds	1991	95 runs, .292 average, just missed leading the league in RBI and just missed the MVP Award.
14	Heinie Manush	1928	Just missed the batting title AND the MVP Award.
15	Willie Stargell	1973	.299 average, just missed the MVP Award.
16	Darin Erstad	1997	
17	Steve Finley	1996	.298 average, 95 RBI, 195 hits.
18	Herman Long	1898	99 Runs Scored AND 99 RBI.
19	Raul Mondesi	1999	99 RBI, 98 runs scored.
20	Mike Sweeney	2001	99 RBI, 97 runs scored, 29 homers.
21	Rich Rollins	1962	96 runs scored, 96 RBI, .298 average.
22	Wally Pipp	1921	
23	Luke Appling	1940	96 runs scored, 197 hits, close to the batting title.
24	Frank Robinson	1957	
25	Yogi Berra	1952	97 runs scored, 98 RBI, missed by two of leading league in home runs.

The most notable seasons for pitchers are all 19-win seasons. Mark Langston in 1991 had 19 wins, missed by one of leading the league in wins, and had a 3.00 ERA… one more out would have made it 2.99. Bert Blyleven in '84 had 19 wins, missed by one of leading the league in wins, and also just missed leading the league in ERA. Bob Gibson in '64, Greg Maddux in 2000, Fernando Valenzuela in '82, Dutch Leonard in 1914…all basically the same sort of near-miss seasons.

And, on the Other Hand

The players who had the longest careers without earning ANY cigar points were:

1. Tim Foli
2. Ted Sizemore
3. Horace Clarke
4. Chico Carrasquel
5. Mike Heath
6. Lee Tannehill
7. Todd Hundley
8. Larry Brown
9. Dal Maxvill
10. Frank Bowerman

In general, these players didn't earn any cigar points because they generally weren't close to any standards of excellence as a hitter. But obviously, they could have had 19 doubles in a season or 9 homers or 9 triples or 9 stolen bases. It just happened that they never did. And, on the pitcher's side:

1. Cy Falkenberg
2. Toad Ramsey
3. Marty Pattin
4. Dave Foutz
5. Charles Nagy
6. Randy Jones
7. Alex Kellner
8. Jersey Bakely
9. Duke Esper
10. Bobby Bolin

Barry Zito had no points through 2006, when I first did the research for this article, but picked up a few points in 2007 for pitching 196 innings, at a cost of roughly $100,000 an inning. Seriously.

Actually, on a certain level this study is kind of a dud.

Cleveland Indians

Cleveland Indians – 2007
Team Overview

Description		Ranking
Won-Lost Record	96-66	
Place	1st of 5 in American League Central	
Runs Scored	811	8th in the majors
Runs Allowed	704	5th in the majors
Home Runs	178	9th in the majors
Home Runs Allowed	146	4th in the majors
Batting Average	.268	14th in the majors
Batting Average Allowed	.268	16th in the majors
Walks Drawn	590	6th in the majors
Walks Given	410	1st in the majors
OPS For	.771	11th in the majors
OPS Against	.729	6th in the majors
Stolen Bases	72	22nd in the majors
Stolen Bases Allowed	93	12th in the majors

Key Players

Pos	Player	G	AB	R	H	2B	3B	HR	RBI	SB	CS	BB	SO	Avg	OBP	Slg	OPS	WS
C	Victor Martinez	147	562	78	169	40	0	25	114	0	0	62	76	.301	.374	.505	.879	29
1B	Ryan Garko	138	484	62	140	29	1	21	61	0	1	34	94	.289	.359	.483	.842	12
2B	Josh Barfield	130	420	53	102	19	3	3	50	14	5	14	90	.243	.270	.324	.594	8
3B	Casey Blake	156	588	81	159	36	4	18	78	4	5	54	123	.270	.339	.437	.776	11
SS	Jhonny Peralta	152	574	87	155	27	1	21	72	4	4	61	146	.270	.341	.430	.771	21
LF	Jason Michaels	105	267	43	72	11	1	7	39	3	4	20	50	.270	.324	.397	.721	7
CF	Grady Sizemore	162	628	118	174	34	5	24	78	33	10	101	155	.277	.390	.462	.852	29
RF	Trot Nixon	99	307	30	77	17	0	3	31	0	0	44	59	.251	.342	.336	.677	4
DH	Travis Hafner	152	545	80	145	25	2	24	100	1	1	102	115	.266	.385	.451	.837	16

Key Pitchers

Pos	Player	G	GS	W	L	Sv	IP	H	R	ER	BB	SO	BR/9	ERA	WS
SP	C.C. Sabathia	34	34	19	7	0	241.0	238	94	86	37	209	10.57	3.21	24
SP	Fausto Carmona	32	32	19	8	0	215.0	199	78	73	61	137	11.34	3.06	22
SP	Paul Byrd	31	31	15	8	0	192.1	239	107	98	28	88	12.77	4.59	12
SP	Jake Westbrook	25	25	6	9	0	152.0	159	78	73	55	93	13.03	4.32	9
SP	Cliff Lee	20	16	5	8	0	97.1	112	73	68	36	66	14.33	6.29	1
CL	Joe Borowski	69	0	4	5	45	65.2	77	39	37	17	58	13.16	5.07	8
RP	Tom Mastny	51	0	7	2	0	57.2	63	30	30	32	52	15.14	4.68	4
RP	Rafael Betancourt	68	0	5	1	3	79.1	51	13	13	9	80	6.81	1.47	16

Who is the best leadoff man on the Indians?

You might expect it to be Grady Sizemore. The Indians did do very well when Grady led off in 2007, scoring .59 runs per inning, which is 5.35 per nine innings, which is very good. But their best performance came when the leadoff man was that great burner, Victor Martinez. The Indians scored 5.98 runs per nine innings when Victor led off. Jhonny Peralta was second on the team, at 5.62 per nine innings, and Sizemore was third.

Victor Martinez – 2007
Performance as Leadoff Man

Innings Led Off:	152	
Team Scored:	101 Runs	.66 per inning
Reached Base Leading Off:	54	
Team Scored:	63 Runs	1.17 per inning
Did Not Reach:	98	
Team Scored:	38 Runs	.39 per inning
Other Innings for Team:	1310	
Team Scored:	710 Runs	.54 per inning

Grady Sizemore – 2007
Performance as Leadoff Man

Innings Led Off:	296	
Team Scored:	176 Runs	.59 per inning
Reached Base Leading Off:	105	
Team Scored:	119 Runs	1.13 per inning
Did Not Reach:	191	
Team Scored:	57 Runs	.30 per inning
Other Innings for Team:	1166	
Team Scored:	635 Run	.54 per inning

Jhonny Peralta – 2007
Performance as Leadoff Man

Innings Led Off:	157	
Team Scored:	98 Runs	.62 per inning
Reached Base Leading Off:	51	
Team Scored:	65 Runs	1.27 per inning
Did Not Reach:	106	
Team Scored:	33 Runs	.31 per inning
Other Innings for Team:	1305	
Team Scored:	713 Runs	.55 per inning

Sizemic Shift

Who pulls the ball more frequently: Travis Hafner or Grady Sizemore?

Sizemore does. 52% of Sizemore's hits over the last two years have gone to right, compared to 38% for Hafner.

66% of Grady's ground balls go to the right side, as opposed to 52% for Hafner.

Sizemore hits just 8% of his ground balls to left, which is less than David Ortiz or Carlos Delgado, and about the same as Jason Giambi or Jim Thome.

The question is: Do they not run a shift on Sizemore because

a) He doesn't look like a guy who would pull all of his grounders, therefore people don't realize that he does, or

b) You can't play that defense against a guy with Sizemore's speed?

As much as I love to be judgmental and uncharitable, I suspect it is more (b) than (a). When you play a Ted Williams shift one of the infielders is really more like a shallow outfielder. Unless Grady hit the ball sharply right at him, that guy couldn't throw out Grady at first anyway, so there would be no point in having him there. And if you stationed a lone sentry on the left side, all Grady would have to do is bunt for a double. It just probably wouldn't work.

Not that it works anyway.

Grady Sizemore – 2007
Hitting Analysis

Batting Left-Handed							1B	2B	3B	HR
Ground Balls to Left	12	Outs	9	Hits	3	Average .250	Hit Type	3 - 0	- 0	- 0
Ground Balls to Center	36	Outs	21	Hits	15	Average .417	Hit Type	14 - 1	- 0	- 0
Ground Balls to Right	104	Outs	83	Hits	21	Average .202	Hit Type	19 - 1	- 1	- 0
Line Drives to Left	16	Outs	4	Hits	12	Average .750	Hit Type	11 - 1	- 0	- 0
Line Drives to Center	36	Outs	7	Hits	29	Average .806	Hit Type	26 - 3	- 0	- 0
Line Drives to Right	44	Outs	8	Hits	36	Average .818	Hit Type	26 - 9	- 1	- 0
Fly Balls to Left	88	Outs	80	Hits	8	Average .093	Hit Type	3 - 5	- 0	- 0
Fly Balls to Center	72	Outs	57	Hits	15	Average .208	Hit Type	1 - 6	- 2	- 6
Fly Balls to Right	56	Outs	28	Hits	28	Average .500	Hit Type	1 - 8	- 1	- 18
Total on Ground Balls	152	Outs	113	Hits	39	Average .257	Hit Type	36 - 2	- 1	- 0
Total on Line Drives	96	Outs	19	Hits	77	Average .802	Hit Type	63 - 13	- 1	- 0
Total on Fly Balls	216	Outs	165	Hits	51	Average .238	Hit Type	5 - 19	- 3	- 24
Total Hit to Left	116	Outs	93	Hits	23	Average .202	Hit Type	17 - 6	- 0	- 0
Total Hit to Center	144	Outs	85	Hits	59	Average .410	Hit Type	41 - 10	- 2	- 6
Total Hit to Right	204	Outs	119	Hits	85	Average .417	Hit Type	46 - 18	- 3	- 18
Bunts	11	Outs	4	Hits	7	Average .636	Hit Type	7 - 0	- 0	- 0
All Balls in Play	475	Outs	301	Hits	174	Average .368	HitType	111 - 34	- 5	- 24

Travis Hafner – 2007
Hitting Analysis

Batting Left-Handed							1B	2B	3B	HR
Ground Balls to Left	28	Outs	17	Hits	11	Average .393	Hit Type	10 - 1	- 0	- 0
Ground Balls to Center	77	Outs	57	Hits	20	Average .260	Hit Type	19 - 1	- 0	- 0
Ground Balls to Right	103	Outs	85	Hits	18	Average .175	Hit Type	17 - 1	- 0	- 0
Line Drives to Left	19	Outs	4	Hits	15	Average .789	Hit Type	12 - 3	- 0	- 0
Line Drives to Center	38	Outs	12	Hits	26	Average .684	Hit Type	20 - 6	- 0	- 0
Line Drives to Right	19	Outs	6	Hits	13	Average .684	Hit Type	8 - 4	- 1	- 0
Fly Balls to Left	61	Outs	47	Hits	14	Average .237	Hit Type	5 - 6	- 1	- 2
Fly Balls to Center	50	Outs	41	Hits	9	Average .184	Hit Type	3 - 1	- 0	- 5
Fly Balls to Right	40	Outs	21	Hits	19	Average .500	Hit Type	0 - 2	- 0	- 17
Total on Ground Balls	208	Outs	159	Hits	49	Average .236	Hit Type	46 - 3	- 0	- 0
Total on Line Drives	76	Outs	22	Hits	54	Average .711	Hit Type	40 - 13	- 1	- 0
Total on Fly Balls	151	Outs	109	Hits	42	Average .288	Hit Type	8 - 9	- 1	- 24
Total Hit to Left	108	Outs	68	Hits	40	Average .377	Hit Type	27 - 10	- 1	- 2
Total Hit to Center	165	Outs	110	Hits	55	Average .335	Hit Type	42 - 8	- 0	- 5
Total Hit to Right	162	Outs	112	Hits	50	Average .312	Hit Type	25 - 7	- 1	- 17
All Balls in Play	435	Outs	290	Hits	145	Average .337	Hit Type	94 - 25	- 2	- 24

C. C. Sabathia started 236 innings in 2007, and failed to finish the inning only 4 times.

Fausto Carmona – 2007
Inning Analysis

Innings Pitched	215.0
Runs Allowed	78
Innings Started	221
Runs in Those Innings	79
Shutout Innings	179
One-Run Innings	17
Two-Run Innings	16
Three-Run Innings	8
Six-Run Innings	1
Got First Man Out	152
Runs Scored in Those Innings	20
Runs/9 Innings	1.18
First Man Reached	69
Runs Scored in Those Innings	59
Runs/9 Innings	7.70
1-2-3 Innings	100
10-pitch Innings (or less)	56
Long Innings (20 or more pitches)	36
Failed to Finish Inning	8

C.C. Sabathia – 2007
Inning Analysis

Innings Pitched	241.0
Runs Allowed	94
Innings Started	243
Runs in Those Innings	94
Shutout Innings	188
One-Run Innings	32
Two-Run Innings	13
Three-Run Inning	6
Four-Run Innings	2
Five-Run Innings	2
Got First Man Out	165
Runs Scored in Those Innings	36
Runs/9 Innings	1.96
First Man Reached	78
Runs Scored in Those Innings	58
Runs/9 Innings	6.69
1-2-3 Innings	106
10-pitch Innings (or less)	58
Long Innings (20 or more pitches)	55
Failed to Finish Inning	4

Carmona Chameleon

In the regular season, Fausto Carmona started 221 innings, in only 9 of which did the opposition score three or more runs.
In the ALCS he started eight innings, of which four resulted in three or more runs.

Cleveland Indians – 2007
Performance by Quality of Start

Game Score	#	ERA	W	-	L
80 and above	6	0.16	5	-	1
70 to 79	17	1.17	12	-	5
60 to 69	29	2.22	20	-	9
50 to 59	31	3.41	23	-	8
40 to 49	40	4.27	27	-	13
30 to 39	20	6.18	8	-	12
20 to 29	10	7.88	1	-	9
Below 20	9	11.01	0	-	9

Most teams are below .500 when their starting pitchers post a Game Score under 50, but Cleveland was 27-13 with a Game Score of 40 to 49.

Fausto

When a pitcher goes from 1-10 to 19-8, there probably is more than one change underlying that. We don't really know; for all we know Fausto Carmona may or may not have changed cars, apartments, dogs, TVs, girlfriends, athletic supporters and pizza delivery services.

We do, however, know one thing that he definitely changed: he junked the change up and concentrated on the splitter. See data below.

Fausto Carmona – 2006
Pitch Type Analysis

Overall		
Total Pitches	1248	
Fastball	935	75%
Curveball	1	0%
Changeup	43	3%
Slider	185	15%
Split Finger	47	4%
Pitchout	1	0%
Not Charted	36	3%

	Vs. RHB		Vs. LHB	
Total Pitches	691		557	
Outs Recorded	121		102	
Fastball	501	73%	434	78%
Curveball	1	0%	0	0%
Changeup	4	1%	39	7%
Slider	161	23%	24	4%
Split Finger	13	2%	34	6%
Pitchout	1	0%	0	0%
Not Charted	10	1%	26	5%

Fausto Carmona – 2007
Pitch Type Analysis

Overall		
Total Pitches	3137	
Fastball	2219	71%
Slider	354	11%
Split Finger	385	12%
Pitchout	3	0%
Not Charted	176	6%

	Vs. RHB		Vs. LHB	
Total Pitches	1401		1736	
Outs Recorded	305		340	
Fastball	983	70%	1236	71%
Slider	209	15%	145	8%
Split Finger	141	10%	244	14%
Pitchout	3	0%	0	0%
Not Charted	65	5%	111	6%

When a pitcher escapes from a bases-loaded, no-out jam without allowing a run, we call that a "Houdini". Cleveland's Paul Byrd recorded two Houdini's in 2007. Both of them against the Rangers. Only four other pitchers had two Houdini's: James Shields with Tampa Bay, Juan Cruz with Arizona, Kevin Cameron with San Diego, and Mark Henrickson with the Los Angeles Dodgers.

Colorado Rockies

Colorado Rockies – 2007
Team Overview

Description		Ranking
Won-Lost Record	90-73	
Place	2nd of 5 in National League West	
Runs Scored	860	5th in the majors
Runs Allowed	758	13th in the majors
Home Runs	171	13th in the majors
Home Runs Allowed	164	14th in the majors
Batting Average	.280	5th in the majors
Batting Average Allowed	.266	13th in the majors
Walks Drawn	622	5th in the majors
Walks Given	504	9th in the majors
OPS For	.791	5th in the majors
OPS Against	.753	13th in the majors
Stolen Bases	100	13th in the majors
Stolen Bases Allowed	96	14th in the majors

Key Players

Pos	Player	G	AB	R	H	2B	3B	HR	RBI	SB	CS	BB	SO	Avg	OBP	Slg	OPS	WS
C	Yorvit Torrealba	113	396	47	101	22	1	8	47	2	1	34	73	.255	.323	.376	.699	6
1B	Todd Helton	154	557	86	178	42	2	17	91	0	1	116	74	.320	.434	.494	.928	22
2B	Kaz Matsui	104	410	84	118	24	6	4	37	32	4	34	69	.288	.342	.405	.746	14
3B	Garrett Atkins	157	605	83	182	35	1	25	111	3	1	67	96	.301	.367	.486	.853	18
SS	Troy Tulowitzki	155	609	104	177	33	5	24	99	7	6	57	130	.291	.359	.479	.838	24
LF	Matt Holliday	158	636	120	216	50	6	36	137	11	4	63	126	.340	.405	.607	1.012	27
CF	Willy Taveras	97	372	64	119	13	2	2	24	33	9	21	55	.320	.367	.382	.748	11
RF	Brad Hawpe	152	516	80	150	33	4	29	116	0	2	81	137	.291	.387	.539	.926	20

Key Pitchers

Pos	Player	G	GS	W	L	Sv	IP	H	R	ER	BB	SO	BR/9	ERA	WS
SP	Jeff Francis	34	34	17	9	0	215.1	234	103	101	63	165	12.71	4.22	14
SP	Josh Fogg	30	29	10	9	0	165.2	194	99	91	59	94	14.45	4.94	6
SP	Aaron Cook	25	25	8	7	0	166.0	178	87	76	44	61	12.36	4.12	9
SP	Jason Hirsh	19	19	5	7	0	112.1	103	63	60	48	75	12.26	4.81	5
SP	Ubaldo Jimenez	15	15	4	4	0	82.0	70	46	39	37	68	12.40	4.28	4
CL	Brian Fuentes	64	0	3	5	20	61.1	46	26	21	23	56	11.15	3.08	10
RP	Manny Corpas	78	0	4	2	19	78.0	63	20	18	20	58	9.81	2.08	15
RP	Jeremy Affeldt	75	0	4	3	0	59.0	47	26	23	33	46	12.66	3.51	5

The 2006 Colorado Rockies drew 8 more walks than their pitchers issued.
In 2007 they drew 118 more walks than their pitchers issued.

Colorado Rockies – 2006
Team Overview

Description		Ranking
Won-Lost Record	76-86	
Place	4th of 5 in National League West	
Runs Scored	813	11th in the majors
Runs Allowed	812	22nd in the majors
Home Runs	157	26th in the majors
Home Runs Allowed	155	3rd in the majors
Batting Average	.270	14th in the majors
Batting Average Allowed	.277	22nd in the majors
Walks Drawn	561	10th in the majors
Walks Given	553	20th in the majors
OPS For	.774	12th in the majors
OPS Against	.785	22nd in the majors
Stolen Bases	85	16th in the majors
Stolen Bases Allowed	99	18th in the majors

Key Players

Pos	Player	G	AB	R	H	2B	3B	HR	RBI	SB	CS	BB	SO	Avg	OBP	Slg	OPS	WS
C	Yorvit Torrealba	65	223	23	55	16	3	7	43	4	3	11	49	.247	.293	.439	.732	6
1B	Todd Helton	145	546	94	165	40	5	15	81	3	2	91	64	.302	.404	.476	.880	21
2B	Jamey Carroll	136	463	84	139	23	5	5	36	10	12	56	66	.300	.377	.404	.781	13
3B	Garrett Atkins	157	602	117	198	48	1	29	120	4	0	79	76	.329	.409	.556	.965	23
SS	Clint Barmes	131	478	57	105	26	4	7	56	5	4	22	72	.220	.264	.335	.598	6
LF	Matt Holliday	155	602	119	196	45	5	34	114	10	5	47	110	.326	.387	.586	.973	19
CF	Cory Sullivan	126	386	47	103	26	10	2	30	10	6	32	100	.267	.321	.402	.722	6
RF	Brad Hawpe	150	499	67	146	33	6	22	84	5	5	74	123	.293	.383	.515	.898	15

Key Pitchers

Pos	Player	G	GS	W	L	Sv	IP	H	R	ER	BB	SO	BR/9	ERA	WS
SP	Jeff Francis	32	32	13	11	0	199.0	187	101	92	69	117	12.17	4.16	13
SP	Josh Fogg	31	31	11	9	0	172.0	206	115	105	60	93	14.23	5.49	6
SP	Jason Jennings	32	32	9	13	0	212.0	206	94	89	85	142	12.48	3.78	14
SP	Aaron Cook	32	32	9	15	0	212.2	242	107	100	55	92	12.87	4.23	12
SP	Byung-Hyun Kim	27	27	8	12	0	155.0	179	103	96	61	129	14.40	5.57	5
CL	Brian Fuentes	66	0	3	4	30	65.1	50	25	25	26	73	11.30	3.44	12
RP	Tom Martin	68	0	2	0	0	60.1	62	37	34	25	46	13.57	5.07	3
RP	Jose Mesa	79	0	1	5	1	72.1	73	32	31	36	39	14.18	3.86	6

The Rockies were 18-26 at the end of a homestand on May 20. They then had a great road trip (5-1), an OK homestand (6-4), a good road trip (4-2) and a good homestand (5-1) to reach 38-34, but a disastrous road trip (1-9) dropped them back to 39-43, and nearly finished them.

From then until September 13 they won their homestands and treaded water on the road:

5-1 at home	5-5 on the road	they're 49-49
4-2 at home	3-3 on the road	56-54
5-2 at home	2-4 on the road	63-60
4-3 at home	3-3 on the road	70-66
4-2 at home	2-2 on the road	76-70

Then it is September 14, and they catch fire:

5-2 at home	6-0 on the road	87-72
3-1 at home		90-73

Colorado Rockies – 2007
Tracking the Season by Segments

	W-L	R	PG	Avg	OR	PG	ERA	W-L
Homestand, April 2 to 4	2-1	21	7.0	.328	15	5.0	4.34	2-1
Road Trip, April 6 to 15	3-6	28	3.1	.221	30	3.3	3.52	5-7
Homestand, April 16 to 22	3-4	21	3.0	.260	41	5.9	5.29	8-11
Road Trip, April 23 to 25	1-2	13	4.3	.282	13	4.3	4.08	9-13
Homestand, April 27 to 29	1-2	18	6.0	.269	22	7.3	5.90	10-15
Road Trip, April 30 to May 9	4-5	41	4.6	.263	57	6.3	6.00	14-20
Homestand, May 10 to 20	4-6	35	3.5	.233	56	5.6	5.23	18-26
Road Trip, May 21 to 27	5-1	27	4.5	.272	15	2.5	2.50	23-27
Homestand, May 28 to June 7	6-4	53	5.3	.304	51	5.1	4.85	29-31
Road Trip, June 8 to 14	4-2	31	5.2	.273	12	2.0	2.04	33-33
Homestand, June 15 to 21	5-1	39	6.5	.308	19	3.2	3.17	38-34
Road Trip, June 22 to July 1	1-9	50	5.0	.264	78	7.8	7.61	39-43
Homestand, July 2 to 8	5-1	51	8.5	.377	29	4.8	4.34	44-44
Road Trip, July 13 to 22	5-5	42	4.2	.221	37	3.7	3.49	49-49
Homestand, July 23 to 29	4-2	39	6.5	.286	25	4.2	3.83	53-51
Road Trip, July 31 to August 5	3-3	31	5.2	.275	24	4.0	3.44	56-54
Homestand, August 6 to 12	5-2	61	8.7	.343	31	4.4	3.29	61-56
Road Trip, August 14 to 19	2-4	26	4.3	.257	33	5.5	5.07	63-60
Homestand, August 20 to 26	4-3	35	5.0	.267	33	4.7	4.02	67-63
Road Trip, August 27 to September 2	3-3	28	4.7	.271	26	4.3	4.50	70-66
Homestand, September 3 to 9	4-2	31	5.2	.270	23	3.8	3.83	74-68
Road Trip, September 10 to 13	2-2	29	7.3	.313	20	5.0	4.84	76-70
Homestand, September 14 to 20	5-2	48	6.9	.340	35	5.0	4.57	81-72
Road Trip, September 21 to 27	6-0	36	6.0	.284	17	2.8	2.59	87-72
Homestand, September 28 to October 1	3-1	26	6.5	.299	16	4.0	3.38	90-73

Johnny Damon and Todd Helton are the same age and both are battling back issues, but whereas Damon in 2007 had his best year on the bases since we've been keeping track of stuff (2002), Helton had just a dreadful year on the bases, ranking as the worst baserunner in the major leagues after having been a good baserunner in previous seasons.

I wish that I could explain this to you, but the truth is that I don't understand it, either; there are a variety of possible explanations, and, as we get more experience with detailed baserunning records, we should start to understand them better. Let's begin by examining the charts on the next page in a little detail:

- Johnny Damon before last season was 36-for-127 going first-to-third on a single; Helton wasn't that different, 34-for-129. But last year Damon moved from first to third on a single 18 times in 34 chances, whereas Helton moved successfully only 5 times in 42 chances.
- In 2003 Todd Helton was on first base when a double was hit 12 times, and scored on 8 of those plays. In 2007 he was on first when a double was hit 10 times, and didn't score on any of those plays.
- In 2003 Helton moved up 28 bases on wild pitches, passed balls, balks, defensive indifference and sacrifice flies—that's what we call "Bases Taken", those five events—and did not run into any outs on the bases. In 2007 he had only 9 bases taken and ran into 10 outs.

Both Damon and Helton represent "types" of players who tend to age well. Helton, a left-handed hitter with some power and good command of the strike zone, is in those ways like Stan Musial, Willie Stargell,

Rafael Palmeiro and Darrell Evans—a class of players who have aged well. Damon is a speed player, and speed players age very well relative to power hitters of the same overall level of ablity.

A superficial interpretation of Helton's baserunning numbers would be that, having slowed down just a step, he found himself unable to do the things that he *thought* he could do, and consequently ran into a bunch of outs. Since our system penalizes players pretty heavily for making outs on the bases, Helton winds up with a Net Gain for the season of negative 34. That *could* be what happened; I don't know that it isn't. But another possibility is simply that he was in the wrong place at the wrong time; people made plays on him that they wouldn't make eight times in ten. That could happen. There are random up and down movements in baserunning as there are in every other area of performance, and Helton's baserunning numbers *could* return to normal next year. We really don't know.

When I was young and knew everything, I thought that baserunning was an essentially negligible part of a team's offense—that on the 250-run spectrum between a very good offense and a very bad offense, baserunning controlled only a small number of runs. Maybe I was right about that; maybe I was wrong, but in either case, let's set that aside as the discussion moves forward. The world is very different now than it was thirty years ago; we have mountains of really good data that just didn't exist then, and our ability to evaluate the impact of baserunning is light years ahead of where it was way back when. Everything that everybody said about baserunning before the year 2000, including me, was really just speculation in the absence of evidence. Now we have real data. It's a better world.

Brad Hawpe hit .378 in clutch situations, driving in an amazing 45 runs in only 74 clutch at-bats. (See Clutch Hitter of the Year article on page 93).

Brad Hawpe – Career
Clutch Hitting

Season	AB	H	2B	3B	HR	RBI	BB	SO	GIDP	Avg	OBP	Slg
2004	11	3	1	0	0	1	1	2	1	.273	.333	.364
2005	30	7	1	1	1	11	7	7	0	.233	.378	.433
2006	66	13	5	0	1	11	8	25	1	.197	.280	.318
2007	74	28	5	1	5	45	15	23	4	.378	.478	.676
Totals	181	51	12	2	7	68	31	57	6	.282	.384	.486

Todd Helton – 2002 - 2007
Baserunning Analysis

Year	1st to 3rd Adv	Opp	2nd to Home Adv	Opp	1st to Home Adv	Opp	DP Opp	GIDP	Bases Taken	BR Outs	BR Gain	SB Gain	Net Gain
2002	8	27	9	21	4	9	134	10	24	6	-3	3	0
2003	11	31	16	25	8	12	170	19	28	0	22	-8	+14
2004	2	21	17	22	7	15	139	12	15	2	7	3	+10
2005	3	16	15	22	4	11	141	14	17	5	0	3	+3
2006	10	34	21	29	4	12	138	10	22	5	11	-1	+10
2007	5	42	19	26	0	10	124	15	9	10	-34	-2	-36
Totals	39	171	97	145	27	69	846	80	115	28	4	-2	+2
		23%		67%		39%		9%					

Johnny Damon – 2002 - 2007
Baserunning Analysis

Year	1st to 3rd Adv	Opp	2nd to Home Adv	Opp	1st to Home Adv	Opp	DP Opp	GIDP	Bases Taken	BR Outs	BR Gain	SB Gain	Net Gain
2002	6	23	19	24	4	12	111	4	31	5	17	19	+36
2003	3	23	19	29	5	9	94	5	22	1	14	18	+32
2004	12	27	11	15	10	15	122	8	29	4	27	3	+30
2005	6	31	22	34	7	10	111	5	26	9	5	16	+21
2006	9	23	21	28	4	8	106	4	23	3	26	5	+31
2007	18	34	17	29	1	7	85	4	21	4	18	21	+39
Totals	54	161	109	159	31	61	629	30	152	26	106	82	+188
		34%		69%		51%		4%					

Manny Corpas retired the side in order 41 times, more than any other major league reliever.

Manny Corpas – 2007
Inning Analysis

Innings Pitched	78.0
Runs Allowed	20
Innings Started	76
Runs in Those Innings	15
Shutout Innings	64
One-Run Innings	9
Two-Run Innings	3
Got First Man Out	54
Runs Scored in Those Innings	5
Runs/9 Innings	.83
First Man Reached	22
Runs Scored in Those Innings	10
Runs/9 Innings	4.09
1-2-3 Innings	41
10-pitch Innings (or less)	22
Long Innings (20 or more pitches)	7
Failed to Finish Inning	4

When Willy Taveras hit a ground ball to the left side of the infield, he beat it out over one third of the time (.383 average).

Willy Taveras – 2007
Hitting Analysis

Batting Left-Handed							1B	2B	3B	HR
Ground Balls to Left	47	Outs	29	Hits	18	Average .383	Hit Type	18 - 0 - 0 - 0
Ground Balls to Center	62	Outs	50	Hits	12	Average .194	Hit Type	12 - 0 - 0 - 0
Ground Balls to Right	28	Outs	21	Hits	7	Average .250	Hit Type	5 - 2 - 0 - 0
Line Drives to Left	8	Outs	2	Hits	6	Average .750	Hit Type	4 - 2 - 0 - 0
Line Drives to Center	23	Outs	5	Hits	18	Average .783	Hit Type	15 - 2 - 1 - 0
Line Drives to Right	14	Outs	5	Hits	9	Average .643	Hit Type	7 - 1 - 1 - 0
Fly Balls to Left	18	Outs	10	Hits	8	Average .471	Hit Type	2 - 4 - 0 - 2
Fly Balls to Center	25	Outs	22	Hits	3	Average .120	Hit Type	1 - 2 - 0 - 0
Fly Balls to Right	41	Outs	40	Hits	1	Average .024	Hit Type	1 - 0 - 0 - 0
Total on Ground Balls	137	Outs	100	Hits	37	Average .270	Hit Type	35 - 2 - 0 - 0
Total on Line Drives	45	Outs	12	Hits	33	Average .733	Hit Type	26 - 5 - 2 - 0
Total on Fly Balls	84	Outs	72	Hits	12	Average .145	Hit Type	4 - 6 - 0 - 2
Total Hit to Left	73	Outs	41	Hits	32	Average .444	Hit Type	24 - 6 - 0 - 2
Total Hit to Center	110	Outs	77	Hits	33	Average .300	Hit Type	28 - 4 - 1 - 0
Total Hit to Right	83	Outs	66	Hits	17	Average .205	Hit Type	13 - 3 - 1 - 0
Bunts	59	Outs	22	Hits	37	Average .712	Hit Type	37 - 0 - 0 - 0
All Balls in Play	325	Outs	206	Hits	119	Average .375	Hit Type	102 - 13 - 2 - 2

Willy Taveras had 37 bunt hits, more than twice as many as anyone else in the majors.

Tulo Time

Rockies' shortstops led the majors in put-outs (281) AND assists (597). The last time one major league team led in both those categories was 1993...Ozzie Smith's last season as a regular, the Cardinals led in both.

You can lead the league in assists by a shortstop if

a) you have outstanding range, or
b) you play behind a ground ball staff.

In this case it wasn't "either"; it was "both".

Jeremy Affeldt's ERA dropped from 6.20 in 2006 to 3.51 in 2007.
In 2006 he threw 17% curves, 12% cut fastballs, 5% changeups.
In 2007 he threw curves 35% of the time—changeups and cut fastballs less than 1%.

Jeremy Affeldt – 2006 Pitch Type Analysis

Overall		
Total Pitches	1682	
Fastball	1059	63%
Curveball	283	17%
Changeup	77	5%
Slider	17	1%
Cut Fastball	199	12%
Not Charted	47	3%

	Vs. RHB		Vs. LHB	
Total Pitches	1170		512	
Out Recorded	202		90	
Fastball	727	62%	332	65%
Curveball	208	18%	75	15%
Changeup	71	6%	6	1%
Slider	11	1%	6	1%
Cut Fastball	119	10%	80	16%
Not Charted	34	3%	13	3%

Jeremy Affeldt – 2007 Pitch Type Analysis

Overall		
Total Pitches	971	
Fastball	555	57%
Curveball	341	35%
Changeup	11	1%
Cut Fastball	3	0%
Pitchout	4	0%
Not Charted	57	6%

	Vs. RHB		Vs. LHB	
Total Pitches	598		373	
Outs Recorded	111		66	
Fastball	326	55%	229	61%
Curveball	214	36%	127	34%
Changeup	11	2%	0	0%
Cut Fastball	2	0%	1	0%
Pitchout	4	1%	0	0%
Not Charted	41	7%	16	4%

Ground Ball Pitchers

Rockies first basemen this year recorded 1,608 putouts, the most in the major leagues. Rays first basemen recorded 1,235 putouts, fewest in the major leagues. If you think about it, that's a fairly phenomenal spread…a difference of almost 400 first base putouts (which is to say, ground ball outs) between the teams.

There is a basis for contrast here. Both of these organizations are 1990s expansion teams, and both of them have tremendous young talent…in fact, in our Young Talent Inventory in *The Bill James Handbook 2008* we ranked them first and second in the major leagues. However, the Rockies have put their talent together into a team; the Rays, while I sincerely believe that they will get there within a year or two, are still working on getting the talent to mesh.

One of the things that made the Rockies' work this year was the ground ball pitchers, as is reflected in the extraordinary putout total of their first basemen. For example, Jeff Francis induced 204 ground outs for the Rockies last year while only 138 batters grounded out against Tampa Bay's Scott Kazmir.

The Rockies for a long time didn't know what to do with their pitching because the park is so peculiar. It's hard to throw a curve or a slider there, because the ball doesn't break normally, and you can't survive walking people.

If my data is right, the 1,608 putouts by Rockies first basemen is

a) Less than the Cardinals had in 2005 (1,696), but

b) More than anybody else has had in the majors in the last 14 years.

What the Rockies have figured out to do with their pitching is to get ground ball pitchers—lots of them. A sinker isn't a difficult pitch to control (relative to other pitches), and it isn't especially vulnerable to the effects of the thin air. There has to be other data that shows this effect.

The Rockies were 18th in the majors in first base putouts in 2005 (1,428), fourth in 2006 (1,535), first last year. The Rays, who are solidly committed to power pitchers, were 29th, 24th and 30th during the same three years.

Todd Helton – 2007
Pitch Analysis

Get a Piece of It

By our count, Todd Helton hit the most foul balls in the majors last year (600). Perhaps not coincidentally, he also was among the hitters who swung and missed least often. He came up empty on only 8% of his swings, seventh-lowest among hitters who saw 1000 pitches.

Overall		
Pitches Seen	2917	
Taken	1738	60%
Swung At	1179	40%
Pitches Taken		
Taken for a Strike	547	31%
Called a ball	1191	69%
Pitches Taken by Pitch Location		
In Strike Zone	547	31%
High	166	10%
Low	429	25%
Inside	134	8%
Outside	462	27%
Swung At		
Missed	89	8%
Fouled Off	600	51%
Put in Play	490	42%
Swung At by Pitch Location		
In Strike Zone	925	78%
High	53	4%
Low	73	6%
Inside	68	6%
Outside	60	5%

The 2007 Major League Clutch Hitter of the Year

Brad Hawpe

Colorado Rockies

Photo courtesy of Ryan McKee/Rich Clarkson and Associates

Previous Winners

2006	2005	2004	2003

Albert Pujols

St. Louis
Cardinals

Andruw Jones

Atlanta
Braves

David Ortiz

Boston
Red Sox

David Ortiz

Boston
Red Sox

.383 with 11 homers, 38 RBI in clutch situations in regular season.

10 clutch home runs, 38 RBI in clutch situations in regular season, plus .471 average, 5 RBI in four games in the playoffs.

.339 average, 1.139 clutch OPS, 7 homers, 33 RBI in clutch situations in regular season, plus a series of game-breaking hits in October.

.307 average, 1.016 clutch OPS, 38 RBI in clutch situations in regular season.

The 2007 Major League Clutch Hitter of the Year

by Bill James

On April 13 in Arizona, the Rockies and D'Backs were tied 3-3 in the seventh inning, two on and two out. Brad Hawpe ripped a double into right field, plating two runners and setting up a 6-3 Colorado victory.

On May 7 in St. Louis, the Rockies and Cardinals were tied 2-2 in the ninth, two out, bases loaded. Brad Hawpe worked a walk from Tyler Johnson, forcing home the game-winning run.

On May 16 against Arizona in Colorado the Rockies and the Snakes were tied 2-2 in the bottom of the sixth—tied up in part because of an earlier solo home run by Brad Hawpe. Sixth inning, two on, two out, Brandon Webb on the mound, Brad Hawpe launched a towering three-run home run, lifting the Rockies to a 5-3 win.

On May 19 against Kansas City, Gil Meche led the Rockies 1-0 with two out in the fourth, man on first. Hawpe homered, making it 2-1, and the Rockies went on to win, 6-4.

No major league player in 2007 had as many big hits as Brad Hawpe—and nobody was close.

On May 25 in San Francisco the Rockies trailed the Giants 3-0 through six innings. Hawpe walked in the seventh and scored the Rockies' first run, then doubled with two out in the 8th to tie the score at 3-3. The Rockies won it in the 9th.

On June 6 against the Astros in Colorado the game was tied 5-5 in the 7th, runners on first and second. Brad Hawpe. Two-run triple to center, 7-5 lead. Rockies win, 8-7.

The next day, June 7, the Rockies trailed 6-4 going into the ninth, 6-5 when Hawpe came to bat with the bases loaded, none out. Hawpe's fly ball tied the score, and the Rockies won 7-6 one batter later.

On June 13 in Fenway Park the Rockies led the Red Sox 3-2 in the fifth inning, two men on, two out, Curt Schilling on the mound. Boom. Hawpe's three-run homer launched the Rockies to 12-2 rout.

On June 16 against Tampa Bay, 0-0 in the first, bases loaded, two out. Grand Slam, Brad Hawpe. 10-5 victory.

On July 6 against Philadelphia the Rockies trailed 6-5 with two out in the ninth, bases empty, Brad Hawpe at the plate, Antonio Alfonseco on the slab. Home Run. Tie Game. Rockies won it in the 11th.

July 18 in Pittsburgh, game tied 1-1 in the fourth, man on first, two out, Ian Snell on the mound. Brad Hawpe. Home Run, 3-1 lead. Rockies win, 5-3.

July 23 against San Diego, game tied 5-5 in the eighth. Man on first, two out, Cla Meredith on the hill. Brad Hawpe. Two-run homer. 7-5 win.

On August 18 in Los Angeles the Dodgers and Rockies had played into the 15th inning. Matt Holliday put the Rockies up 5-4, and a two-run single by Brad Hawpe made it 7-4. Rockies won, 7-4.

On August 25 against Washington, game tied 1-1 in the fourth. Brad Hawpe. Two-run homer, 3-1 lead. 5-1 victory.

On August 31 in Arizona, Diamondbacks lead the Rockies 3-0 though seven. Eighth inning, Brad Hawpe doubles, putting runners on second and third, and the Rockies cut the score to 3-2. Hawpe walks in the ninth to load the bases, Rockies tie the score at three, and then hits a two-run single in the 10th. Rockies win, 7-3.

On September 4 against the Giants, Rockies and Giants tied 5-5 in the 9th. Brad Hawpe at the plate, man on second, one out. Walk-off single.

On September 19 against the Dodgers, the Rockies trailed 5-4 in the bottom of the eighth. Brad Hawpe's two-run homer put the Rockies on top, 6-5. Rockies win, 6-5.

On September 21 in San Diego the Rockies and the Padres were tied up, 0-0 through six. Brad Hawpe singles in the seventh, putting the Rockies ahead, 1-0, but the Padres tied it up in the ninth. 1-1 through 10, 11, 12, 13. 14th inning, Brad Hawpe hits a solo home run. Rockies win, 2-1.

September 22 in San Diego, Rockies' six-game winning streak has put them back in the race with a week to play. Every at bat is clutch now—and MVP candidate Matt Holliday is out with an oblique strain. Brad Hawpe goes 4-for-4, drives in two runs. Rockies win, 6-2.

Next day, September 23 in San Diego, Holliday still out, Greg Maddux on the mound. Hawpe chips in a single, a homer, and two walks. Rockies win their eighth in a row, 7-3. Pull to within one game of the division lead.

September 24 in LA, Hawpe drives in another run in a 9-7 victory. Rockies stay one game behind.

September 27 in LA, Rockies still winning. Brad Hawpe goes 3-for-5, single, double and a homer, 4 RBI. Rockies win, 10-4.

The Rockies lost on September 28 but resumed their historic hot streak on September 29, Hawpe driving in a run in each game. On September 30, the last day of the regular season, the Rockies faced first-place Arizona. A loss would end their season. The game was scoreless into the bottom of the sixth, man on first, two out, Hawpe at the plate. Double. Rockies up, 1-0. In the eighth, with the Rockies up 2-1, he doubled again, driving home two more runs. The Rockies won, 4-3, forcing a one game playoff with San Diego.

The Rockies cruised through the first two rounds of the playoffs, needing no heroics from Hawpe and receiving none. They had a long layoff before the World Series, and could never get their offense re-started during the series, including Hawpe, who struck out eight times in the four-game series—and still had a .563 slugging percentage for the series, with a home run in the final game. For the post-season as a whole his numbers were respectable: .282 average, .404 on base percentage, .410 slugging.

Over the course of a long season everybody has his moments. No major league player in 2007 had as many big hits as Brad Hawpe—and nobody was close. Many major league regulars drive in less than 10 clutch runs in a season. Only a few get to 20. Hawpe, by our count, drove in 45 clutch runs. We are pleased to name him the 2007 Major League Clutch Hitter of the Year.

The Rockies lost on September 28 but resumed their historic hot streak on September 29, Hawpe driving in a run in each game.

Detroit Tigers

Detroit Tigers – 2007
Team Overview

Description		Ranking
Won-Lost Record	88-74	
Place	2nd of 5 in American League Central	
Runs Scored	887	3rd in the majors
Runs Allowed	797	19th in the majors
Home Runs	177	10th in the majors
Home Runs Allowed	174	21st in the majors
Batting Average	.287	2nd in the majors
Batting Average Allowed	.266	12th in the majors
Walks Drawn	474	27th in the majors
Walks Given	566	21st in the majors
OPS For	.802	4th in the majors
OPS Against	.765	17th in the majors
Stolen Bases	103	12th in the majors
Stolen Bases Allowed	73	5th in the majors

Key Players

Pos	Player	G	AB	R	H	2B	3B	HR	RBI	SB	CS	BB	SO	Avg	OBP	Slg	OPS	WS
C	Ivan Rodriguez	129	502	50	141	31	3	11	63	2	2	9	96	.281	.294	.420	.714	12
1B	Sean Casey	143	453	40	134	30	1	4	54	2	2	39	42	.296	.353	.393	.746	9
2B	Placido Polanco	142	587	105	200	36	3	9	67	7	3	37	30	.341	.388	.458	.846	24
3B	Brandon Inge	151	508	64	120	25	2	14	71	9	2	47	150	.236	.312	.376	.688	12
SS	Carlos Guillen	151	564	86	167	35	9	21	102	13	8	55	93	.296	.357	.502	.859	19
LF	Craig Monroe	99	343	47	76	19	0	11	55	0	3	20	94	.222	.264	.373	.637	3
CF	Curtis Granderson	158	612	122	185	38	23	23	74	26	1	52	141	.302	.361	.552	.913	25
RF	Magglio Ordonez	157	595	117	216	54	0	28	139	4	1	76	79	.363	.434	.595	1.029	34
DH	Gary Sheffield	133	494	107	131	20	1	25	75	22	5	84	71	.265	.378	.462	.839	16

Key Pitchers

Pos	Player	G	GS	W	L	Sv	IP	H	R	ER	BB	SO	BR/9	ERA	WS
SP	Justin Verlander	32	32	18	6	0	201.2	181	88	82	67	183	11.92	3.66	16
SP	Jeremy Bonderman	28	28	11	9	0	174.1	193	105	97	48	145	12.65	5.01	7
SP	Nate Robertson	30	30	9	13	0	177.2	199	98	94	63	119	13.42	4.76	8
SP	Chad Durbin	36	19	8	7	1	127.2	133	71	67	49	66	13.39	4.72	6
SP	Mike Maroth	13	13	5	2	0	78.1	97	47	44	33	28	15.28	5.06	3
CL	Todd Jones	63	0	1	4	38	61.1	64	29	29	23	33	12.77	4.26	8
RP	Bobby Seay	58	0	3	0	1	46.1	38	12	12	15	38	10.68	2.33	6
RP	Jason Grilli	57	0	5	3	0	79.2	81	46	42	32	62	13.33	4.74	4

Justin Verlander – 2007
Runs Allowed Analysis

Reached by Single:	126	Scored: 34	27%
Reached by Double:	33	Scored: 15	45%
Reached by Triple:	2	Scored: 1	50%
Reached by Homer:	20		
Reached by Walk:	67	Scored: 16	24%
Reached by HBP:	19	Scored: 0	0%
Reached by Error:	6	Scored: 1	17%
Reached by FC - All Safe:	3	Scored: 1	33%
Reached by FC - Out:	18	Scored: 0	0%
Total On Base	294	Scored: 90	31%
Stolen Bases Allowed:	4	Scored: 1	25%
Caught Stealing:	1	Scored: 0	0%
Steal Attempts:	5	Scored: 1	20%
Intentional Walks:	3	Scored: 0	0%

Byung-Hyun Kim – 2007
Runs Allowed Analysis

Reached by Single:	82	Scored: 25	30%
Reached by Double:	25	Scored: 16	64%
Reached by Triple:	4	Scored: 3	75%
Reached by Homer:	20		
Reached by Walk:	68	Scored: 16	23%
Reached by HBP:	16	Scored: 7	44%
Reached by Error:	7	Scored: 3	43%
Reached by FC - All Safe:	1	Scored: 0	0%
Reached by FC - Out:	8	Scored: 0	0%
Total On Base	231	Scored:118	51%
Stolen Bases Allowed:	23	Scored: 13	57%
Caught Stealing:	6	Scored: 1	17%
Steal Attempts:	29	Scored: 14	48%
Intentional Walks:	3	Scored: 0	0%

Justin Verlander also led the majors in wild pitches (17).

The last pitcher to lead the majors in hit batsmen and wild pitches was Tom Murphy in 1969, 16 wild pitches, 21 hit batsmen. Roy Parmalee, a National League pitcher famous for his explosive but uncontrollable fastball, led the majors in both categories in both 1933 and 1937, and was the last pitcher to have a winning record while doing this. He was 13-8 in 1933.

Over his last two seasons here, the Detroit Tigers were 16-6 in games started by Mike Maroth — 7-2 in 2006, 9-4 in 2007.

Detroit Tigers – 2006
Performance by Starting Pitcher

Games Started By	G	RS	RA	Won	Lost
Bonderman, Jeremy	34	165	155	18	16
Rogers, Kenny	33	195	126	24	9
Robertson, Nate	32	125	122	15	17
Verlander, Justin	30	169	117	19	11
Miner, Zach	16	91	78	9	7
Maroth, Mike	9	37	28	7	2
Ledezma, Wil	7	34	38	3	4
Colon, Roman	1	6	11	0	1
Team Totals	162	822	675	95	67

Detroit Tigers – 2007
Performance by Starting Pitcher

Games Started By	G	RS	RA	Won	Lost
Verlander, Justin	32	196	135	22	10
Robertson, Nate	30	137	158	11	19
Bonderman, Jeremy	28	153	141	15	13
Durbin, Chad	19	106	96	9	10
Maroth, Mike	13	84	69	9	4
Miller, Andrew	13	81	66	7	6
Rogers, Kenny	11	53	54	6	5
Jurrjens, Jair	7	33	23	6	1
Tata, Jordan	3	16	21	1	2
Vasquez, Virgil	3	15	29	0	3
Bazardo, Yorman	2	12	3	2	0
Miner, Zach	1	1	2	0	1
Team Totals	162	887	797	88	74

Curtis Granderson – 2007
Runs Scored Analysis

Reached on		Runs Scored After	
Home Runs	23		23
Triples	23	Scored after Triple	13
Doubles	38	Scored after Double	19
Singles	101	Scored after Single	40
Walk/HBP	57	Scored after Walk/HBP	20
Reached on Error	5	Scored after ROE	3
Reached on Forceout	11	Vultured Runs	3
Inserted as Pinch Runner	1	Runs as pinch runner	1
		Total Runs Scored	122

Brought in by		Driven in by	
Single	46	Placido Polanco	27
Double	17	Magglio Ordonez	26
Triple	1	Himself	23
His own home run	23	Gary Sheffield	18
Other home run	7	Carlos Guillen	8
Sac Fly	13	No RBI	4
Walk, Error, or Other	15	Sean Casey	4
		Ivan Rodriguez	3
		Marcus Thames	3
		Ryan Raburn	2
		Neifi Perez	1
		Craig Monroe	1
		Brandon Inge	1
		Cameron Maybin	1

Since 2002 Kenny Rogers is 15-3 with a 3.13 ERA when facing a team with a winning percentage below .400.

When facing a team with a winning percentage over .600 he is 1-4 in ten starts with an ERA of 8.10.

Kenny Rogers
Career Records Against Quality of Opposition

Opponent	G	IP	W	L	SO	BB	ERA
.600 teams	10	50.0	1	4	32	22	8.10
.500 - .599 teams	78	492.0	37	17	248	160	3.59
.400 - .499 teams	64	393.2	25	21	205	110	4.64
sub .400 teams	24	144.0	15	3	86	34	3.13

Jeremy Bonderman last year threw 941 sliders, third-most in the majors, while Justin Verlander threw none.

Jeremy Bonderman – 2007
Pitch Type Analysis

Overall		
Total Pitches	2725	
Fastball	1556	57%
Changeup	174	6%
Slider	941	35%
Pitchout	17	1%
Not Charted	37	1%

	Vs. RHB		Vs. LHB	
Total Pitches	1170		1555	
Outs Recorded	219		304	
Fastball	644	55%	912	59%
Changeup	24	2%	150	10%
Slider	489	42%	452	29%
Pitchout	1	0%	16	1%
Not Charted	12	1%	25	2%

Justin Verlander – 2007
Pitch Type Analysis

Overall		
Total Pitches	3354	
Fastball	2059	61%
Curveball	623	19%
Changeup	621	19%
Pitchout	3	0%
Not Charted	48	1%

	Vs. RHB		Vs. LHB	
Total Pitches	1522		1832	
Outs Recorded	282		323	
Fastball	917	60%	1142	62%
Curveball	372	24%	251	14%
Changeup	212	14%	409	22%
Pitchout	1	0%	2	0%
Not Charted	20	1%	28	2%

Magglio Ordonez – 2007
Skills Assessment

Hitting for Average:	99th percentile	100th percentile among right fielders
Hitting for Power:	80th percentile	87th percentile among right fielders
Plate Discipline:	74th percentile	79th percentile among right fielders
Running:	33rd percentile	26th percentile among right fielders

Magglio Ordonez's drove in 48 runs with singles, the most in the majors. He also drove in 30 runs with doubles, which also was most in the majors.

Magglio Ordonez – 2007
RBI Analysis

Hits		RBI Hits		RBI Total		Drove In	
Home Runs:	28			RBI on Home Runs:	47	Curtis Granderson	25
Triples:	0	RBI Triples:	0	RBI on Triples:	0	Omar Infante	2
Doubles:	54	RBI Doubles:	22	RBI on Doubles:	30	Brandon Inge	4
Singles:	134	RBI Singles:	42	RBI on Singles:	48	Craig Monroe	4
				Sacrifice Flies:	4	Neifi Perez	3
		Other RBI: Walks	2			Timo Perez	1
		Other RBI: Ground Outs	4	Total Other:	10	Placido Polanco	36
						Ryan Raburn	4
				Total RBI:	139	Ivan Rodriguez	3
						Gary Sheffield	28
						Marcus Thames	1
						His Own Bad Self	28
						Total	139

Atypical Seasons

by Bill James

1) There are 11,364 players in history, through 2006, who had 500 or more plate appearances in a season.

2) Only 444 of those players (4%) finished the season with the exact hit total you would expect if you simply multiplied their career batting average times their season's at bats. And many of those were players who only played one year in the majors.

3) Only one-third of regular players finish the season within five hits of their career batting average.

4) Less than two-thirds are within ten hits.

5) By decade the total number of players with 500 plate appearances is:

1870s—zero
1880s—296
1890s—649
1900s—736
1910s—807
1920s—791
1930s—813
1940s—753
1950s—732
1960s—962
1970s—1256
1980s—1181
1990s—1269
2000-2006—1119

The straightforward general question, as always, divides into picayune smaller questions.

6) Through 2006 there have been 3,166 players who hit .300 in 500 or more plate appearances—28% of all hitters.

7) There are more than twice as many .300 hitters as hitters with .400 on-base percentages.

8) There are almost twice as many .300 hitters as hitters with .500 slugging percentages.

9) Barry Bonds career divides in half like a peanut.

10) I am really sick of talking about Barry Bonds.

These were among the things I discovered when I set out to answer a simple question: what player had the most atypical season in baseball history? The straightforward general question, as always, divides into picayune smaller questions, which have answers that turn out to be not as interesting as I thought they would be.

The player who missed his career batting average by the widest margin was: Hugh Duffy in 1894. Different sources give different batting averages for Duffy in 1894, but his average, whatever it was, was astronomical. His career batting average was "only" .324, so when he hit .440 in 1894—which is the figure I'm using, but the conclusion won't change if you use a different one—when he hit .440 in 1894, he overshot his career average by a whopping 62 hits.

The reason this list is less interesting than I thought it would be is that I was looking for players who had atypical seasons, and that's not exactly what I found. What I found was a bunch of guys from the 1890s. Batting norms were extremely unstable in the 1890s—starting out very low in the early 1890s, shooting up to historic highs in the mid-1890s, after the pitching mound was moved back to its current distance, and then crashing again at the turn of the century, entering the dead ball era. Because of this, the seven most off-the-norm batting averages of all time were all posted between 1887 and 1901.

As I've written somewhere, or if I haven't I will, I have come to believe that we made a mistake in re-labeling 19th century baseball as major league baseball. When I was young, 19th century baseball was

1) almost entirely ignored,
2) little known and less understood, and
3) not considered to be major league baseball when it was referenced.

A line was drawn across baseball history. Post-1900 was "modern" baseball history, and 19th century baseball was like the edge of the ocean on medieval maps: Here Be Monsters. The first generation of serious baseball researchers, led by Lee Allen, erased that line. For many years I supported that decision. In recent years I have come to see it as a mistake. It was a wonderful thing that 19th century baseball was re-discovered, because it is extremely fascinating and we wouldn't have major league baseball without it. We should have re-examined it, but we should not have re-labeled it, because, when you look at it, 19th century baseball really has almost none of the characteristics of "major league" baseball.

But it's there, and I don't want to push myself out on an island by treating this material different than every-

When you look at it, 19th century baseball really has almost none of the characteristics of "major league" baseball.

one else, so...the seven most atypical seasons in major league history are all from 1887 to 1901. The most atypical batting performances since 1901 are:

1. Norm Cash, 1961. Cash in 1961 had 535 at bats, and Cash had a career batting average of .271. We thus would have expected him to have 145 hits that season. He actually had 193 hits—+48 hits.
2. Jesse Burkett, 1905, -47 hits.
3. George Sisler, 1922, +47 hits.
4. Darren Erstad, 2000, +47 hits.
5. Charlie Gehringer, 1941, -44 hits.
6. Cy Seymour, 1905, +43 hits.
7. Bill Sweeney, 1912, +43 hits.
8. Chuck Klein, 1930, +43 hits.
9. Heinie Zimmerman, 1912, +43 hits.
10. George Sisler, 1920, +42 hits.

What I really was looking for was the seasons like Cash's and Erstad's, and, since Erstad is still around, let's talk for a moment about him.

In theory, I should have banned Erstad from the list, since he is still active, and we don't really know how far above his career norm his 2000 season will be, once his norms are fixed by retirement. But I decided not to exclude him from the list, because it seems extremely unlikely that Erstad will improve his career batting average from here on out. His career average entering this season was .286. There's about a 99% chance his career average will wind up lower than that.

That means that Erstad, who is already within one hit of having the greatest hit discrepancy from his career norm since 1901, is very likely, once he retires, to move ahead of Cash, and to actually have the greatest hit discrepancy since 1901. Erstad's 2000 season, when he had 240 hits, is among the greatest fluke seasons of all time.

There are really only three seasons on this list—Cash, Erstad, and Seymour—which represent the type of season I was trying to find, which is atypical seasons. The other things we find with this search are:

1) Seasons at the very beginning and very end of careers. Charlie Gehringer in 1941 and Jesse Burkett in 1905 weren't having aberrant seasons; they just couldn't play anymore. Al Kaline, 1954, turns up on several of these lists. He was 19; he just wasn't really Al Kaline yet.

2) Players who had their best seasons in atypical years. 1930, of course, was an atypical season, and 1911-1912 was a little hiatus of the Dead Ball era. The cork-center baseball was introduced in 1911. For a year or two bat-

ting numbers jumped. But the practice of scratching or defacing the baseball, which really began in 1910, progressed rapidly after 1912, and dragged baseball back into the Dead Ball era.

3) Players whose level of ability actually changed because of injury, like George Sisler, who was a career .361 before his illness, .320 afterward.

4) Players who were early in their career or late in their career at a time when the game underwent a seismic shift in run production levels.

Those things are instructive, and interesting in their own way, but not exactly what I was looking for. Ed Delahanty, a career .346 hitter, hit just .243 in 1891, which is the greatest batting average under-achievement of all time. But the National League batting average jumped from .245 to .309 between 1892 and 1894, and the change in the league actually explains most of the change in Delahanty's record.

Looking for "true aberrations", rather than one of the four things listed above, here are a few:

Joe Torre, 1971 (+41 hits)
Luke Appling, 1936 (+41)
Bret Boone, 2001 (+41)
Miguel Dilone, 1980 (+40)
Mickey Vernon, 1946 (+39)
Andres Galarraga, 1993 (+39)
Carson Bigbee, 1922 (+39)
George Brett, 1980 (+38)
Adrian Beltre, 2004 (+38)
John Olerud, 1993 (+38)
Rod Carew, 1977 (+37)
Cito Gaston, 1970 (+36)
Wade Boggs, 1992 (-36)
Al Simmons, 1935 (-36)
Carlos Delgado, 2000 (+36)
Tommy Davis, 1962 (+35)
Alan Trammell, 1987 (+35)
George Scott, 1968 (-34)

There is no player in history who EXACTLY matched his career batting average in a season of 500 or more at bats—hundreds of players who matched it to three decimals, but no one who EXACTLY matched it, other than the one-year players. That was a surprise to me, also; I would have guessed that there would be some player who hit exactly .300 for both career and season, or .250, or who went exactly 2-for-each-7 or 3-for-each-11 or 4-for-each-15 or something, both for a season and a career.

While I was looking for most atypical batting averages (actually, most atypical hit totals), I also looked for seasons with atypical on base percentages, slugging percentages, OPS, and home run totals. These lists tend to be dominated on both ends by Barry Bonds. Bonds has such an unusual career progression, with such extraordinary totals, that he tends to have seasons at the top and bottom of both lists. And…you know, everything's been said about Barry Bonds, so I'm just going to skip that. Other things you might want to know about the study:

1) The greatest over-performance in on base percentage that wasn't Bonds was Norm Cash in '61 (+75 times on base).

2) The greatest under-performance ever was Hughie Jennings in 1892.

3) The greatest "legitimate under-performance", not explained by age or seismic shifts, was probably Ozzie Smith in 1979 (-49 times on base).

4) The greatest slugging percentage over-achievement in a season was Duffy in 1894, again (+132 bases), followed by Luis Gonzalez in 2001 (+124 bases) and Brady Anderson in 1996 (+123).

5) Barry Bonds in 1989 was the only player ever who was 100 total bases BELOW his career norm (-106), although this could change (but probably won't) when his career norms are finished settling.

6) To figure the "OPS discrepancy" I multiplied the player's OPS times his plate appearances.

7) The greatest discrepancy ever which isn't Bonds or Duffy was Sammy Sosa in 2001 (+207).

8) The greatest under-achievement in OPS which wasn't Bonds or the early 1890s was Mark McGwire in 1991 (-157 bases).

9) Barry Bonds' 2001 home run rate is almost exactly twice his career norm.

10) The greatest home run over-production in a season that wasn't Bonds was Gonzalez the same season (+33 homers), followed by Brady Anderson, Maris, Davey Johnson, Hack Wilson in '30, Tilly Walker in '22, Adrian Beltre in 2004, Sammy Sosa in 2001, Hank Greenberg in 1938, Jay Bell in 1999, and Carl Yastrzemski in 1967.

11) The greatest home run under-production in a season that wasn't Bonds was Rafael Palmeiro in 1988 (-24), followed by several more steroid-era players…McGwire in '91, Palmeiro again in '89, Sosa in 1990, etc.

12) Two of the greatest home run under-producers of all time were teammates: Kirby Puckett and Gary Gaetti in 1984. Puckett hit no homers (-16), Gaetti hit only 5 (-19). Suggesting the possibility that the Twins' two World Championships may have been aided by their team being among the first to discover…well, I'd better not go there. Nor will I point out that Gaetti was bald and had acne and Puckett died young.

There are really only three seasons on this list—Cash, Erstad, and Seymour—which represent the type of season I was trying to find, which is atypical seasons.

Florida Marlins

Florida Marlins – 2007
Team Overview

Description		Ranking
Won-Lost Record	71-91	
Place	5th of 5 in National League East	
Runs Scored	790	13th in the majors
Runs Allowed	891	29th in the majors
Home Runs	201	4th in the majors
Home Runs Allowed	176	24th in the majors
Batting Average	.267	16th in the majors
Batting Average Allowed	.285	28th in the majors
Walks Drawn	521	18th in the majors
Walks Given	661	28th in the majors
OPS For	.784	7th in the majors
OPS Against	.806	29th in the majors
Stolen Bases	105	11th in the majors
Stolen Bases Allowed	94	13th in the majors

Key Players

Pos	Player	G	AB	R	H	2B	3B	HR	RBI	SB	CS	BB	SO	Avg	OBP	Slg	OPS	WS
C	Miguel Olivo	122	452	43	107	20	4	16	60	3	2	14	123	.237	.262	.405	.667	7
1B	Mike Jacobs	114	426	57	113	27	2	17	54	1	2	31	101	.265	.317	.458	.775	7
2B	Dan Uggla	159	632	113	155	49	3	31	88	2	1	68	167	.245	.326	.479	.805	16
3B	Miguel Cabrera	157	588	91	188	38	2	34	119	2	1	79	127	.320	.401	.565	.965	29
SS	Hanley Ramirez	154	639	125	212	48	6	29	81	51	14	52	95	.332	.386	.562	.948	27
LF	Josh Willingham	144	521	75	138	32	4	21	89	8	1	66	122	.265	.364	.463	.827	19
CF	Alfredo Amezaga	133	400	46	105	14	9	2	30	13	7	35	52	.263	.324	.358	.682	5
RF	Jeremy Hermida	123	429	54	127	32	1	18	63	3	4	47	105	.296	.369	.501	.870	13

Key Pitchers

Pos	Player	G	GS	W	L	Sv	IP	H	R	ER	BB	SO	BR/9	ERA	WS
SP	Dontrelle Willis	35	35	10	15	0	205.1	241	131	118	87	146	14.99	5.17	7
SP	Scott Olsen	33	33	10	15	0	176.2	226	134	114	85	133	15.89	5.81	1
SP	Sergio Mitre	27	27	5	8	0	149.0	180	88	77	41	80	13.95	4.65	4
SP	Byung-Hyun Kim	23	19	9	5	0	109.2	114	74	66	62	102	15.59	5.42	3
SP	Rick Vanden Hurk	18	17	4	6	0	81.2	94	63	62	48	82	15.98	6.83	0
CL	Kevin Gregg	74	0	0	5	32	84.0	63	34	33	40	87	11.68	3.54	10
RP	Taylor Tankersley	67	0	6	1	1	47.1	42	22	21	29	49	14.07	3.99	4
RP	Matt Lindstrom	71	0	3	4	0	67.0	66	27	23	21	62	12.09	3.09	5

The Marlins' defense really let their pitchers down this season.

They led the league in errors.

They allowed 98 unearned runs; the other National League teams averaged 55 unearned runs allowed.

Their batting average allowed climbed from .267 in 2006 to .285. Only one point of that climb was from increased home runs allowed.

The pitchers' walks per nine innings did increase from 3.9 to 4.1, but their strikeouts per nine also climbed from 6.8 to 7.1.

When Your Best Starting Pitcher Is Sergio Mitre...

The Florida Marlins had 106 starts with a Game Score under 50—easily the highest total in baseball.

Florida Marlins – 2007
Performance by Quality of Start

Game Score	#	ERA	W	-	L
70 to 79	4	0.75	4	-	0
60 to 69	17	2.32	12	-	5
50 to 59	35	3.81	19	-	16
40 to 49	47	4.45	25	-	22
30 to 39	29	5.69	7	-	22
20 to 29	15	7.93	2	-	13
Below 20	15	9.28	2	-	13

Plop, Plop, Fizz, Fizz

Over the last seven seasons the Florida Marlins have had seven different pitchers lead the team in saves. For ten points and a chance at a bonus finger, which of the following pitchers is NOT on the list of Marlins' save leaders, 2001 to 2007:

Antonio Alfonseca	Armando Benitez
Vladimir Nunez	Todd Jones
Chad Fox	Joe Borowski
Ugueth Urbina	Kevin Gregg

For 2008, my money is on Renyel Pinto. The answer, by the way, is something that rhymes with "Mad Crocks".

Florida Marlins – 2007
Performance by Starting Pitcher

Games Started By	G	RS	RA	Won	Lost
Willis, Dontrelle	35	186	182	17	18
Olsen, Scott	33	153	179	17	16
Mitre, Sergio	27	126	138	11	16
Kim, Byung-Hyun	19	114	98	11	8
Vanden Hurk, Rick	17	82	108	6	11
Obermueller, Wes	7	34	38	3	4
Sanchez, Anibal	6	31	29	2	4
Barone, Daniel	6	21	31	2	4
Nolasco, Ricky	4	11	22	1	3
Seddon, Chris	4	22	32	1	3
Johnson, Josh	4	10	34	0	4
Team Totals	162	790	891	71	91

Jeremy Hermida has hit 51 fly balls to right field in his career, of which 22 have been home runs. He has hit 100 fly balls to left, of which not a single one has left the yard.

Jeremy Hermida – Career
Hitting Analysis

Batting Left-Handed								1B	2B	3B	HR
Ground Balls to Left	36	Outs	29	Hits	7	Average	.194	Hit Type	7 - 0	- 0	- 0
Ground Balls to Center	89	Outs	59	Hits	30	Average	.337	Hit Type	30 - 0	- 0	- 0
Ground Balls to Right	129	Outs	105	Hits	24	Average	.186	Hit Type	19 - 5	- 0	- 0
Line Drives to Left	31	Outs	6	Hits	25	Average	.806	Hit Type	16 - 9	- 0	- 0
Line Drives to Center	47	Outs	17	Hits	30	Average	.652	Hit Type	24 - 6	- 0	- 0
Line Drives to Right	43	Outs	7	Hits	36	Average	.837	Hit Type	20 - 13	- 1	- 2
Fly Balls to Left	100	Outs	80	Hits	20	Average	.204	Hit Type	8 - 12	- 0	- 0
Fly Balls to Center	59	Outs	45	Hits	14	Average	.237	Hit Type	5 - 5	- 1	- 3
Fly Balls to Right	51	Outs	25	Hits	26	Average	.520	Hit Type	1 - 3	- 0	- 22
Total on Ground Balls	254	Outs	193	Hits	61	Average	.240	Hit Type	56 - 5	- 0	- 0
Total on Line Drives	121	Outs	30	Hits	91	Average	.758	Hit Type	60 - 28	- 1	- 2
Total on Fly Balls	210	Outs	150	Hits	60	Average	.290	Hit Type	14 - 20	- 1	- 25
Total Hit to Left	167	Outs	115	Hits	52	Average	.315	Hit Type	31 - 21	- 0	- 0
Total Hit to Center	195	Outs	121	Hits	74	Average	.381	Hit Type	59 - 11	- 1	- 3
Total Hit to Right	223	Outs	137	Hits	86	Average	.387	Hit Type	40 - 21	- 1	- 24
Bunts	12	Outs	8	Hits	4	Average	.444	Hit Type	4 - 0	- 0	- 0
All Balls in Play	597	Outs	381	Hits	216	Average	.366	Hit Type	134 - 53	- 2	- 27

Alfredo Amezaga went 4-for-40 (.100) in the clutch in 2007, and is now a .136 career hitter in clutch situations.

Alfredo Amezaga – Career
Clutch Hitting

Season	AB	H	2B	3B	HR	RBI	BB	SO	GIDP	Avg	OBP	Slg
2003	6	1	0	0	0	0	2	3	0	.167	.375	.167
2004	13	2	1	0	0	0	1	3	0	.154	.214	.231
2006	22	4	1	0	0	1	3	4	0	.182	.333	.227
2007	40	4	0	0	0	8	5	8	0	.100	.208	.100
Totals	81	11	2	0	0	9	11	18	0	.136	.258	.160

How did right-handed hitter Cody Ross go from a .212 average and .396 slugging percentage in 2006 to a .335 average and .653 slugging percentage in '07? Part of it was the fact that he pulled the ball a lot more. In '06, 40% of his balls in play were hit to left, but in '07, 57% went to left. And when he pulls the ball in the air, he's dangerous as hell. In '06, he hit 22 fly balls to left, and 12 of them cleared the fence; in '07, he hit 23 to left and came away with nine homers.

Cody Ross – 2006
Hitting Analysis

Batting Right-Handed								1B		2B		3B		HR
Fly Balls to Left	22	Outs	9	Hits	13	Average	.591	Hit Type	0	-	1	-	0	- 12
Fly Balls to Center	31	Outs	28	Hits	3	Average	.100	Hit Type	0	-	2	-	0	- 1
Fly Balls to Right	35	Outs	31	Hits	4	Average	.118	Hit Type	1	-	1	-	2	- 0
Total Hit to Left	83	Outs	49	Hits	34	Average	.410	Hit Type	17	-	5	-	0	- 12
Total Hit to Center	67	Outs	53	Hits	14	Average	.212	Hit Type	8	-	5	-	0	- 1
Total Hit to Right	55	Outs	42	Hits	13	Average	.241	Hit Type	9	-	2	-	2	- 0
All Balls in Play	206	Outs	145	Hits	61	Average	.300	Hit Type	34	-	12	-	2	- 13

Cody Ross – 2007
Hitting Analysis

Batting Right-Handed								1B		2B		3B		HR
Fly Balls to Left	23	Outs	10	Hits	13	Average	.565	Hit Type	1	-	3	-	0	- 9
Fly Balls to Center	17	Outs	13	Hits	4	Average	.250	Hit Type	0	-	3	-	0	- 1
Fly Balls to Right	12	Outs	11	Hits	1	Average	.083	Hit Type	0	-	1	-	0	- 0
Total Hit to Left	77	Outs	40	Hits	37	Average	.481	Hit Type	14	-	13	-	0	- 10
Total Hit to Center	38	Outs	23	Hits	15	Average	.405	Hit Type	11	-	3	-	0	- 1
Total Hit to Right	21	Outs	15	Hits	6	Average	.286	Hit Type	2	-	3	-	0	- 1
All Balls in Play	136	Outs	78	Hits	58	Average	.430	Hit Type	27	-	19	-	0	- 12

The Florida Marlins were 36-22 when they got the leadoff man on 4 or more times a game, 35-69 when it was 3 or less.

Florida Marlins – 2007
Record by Leadoff Hitter Reached

Leadoff Hitter Reached	W	-	L
6 times	5	-	3
5 times	6	-	3
4 times	25	-	16
3 times	18	-	32
2 times	10	-	20
1 times	6	-	13
0 times	1	-	4
Total, 4 or more LO men on	36	-	22
Total, 3 or less LO men on	35	-	69

The largest platoon differential in the majors last year was by Dontrelle Willis, who limited left-handed hitters to a .142 slugging percentage, but had the bejeezus beaten out of him by right-handers. (This is not a fluke—he is always very tough on lefties.)

The major league pitcher who threw the most fastballs last year was:

Dontrelle Willis, 2,652 fastballs.

Thirty-nine percent of the balls Miguel Olivo swung at last year were out of the strike zone. No other Marlins regular had a figure over 30%.

Dontrelle Willis – 2007
Pitch Type Analysis

Overall

Total Pitches	3491	
Fastball	2652	76%
Changeup	199	6%
Slider	561	16%
Pitchout	5	0%
Not Charted	74	2%

	Vs. RHB		Vs. LHB	
Total Pitches	3031		460	
Outs Recorded	518		98	
Fastball	2303	76%	349	76%
Changeup	189	6%	10	2%
Slider	468	15%	93	20%
Pitchout	5	0%	0	0%
Not Charted	66	2%	8	2%

Miguel Olivo – 2007
Pitch Analysis

Overall

Pitches Seen	1585	
Taken	694	44%
Swung At	891	56%

Pitches Taken

Taken for a Strike	218	31%
Called a ball	476	69%

Pitches Taken by Pitch Location

In Strike Zone	218	31%
High	76	11%
Low	222	32%
Inside	68	10%
Outside	110	16%

Swung At

Missed	291	33%
Fouled Off	270	30%
Put in Play	330	37%

Swung At by Pitch Location

In Strike Zone	545	61%
High	51	6%
Low	148	17%
Inside	17	2%
Outside	130	15%

I was going to leave that note at that, but Willis' platoon splits are truly phenomenal. He was the only major league pitcher last year to pitch 200 innings, or anything like 200 innings, without giving up a home run to a left-handed batter. But he led the majors in home runs given up to right-handed hitters (29), and, worse yet, also in doubles (51).

Momma Likes You (All) Better

Scott Olsen pitched 176.2 innings in 2007 allowing 134 runs, 114 earned. He gave up 20 unearned runs, thanks to 14 errors behind him on the field while he was pitching. The Marlins' relief trio of Kevin Gregg, Taylor Tankersley and Matt Lindstrom pitched more innings than Olsen (198.1), yet only 3 errors were committed while they pitched. The trio only "suffered" six unearned runs against them.

Scott Olsen – 2007
Runs Allowed Analysis

Reached by Single:	150	Scored:	47	31%
Reached by Double:	45	Scored:	24	53%
Reached by Triple:	2	Scored:	2	100%
Reached by Homer:	29			
Reached by Walk:	85	Scored:	20	24%
Reached by HBP:	1	Scored:	0	0%
Reached by Error:	14	Scored:	8	57%
Reached by FC - All Safe:	1	Scored:	1	100%
Reached by FC - Out:	17	Scored:	2	12%
Total On Base	344	Scored:	141	41%
Stolen Bases Allowed:	10	Scored:	4	40%
Caught Stealing:	6	Scored:	0	0%
Steal Attempts:	16	Scored:	4	25%
Intentional Walks:	4	Scored:	1	25%

Even the Wins Weren't So Winning

Dontrelle Willis' ERA in his victories was 4.30, the highest of any pitcher with 10 or more wins. Teammate Scott Olsen was fourth-highest (3.60).

Dontrelle Willis – 2007
Decision Analysis

Group	G	IP	W	L	Pct	H	R	SO	BB	ERA
Wins	10	67.0	10	0	1.000	70	34	57	19	4.30
Losses	15	86.0	0	15	.000	118	70	55	41	6.38
No Decisions	10	52.1	0	0	—	53	27	34	27	4.30

Quality Starts: 6 in Wins, 5 in Losses, 5 in no-decisions

Scott Olsen – 2007
Decision Analysis

Group	G	IP	W	L	Pct	H	R	SO	BB	ERA
Wins	10	60.0	10	0	1.000	53	28	51	25	3.60
Losses	15	72.0	0	15	.000	116	79	50	38	7.88
No Decisions	8	44.2	0	0	—	57	27	32	22	5.44

Quality Starts: 5 in Wins, 2 in Losses, 4 in no-decisions

Houston Astros

Houston Astros – 2007
Team Overview

Description		Ranking
Won-Lost Record	73-89	
Place	4th of 6 in National League Central	
Runs Scored	723	24th in the majors
Runs Allowed	813	20th in the majors
Home Runs	167	17th in the majors
Home Runs Allowed	206	30th in the majors
Batting Average	260	23rd in the majors
Batting Average Allowed	.273	21st in the majors
Walks Drawn	547	9th in the majors
Walks Given	510	12th in the majors
OPS For	.742	22nd in the majors
OPS Against	.791	25th in the majors
Stolen Bases	65	25th in the majors
Stolen Bases Allowed	84	8th in the majors

Key Players

Pos	Player	G	AB	R	H	2B	3B	HR	RBI	SB	CS	BB	SO	Avg	OBP	Slg	OPS	WS
C	Brad Ausmus	117	349	38	82	16	3	3	25	6	1	37	74	.235	.318	.324	.642	7
1B	Lance Berkman	153	561	95	156	24	2	34	102	7	3	94	125	.278	.386	.510	.896	24
2B	Craig Biggio	141	517	68	130	31	3	10	50	4	3	23	112	.251	.285	.381	.666	6
3B	Morgan Ensberg	85	224	36	52	10	0	8	31	0	1	31	48	.232	.323	.384	.707	5
SS	Mark Loretta	133	460	52	132	23	2	4	41	1	2	44	41	.287	.352	.372	.724	12
LF	Carlos Lee	162	627	93	190	43	1	32	119	10	5	53	63	.303	.354	.528	.882	21
CF	Hunter Pence	108	456	57	147	30	9	17	69	11	5	26	95	.322	.360	.539	.899	18
RF	Luke Scott	132	369	49	94	28	5	18	64	3	1	53	95	.255	.351	.504	.855	11

Key Pitchers

Pos	Player	G	GS	W	L	Sv	IP	H	R	ER	BB	SO	BR/9	ERA	WS
SP	Roy Oswalt	33	32	14	7	0	212.0	221	80	75	60	154	12.23	3.18	17
SP	Wandy Rodriguez	31	31	9	13	0	182.2	179	102	93	62	158	12.12	4.58	7
SP	Woody Williams	33	31	8	15	0	188.0	216	114	110	53	101	13.45	5.27	4
SP	Chris Sampson	24	19	7	8	0	121.2	138	64	62	30	51	12.95	4.59	5
SP	Matt Albers	31	18	4	11	0	110.2	127	77	72	50	71	14.96	5.86	0
CL	Brad Lidge	66	0	5	3	19	67.0	54	29	25	30	88	11.82	3.36	10
RP	Chad Qualls	79	0	6	5	5	82.2	84	29	28	25	78	12.19	3.05	9
RP	Trever Miller	76	0	0	0	1	46.1	45	26	25	23	46	13.99	4.86	2

The Epic of Craig Biggio

I wonder how many people even remember anymore that Craig Biggio came to the majors as a catcher? Biggio wasn't much of a catcher, honestly, but he was a major league regular catcher for three and a half years. This was ages ago. When I heard that the Astros were taking their young catcher and moving him to second base I thought, "Yeah, right; that'll work great." I would have given you 20-1 odds it would fail. I've been a baseball fan a long time. Moves like that always fail.

Biggio made it work, however, and I was thrilled to be wrong. It was such an unusual thing to see a player who could make a transition like that at the major league level, from catcher to second base. It required something that you don't often see, an exceptional level of determination, dedication and adaptability.

Gradually, over the years after that, Craig Biggio emerged as my favorite player. I had a Craig Biggio pennant on my wall. The only other one I ever had was George Brett. I was never an Astros fan; that wasn't it. It had to do with something Dan Okrent had asked me, when he was working on an article for *Sports Illustrated* in 1980. "Bill," he said, "you write about the player with subtle skills, the player who isn't a recognized star but who is just as valuable as the star because of his combination of skills. Who is the player that best exemplifies that other kind of star?"

I couldn't come up with anybody. I finally pointed toward Al Bumbry, who was that kind of a player in 1980, but not consistently throughout his career. I loved Craig Biggio because he was the perfect answer to that question. He was the player who wasn't a star, but who was just as valuable as the superstars because of his exceptional command of a collection of little skills—getting on base, and avoiding the double play, and stealing a base here and there, and playing defense. Here was the guy who scored 120 runs every year because he hit 45 or 50 doubles every year and walked 70 to 90 times a year and led the majors in being hit with the pitch and hardly ever grounded into a double play and somehow stole 25 to 50 bases every year although he really had very average speed.

You have to understand, when I wrote in 1998 that Craig Biggio was one of the five greatest second basemen of all time, people thought I was nuts. Very few people at that time saw him as a special player. I liked that, too—I liked people thinking I was out on a limb about something when I knew I was right. I loved doing a point-by-point summary comparing Craig Biggio to Ken Griffey Jr., and showing Biggio was actually as valuable, in his best seasons, as Griffey. Griffey at that time was generally regarded as the best player in baseball. In 1997 Griffey outhomered Biggio 56-22, in 1998 56-20. But Biggio had a higher batting average, more doubles and triples, more stolen bases with a better stolen base percentage, was hit by pitches an additional 20 times a year and grounded into fewer double plays. He had as many walks and fewer strikeouts. It was pretty obvious that, if you added together all of Biggio's advantages, Biggio was, at a minimum, on the same level.

Later on, after an injury, the Astros needed a center fielder. Craig Biggio raised his hand and said "I can play center. We've got other guys here who can cover second; put me in center." Later he moved back to second. It's an amazing thing, absolutely amazing. Who else could cover you at three of the four up-the-middle defensive positions? Nobody.

But in the last years of his career, my affection for Biggio started to fade, I'm afraid. As he moved closer to 3,000 career hits there came a general recognition of his status as a star player, which severed the bond that I felt to him when he was deserving of recognition that he wasn't getting. Yes, he moved to center field and yes, he moved back to second base when they needed him back at second base, but in all candor, he was pretty awful in center field, and he was pretty awful defensively back at second base. I got tired of pretending not to notice.

At some point, Biggio was hanging around to get 3,000 hits. On the one hand I was happy for him that he was going to get his 3,000 hits and pleased that he had proven to everybody that he was a great player, but it's not something I really admire, hanging around to pursue personal goals. He couldn't hit a good pitcher—never could, really. His career batting average in post-season play was .234, OPS somewhere around .600. His clutch hitting record is miserable.

We have this profile in the online…Batting Performance by Quality of Opposing Pitcher. Of course, over time, almost everybody is going to hit better against weaker pitchers. I doubt that anybody was as consistent or extreme about it as Biggio was. In 2003 he hit .354 against pitchers with ERAs over 5.25 (64 for 181), but .143 against pitchers with ERAs under 3.50 (19 for 133). In 2004 he hit .382 with 10 homers in 110 at bats against pitchers with ERAs over 5.25. Every year he has had huge good pitcher/bad pitcher splits.

I'm not picking on him, I hope, but the reason that Biggio struggled in clutch situations and against good pitchers couldn't be more obvious. He was an overachiever, and he knew what he was doing. Against a weak pitcher, a pitcher not really in command of his material, Biggio could take control of the at bat and drive it toward a good conclusion. When the pitcher was not really focused, Biggio was. But when the pressure was on and there was somebody on the mound who knew what he was doing, Biggio had limited ability to step up. Maybe this was not as true in the 1990s. I hope. We'll figure the data and put it online.

I'll still say today, if there was a draft and you could look ahead and say "OK, that guy's going to be Ken Griffey, that guy's going to be Frank Thomas, that guy's going to be Juan Gonzalez, that guy's going to be Tom Glavine, that guy's going to be Craig Biggio", just give me Biggio and I'll take my chances. Maybe that's not what the numbers say is the right answer, but Biggio was the guy who would do whatever needed to be done. Makes it a lot easier to build a team.

And then the story went on a little too long. You ever go to a movie, it's pretty good for about an hour and a half but then the story is over but it's like the director can't find the ending so it goes on for another half-hour looking for some way to tie things together? That's kind of Biggio's career; it was over, and then it went on for quite awhile.

Craig Biggio
Clutch Hitting

Season	AB	H	2B	3B	HR	RBI	BB	SO	GIDP	Avg	OBP	Slg
2002	49	13	3	0	0	15	3	9	2	.265	.321	.327
2003	75	19	5	0	2	15	8	11	1	.253	.341	.400
2004	34	6	0	0	0	6	4	7	0	.176	.275	.176
2005	57	12	2	0	2	11	5	9	0	.211	.324	.351
2006	58	12	1	0	2	12	3	10	3	.207	.242	.328
2007	34	8	2	0	2	12	2	10	0	.235	.289	.471
Totals	307	70	13	0	8	71	25	56	6	.228	.303	.349

Craig Biggio – 2003
Batting Performance by Quality of Opposing Pitcher

	AB	H	HR	RBI	Avg	OPS
Pitcher with ERA <= 3.50	133	19	3	7	.143	.503
Pitcher with ERA 3.51 to 4.25	165	38	3	14	.230	.691
Pitcher with ERA 4.26 to 5.25	149	45	3	21	.302	.800
Pitcher with ERA over 5.25	181	64	6	20	.354	.985

Craig Biggio – 2004
Batting Performance by Quality of Opposing Pitcher

	AB	H	HR	RBI	Avg	OPS
Pitcher with ERA <= 3.50	156	37	5	12	.237	.698
Pitcher with ERA 3.51 to 4.2	195	47	8	18	.241	.741
Pitcher with ERA 4.26 to 5.25	172	52	1	12	.302	.748
Pitcher with ERA over 5.25	110	42	10	21	.382	1.168

Canned Corn Manufacturer

Over the past two years, Orlando Palmeiro has hit 57 fly balls. All but three have been caught.

Orlando Palmeiro – 2006
Hitting Analysis

Batting Left-Handed								1B	2B	3B	HR
Ground Balls to Left	10	Outs	6	Hits	4	Average	.400	Hit Type	3 - 1 - 0 - 0
Ground Balls to Center	13	Outs	10	Hits	3	Average	.231	Hit Type	3 - 0 - 0 - 0
Ground Balls to Right	18	Outs	15	Hits	3	Average	.167	Hit Type	2 - 1 - 0 - 0
Line Drives to Left	9	Outs	3	Hits	6	Average	.667	Hit Type	3 - 3 - 0 - 0
Line Drives to Center	12	Outs	4	Hits	8	Average	.667	Hit Type	7 - 1 - 0 - 0
Line Drives to Right	7	Outs	4	Hits	3	Average	.429	Hit Type	2 - 0 - 1 - 0
Fly Balls to Left	15	Outs	14	Hits	1	Average	.067	Hit Type	1 - 0 - 0 - 0
Fly Balls to Center	10	Outs	10	Hits	0	Average	.000	Hit Type	0 - 0 - 0 - 0
Fly Balls to Right	5	Outs	5	Hits	0	Average	.000	Hit Type	0 - 0 - 0 - 0
Total on Ground Balls	41	Outs	31	Hits	10	Average	.244	Hit Type	8 - 2 - 0 - 0
Total on Line Drives	28	Outs	11	Hits	17	Average	.607	Hit Type	12 - 4 - 1 - 0
Total on Fly Balls	30	Outs	29	Hits	1	Average	.033	Hit Type	1 - 0 - 0 - 0
Total Hit to Left	34	Outs	23	Hits	11	Average	.324	Hit Type	7 - 4 - 0 - 0
Total Hit to Center	35	Outs	24	Hits	11	Average	.314	Hit Type	10 - 1 - 0 - 0
Total Hit to Right	30	Outs	24	Hits	6	Average	.200	Hit Type	4 - 1 - 1 - 0
Bunts	5	Outs	3	Hits	2	Average	.667	Hit Type	2 - 0 - 0 - 0
All Balls in Play	104	Outs	74	Hits	30	Average	.294	Hit Type	23 - 6 - 1 - 0

Orlando Palmeiro – 2007
Hitting Analysis

Batting Left-Handed								1B	2B	3B	HR
Ground Balls to Left	12	Outs	9	Hits	3	Average	.250	Hit Type	3 - 0 - 0 - 0
Ground Balls to Center	16	Outs	13	Hits	3	Average	.188	Hit Type	3 - 0 - 0 - 0
Ground Balls to Right	19	Outs	15	Hits	4	Average	.211	Hit Type	3 - 1 - 0 - 0
Line Drives to Left	5	Outs	4	Hits	1	Average	.200	Hit Type	1 - 0 - 0 - 0
Line Drives to Center	7	Outs	2	Hits	5	Average	.714	Hit Type	5 - 0 - 0 - 0
Line Drives to Right	6	Outs	1	Hits	5	Average	.833	Hit Type	5 - 0 - 0 - 0
Fly Balls to Left	13	Outs	13	Hits	0	Average	.000	Hit Type	0 - 0 - 0 - 0
Fly Balls to Center	6	Outs	6	Hits	0	Average	.000	Hit Type	0 - 0 - 0 - 0
Fly Balls to Right	7	Outs	5	Hits	2	Average	.286	Hit Type	0 - 2 - 0 - 0
Total on Ground Balls	47	Outs	37	Hits	10	Average	.213	Hit Type	9 - 1 - 0 - 0
Total on Line Drives	18	Outs	7	Hits	11	Average	.611	Hit Type	11 - 0 - 0 - 0
Total on Fly Balls	26	Outs	24	Hits	2	Average	.077	Hit Type	0 - 2 - 0 - 0
Total Hit to Left	30	Outs	26	Hits	4	Average	.133	Hit Type	4 - 0 - 0 - 0
Total Hit to Center	29	Outs	21	Hits	8	Average	.276	Hit Type	8 - 0 - 0 - 0
Total Hit to Right	32	Outs	21	Hits	11	Average	.344	Hit Type	8 - 3 - 0 - 0
Bunts	6	Outs	5	Hits	1	Average	.250	Hit Type	1 - 0 - 0 - 0
All Balls in Play	97	Outs	73	Hits	24	Average	.253	Hit Type	21 - 3 - 0 - 0

Houston Astros – 2007
Games Played by Opening Day Starter at Each Position

Pos	Player	Starts
C	Ausmus	102
1B	Berkman	150
2B	Biggio	116
3B	Ensberg	52
SS	Everett	62
LF	Lee	160
CF	Burke	71
RF	Scott	92
	Total	805

Houston's opening-day starters accounted for 62% of their regular season starting lineup.

Only three of Houston's Opening Day starters last year were in the lineup for more than 102 games.

In his eleven no-decisions in 2007, Roy Oswalt had seven quality starts and a 2.63 ERA.

Roy Oswalt – 2007
Decision Analysis

Group	G	IP	W	L	Pct	H	R	SO	BB	ERA
Wins	14	94.0	14	0	1.000	85	24	77	25	2.20
Losses	7	45.2	0	7	.000	59	33	25	17	6.11
Holds	1	0.1	0	0	—	0	0	0	0	0.00
No Decisions	11	72.0	0	0	—	77	23	52	18	2.63

Quality Starts: 12 in Wins, 2 in Losses, 7 in no-decisions

The worst seat in baseball in 2007 was to be an Astros fan in the second inning. After the first inning, the Astros were ahead in 48 games, behind in only 38, ten games over 500.

After the second inning, they were ahead in 49 but behind in 63—a 24-game slide in the standings in one inning.

Houston Astros – 2007
Innings Ahead/Behind/Tied

Inning	1	2	3	4	5	6	7	8	9	Extra	Final
Ahead	48	49	57	63	66	65	62	64	64	9	73
Behind	38	63	63	76	84	81	78	77	78	10	89
Tied	76	50	42	23	12	16	22	20	19	35	—

In 2007, Wandy Rodriguez 1) junked his slider, and 2) threw his fastball more often. He also 1) boosted his strikeout rate by 20%, and 2) improved his ERA by more than a full run.

Wandy Rodriguez – 2006
Pitch Type Analysis

Overall		
Total Pitches	2275	
Fastball	1378	61%
Curveball	469	21%
Changeup	204	9%
Slider	105	5%
Cut Fastball	38	2%
Pitchout	1	0%
Not Charted	80	4%

	Vs. RHB		Vs. LHB	
Total Pitches	1731		544	
Outs Recorded	312		95	
Fastball	1025	59%	353	65%
Curveball	343	20%	126	23%
Changeup	183	11%	21	4%
Slider	70	4%	35	6%
Cut Fastball	37	2%	1	0%
Pitchout	1	0%	0	0%
Not Charted	72	4%	8	1%

Wandy Rodriguez – 2007
Pitch Type Analysis

Overall		
Total Pitches	3036	
Fastball	2004	66%
Curveball	730	24%
Changeup	248	8%
Pitchout	4	0%
Not Charted	50	2%

	Vs. RHB		Vs. LHB	
Total Pitches	2542		494	
Outs Recorded	452		95	
Fastball	1638	64%	366	74%
Curveball	628	25%	102	21%
Changeup	232	9%	16	3%
Pitchout	4	0%	0	0%
Not Charted	40	2%	10	2%

Wandy Rodriguez won only nine games in 2007, but he allowed one run or less in all nine of those wins. His ERA in the games he won was 0.89.

Wandy Rodriguez – 2007
Decision Analysis

Group	G	IP	W	L	Pct	H	R	SO	BB	ERA
Wins	9	60.2	9	0	1.000	42	6	48	13	0.89
Losses	13	67.0	0	13	.000	87	71	59	29	8.46
No Decisions	9	55.0	0	0	—	50	25	51	20	3.93
Quality Starts: 7 in Wins, 2 in Losses, 6 in no-decisions										

Brad Lidge's opponent batting lines from 2006 and 2007:

Year	Avg	OBP	Slg
2006	.238	.332	.403
2007	.219	.312	.409

Isn't it hard to believe, from just looking at those two lines, that his ERAs in those two seasons were nearly two full runs apart? In 2006 his ERA was 5.28, and in 2007 it was 3.36. So...which one was "right"? Answer: neither. Opponent batting lines like the ones above usually produce ERAs in the low-fours. His actual ERA in 2006 was at least a full run higher than it should have been, and in '07 it missed the mark in the other direction by about three-quarters of a run.

Brad Lidge
Record of Opposing Batters

Season	AB	R	H	2B	3B	HR	RBI	BB	SO	SB	CS	GIDP	Avg	OBP	Slg	OPS
2002	36	6	12	4	0	0	5	9	12	2	0	1	.333	.467	.444	.911
2003	297	36	60	14	2	6	32	42	97	5	6	6	.202	.301	.323	.624
2004	328	21	57	6	4	8	23	30	157	2	5	5	.174	.243	.290	.533
2005	260	21	58	11	0	5	26	23	103	5	2	1	.223	.286	.323	.609
2006	290	47	69	12	3	10	42	36	104	7	0	2	.238	.322	.403	.726
2007	247	29	54	14	3	9	30	30	88	3	0	3	.219	.303	.409	.712

You Don't Have To Be in Colorado for Things to Be Rocky...

The Astros were 3-15 in Jason Jennings' starts. No team had a worse record for a starting pitcher who made a dozen starts.

Houston Astros – 2007
Performance by Starting Pitcher

Games Started By	G	RS	RA	Won	Lost
Oswalt, Roy	32	150	121	19	13
Rodriguez, Wandy	31	157	151	16	15
Williams, Woody	31	126	163	13	18
Sampson, Chris	19	92	103	9	10
Jennings, Jason	18	66	112	3	15
Albers, Matt	18	66	107	5	13
Backe, Brandon	5	32	17	4	1
Gutierrez, Juan	3	18	17	2	1
Paulino, Felipe	3	12	14	2	1
Patton, Troy	2	4	8	0	2
Team Totals	162	723	813	73	89

Absolute Rookies

In 1984 Buck Martinez played 100 games for the first and only time in his career. He had been in the majors since 1969, and had played 824 games before the start of his first 100-game season. This is an all-time record; no other player ever had his first 100-game season that late in his career.

On the other hand you have the "absolute rookies", the players who play 100 games in a season after having had *no* prior major league experience, not even one game.

Hunter Pence of Houston, one of the best rookies of 2007, was an absolute rookie, as were Alex Gordon, Mark Reynolds and Ryan Braun.

There aren't that many absolute rookies anymore. It used to be common that a player would finish out his minor league apprenticeship in one season, earn a job in spring training, and be the team's regular right fielder or regular second baseman or whatever that year. It doesn't happen much anymore.

At least, that's what I thought before I studied the issue. One of the best things about doing research is that sometimes you discover that what you thought you knew just wasn't right. I looked at all major league players playing 100 games for the first time in a season, going all the way back to 1876 (although nobody played 100 games in a season until 1884.)

From 1880 to 1959 the percentage of first-year 100-game players who were absolute rookies was fairly constant at 25%. It went up and down because of various things, but overall, it was 25.4% from 1880-1899 and 24.7% from 1950-1959, and fairly steady in between.

In 1960 it dropped suddenly to about 14%. It was 14% in the 1960s, 14% in the 1970s and 14% in the 1980s, dropped to 10% in the 1990s—and has been a little over 15% since 2000. In other words, the number of absolute rookies actually is going up recently, not down.

There was something that always appealed to me about the old practice of jumping a player straight into a major league job at the start of a season, something about the clean transition from minor leaguer to major leaguer, but it isn't necessarily the best idea. A new major league player goes through several phases—a rubber-necking phase (oh, my God, that was *Carlos Delgado*), a confusion and consternation phase (but everybody told me you don't have to do that anymore when you get the major leagues), an intimidation phase (if *everybody* up here has a slider like that, I'm toast), an annoyance phase (how many TV stations are there in Cleveland, anyway?), an I'm-a-big-leaguer phase (I was talking to Carlos Delgado about that just the other day), etc. From the team's standpoint, you'd prefer to get the new player through as many of these phases as possible before you start actually depending on him to help you win baseball games. Give him a taste of the big leagues, let him hang around in September, call him up to be a fourth outfielder for a week when you've got an injury, keep him around another September; when you finally need him to play he is through most of the phases and ready to focus on the game.

That keeps the number of first-time regulars who are absolute rookies low, but two things are driving it back up. One is the players coming over from Japan, many of whom are first-time major leaguers at a more advanced age, like Akinori Iwamura in 2007 or Kenji Johjima in 2006. There are just a few of those guys, and that's really not what is driving the number a little higher. The bigger factor is the six-year free agent clock. If you have a player with a big future, like Ryan Braun or Alex Gordon, you probably don't want to start the clock moving for him—or even to start him moving toward arbitration—until you're fairly convinced that he is ready to go from a skills standpoint.

The Turk Farrell Award

by Bill James

Part I

In 1962 a pitcher named Turk Farrell lost 20 games for the Houston Astros. He wasn't a bad pitcher; he was a good pitcher pitching for a bad team. An effective reliever in '57, '58 and '60, Farrell had a bad year in '61, and found himself in the starting rotation of a first-year expansion team in '62. Pitching 242 innings, Farrell struck out 203 batters (fourth in the league), walked only 55 (he was sixth in the league in fewest walks/9 innings), and posted a 3.02 ERA (seventh best in the league). He finished 10 and 20.

In the spring of '63 the *Saturday Evening Post* printed an article entitled, as I recall, "It Takes a Hell of a Pitcher to Lose 20 Games." (Even in 1963, media entities liked to push the boundaries of taste. But in 1963, using the word "Hell" in the title of an article was considered pushing the boundaries. Seriously.)

In my mind, Turk Farrell, 1962, has always represented the epitome of a really good pitcher stuck with a really bad record because his team couldn't plant their spikes on home plate.

Anyway, that season and that article made quite an impression on me. I was young at the time. (God was young at the time.) In my mind, Turk Farrell, 1962, has always represented the epitome of a really good pitcher stuck with a really bad record because his team couldn't plant their spikes on home plate. It always seemed to me that there should be some sort of recognition for these pitchers, and so, with the Bill James Online, we have decided to start one: The Turk Farrell Award.

The Turk Farrell Award will be "given" each year (don't expect hardware) to the pitcher who best represents the idea that a really good pitcher doesn't have to have a really good record, necessarily. To be eligible for the Turk Farrell Award, the pitcher must
a) make fifteen or more starts, and
b) have a losing record.

That will give us a fairly long list of eligible turkeys. I started out thinking that I would just name the BEST eligible pitcher of each year as the Turk Farrell winner, choosing the best by the Season Score method (explained briefly in the "Medley" article of this book, explained in more detail in Bill James Online). But the Season Score method gives the pitcher credit for wins, subtracts points for losses. For our present purposes, that's backward. Suppose that two pitchers each pitch the same number of innings, have the same strikeouts, the same walks, the same ERA, the same saves. If one of those guys goes 14-15 and the other one goes 10-22, the Season Score method would give the award to the guy who goes 14-15. That's not right; we're trying to find the guy who has a really BAD record despite pitching well.

I modified the scoring system so that the pitcher's "Turk Farrell Score" is his season's score, plus 15 times (Losses minus Wins). In 1910 Ed Walsh pitched 369.2 innings with a 1.27 ERA, striking out 258 batters and walking only 61. Despite this Gibsonesque ERA, Walsh wound up the year with a losing record, 18-20, and the highest Turk Farrell Score of the 20th century, 389.

Since then, the highest Turk Farrell Score was by: Turk Farrell, 1962. Turk Farrell had a Turk Farrell Score of 296.

Part II

What I am really writing about here is not Turk Farrell, but unlucky pitchers. I am using the mythical Turk Farrell Award and the arbitrary Turk Farrell formula to organize a discussion about the unluckiest pitchers who ever lived. In a minute, I'll give you the Turk Farrell Award winners for each season since 1956, but actually, what is most interesting are the *really* unlucky pitchers, the historically significant turkeys:

1870s

George Bradley, 1879. Bradley pitched 487.0 innings with a 2.85 ERA, walking only 26 hitters, or less than one per two games. He finished with a better batting average (.247) than Winning Percentage (.245); he was 13-40. Turk Farrell Score: 514.

1880s

Will White, 1880. White pitched 517.1 innings with a better-than-league 2.14 ERA, but finished with 18 wins, 42 losses. His Turk Farrell Score: an all-time record 546.

1890s

The Baseball War of 1890, which featured a start-up league run by the players, brought the 19-year-old Amos Rusie to New York. Rusie led all three major leagues in strikeouts (341) and walks (289), posted a 2.56 ERA in 549 innings—but finished 29-34. His Turk Farrell Score, 285, was the highest of the decade.

1900s

The first decade of the 20th century still had sort-of 19th-century pitching records, and, entering the spitball/dead ball era, very low ERAs. Numerous pitchers had Turk Farrells scores higher than Farrell. The highest of them: Cy Young in 1905. Young pitched 321 innings with a 1.82 ERA and a 7-to-1 strikeout/walk ratio (210-30)—but finished 18-19. Turk Farrell Score: 323. Young also had the highest Turk Farrell Score of 1906, when he finished 13-21. Walter Johnson had the highest in 1909.

What I am really writing about here is not Turk Farrell, but unlucky pitchers.

1910s

Ed Walsh, as mentioned (389).

1920s

Batting totals shot up in the 1920s, and Scott Perry's 3.61 ERA in 1920 was better than the league average (3.79). But he went 11-25, Turk Farrell Score of 226. (Season Scores are not park- or era-adjusted, so the numbers rise and fall inversely to league ERAs.) Perry barely beat out Red Ruffing, 1928 (224, stats similar to Perry's)—which would have made four straight decades that the highest Turk Farrell Score was posted by a Hall of Famer.

1930s

Paul Derringer's 1933 season, when he finished 7-27 despite a better-than-league ERA, is one of the most famous

hard-luck seasons of all time. His Turk Farrell Score, 284, was by far the highest of the decade.

1940s

Ken Raffensberger, 1944 Phillies. He was 13-20 with a 3.06 ERA—but there were a lot of young men that summer who would have considered him damned lucky. Turk Farrell Score: 237.

Raffensberger would also have won the award in 1946, 1950 and 1951, and would have been well up the list in several other seasons. Seventy-two runs better than league over the course of his career (park-adjusted) but 35 games under .500 (119-154), Raffensberger is truly one of the toughest-luck pitchers of all time. With better luck, he could have won 20 games three or four times.

1950s

Warren Spahn had the same ERA in 1952 that he had in 1951—2.98. In 1951 he was his usual 22-14. In 1952 he dropped to 14-19—and posted the second-highest Turk Farrell Score of the decade at 243.

Beating him by one point, but keeping the award in Hall of Fame fingers, was Robin Roberts, 1957. Roberts, who had won 20 games from 1950 through 1955 and was the best pitcher in the majors in several of those seasons, lost 20 for the only time in his career in 1957, finishing 10-22 with a 4.07 ERA.

1960s

Turk Farrell, 1962, 296.

1970s

Jerry Koosman, 1977—8-20 despite 192 strikeouts and a 3.49 ERA. Koosman had won 20 games the year before and would win 20 again with the Twins two years later, but the '77 Mets did not have a hitter with more than 12 home runs. Turk Farrell Score, 245.

1980s

Nolan Ryan in 1987 led the National League in strikeouts (270) and ERA (2.76)—but finished 8-16, one away from also leading the league in losses. Turk Farrell Score: 266.

1990s

Pitching for the Cleveland Indians between 1959 and 1993 was rarely lucky. Greg Swindell, 1991: 238 innings, 3.49 ERA, 169-31 K/W ratio. Finished 9-16. The team lost 105 games. Turk Farrell Score: 237.

2000s

Ben Sheets in 2004 had a truly remarkable season, striking out 264, walking only 32, posting a 2.70 ERA against a league average of 4.31, and yet finishing just 12-14. They gave the Cy Young Award to the great Roger Clemens, but Sheets had more strikeouts, fewer walks and a better ERA. If we tweaked the formula a little bit, he could rank as the unluckiest pitcher of all time. As it is, we have him at 285—the highest Turk Farrell Score since Turk Farrell himself.

Part III

Suppose that, in 1956, when they started giving out Cy Young Awards, they had also started giving out Turk Farrell Awards. That would have been remarkable foresight because, at that time, Turk Farrell was in the minor leagues. If they had started giving out Turk Farrell Awards at that time, they would probably have called them Ned Garver Awards or Murry Dickson Awards.

This is ducking the question, which is: Who would have won them? Awards which exist only in theory (such as the Turk Farrell and Nolan Ryan Awards in this book) are, in general, not quite as prestigious as those awards that are actually presented. Also, awards which are given out at the time are generally preferred over those which are "given out" only as electronic hyperspace bubbles 50 years later, and awards which are supported by an actual consensus of opinion are preferred awards compared to those which are determined by addition and subtraction of statistical totals.

This award, then, is the worst of the worst of the worst, the serial child molester of the baseball awards universe. Without further ado, the winner of the 1956 Turk Farrell Award is: Ron Kline.

Kline was 14-18 with a 3.38 ERA. Hey, he lasted a lot longer than Don Newcombe did. Newcombe, who won the first Cy Young Award that year, pitched 268 innings with a 3.08 ERA. Kline pitched almost the same number of innings (264) with a not-dissimilar ERA (3.38), but whereas Newk finished 27-7, Kline was 14-18. Newcome was 37-42 in the rest of his career, 3.84 ERA. Kline was 94-106 for the rest of his career, 3.69 ERA, and also registered more than 100 saves. We win.

The full list of Turk Farrell Award winners is given below; we only give one per season. A few notes thereon:

1957: Through the first half of the 1950s, Robin Roberts was the best starting pitcher in baseball, and Warren Spahn was the second-best starting pitcher in the National League. In '57 Spahn became the first future Hall of Famer to win the Cy Young Award—and Roberts, going 10-22, became the first Hall of Famer to win the Turk Farrell Award.

The frequency with which future Hall of Famers win the Turk Farrell Award is not as high as the frequency with which they win the Cy Young Award, but it is not negligible, either. Future Hall of Famers have won six Turk Farrells so far, and that number will go up when Roger Clemens, Bert Blyleven and Jose DeLeon are elected to the Hall of Fame.

1959: In 1957 Robin Roberts won the Farrell Award, with Bob Friend second; in '59 it was Friend first and Roberts second. Friend was also fourth in the standings in '61 and won the award again in '64, while Roberts was also third in the standings in 1960.

1960: Jim Bunning, who won the Turk Farrell Award in 1960, was actually probably the best pitcher in the American League that year. This may be the only time over the last 50 years that a pitcher with a losing record was actually the best pitcher in the league, although one can make an argument for Ben Sheets in 2004.

1961: Pedro Ramos, who was a perennial contender for the Farrell Award from 1958 on, finally broke through with an 11-20 mark in 1961. He had finished second in 1960 (the standings going Jim Bunning, Ramos, Robin Roberts). Ramos was a colorful Cuban who liked to claim that he was the fastest runner in baseball—he was pretty fast—and talked openly about how much he would like to pitch for the Yankees some day, said he would win 20 games a year if he was a Yankee, which is not entirely true but not entirely nonsense, either. He was always challenging Mickey Mantle to a footrace, trying to show everybody how fast he was. His Cuban running mate, Camilo Pascual, was also a Turk Farrell Award contender for several years.

1962: In '62, when Farrell himself won the award, there were three National League pitchers on the two expansion teams who would have won the award in a more normal year—Farrell, Roger Craig, and Ken Johnson. Craig had a famous long losing streak in 1963, losing I think eighteen straight games to fall to 2 and 20 at one point—this after he had lost 24 games the year before. He wasn't a *good* pitcher, but he wasn't *that* bad; he got to 2 and 20 with an ERA under 4.00. Ken Johnson lost so many 1-0 games in Houston that they had a "runs for Johnson" night, at which any woman who came to the game with a run in her stocking was admitted for half price or something. Johnson pitched and lost the game, 1-0. At least as I remember.

1967: Gaylord Perry won the Award, with two other Hall of Famers, Don Drysdale and Catfish Hunter, finishing second and third. Drysdale was also the runner-up in '66.

This award, then, is the worst of the worst of the worst, the serial child molester of the baseball awards universe.

The frequency with which future Hall of Famers win the Turk Farrell Award is not as high as the frequency with which they win the Cy Young Award, but it is not negligible, either.

1969: I have commented in other places that there is a superficial similarity in the career records of Don Sutton and Steve Carlton. Sutton was second in the Turk Farrell standings in 1969 and again ten years later, 1979, and appeared on the lists as early as 1967 and as late as 1983. Carlton who finished third in 1970, won the award in '73 and won it again ten years later, in 1983. Mickey Lolich was also a serious Turk Farrell contender numerous times between 1970 and 1976.

1971: Dave Roberts had a famous tough-luck season in 1971, finishing 14-17 with a 2.10 ERA. It was a remarkable season, and he could be seen as ranking much higher on this list than we have him. Although he did win the Turk Farrell Award in 1971, he could very well be seen as hard-luck pitcher of the decade for the 1970s, and even as the equal of Turk Farrell. The formula isn't knocked out by him because his strikeout/walk ratio wasn't that good, but he was a ground ball pitcher, supported by a league-leading 37 ground ball double plays that year.

1976: Blyleven in '76 had nine starts in which he pitched 76 innings with a 2.12 ERA, but finished 0 and 9.

1977-78: Jerry Koosman became the first pitcher to win the award in back-to-back seasons, the two tough-luck seasons bookended by 20-win seasons. Koosman would win a third Turk Farrell Award in '81—the only three-time winner. Friend, Carlton, Jose DeLeon and Javier Vazquez have won it twice.

1986: Bob Welch won the Award, winning only 7 games despite a 3.28 ERA in 33 starts. But he more than got even in 1990.

1993: Doug Drabek with Barry Bonds on his team: 22-6, Cy Young. Doug Drabek without Barry Bonds: 9-18, Turk Farrell. Seven pitchers have won the Turk Farrell Award and also, in other seasons, the Cy Young Award—Gaylord Perry, Steve Carlton, Fernando Valenzuela, Frank Viola, Bob Welch, Doug Drabek and Roger Clemens. Robin Roberts, Jim Bunning, Bert Blyleven, Nolan Ryan, Jerry Koosman, Frank Tanana, Mike Mussina and Curt Schilling won the Turk Farrell Award—but never the Cy Young.

2002: Ben Sheets, who had the remarkable year in 2004, also was second in 2002.

2003: In the early days of the Turk Farrell Award, many of the award winners were 20-game losers. After 1980 the switch to five-man rotations and the hypersensitivity of managers who didn't want to "embarrass" their pitchers led to the disappearance of 20-game losers, until Mike Maroth managed to lose 21 in 2003.

This set up a Turk Farrell battle between Curt Schilling, who was a very good pitcher but lost only 9 games, and Mike Maroth, who lost 21 games but wasn't really a very good pitcher. Schilling, who was openly disappointed not to get the Cy Young Award in 2002, was no doubt pleased to receive the Farrell award in 2003—or would have been, if he'd heard about it.

2007: Turk Farrell Award winner Matt Cain had 22 Quality Starts, the same number as Arizona's Brandon Webb. Webb went 17-2 in his Quality Starts. Cain went 6-8.

First	Last	Year	G	IP	Won		Lost	SO	BB	ERA	Turk Farrell Score
Ron	Kline	1956	44	264.0	14	-	18	125	81	3.38	166
Robin	Roberts	1957	39	250.0	10	-	22	128	43	4.07	244
Jack	Harshman	1958	34	236.0	12	-	15	161	75	2.90	189
Bob	Friend	1959	35	235.0	8	-	19	104	52	4.02	193
Jim	Bunning	1960	36	252.0	11	-	14	201	64	2.79	217
Pedro	Ramos	1961	42	264.0	11	-	20	174	79	3.95	219
Turk	Farrell	1962	43	242.0	10	-	20	203	55	3.01	296
Roger	Craig	1963	46	236.0	5	-	22	108	58	3.78	247
Bob	Friend	1964	35	240.0	13	-	18	128	50	3.34	195

First	Last	Year	G	IP	Won		Lost	SO	BB	ERA	Turk Farrell Score
Jack	Fisher	1965	43	254.0	8	-	24	116	68	3.93	242
Dick	Ellsworth	1966	38	269.0	8	-	22	144	51	3.98	255
Gaylord	Perry	1967	39	293.0	15	-	17	230	84	2.61	245
Ray	Sadecki	1968	38	254.0	12	-	18	206	70	2.91	246
Denny	Lemaster	1969	38	245.0	13	-	17	173	72	3.16	201
Bob	Johnson	1970	40	214.0	8	-	13	206	82	3.07	203
Dave	Roberts	1971	37	269.2	14	-	17	135	61	2.10	216
Pat	Dobson	1972	38	268.0	16	-	18	161	69	2.65	208
Steve	Carlton	1973	40	293.1	13	-	20	223	113	3.90	207
Frank	Tanana	1974	39	268.2	14	-	19	180	77	3.12	219
Rick	Reuschel	1975	38	234.0	11	-	17	155	67	3.73	187
Bert	Blyleven	1976	36	297.2	13	-	16	219	81	2.87	230
Jerry	Koosman	1977	32	226.2	8	-	20	192	81	3.49	245
Jerry	Koosman	1978	38	235.1	3	-	15	160	84	3.75	196
Bob	Shirley	1979	49	205.0	8	-	16	117	59	3.38	176
Brian	Kingman	1980	32	211.1	8	-	20	116	82	3.83	183
Jerry	Koosman	1981	27	121.1	4	-	13	76	41	4.01	148
Bruce	Berenyi	1982	34	222.1	9	-	18	157	96	3.36	184
Steve	Carlton	1983	37	283.2	15	-	16	275	84	3.11	244
Fernando	Valenzuela	1984	34	261.0	12	-	17	240	106	3.03	221
Jose	DeLeon	1985	31	162.2	2	-	19	149	89	4.70	205
Bob	Welch	1986	33	235.2	7	-	13	183	55	3.28	207
Nolan	Ryan	1987	34	211.2	8	-	16	270	87	2.76	266
Mike	Moore	1988	37	228.2	9	-	15	182	63	3.78	197
Frank	Viola	1989	36	261.0	13	-	17	211	74	3.66	211
Jose	DeLeon	1990	32	182.2	7	-	19	164	86	4.43	190
Greg	Swindell	1991	33	238.0	9	-	16	169	31	3.48	237
Melido	Perez	1992	33	247.2	13	-	16	218	93	2.87	206
Doug	Drabek	1993	34	237.2	9	-	18	157	60	3.79	212
Andy	Benes	1994	25	172.1	6	-	14	189	51	3.86	207
Tom	Candiotti	1995	30	190.1	7	-	14	141	58	3.50	173
Roger	Clemens	1996	34	242.2	10	-	13	257	106	3.63	182
Kevin	Appier	1997	34	235.2	9	-	13	196	74	3.40	184
Jon	Lieber	1998	29	171.0	8	-	14	138	40	4.11	172
Steve	Trachsel	1999	34	205.1	8	-	18	149	64	5.57	162
Mike	Mussina	2000	34	237.2	11	-	15	210	46	3.79	221
Bobby	Jones	2001	33	195.0	8	-	19	113	38	5.12	185
Javier	Vazquez	2002	34	230.1	10	-	13	179	49	3.91	178
Curt	Schilling	2003	24	168.0	8	-	9	194	32	2.95	186
Ben	Sheets	2004	34	237.0	12	-	14	264	32	2.70	285
Javier	Vazquez	2005	33	215.2	11	-	15	192	46	4.42	191
Jake	Peavy	2006	32	202.1	11	-	14	215	62	4.09	187
Matt	Cain	2007	32	200.0	7	-	16	163	79	3.65	185

Kansas City Royals

Kansas City Royals – 2007
Team Overview

Description		Ranking
Won-Lost Record	69-93	
Place	5th of 5 in American League Central	
Runs Scored	706	27th in the majors
Runs Allowed	778	17th in the majors
Home Runs	102	30th in the majors
Home Runs Allowed	168	17th in the majors
Batting Average	.261	22nd in the majors
Batting Average Allowed	.277	25th in the majors
Walks Drawn	428	29th in the majors
Walks Given	520	15th in the majors
OPS For	.710	29th in the majors
OPS Against	.785	24th in the majors
Stolen Bases	78	20th in the majors
Stolen Bases Allowed	70	4th in the majors

Key Players

Pos	Player	G	AB	R	H	2B	3B	HR	RBI	SB	CS	BB	SO	Avg	OBP	Slg	OPS	WS
C	John Buck	113	347	41	77	18	0	18	48	0	1	36	92	.222	.308	.429	.738	7
1B	Ross Gload	102	320	37	92	22	3	7	51	2	2	16	39	.288	.318	.441	.759	7
2B	Mark Grudzielanek	116	453	70	137	32	3	6	51	1	2	23	60	.302	.346	.426	.772	12
3B	Alex Gordon	151	543	60	134	36	4	15	60	14	4	41	137	.247	.314	.411	.725	12
SS	Tony F Pena	152	509	58	136	25	7	2	47	5	6	10	78	.267	.284	.356	.640	11
LF	Emil Brown	113	366	44	94	13	1	6	62	12	2	24	71	.257	.300	.347	.647	8
CF	David DeJesus	157	605	101	157	29	9	7	58	10	4	64	83	.260	.351	.372	.722	15
RF	Mark Teahen	144	544	78	155	31	8	7	60	13	5	55	127	.285	.353	.410	.763	15
DH	Billy Butler	92	329	38	96	23	2	8	52	0	0	27	55	.292	.347	.447	.794	7

Key Pitchers

Pos	Player	G	GS	W	L	Sv	IP	H	R	ER	BB	SO	BR/9	ERA	WS
SP	Brian Bannister	27	27	12	9	0	165.0	156	76	71	44	77	11.24	3.87	11
SP	Gil Meche	34	34	9	13	0	216.0	218	98	88	62	156	11.79	3.67	13
SP	Odalis Perez	26	26	8	11	0	137.1	178	90	85	50	64	15.20	5.57	3
SP	Jorge de la Rosa	26	23	8	12	0	130.0	160	88	84	53	82	14.95	5.82	3
SP	Zack Greinke	52	14	7	7	1	122.0	122	52	50	36	106	11.88	3.69	9
CL	Joakim Soria	62	0	2	3	17	69.0	46	20	19	19	75	8.61	2.48	13
RP	Jimmy Gobble	74	0	4	1	1	53.2	56	23	18	23	50	13.58	3.02	5
RP	David Riske	65	0	1	4	4	69.2	61	19	19	27	52	11.50	2.45	8

One of the best leadoff men in the major leagues is languishing on the Kansas City Royals' bench.

I am not here to criticize the Royals' decision not to play Esteban German more, or to second-guess them. The Royals deserve credit and praise for rescuing German from a life in the minor leagues, not criticism for the incompleteness of their insight.

Still, suppose that you did a search for the top leadoff men in the major leagues. OK; I did the search for you. I ranked all major league players from 2007 based on

1) Career on-base percentage,
2) Speed, and
3) Power (ranked inversely on power).

Brief digression. Somebody will argue that it is inappropriate to select a leadoff man based on the *lack* of power, since a leadoff home run is not in itself a bad thing. This is a valid argument in certain contexts, not a valid argument in others. Suppose that you are the General Manager of some team and are looking for a leadoff man. The power is certainly relevant, because if a player has power that creates an inefficient utilization of resources issue. If you look for the best leadoff men and you don't screen out power, you get David Wright and Carlos Beltran and Chase Utley as leadoff guys. You can't really afford to pursue those options.

So anyway, this is the list of the leadoff men that I came up with—not a perfect list, and we'll discuss the problems at the end:

1. Reggie Willits, Angels
2. Ichiro
3. Norris Hopper, Reds
4. Luis Castillo, not sure who he's with anymore
5. Esteban German
6. Kenny Lofton
7. Bobby Abreu
8. Joe Mauer
9. Derek Jeter
10. Chone Figgins

Norris Hopper is problematic because, while he has a .332 career batting average at this moment, it is difficult to state with confidence that he is in fact a .332 hitter. If he *is* a legitimate .332 hitter, which is slightly less likely than the possibility that he is the Easter bunny, then he will certainly emerge as a star leadoff man. Reggie Willits has, to an extent, the same problem: we are not yet entirely confident that his .393 career on base percentage is the real deal.

Anyway, taking this list for what it is worth, it creates an argument that Esteban German should have been in the lineup for the last two years. I am not trying to make that argument. Two years ago the Royals got Esteban German for a Rule 5 draft pick, not really knowing what they had. At the same time they signed Mark Grudzielanek to a more substantial contract. Grudzielanek has hit about .300 over the last two years, and he is a better defensive second baseman than German. The Royals two years ago didn't really know what they had in Esteban German, and to an extent, they still don't. He's hit .326 one year, .264 the other. There is a big difference between a .326 hitter and a .264 hitter. We still don't really know which one he is.

But going forward from now, Esteban German needs to play. Yes, he's not a Gold Glove second baseman, but he's not a *bad* second baseman, either. He's pretty average. He is a better player than Grudzielanek. He's a bad third baseman and has yet to prove that he can play the outfield. If the only place he can play is second base, second base should be his. Look at the Royals' runs scored with Esteban German leading off. Over the last two seasons German has led off in 172 innings, and the Royals have scored 6.02 runs per nine innings when he has. They don't score that often with anybody else leading off. They haven't scored that often with David DeJesus leading off. German lost two or three years of his career when he should have been in the majors but wasn't. It is time to hand him the keys and let him see if he can drive the offense.

Esteban German – 2006
Impact by Position in Inning

Position	Innings	Runs	Runs/Inning	Runs/RBI
Leading Off	76	58	.76	18/1
Batting Second	100	48	.48	10/5
Batting Third	56	31	.55	5/5
Batting Fourth	53	41	.77	5/11
Batting 5th or later	46	101	2.20	3/12

Esteban German – 2007
Impact by Position in Inning

Position	Innings	Runs	Runs/Inning	Runs/RBI
Leading Off	96	57	.59	18/1
Batting Second	127	63	.50	12/7
Batting Third	67	38	.57	7/4
Batting Fourth	62	49	.79	7/12
Batting 5th or later	53	122	2.30	5/13

Question: What do Buddy Bell, Stan Hack, Gary Gaetti, Ron Santo, Doug DeCinces, Mike Schmidt, Jimmy Dykes, Pie Traynor, Vinny Castilla, George Brett, Sal Bando, Adrian Beltre, Aramis Ramirez, Tim Wallach, Ron Ventura, Ken Caminiti, Brooks Robinson, Eddie Yost, Matt Williams, Clete Boyer and George Kell all have in common?

Answer: None of them hit as well their first year as Alex Gordon did.

OK, this is only arguably true; all of those players had lower OPS than Gordon (in their first season with significant playing time), but if you use some other measure of offensive effectiveness and adjust it for the league runs scored level, some of them are probably ahead of Gordon. George Brett and Pie Traynor each hit .282 their first year, 35 points higher than Gordon, but their slugging percentages were significantly lower than Gordon's, and their on-base percentage not more than a few points higher. George Kell hit .268 with no homers and 22 walks in 139 games in 1944, but if you adjust that for war-time run scoring levels, he might be OK. Mike Schmidt hit .196 as a rookie, Adrian Beltre .215, Matt Williams .188. Brooks Robinson hit .238 with 3 homers, 32 RBI in 145 games. Ed Yost drove in 14 runs in 115 games. Ron Cey hit almost the same as Gordon—.245 with 15 homers—while DeCinces, Dykes, Bando and Buddy Bell all hit over .250, but barely and with little power.

In history there are very few rookie third basemen who have had outstanding years. Only a handful of third basemen have won the Rookie of the Year award, and almost all of those either had disappointing careers or moved quickly to another position (Bob Horner, Chris Sabo, Eric Hinske and John Castino in the former category, Dick Allen and Albert Pujols in the latter.)

By the way, did Chewbacca ever win the Wookie of the Year Award? Maybe he wins it every year. Anyway, my point was: the really good third basemen always seem to struggle their first year up. In the last edition of the Historical Abstract a few years ago I discussed the shortage of quality third basemen in this generation, as contrasted with the abundance of fine third basemen in the 1970s. These things are circular. In the 2005 amateur draft, three of the first five players taken were third basemen—Gordon, Ryan Zimmerman and Ryan Braun. They're all in the majors now, Braun and Gordon rookies last year, so...who do you want? Mark Reynolds, Kevin Kouzmanoff and Josh Fields fans... you can play, too. You're not going to win, but we'll let you in the game.

I'm not saying that in the long run Gordon is going to be better than Braun or Zimmerman. I'm not saying that, quite. Gordon hit .173 in April and .195 in May, but hit .285 from June 7 to the end of the season. Braun is a debatable third baseman, and Zimmerman isn't a legitimate middle-of-the-order hitter yet, although he may be later on. Third base is a difficult position, in that third basemen are expected to field almost like shortstops and to hit almost like corner outfielders. Historically, a lot of the third baseman who have stepped in ready to go from an offensive standpoint, like Dick Allen, Bill Madlock, Kevin Seitzer, Miguel Cabrera and Wade Boggs, have not really been ready as defensive players.

Robin Ventura hit .249 with 5 homers in 493 at bats his first year. Ken Caminiti hit .246 with 3 homers. I have named most of the best third basemen in baseball history here. Most of them hit about like Gordon their first year up.

I feel like I should have said something about the best young third baseman in baseball, who is obviously David Wright. Gordon is just one year younger than Wright and Cabrera, who are established stars. I doubt that he will ever catch up to Wright. The other guys, Braun, Zimmerman, Reynolds, Kouzmanoff, Fields, Cabrera, Garrett Atkins...they're all good. I wouldn't trade Gordon for any of them.

Brian Bannister last year gave up 30 doubles to left-handed hitters—the most of any major league pitcher—but only 7 homers. That's a lot better than, say, Woody Williams, who gave up only 20 doubles to lefties, but 22 homers.

Brian Bannister
Record of Opposing Batters

Season	AB	R	H	2B	3B	HR	RBI	BB	SO	SB	CS	GIDP	Avg	OBP	Slg	OPS
2006	142	18	34	6	2	4	18	22	19	7	1	1	.239	.342	.394	.736
2007	626	76	156	47	4	15	72	44	77	7	5	14	.249	.299	.409	.708

Gil Meche pitched nearly as well in his no-decisions (2.89 ERA) as he did in his victories (2.40). He had nine quality starts in his 12 no-decisions.

Gil Meche – 2007
Decision Analysis

Group	G	IP	W	L	Pct	H	R	SO	BB	ERA
Wins	9	60.0	9	0	1.000	53	20	48	10	2.40
Losses	13	81.1	0	13	.000	91	50	51	25	5.31
No Decisions	12	74.2	0	0	—	74	28	57	27	2.89
Quality Starts: 8 in Wins, 6 in Losses, 9 in no-decisions										

Kansas City Royals – 2007
Performance by Starting Pitcher

The Royals have gotten 10 or more starts from six pitchers in each of the last three seasons. Among those 18 pitcher seasons, only once did the Royals have a winning record. This past season, Kansas City managed 15 wins against 12 losses when Brian Bannister started the game. Bannister finished the season with a 12-9 record with the Royals playing .500 (3-3) in his no-decision starts.

Games Started By	G	RS	RA	Won	Lost
Meche, Gil	34	132	135	15	19
Bannister, Brian	27	126	115	15	12
Perez, Odalis	26	106	138	11	15
de la Rosa, Jorge	23	129	109	10	13
Greinke, Zack	14	47	64	5	9
Davies, Kyle	11	44	69	3	8
Elarton, Scott	9	54	56	4	5
Nunez, Leo	6	32	17	4	2
Buckner, Billy	5	18	31	1	4
Duckworth, Brandon	3	7	17	0	3
Thomson, John	2	6	6	1	1
Hochevar, Luke	1	2	4	0	1
Hudson, Luke	1	3	17	0	1
Team Totals	162	706	778	69	93

Joakim Soria and David Riske had nearly identical ERAs (2.48 for Soria, 2.45 for Riske), but their opponent batting lines reveal that Soria was vastly more effective. Batters hit .187 and slugged .264 against Soria, and hit .240 and slugged .394 against Riske. Soria's Component ERA was 1.63. Riske's was 3.46.

David Riske
Record of Opposing Batters

Season	AB	R	H	2B	3B	HR	RBI	BB	SO	SB	CS	GIDP	Avg	OBP	Slg	OPS
2002	191	32	49	9	1	8	39	35	65	6	2	5	.257	.372	.440	.812
2003	265	21	52	10	0	9	26	20	82	4	2	6	.196	.253	.336	.589
2004	288	32	69	17	0	11	41	41	78	2	0	7	.240	.334	.413	.748
2005	265	28	55	9	1	11	30	15	48	2	1	7	.208	.250	.374	.624
2006	166	20	40	10	0	6	28	17	28	3	1	3	.241	.312	.410	.721
2007	254	19	61	13	1	8	30	27	52	4	1	6	.240	.313	.394	.707

Joakim Soria
Record of Opposing Batters

Season	AB	R	H	2B	3B	HR	RBI	BB	SO	SB	CS	GIDP	Avg	OBP	Slg	OPS
2007	246	20	46	8	1	3	18	19	75	0	0	2	.187	.245	.264	.510

In 2003, the Kansas City Royals were ahead 46 times, behind 43 times after the first inning. They continued to lead throughout the game, having a winning record at the end of every inning except the second:

Kansas City Royals – 2003
Innings Ahead/Behind/Tied

Inning	1	2	3	4	5	6	7	8	9	Extra	Final
Ahead	46	54	72	77	77	84	83	81	78	5	83
Behind	43	57	66	69	72	63	66	71	75	4	79
Tied	73	51	24	16	13	15	13	10	9	7	—

Since 2003, the Royals have been behind more often than ahead at the conclusion of each inning every year.

Kansas City rookie Brian Bannister was very impressive last year, pitching like a veteran and winning 12 games for a team that doesn't sneer at 12-game winners. There is a lot to like about Bannister. His control was excellent. He mixes up four secondary pitches to keep the pressure off his fastball. He gets some ground balls. He is composed and focused on the mound. He is very tough to run on. The on-base percentage of batters facing him was under .300.

At the same time you have to say: Bannister won 12 games with 77 strikeouts. History shows that that kind of a ratio is almost always unsustainable.

There has been only one pitcher in the last twenty years who won 100 games with a strikeout/win ratio less than 6.50 to 1, that being Kirk Rueter. There aren't a lot of guys who have ratios under ten to one.

From 1997 through 2006 there were eighteen starting pitchers who won 11 to 13 games with 70 to 85 strikeouts and a winning record. Their aggregate won-lost record was 183-129. The following season, the aggregate won-lost record or those pitchers was 94-139, average ERA of 5.69.

Bannister's ratio of strikeouts to wins was the sixth-lowest in the majors. On the bottom ten list for 2006 you have two pitchers who were able to sustain their performance level in 2007 (Chien-Ming Wang and Carlos Silva) and eight who had disappointing seasons in 2007 (Gustavo Chacin, Adam Eaton, Jon Garland, Kenny Rogers, Jeremy Sowers, Steve Trachsel, and Dave and Woody Williams).

Ten Lowest Strikeout/Win Ratios – 2007

Name	Team	W	L	SO	Strikeouts Per Win
Kyle Kendrick	Philadelphia Phillies	10	4	49	4.90
Horacio Ramirez	Seattle Mariners	8	7	40	5.00
Chien-Ming Wang	New York Yankees	19	7	104	5.47
Paul Byrd	Cleveland Indians	15	8	88	5.87
Noah Lowry	San Francisco Giants	14	8	87	6.21
Brian Bannister	Kansas City Royals	12	9	77	6.42
Tim Wakefield	Boston Red Sox	17	12	110	6.47
Brad Thompson	St. Louis Cardinals	8	6	53	6.63
J.D. Durbin	Mostly Philadelphia	6	5	40	6.67
Tom Glavine	New York Mets	13	8	89	6.85

Los Angeles Angels

Los Angeles Angels – 2007
Team Overview

Description		Ranking
Won-Lost Record	94-68	
Place	1st of 4 in American League West	
Runs Scored	822	6th in the majors
Runs Allowed	731	9th in the majors
Home Runs	123	27th in the majors
Home Runs Allowed	151	8th in the majors
Batting Average	.284	4th in the majors
Batting Average Allowed	.266	11th in the majors
Walks Drawn	507	21st in the majors
Walks Given	477	4th in the majors
OPS For	.762	14th in the majors
OPS Against	.739	9th in the majors
Stolen Bases	139	3rd in the majors
Stolen Bases Allowed	107	23rd in the majors

Key Players

Pos	Player	G	AB	R	H	2B	3B	HR	RBI	SB	CS	BB	SO	Avg	OBP	Slg	OPS	WS
C	Mike Napoli	75	219	40	54	11	1	10	34	5	2	33	63	.247	.351	.443	.794	8
1B	Casey Kotchman	137	443	64	131	37	3	11	68	2	4	53	43	.296	.372	.467	.840	15
2B	Howie Kendrick	88	338	55	109	24	2	5	39	5	4	9	61	.322	.347	.450	.796	9
3B	Chone Figgins	115	442	81	146	24	6	3	58	41	12	51	81	.330	.393	.432	.825	21
SS	Orlando Cabrera	155	638	101	192	35	1	8	86	20	4	44	64	.301	.345	.397	.742	25
LF	Garret Anderson	108	417	67	124	31	1	16	80	1	0	27	54	.297	.336	.492	.827	13
CF	Gary Matthews Jr.	140	516	79	130	26	3	18	72	18	4	55	102	.252	.323	.419	.742	14
RF	Vladimir Guerrero	150	574	89	186	45	1	27	125	2	3	71	62	.324	.403	.547	.950	29
DH	Shea Hillenbrand	53	197	19	50	5	0	3	22	0	2	5	18	.254	.275	.325	.599	0

Key Pitchers

Pos	Player	G	GS	W	L	Sv	IP	H	R	ER	BB	SO	BR/9	ERA	WS
SP	John Lackey	33	33	19	9	0	224.0	219	87	75	52	179	11.37	3.01	21
SP	Kelvim Escobar	30	30	18	7	0	195.2	182	79	74	66	160	11.55	3.40	18
SP	Jered Weaver	28	28	13	7	0	161.0	178	77	70	45	115	12.58	3.91	12
SP	Joe Saunders	18	18	8	5	0	107.1	129	56	53	34	69	13.75	4.44	7
SP	Ervin Santana	28	26	7	14	0	150.0	174	103	96	58	126	14.40	5.76	3
CL	Francisco Rodriguez	64	0	5	2	40	67.1	50	22	21	34	90	11.36	2.81	15
RP	Darren Oliver	61	0	3	1	0	64.1	58	31	27	23	51	11.47	3.78	5
RP	Scot Shields	71	0	4	5	2	77.0	62	36	33	33	77	11.57	3.86	8

Baaaad Ball Hitter

In 2007 Albert Pujols took 556 pitches for a strike, and swung at 241 pitches outside the strike zone.

Vladimir Guerrero took 139 pitches for a strike, and swung at 616 pitches outside the strike zone.

Here's something you never read in a scouting report: *This kid reminds me of a young Vladimir Guerrero.* Vladimir is one of those players you just have to love because he is unique, like Sheffield and Ichiro and El Duque and David Wells and David Eckstein. Eckstein is unique, but nonetheless every infielder under 5'8" is supposed to be the next David Eckstein. Vladimir is *so* unique that nobody would dare.

You think he is starting to learn the strike zone, starting to reign in his free-swinging ways? Think again. In 2005 Vladimir swung at 303 pitches outside the strike zone. Last year he almost doubled that.

This is Vladimir's pitches Taken for a Strike (TS) and Swung at Outside the Zone (SOZ) since 2004:

Year	TS	SOZ
2004	112	281
2005	131	303
2006	121	428
2007	139	604

Would Guerrero be a better hitter if he tended to his strike zone? I doubt it. First, I don't see how you *can* be much scarier, as a hitter, than Vladimir is. Second, part of what makes him great is his absolute conviction that he can hit anything. He has dispensed with the normal balancing act that slows down normal hitters (Should I swing at that one or let it go by?) If he can get to it and it's not some off-speed pitch that will throw off his timing, he's going for it. It's not the way you teach a kid to play baseball, but it works for him.

Vladimir Guerrero – 2007
Pitch Analysis

Overall		
Pitches Seen	2037	
Taken	878	43%
Swung At	1159	57%

Pitches Taken		
Taken for a Strike	139	16%
Called a ball	739	84%

Pitches Taken by Pitch Location		
In Strike Zone	139	16%
High	92	10%
Low	290	33%
Inside	137	16%
Outside	220	25%

Swung At		
Missed	231	20%
Fouled Off	410	35%
Put in Play	518	45%

Swung At by Pitch Location		
In Strike Zone	543	47%
High	50	4%
Low	224	19%
Inside	233	20%
Outside	109	9%

Albert Pujols – 2007
Pitch Analysis

Overall		
Pitches Seen	2678	
Taken	1657	62%
Swung At	1021	38%

Pitches Taken		
Taken for a Strike	556	34%
Called a ball	1101	66%

Pitches Taken by Pitch Location		
In Strike Zone	556	34%
High	196	12%
Low	451	27%
Inside	141	9%
Outside	307	19%

Swung At		
Missed	114	11%
Fouled Of	392	38%
Put in Play	515	50%

Swung At by Pitch Location		
In Strike Zone	776	76%
High	51	5%
Low	77	8%
Inside	31	3%
Outside	82	8%

A Zone of His Own

About one-half of the pitches thrown in the major leagues are in the strike zone; a little more than half for some hitters, a little less than half for others. With the exception of one hitter, the "in the zone percentage" for every major league hitter seeing 500 or more pitches was between 41 and 59.

The exception, however, was not at 40.8%, or 40.4%, or 40%, or 39% or 38. Of the 2,037 pitches thrown to Vladimir Guerrero, only an astonishing 32% were in the strike zone. On the spectrum of strikes seen, the next-lowest hitter was as close to the middle as he was to Vladimir.

Until last year, right-hander Francisco Rodriguez 1) always had thrown almost all fastballs and sliders, and 2) always had been less effective against lefthanded hitters. But last year, he began throwing his changeup much more often to lefthanded hitters (20% of the time), and was more effective against lefties than righties for the first time in his career.

Francisco Rodriguez – 2006
Pitch Type Analysis

Overall		
Total Pitches	1218	
Fastball	670	55%
Curveball	37	3%
Changeup	24	2%
Slider	466	38%
Pitchout	4	0%
Not Charted	17	1%

	Vs. RHB		Vs. LHB	
Total Pitches	609		609	
Outs Recorded	115		104	
Fastball	348	57%	322	53%
Curveball	12	2%	25	4%
Changeup	0	0%	24	4%
Slider	241	40%	225	37%
Pitchout	4	1%	0	0%
Not Charted	4	1%	13	2%

Francisco Rodriguez – 2007
Pitch Type Analysis

Overall		
Total Pitches	1200	
Fastball	612	51%
Changeup	114	10%
Slider	468	39%
Pitchout	4	0%
Not Charted	2	0%

	Vs. RHB		Vs. LHB	
Total Pitches	639		561	
Outs Recorded	111		91	
Fastball	383	60%	229	41%
Changeup	1	0%	113	20%
Slider	252	39%	216	39%
Pitchout	1	0%	3	1%
Not Charted	2	0%	0	0%

We Don't Need No Stinkin' Homers

No club had a winning record when it was held homerless, but the Angels came the closest, with a record of 39-44. They also were held homerless more often than any team except the Twins and Royals.

Los Angeles Angels – 2007
Record by Home Runs

Home Runs	W – L
0 homers	39 - 44
1 homer	32 - 13
2 homers	18 - 9
3 or more homers	5 - 2

It Don't Matter to Me How You Throw

When he put the ball in play, Chone Figgins hit .404 in 2007. He batted .404 from the left side of the plate and .405 from the right side.

Chone Figgins – 2007
Hitting Analysis

Total					1B	2B	3B	HR
Ground Balls to Left	41	Outs 31	Hits 10	Average .244	Hit Type 10	- 0	- 0	- 0
Ground Balls to Center	51	Outs 33	Hits 18	Average .353	Hit Type 18	- 0	- 0	- 0
Ground Balls to Right	80	Outs 65	Hits 15	Average .188	Hit Type 15	- 0	- 0	- 0
Line Drives to Left	35	Outs 8	Hits 27	Average .771	Hit Type 21	- 6	- 0	- 0
Line Drives to Center	32	Outs 4	Hits 28	Average .875	Hit Type 26	- 2	- 0	- 0
Line Drives to Right	29	Outs 4	Hits 25	Average .862	Hit Type 14	- 8	- 3	- 0
Fly Balls to Left	45	Outs 37	Hits 8	Average .205	Hit Type 2	- 4	- 2	- 0
Fly Balls to Center	23	Outs 19	Hits 4	Average .182	Hit Type 3	- 0	- 1	- 0
Fly Balls to Right	27	Outs 18	Hits 9	Average .346	Hit Type 2	- 4	- 0	- 3
Total on Ground Balls	172	Outs 129	Hits 43	Average .250	Hit Type 43	- 0	- 0	- 0
Total on Line Drives	96	Outs 16	Hits 80	Average .833	Hit Type 61	- 16	- 3	- 0
Total on Fly Balls	95	Outs 74	Hits 21	Average .241	Hit Type 7	- 8	- 3	- 3
Total Hit to Left	121	Outs 76	Hits 45	Average .391	Hit Type 33	- 10	- 2	- 0
Total Hit to Center	106	Outs 56	Hits 50	Average .476	Hit Type 47	- 2	- 1	- 0
Total Hit to Right	136	Outs 87	Hits 49	Average .363	Hit Type 31	- 12	- 3	- 3
Bunts	8	Outs 6	Hits 2	Average .333	Hit Type 2	- 0	- 0	- 0
All Balls in Play	371	Outs 225	Hits 146	Average .404	Hit Type 113	- 24	- 6	- 3

Chone Figgins – 2007 Batting Right-Handed
Hitting Analysis

Batting Right-Handed								1B	2B	3B	HR
Ground Balls to Left	7	Outs	7	Hits	0	Average	.000	Hit Type	0 - 0 - 0 - 0
Ground Balls to Center	9	Outs	6	Hits	3	Average	.333	Hit Type	3 - 0 - 0 - 0
Ground Balls to Right	12	Outs	11	Hits	1	Average	.083	Hit Type	1 - 0 - 0 - 0
Line Drives to Left	1	Outs	0	Hits	1	Average	1.000	Hit Type	0 - 1 - 0 - 0
Line Drives to Center	11	Outs	2	Hits	9	Average	.818	Hit Type	8 - 1 - 0 - 0
Line Drives to Right	10	Outs	1	Hits	9	Average	.900	Hit Type	5 - 2 - 2 - 0
Fly Balls to Left	3	Outs	2	Hits	1	Average	.333	Hit Type	0 - 1 - 0 - 0
Fly Balls to Center	8	Outs	7	Hits	1	Average	.143	Hit Type	1 - 0 - 0 - 0
Fly Balls to Right	10	Outs	7	Hits	3	Average	.300	Hit Type	0 - 3 - 0 - 0
Total on Ground Balls	28	Outs	24	Hits	4	Average	.143	Hit Type	4 - 0 - 0 - 0
Total on Line Drives	22	Outs	3	Hits	19	Average	.864	Hit Type	13 - 4 - 2 - 0
Total on Fly Balls	21	Outs	16	Hits	5	Average	.250	Hit Type	1 - 4 - 0 - 0
Total Hit to Left	11	Outs	9	Hits	2	Average	.182	HitType	0 - 2 - 0 - 0
Total Hit to Center	28	Outs	15	Hits	13	Average	.481	Hit Type	12 - 1 - 0 - 0
Total Hit to Right	32	Outs	19	Hits	13	Average	.406	Hit Type	6 - 5 - 2 - 0
Bunts	6	Outs	4	Hits	2	Average	.500	Hit Type	2 - 0 - 0 - 0
All Balls in Play	77	Outs	47	Hits	30	Average	.405	Hit Type	20 - 8 - 2 - 0

Chone Figgins – 2007 Batting Left-Handed
Hitting Analysis

Batting Left-Handed								1B	2B	3B	HR
Ground Balls to Left	34	Outs	24	Hits	10	Average	.294	Hit Type	10 - 0 - 0 - 0
Ground Balls to Center	42	Outs	27	Hits	15	Average	.357	Hit Type	15 - 0 - 0 - 0
Ground Balls to Right	68	Outs	54	Hits	14	Average	.206	Hit Type	14 - 0 - 0 - 0
Line Drives to Left	34	Outs	8	Hits	26	Average	.765	Hit Type	21 - 5 - 0 - 0
Line Drives to Center	21	Outs	2	Hits	19	Average	.905	Hit Type	18 - 1 - 0 - 0
Line Drives to Right	19	Outs	3	Hits	16	Average	.842	Hit Type	9 - 6 - 1 - 0
Fly Balls to Left	42	Outs	35	Hits	7	Average	.194	Hit Type	2 - 3 - 2 - 0
Fly Balls to Center	15	Outs	12	Hits	3	Average	.200	Hit Type	2 - 0 - 1 - 0
Fly Balls to Right	17	Outs	11	Hits	6	Average	.375	Hit Type	2 - 1 - 0 - 3
Total on Ground Balls	144	Outs	105	Hits	39	Average	.271	Hit Type	39 - 0 - 0 - 0
Total on Line Drives	74	Outs	13	Hits	61	Average	.824	Hit Type	48 - 12 - 1 - 0
Total on Fly Balls	74	Outs	58	Hits	16	Average	.239	Hit Type	6 - 4 - 3 - 3
Total Hit to Left	110	Outs	67	Hits	43	Average	.413	Hit Type	33 - 8 - 2 - 0
Total Hit to Center	78	Outs	41	Hits	37	Average	.474	Hit Type	35 - 1 - 1 - 0
Total Hit to Right	104	Outs	68	Hits	36	Average	.350	Hit Type	25 - 7 - 1 - 3
Bunts	2	Outs	2	Hits	0	Average	.000	Hit Type	0 - 0 - 0 - 0
All Balls in Play	294	Outs	178	Hits	116	Average	.404	Hit Type	93 - 16 - 4 - 3

The Angels leftfielders are mirror images of each other in their skills assessment:

Garret Anderson
Hitting for Power: 60th percentile
Running: 52nd percentile
Plate Discipline: 5th percentile

Reggie Willits
Hitting for Power: 2nd percentile
Running: 78th percentile
Plate Discipline: 92nd percentile

Except in hitting for average:

Hitting for Average: 71st percentile   Hitting for Average: 65th percentile

Garret Anderson – 2007
Skills Assessment

Hitting for Average:	71st percentile	72nd percentile among left fielders
Hitting for Power:	60th percentile	46th percentile among left fielders
Running:	52nd percentile	45th percentile among left fielders
Plate Discipline:	5th percentile	9th percentile among left fielders

Reggie Willits – 2007
Skills Assessment

Plate Discipline:	92nd percentile	93rd percentile among left fielders
Running:	78th percentile	85th percentile among left fielders
Hitting for Average:	65th percentile	70th percentile among left fielders
Hitting for Power:	2nd percentile	7th percentile among left fielders

Playing to the Level of the Competition
Bartolo Colon's ERA gets better against the better teams.

Bartolo Colon
Career Records Against Quality of Opposition

Opponent	G	IP	W	L	SO	BB	ERA
.600 teams	13	86.0	7	3	69	30	3.56
.500 - .599 teams	62	420.0	32	24	257	106	3.90
.400 - .499 teams	68	434.0	32	22	319	128	4.23
sub .400 teams	20	122.0	10	5	99	27	4.72

Kelvim Escobar has one of the deepest repertoires of any major league pitcher. Against righthanded hitters, he regularly makes use of six different pitches. With a lefty at the plate, he generally whittles his choices down to four.

Kelvim Escobar – 2007
Pitch Type Analysis

Overall		
Total Pitches	3041	
Fastball	1558	51%
Curveball	272	9%
Changeup	376	12%
Slider	342	11%
Split Finger	343	11%
Cut Fastball	125	4%
Pitchout	5	0%
Not Charted	20	1%

	Vs. RHB		Vs. LHB	
Total Pitches	1549		1492	
Outs Recorded	302		285	
Fastball	776	50%	782	52%
Curveball	91	6%	181	12%
Changeup	156	10%	220	15%
Slider	291	19%	51	3%
Split Finger	114	7%	229	15%
Cut Fastball	110	7%	15	1%
Pitchout	1	0%	4	0%
Not Charted	10	1%	10	1%

The Nolan Ryan Award

by Bill James

I know there are probably none of you in the audience who don't remember Nolan Ryan, but as an organizing device, I'm going to pretend there are anyway. Nolan Ryan was the ultimate power pitcher. Ryan threw harder than any other pitcher of his generation or perhaps any generation, and it wasn't like he did this once. Ryan could stand on the mound and throw a hundred miles an hour for 9 innings, 10 innings, 11, 12, 13. He would throw more than 200 pitches in a game, come back three days later ready to do it again. He did this for years in a four-man rotation, switched to a five-man rotation and pitched another fifteen years. He threw no-hitters almost as a matter of routine. He holds the single-season record for strikeouts, and broke the career record for strikeouts by some ridiculous margin.

Nolan Ryan was Roger Clemens' boyhood idol, but whereas Clemens became a genuinely great pitcher, Ryan was not. Ryan was the most *impressive* pitcher who ever lived. He did absolutely phenomenal things with such regularity that people took it for granted. But he was not a great pitcher because he never compromised, which means that he never adjusted. He was, in a sense, a perpetual rookie. He was out there to strike the hitter out—period, even when he was 44 years old. He could be behind the number-eight hitter 2-0 with the bases empty, and in his mind he was still working on a strikeout. The concept of "let him hit it and see what happens" absolutely wasn't there for him.

He won a huge number of games, true (324), but he lost almost as many. He holds the career record for strikeouts by a wide margin—and the record for walks by an even wider margin. He holds the career record for wild pitches. He did nothing at all to stop the running game, allowing 757 stolen bases in his career, which is almost certainly a record...anyway he led the league in stolen bases allowed eight times. He committed 90 errors in his career, with a career fielding percentage of .895. His positive numbers will stagger you, but his negative numbers will knock you out.

To win an award properly commemorating Nolan Ryan, then, requires not merely that you win games but also that you lose them, and lose them with style. It requires that you be an iron man, and also that you be a wild man, or at least a wild pitcher. There is a formula for this...of course, as I have written, awards based directly on statistics are silly and superfluous, but we're not handing out any actual hardware here, we're just having a little fun with it. The formula is this:

Wins
Times Losses
Times Strikeouts
Times Walks
Divided by Innings Pitched

And the 2007 Nolan Ryan Award winner is: Carlos Zambrano. Zambrano actually almost won it in 2006, as well, and to put Nolan Ryan in a little bit of perspective, Zambrano over those two years, being the major leagues' most unreformed power pitcher, has had a total of 387 strikeouts, 216 walks, which interestingly enough isn't that far from what Nolan Ryan would do in one season. If you could put Nolan Ryan in perspective he wouldn't be so fascinating; what is so compelling about him is that you can't put him in perspective. He is so far outside the norms of history that there's really no way to put a frame of reference around him. If Carlos Zambrano pitched another hundred innings and increased his strikeouts and walks per inning by about 30%, he'd be close to Ryan.

> *To win an award properly commemorating Nolan Ryan, then, requires not merely that you win games but also that you lose them, and lose them with style. It requires that you be an iron man, and also that you be a wild man, or at least a wild pitcher.*

Anyway, this being based on a formula, we can figure Amos Rusie, Bobo Newsom, Bob Feller, Sam McDowell and the young Randy Johnson; Randy was Ryanesque in his early years, but then decided to stop walking so many people and losing so many games. This is the year-by-year list:

	1880—Jim McCormick	1890—Amos Rusie
	1881—George Derby	1891—Amos Rusie
	1882—Jim McCormick	1892—Amos Rusie
	1883—Tim Keefe	1893—Amos Rusie
	1884—Dupee Shaw	1894—Amos Rusie
	1885—Hardie Henderson	1895—Amos Rusie
1876—Jim Devlin	1886—Toad Ramsey	1896—Pink Hawley
1877—Jim Devlin	1887—Toad Ramsey	1897—Doc McJames
1878—Will White	1888—Ed Seward	1898—Cy Seymour
1879—Will White	1889—Mark Baldwin	1899—Cy Seymour

Cy Seymour switched to the outfield after an arm injury, and was perhaps the best player in baseball in 1905. Moving on.

1900—Noodles Hahn	1910—Walter Johnson	1920—Ferdie Schupp
1901—Wild Bill Donovan	1911—Pete Alexander	1921—Red Faber
1902—Vic Willis	1912—Ed Walsh	1922—Red Faber
1903—Christy Mathewson	1913—Tom Seaton	1923—Dazzy Vance
1904—Rube Waddell	1914—Earl Moseley	1924—Burleigh Grimes
1905—Orval Overall	1915—Al Schulz	1925—Sam Jones
1906—Cy Falkenberg	1916—Elmer Myers	1926—George Uhle
1907—Ed Walsh	1917—Pete Schneider	1927—Charlie Root
1908—Nap Rucker	1918—Walter Johnson	1928—George Pipgras
1909—Nap Rucker	1919—Jim Shaw	1929—George Earnshaw

Several Hall of Famers in this group. Christy Mathewson doesn't sound right, but in 1903 Matty was 22 years old and walked 100 men, although even so he won 30 games. Several of these guys stayed around long enough to become more mature pitchers. Most do not; most Nolan Ryan Award winners burn themselves out before they stop walking people.

1930—George Earnshaw	1940—Bob Feller	1950—Warren Spahn
1931—Wes Ferrell	1941—Bob Feller	1951—Warren Spahn
1932—Bump Hadley	1942—Johnny Vander Meer	1952—Early Wynn
1933—Bump Hadley	1943—Johnny Vander Meer	1953—Billy Pierce
1934—Bobo Newsom	1944—Bill Voiselle	1954—Bob Turley
1935—Dizzy Dean	1945—Hal Newhouser	1955—Sam Jones
1936—Van Lingle Mungo	1946—Bob Feller	1956—Herb Score
1937—Bobo Newsom	1947—Hal Newhouser	1957—Early Wynn
1938—Bobo Newsom	1948—Bob Feller	1958—Sam Jones
1939—Bob Feller	1949—Bob Lemon	1959—Sam Jones

If you could put Nolan Ryan in perspective he wouldn't be so fascinating; what is so compelling about him is that you can't put him in perspective.

Most of these pitchers—almost all of whom either are with the Cubs or were at the time—have gotten hurt after having a couple of 15-14 seasons with 112 walks. The Cubs just love these guys, and are determined to prove that they can win with them.

The Sam Jones who won in 1925 and the Sam Jones who won numerous times in the fifties and sixties are not the same person, obviously. Sad Sam Jones, who won 229 games between 1914 and 1935, was a skinny, off-speed pitcher with funny ears who had kind of an atypical year in 1925, when the Yankees finished seventh. The Sam Jones from the fifties was a big square-shouldered fireballer who came in from the Negro Leagues, pitched with a toothpick in his mouth. He and Herb Score were teammates at Indianapolis in 1954. Wasn't nobody digging in on that team, I'll tell you that.

1960—Sam Jones	1970—Sam McDowell	1980—Steve Carlton
1961—Sandy Koufax	1971—Bill Stoneman	1981—Mario Soto
1962—Joey Jay	1972—Nolan Ryan	1982—Steve Carlton
1963—Steve Barber	1973—Nolan Ryan	1983—Steve Carlton
1964—Bob Veale	1974—Nolan Ryan	1984—Fernando Valenzuela
1965—Sam McDowell	1975—Nolan Ryan	1985—Mario Soto
1966—Denny McLain	1976—Nolan Ryan	1986—Mark Langston
1967—Sam McDowell	1977—Nolan Ryan	1987—Mark Langston
1968—Sam McDowell	1978—J. R. Richard	1988—Charlie Hough
1969—Sam McDowell	1979—Phil Niekro	1989—Mark Langston

If we banned knuckleballers from the list, the winners would be Nolan Ryan in '79 and Dave Stewart in '88. Steve Carlton is an exception to the rule, in that he won the award several times as an aging pitcher, having not won it when he was younger—because of Nolan Ryan. Carlton, who finished second to Ryan in '74, was a couple of years older than Nolan, but he had a fantastic conditioning regimen that enabled him to become baseball's hardest-working pitcher in his late thirties.

1990—Bobby Witt	2000—Matt Clement
1991—Randy Johnson	2001—Ryan Dempster
1992—Randy Johnson	2002—Kazuhisa Ishii
1993—Randy Johnson	2003—Kerry Wood
1994—Juan Guzman	2004—Oliver Perez
1995—Chuck Finley	2005—Chris Capuano
1996—Al Leiter	2006—Ted Lilly
1997—Hideo Nomo	2007—Carlos Zambrano
1998—Randy Johnson	
1999—Russ Ortiz	

Yeah, that's right. The list for the last ten years confirms my intuition, which was that there really hasn't been a pitcher in the Nolan Ryan/Sam McDowell/Mark Langston/Young Randy Johnson mode for several years. Zambrano, having led the majors twice in a row in walks, is as close to that as we have come, but the Nolan Ryan Award has been the kiss of death since 2000. Most of these pitchers—almost all of whom either are with the Cubs or were at the time—have gotten hurt after having a couple of 15-14 seasons with 112 walks. The Cubs just love these guys, and are determined to prove that they can win with them. And, you know, good luck with that; I like power pitchers, too.

Los Angeles Dodgers

Los Angeles Dodgers – 2007
Team Overview

Description		Ranking
Won-Lost Record	82-80	
Place	4th of 5 in National League West	
Runs Scored	735	21st in the majors
Runs Allowed	727	8th in the majors
Home Runs	129	26th in the majors
Home Runs Allowed	146	4th in the majors
Batting Average	.275	8th in the majors
Batting Average Allowed	.261	8th in the majors
Walks Drawn	511	20th in the majors
Walks Given	518	13th in the majors
OPS For	.743	21st in the majors
OPS Against	.725	5th in the majors
Stolen Bases	137	5th in the majors
Stolen Bases Allowed	96	14th in the majors

Key Players

Pos	Player	G	AB	R	H	2B	3B	HR	RBI	SB	CS	BB	SO	Avg	OBP	Slg	OPS	WS
C	Russell Martin	151	540	87	158	32	3	19	87	21	9	67	89	.293	.374	.469	.843	22
1B	James Loney	96	344	41	114	18	4	15	67	0	1	28	48	.331	.381	.538	.919	16
2B	Jeff Kent	136	494	78	149	36	1	20	79	1	3	57	61	.302	.375	.500	.875	17
3B	Nomar Garciaparra	121	431	39	122	17	0	7	59	3	1	31	41	.283	.328	.371	.700	11
SS	Rafael Furcal	138	581	87	157	23	4	6	47	25	6	55	68	.270	.333	.355	.687	15
LF	Luis Gonzalez	139	464	70	129	23	2	15	68	6	2	56	56	.278	.359	.433	.793	12
CF	Juan Pierre	162	668	96	196	24	8	0	41	64	15	33	37	.293	.331	.353	.685	12
RF	Andre Ethier	153	447	50	127	32	2	13	64	0	4	46	68	.284	.350	.452	.802	13

Key Pitchers

Pos	Player	G	GS	W	L	Sv	IP	H	R	ER	BB	SO	BR/9	ERA	WS
SP	Brad Penny	33	33	16	4	0	208.0	199	75	70	73	135	11.99	3.03	20
SP	Derek Lowe	33	32	12	14	0	199.1	194	100	86	59	147	11.47	3.88	11
SP	Chad Billingsley	43	20	12	5	0	147.0	131	56	54	64	141	12.12	3.31	12
SP	Randy Wolf	18	18	9	6	0	102.2	110	55	54	39	94	13.59	4.73	5
SP	Mark Hendrickson	39	15	4	8	0	122.2	142	75	71	29	92	12.62	5.21	3
CL	Takashi Saito	63	0	2	1	39	64.1	33	10	10	13	78	6.85	1.40	17
RP	Joe Beimel	83	0	4	2	1	67.1	63	30	29	24	39	11.76	3.88	6
RP	Jonathan Broxton	83	0	4	4	2	82.0	69	30	26	25	99	10.43	2.85	10

Maybe They Were Just Waiting for Their Fans to Arrive

After the first three innings the 2007 Dodgers were 19 games under .500—ahead in 53 games, behind in 72. After that they were pretty good, improving by 10½ games from the start of the fourth inning to the end of the game.

We generally believe that lineup construction is not a big issue, but one can't help but assume that this is tied to the Dodgers' slightly peculiar decision to bat their worst hitters first and second, which generally means that those hitters would hit twice in the first three innings. The Dodgers had a lower on-base percentage AND a lower slugging percentage from the #1 and #2 spots in the batting order than from any spot 3 through 8.

Los Angeles Dodgers – 2007
Innings Ahead/Behind/Tied

Inning	1	2	3	4	5	6	7	8	9	Extra	Final
Ahead	41	49	53	54	64	71	72	75	73	9	82
Behind	45	61	72	73	69	71	76	75	76	4	80
Tied	76	52	37	35	29	20	14	12	13	19	—

Los Angeles Dodgers – 2007
Productivity by Batting Order Position

Pos	Players	Avg	OBP	Slg	OPS
1	Furcal (130g), Pierre (31g)	.273	.327	.361	.687
2	Pierre (123g)	.283	.327	.348	.675
3	Garciaparra (65g), Martin (42g), Kemp (27g)	.310	.356	.440	.796
4	Kent (132g),Gonzalez (20g)	.293	.365	.506	.871
5	Gonzalez (97g)	.261	.337	.411	.748
6	Martin (71g),Garciaparra (22g)	.277	.355	.433	.788
7	Ethier (55g), Loney (35g)	.300	.358	.463	.821
8	Ethier (35g), Martinez (26g), Abreu (19g)	.260	.331	.379	.710
9	Penny (31g), Lowe (30g), Billingsley (19g)	.206	.267	.307	.573
	Total	.275	.337	.406	.743

In 2003, Nomar Garciaparra pulled 27% of his fly balls and 72% of his ground balls to left field.
In 2007, only 18% of his fly balls and 57% of his ground balls were pulled to left.

Nomar Garciaparra – 2003
Hitting Analysis

Batting Right-Handed							1B	2B	3B	HR
Ground Balls to Left	144	Outs 114	Hits 30	Average .208	Hit Type		26	4	0	0
Ground Balls to Center	42	Outs 27	Hits 15	Average .357	Hit Type		15	0	0	0
Ground Balls to Right	13	Outs 10	Hits 3	Average .231	Hit Type		3	0	0	0
Line Drives to Left	73	Outs 20	Hits 53	Average .726	Hit Type		34	16	1	2
Line Drives to Center	38	Outs 10	Hits 28	Average .737	Hit Type		23	3	1	1
Line Drives to Right	17	Outs 3	Hits 14	Average .824	Hit Type		11	1	2	0
Fly Balls to Left	75	Outs 47	Hits 28	Average .389	Hit Type		0	7	1	20
Fly Balls to Center	97	Outs 82	Hits 15	Average .163	Hit Type		3	4	4	4
Fly Balls to Right	107	Outs 95	Hits 12	Average .114	Hit Type		5	2	4	1
Total on Ground Balls	199	Outs 151	Hits 48	Average .241	Hit Type		44	4	0	0
Total on Line Drives	128	Outs 33	Hits 95	Average .742	Hit Type		68	20	4	3
Total on Fly Balls	279	Outs 224	Hits 55	Average .204	Hit Type		8	13	9	25
Total Hit to Left	292	Outs 181	Hits 111	Average .384	Hit Type		60	27	2	22
Total Hit to Center	177	Outs 119	Hits 58	Average .337	Hit Type		41	7	5	5
Total Hit to Right	137	Outs 108	Hits 29	Average .215	Hit Type		19	3	6	1
Bunts	2	Outs 2	Hits 0	Average .000	Hit Type		0	0	0	0
All Balls in Play	608	Outs 410	Hits 198	Average .332	Hit Type		120	37	13	28

Nomar Garciaparra – 2007
Hitting Analysis

Batting Right-Handed							1B	2B	3B	HR
Ground Balls to Left	98	Outs 71	Hits 27	Average .276	Hit Type		26	1	0	0
Ground Balls to Center	58	Outs 42	Hits 16	Average .276	Hit Type		16	0	0	0
Ground Balls to Right	15	Outs 10	Hits 5	Average .333	Hit Type		5	0	0	0
Line Drives to Left	33	Outs 11	Hits 22	Average .688	Hit Type		19	3	0	0
Line Drives to Center	31	Outs 11	Hits 20	Average .645	Hit Type		16	4	0	0
Line Drives to Right	12	Outs 5	Hits 7	Average .583	Hit Type		6	1	0	0
Fly Balls to Left	26	Outs 15	Hits 11	Average .440	Hit Type		5	2	0	4
Fly Balls to Center	55	Outs 48	Hits 7	Average .132	Hit Type		3	1	0	3
Fly Balls to Right	66	Outs 59	Hits 7	Average .106	Hit Type		2	5	0	0
Total on Ground Balls	171	Outs 123	Hits 48	Average .281	Hit Type		47	1	0	0
Total on Line Drives	76	Outs 27	Hits 49	Average .653	Hit Type		41	8	0	0
Total on Fly Balls	147	Outs 122	Hits 25	Average .174	Hit Type		10	8	0	7
Total Hit to Left	157	Outs 97	Hits 60	Average .387	Hit Type		50	6	0	4
Total Hit to Center	144	Outs 101	Hits 43	Average .303	Hit Type		35	5	0	3
Total Hit to Right	93	Outs 74	Hits 19	Average .204	Hit Type		13	6	0	0
All Balls in Play	394	Outs 272	Hits 122	Average .313	Hit Type		98	17	0	7

Those of us in the stat analysis community tend not to be bullish on Juan Pierre or anybody who even looks like Juan Pierre. However, the charts "Impact by Position in the Inning" and "Performance As Leadoff Man" show clearly that his teams have done much, much better in the innings that Pierre has led off for them than I would have guessed. The runs scored per inning by his teams when he has led off are NOT bad; they're actually quite good.

To an extent this is negated by the fact that you can't always get him leading off in the inning, and his impact on the team when he bats second or third in the inning (or later) is astonishingly awful. In 2006 his team scored less than 2.50 runs per nine innings when Pierre was the number three hitter in the inning.

This figure is driven down by the fact that when Pierre was the number three hitter in the inning, the pitcher was often or usually the number two hitter. Still…try to find another leadoff hitter who has the same data.

Juan Pierre – 2006
Impact by Position in Inning

Position	Innings	Runs	Runs/Inning	Runs/RBI
Leading Off	303	186	.61	53/2
Batting Second	139	69	.50	20/1
Batting Third	136	39	.29	6/8
Batting Fourth	82	37	.45	3/2
Batting 5th or later	90	208	2.31	5/27

Juan Pierre – 2007
Impact by Position in Inning

Position	Innings	Runs	Runs/Inning	Runs/RBI
Leading Off	173	96	.55	32/0
Batting Second	262	154	.59	43/1
Batting Third	136	68	.50	15/9
Batting Fourth	72	43	.60	3/13
Batting 5th or later	86	157	1.83	3/18

Juan Pierre – 2007
Performance as Leadoff Man

Innings Led Off:	173		
Team Scored:		96 Runs	.55 per inning
Reached Base Leading Off:	58		
Team Scored:		69 Runs	1.19 per inning
Did Not Reach:	115		
Team Scored:		27 Runs	.23 per inning
Other Innings for Team:	1288		
Team Scored:		639 Runs	.50 per inning

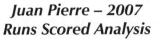

Ichiro Suzuki in 2007 led the majors in singles (203), but Juan Pierre led the majors in runs scored after hitting a single (64).

Magglio Ordonez led the majors in doubles (54), but David Ortiz led the majors in runs scored after hitting a double (28).

Curtis Granderson led the majors in triples (23), but Jimmy Rollins led in runs scored after hitting a triple (15).

Barry Bonds led the majors in reaching base by a walk or hit batsman (135), but Grady Sizemore led in the runs scored after reaching on a walk or hit batsman (37).

I believe that Pierre also tied for the major league lead in Vultured Runs, which are runs scored after grounding into a forceout (thus replacing the runner who had earned his way on base). Pierre and Bobby Abreu each scored 6 times after taking another player's spot, which is the most of any player that I am aware of.

Juan Pierre – 2007
Runs Scored Analysis

Reached on		Runs Scored After	
Triples	8	Scored after Triple	4
Doubles	24	Scored after Double	9
Singles	164	Scored after Single	64
Walk/HBP	39	Scored after Walk/HBP	11
Reached on Error	6	Scored after ROE	2
Reached on Forceout	28	Vultured Runs	6
		Total Runs Scored	96

Brought in by		Driven in by	
Single	40	Jeff Kent	26
Double	19	Russell Martin	17
Triple	3	Luis Gonzalez	13
Other home run	11	Nomar Garciaparra	13
Sac Fly	9	James Loney	8
Walk, Error, or Other	14	No RBI	5
		Matt Kemp	4
		Ramon Martinez	3
		Tony Abreu	2
		Andre Ethier	2
		Himself	1
		Mark Sweeney	1
		Rafael Furcal	1

Luis Gonzalez seems to have lost the ability to hit the elite pitchers. He also hit .193 against pitchers with ERAs under 3.50 in 2006:

Luis Gonzalez – 2007
Batting Performance by Quality of Opposing Pitcher

	AB	H	HR	RBI	Avg	OPS
Pitcher with ERA <= 3.50	115	25	2	9	.217	.589
Pitcher with ERA 3.51 to 4.25	133	37	3	16	.278	.758
Pitcher with ERA 4.26 to 5.25	118	33	4	22	.280	.827
Pitcher with ERA over 5.25	97	33	6	21	.340	1.031

Change for the Better

Brad Penny threw his changeup more than twice as often in 2007 as he had in 2006, and cut more than a run off his ERA. Unlike most pitchers, he did not save it mostly for opposite-side hitters — he relied on it heavily against both lefthanded and righthanded hitters.

Brad Penny – 2006
Pitch Type Analysis

Overall		
Total Pitches	3235	
Fastball	2353	73%
Curveball	616	19%
Changeup	179	6%
Slider	3	0%
Split Finger	25	1%
Pitchout	10	0%
Not Charted	49	2%

	Vs. RHB		Vs. LHB	
Total Pitches	1569		1666	
Outs Recorded	272		295	
Fastball	1170	75%	1183	71%
Curveball	310	20%	306	18%
Changeup	51	3%	128	8%
Slider	3	0%	0	0%
Split Finger	7	0%	18	1%
Pitchout	3	0%	7	0%
Not Charted	25	2%	24	1%

Brad Penny – 2007
Pitch Type Analysis

Overall		
Total Pitches	3227	
Fastball	2292	71%
Curveball	404	13%
Changeup	499	15%
Pitchout	12	0%
Not Charted	20	1%

	Vs. RHB		Vs. LHB	
Total Pitches	1708		1519	
Outs Recorded	323		301	
Fastball	1271	74%	1021	67%
Curveball	193	11%	211	14%
Changeup	230	13%	269	18%
Pitchout	1	0%	11	1%
Not Charted	13	1%	7	0%

Milwaukee Brewers

Milwaukee Brewers – 2007
Team Overview

Description		Ranking
Won-Lost Record	83-79	
Place	2nd of 6 in National League Central	
Runs Scored	801	11th in the majors
Runs Allowed	776	15th in the majors
Home Runs	231	1st in the majors
Home Runs Allowed	161	12th in the majors
Batting Average	.262	21st in the majors
Batting Average Allowed	.269	18th in the majors
Walks Drawn	501	24th in the majors
Walks Given	507	10th in the majors
OPS For	.785	6th in the majors
OPS Against	.754	14th in the majors
Stolen Bases	96	15th in the majors
Stolen Bases Allowed	99	20th in the majors

Key Players

Pos	Player	G	AB	R	H	2B	3B	HR	RBI	SB	CS	BB	SO	Avg	OBP	Slg	OPS	WS
C	Johnny Estrada	120	442	40	123	25	0	10	54	0	0	12	43	.278	.296	.403	.699	7
1B	Prince Fielder	158	573	109	165	35	2	50	119	2	2	90	121	.288	.395	.618	1.013	27
2B	Rickie Weeks	118	409	87	96	21	6	16	36	25	2	78	116	.235	.374	.433	.807	14
3B	Ryan Braun	113	451	91	146	26	6	34	97	15	5	29	112	.324	.370	.634	1.004	22
SS	J.J. Hardy	151	592	89	164	30	1	26	80	2	3	40	73	.277	.323	.463	.786	19
LF	Geoff Jenkins	132	420	45	107	24	2	21	64	2	2	32	116	.255	.319	.471	.790	11
CF	Bill Hall	136	452	59	115	35	0	14	63	4	5	40	128	.254	.315	.425	.740	10
RF	Corey Hart	140	505	86	149	33	9	24	81	23	7	36	99	.295	.353	.539	.892	21

Key Pitchers

Pos	Player	G	GS	W	L	Sv	IP	H	R	ER	BB	SO	BR/9	ERA	WS
SP	Jeff Suppan	34	34	12	12	0	206.2	243	113	106	68	114	14.02	4.62	9
SP	David Bush	33	31	12	10	0	186.1	217	110	106	44	134	13.14	5.12	6
SP	Ben Sheets	24	24	12	5	0	141.1	138	62	60	37	106	11.21	3.82	10
SP	Claudio Vargas	29	23	11	6	1	134.1	153	80	76	54	107	14.00	5.09	5
SP	Chris Capuano	29	25	5	12	0	150.0	170	93	85	54	132	13.92	5.10	5
CL	Francisco Cordero	66	0	0	4	44	63.1	52	23	21	18	86	10.09	2.98	12
RP	Brian Shouse	73	0	1	1	1	47.2	46	19	16	14	32	11.71	3.02	5
RP	Derrick Turnbow	77	0	4	5	1	68.0	44	36	35	46	84	12.18	4.63	6

Dodgertown, 2008

From 1970 through 1973 the Los Angeles Dodgers came up with a formidable list of young players—Bill Buckner, Ron Cey, Joe Ferguson, Steve Garvey, Billy Grabarkewitz, Von Joshua, Lee Lacy, Dave Lopes, Tom Paciorek, Bill Russell, Bobby Valentine, Steve Yeager. The problem was that while the talent level was remarkable, the pieces didn't fit. They had two catchers, Ferguson and Yeager, no first baseman, no second baseman, three third basemen (Grabarkewitz, Cey and Garvey), and a bunch of singles-hitting outfielders. Making a baseball team out of this was like a jigsaw puzzle made up of the pieces from three different puzzles—and then, to make it worse, their young shortstop got hurt. Bobby Valentine, quite possibly was the best player in the group, essentially lost his career to a series of leg injuries.

The Dodgers were a very well-run organization at that time, a kind of baseball corporation, and they sorted it out extremely well. They moved one of the catchers (Joe Ferguson) to the outfield, moved an outfielder to shortstop (Bill Russell) and another one to second base (Davey Lopes), moved Steve Garvey and Bill Buckner both to first base and let them fight it out for the first base job. Garvey won; Buckner was traded. They imported a bunch of veteran, power-hitting outfielders by trade and free agency (Dusty Baker, Jimmy Wynn, Reggie Smith, Rick Monday), and came out of it with a good team.

Where the Dodgers were in 1971 or 1972, that's about where the Brewers are now. Their talent is just eye-popping, but it's hard to see how they're going to make a baseball team out of it. Maybe Ryan Braun will master third base, but frankly, I'm not optimistic. I think, in the end, they're going to have to trade either Fielder or Braun because they just can't play them both. They've got Hall and Hardy, both of whom claim to be shortstops but neither of whom really is, and they've got Rickie Weeks, who is kind of a second baseman. Maybe. It's a good problem, but it's a problem all the same.

As the chart (below) shows, Prince Fielder in 2007 hit 18 home runs to center field. This seems to me truly exceptional straightaway power. I can't remember ever before seeing a player who hit that many home runs to center, although it may have happened. I checked the obvious guys for whom we have data…didn't find anybody who could match it.

Prince Fielder – 2007
Hitting Analysis

Batting Left-Handed							1B	2B	3B	HR
Ground Balls to Left	24	Outs 19	Hits 5	Average .208	Hit Type		5 -	0 -	0 -	0
Ground Balls to Center	49	Outs 39	Hits 10	Average .204	HitType		10 -	0 -	0 -	0
Ground Balls to Right	86	Outs 74	Hits 12	Average .140	Hit Type		11 -	1 -	0 -	0
Line Drives to Left	25	Outs 7	Hits 18	Average .720	Hit Type		10 -	8 -	0 -	0
Line Drives to Center	22	Outs 3	Hits 19	Average .864	Hit Type		12 -	6 -	1 -	0
Line Drives to Right	41	Outs 14	Hits 27	Average .659	Hit Type		17 -	8 -	0 -	2
Fly Balls to Left	68	Outs 51	Hits 17	Average .250	Hit Type		7 -	4 -	1 -	5
Fly Balls to Center	84	Outs 55	Hits 29	Average .354	Hit Type		6 -	5 -	0 -	18
Fly Balls to Right	57	Outs 29	Hits 28	Average .509	Hit Type		0 -	3 -	0 -	25
Total on Ground Balls	159	Outs 132	Hits 27	Average .170	Hit Type		26 -	1 -	0 -	0
Total on Line Drives	88	Outs 24	Hits 64	Average .727	Hit Type		39 -	22 -	1 -	2
Total on Fly Balls	209	Outs 135	Hits 74	Average .361	Hit Type		13 -	12 -	1 -	48
Total Hit to Left	117	Outs 77	Hits 40	Average .342	Hit Type		22 -	12 -	1 -	5
Total Hit to Center	155	Outs 97	Hits 58	Average .379	Hit Type		28 -	11 -	1 -	18
Total Hit to Right	184	Outs 117	Hits 67	Average .368	Hit Type		28 -	12 -	0 -	27
All Balls in Play	456	Outs 291	Hits 165	Average .365	Hit Type		78 -	35 -	2 -	50

Can a good pitcher stop Prince Fielder?
Could last year, anyway. Prince Fielder in 2007 hit .182 against the league's best pitchers, with less than one home run per 18 at bats.
Against weak pitchers hit .348 with a homer every 7 at bats.
No other top power hitter had such a dramatic split.

Prince Fielder – 2007
Batting Performance by Quality of Opposing Pitcher

	AB	H	HR	RBI	Avg	OPS
Pitcher with ERA <= 3.50	110	20	6	12	.182	.682
Pitcher with ERA 3.51 to 4.25	148	46	14	38	.311	1.052
Pitcher with ERA 4.26 to 5.25	160	45	8	23	.281	.917
Pitcher with ERA over 5.25	155	54	22	46	.348	1.307

Albert Pujols – 2007
Batting Performance by Quality of Opposing Pitcher

	AB	H	HR	RBI	Avg	OPS
Pitcher with ERA <= 3.50	111	30	7	19	.270	.892
Pitcher with ERA 3.51 to 4.25	179	58	11	30	.324	.993
Pitcher with ERA 4.26 to 5.25	147	46	5	21	.313	.910
Pitcher with ERA over 5.25	128	51	9	33	.398	1.189

Chris Capuano's ERA was 5.10 in 150 innings for the Brewers last year.
Claudio Vargas ERA was 5.09 in 134.3

The Brewers were 7-18 in Chris Capuano's 25 starts.
They were 16-7 when Vargas started.

The Brewers scored 3.68 runs per game when Chris Capuano started.
Vargas support was 5.78 runs per game.

Milwaukee – 2007
Performance by Starting Pitcher

Games Started By	G	RS	RA	Won	Lost
Suppan, Jeff	34	172	151	18	16
Bush, David	31	145	173	14	17
Capuano, Chris	25	92	146	7	18
Sheets, Ben	24	139	95	15	9
Vargas, Claudio	23	133	96	16	7
Gallardo, Yovani	17	90	79	9	8
Villanueva, Carlos	6	20	24	4	2
Parra, Manny	2	10	12	0	2
Team Totals	162	801	776	83	79

The Days and Nights of Rickie Weeks

Answer: Rickie Weeks and Barry Bonds.

Question: Who are the only two players since 1900 to score 85 runs in a season with less than 100 hits? Barry Bonds, 1999, and Rickie Weeks, 2007.

If you are in a fantasy league and looking for a player whose career might take off in 2008, I would recommend that you look carefully at Rickie Weeks. If you're not in a fantasy league and could care less about that, I recommend that you look at Rickie Weeks anyway, because he's really weird and interesting.

With a small increase in playing time, Rickie Weeks increased his walks last year from 30 to 78—and yet his on-base percentage hardly increased at all! It's an amazing mix of facts. First of all, there are very, very few players who increase their walk rate in a season from 73 walks per 1000 plate appearances to 154. Those that do, you would assume they would show a spike in on base percentage. The only other player in history who had as large an increase in walks and as small an increase in on base percentage, oddly enough, is Jason Lane of Houston—also in 2007.

In his last year at Southern University in Baton Rouge, Rickie Weeks hit .483 with a .948 slugging percentage. That was down from the previous year, when he had hit .495 and slugged .995. Weeks was the second player taken in the draft in 2003, but the averages are part of the problem: you don't hit .500 in college if you're playing good competition.

Weeks bashed his way through the minor leagues in less than two years, and here again we see the problem. Weeks arrived in the majors having had neither the time nor the opportunity to have learned the finer points of the game. One year ago, I would not have been optimistic about Weeks' chance to become a legitimately good player. I saw him as a player who had tremendous ability, but who would probably have a so-so career because of

a) defense, and
b) lack of command of the strike zone.

But while Weeks did not have a breakthrough year in 2007, he did show tremendous progress on those things he needed to work on. As a second baseman in 2005 and 2006 he had a double plays-to-errors ratio about 3-to-1. That's unacceptable; that's like hitting .160. It will end your career as a second baseman. Last year the ratio was almost 6-to-1. He needs it to be about 10-to-1, but 6-to-1 is a step in the right direction.

As a hitter he took a big step forward and a big step back, his batting average dropping from .279 to .235. It's just my intuition, but my intuition is that, in the big picture, the step forward was more significant than the step back. Last year he was forcing himself to take pitches, forcing himself to work the count. Many times the things that you have to force yourself to do one year are kind of natural to you the next year. Probably Weeks will stop forcing himself to take pitches next year, and probably his walk total will drop off—but he wouldn't even think about chasing the really bad pitches that used to get him into trouble. The result may be that he may hit .285 and have a .380 on base percentage and hit for a little power, and play second base and steal 40 bases. That's a player.

Rickie Weeks – 2007
Skills Assessment

Running:	93rd percentile	95th percentile among second basemen
Plate Discipline:	60th percentile	62nd percentile among second basemen
Hitting for Power:	48th percentile	79th percentile among second basemen
Hitting for Average:	27th percentile	26th percentile among second basemen

Who was the biggest pull hitter on the Brewers last year. Prince Fielder? Ryan Braun? Geoff Jenkins? Would you believe…Craig Counsell? He pulled the ball 52% of the time. No one else on the club pulled the ball more than half the time.

Craig Counsell – 2007
Hitting Analysis

Batting Left-Handed							1B	2B	3B	HR
Ground Balls to Left	10	Outs	6	Hits	4	Average .400	Hit Type	2 - 2 - 0 - 0
Ground Balls to Center	21	Outs	14	Hits	7	Average .333	Hit Type	7 - 0 - 0 - 0
Ground Balls to Right	75	Outs	58	Hits	17	Average .227	Hit Type	12 - 5 - 0 - 0
Line Drives to Left	8	Outs	3	Hits	5	Average .625	Hit Type	4 - 1 - 0 - 0
Line Drives to Center	8	Outs	3	Hits	5	Average .625	Hit Type	4 - 0 - 1 - 0
Line Drives to Right	19	Outs	11	Hits	8	Average .421	Hit Type	5 - 2 - 1 - 0
Fly Balls to Left	25	Outs	22	Hits	3	Average .120	Hit Type	3 - 0 - 0 - 0
Fly Balls to Center	39	Outs	34	Hits	5	Average .132	Hit Type	4 - 1 - 0 - 0
Fly Balls to Right	24	Outs	20	Hits	4	Average .174	Hit Type	0 - 1 - 0 - 3
Total on Ground Balls	106	Outs	78	Hits	28	Average .264	Hit Type	21 - 7 - 0 - 0
Total on Line Drives	35	Outs	17	Hits	18	Average .514	Hit Type	13 - 3 - 2 - 0
Total on Fly Balls	88	Outs	76	Hits	12	Average .140	Hit Type	7 - 2 - 0 - 3
Total Hit to Left	43	Outs	31	Hits	12	Average .279	Hit Type	9 - 3 - 0 - 0
Total Hit to Center	68	Outs	51	Hits	17	Average .254	Hit Type	15 - 1 - 1 - 0
Total Hit to Right	118	Outs	89	Hits	29	Average .248	Hit Type	17 - 8 - 1 - 3
Bunts	14	Outs	10	Hits	4	Average .500	Hit Type	4 - 0 - 0 - 0
All Balls in Play	243	Outs	181	Hits	62	Average .264	Hit Type	45 - 12 - 2 - 3

When He Was Good...

Rookie Yovani Gallardo had a 1.06 ERA in his nine wins, and a 2.56 ERA in his six no-deicisons, but a 13.74 ERA in his five losses. Nearly two-thirds of the earned runs he allowed all year came in those five losses.

Yovani Gallardo – 2007
Decision Analysis

Group	G	IP	W	L	Pct	H	R	SO	BB	ERA
Wins	9	59.2	9	0	1.000	46	7	47	19	1.06
Losses	5	19.0	0	5	.000	38	32	19	10	13.74
No Decisions	6	31.2	0	0	—	19	9	35	8	2.56
Quality Starts: 9 in Wins, 0 in Losses, 3 in no-decisions										

They Don't Pay Me to Walk

Johnny Estrada swung at 63% of the pitches he saw, highest in the majors among players who batted 400 times. He swung at a pitch out of the strike zone more than twice as often as he took a called strike. Estrada's walks for the four seasons since he became a regular: 39, 20, 13, and 12.

They Don't Pay to Run, Either

Johnny Estrada still has no triples in his career and no stolen bases. Even Bengie Molina has 4 triples and 3 stolen bases. The leaders for most career plate appearances, no triples:

1. Johnny Estrada   2189
2. Jason Phillips   1537
3. Mark Parent   1080

The leaders for most career plate appearances, no stolen bases:

1. Russ Nixon   2714
2t. Johnny Estrada   2189
2t. Aaron Robinson   2189

Ray King – 2007
Pitch Type Analysis

Overall		
Total Pitches	609	
Fastball	252	41%
Changeup	22	4%
Slider	325	53%
Not Charted	10	2%

	Vs. RHB		Vs. LHB	
Total Pitches	302		307	
Outs Recorded	57		62	
Fastball	172	57%	80	26%
Changeup	20	7%	2	1%
Slider	106	35%	219	71%
Not Charted	4	1%	6	2%

Johnny Estrada – 2007
Pitch Analysis

Overall		
Pitches Seen	1374	
Taken	507	37%
Swung At	867	63%
Pitches Taken		
Taken for a Strike	141	28%
Called a ball	366	72%
Pitches Taken by Pitch Location		
In Strike Zone	141	28%
High	74	15%
Low	110	22%
Inside	56	11%
Outside	126	25%
Swung At		
Missed	114	13%
Fouled Off	346	40%
Put in Play	407	47%
Swung At by Pitch Location		
In Strike Zone	565	65%
High	63	7%
Low	126	15%
Inside	35	4%
Outside	78	9%

Slider Kings

Larry Andersen, who pitched in the majors from 1975 to 1994, was famous for three things:
1) He was tremendously funny,
2) He was traded for Jeff Bagwell, and
3) At the end of his career he threw his slider 90% of the time.

You kind of have to have context to understand how unusual that is. More than 90% of major league pitchers throw their fastball more than 50% of the time. In the other 8 or 9%, most still throw the fastball more than any other pitch.

There are NO major league starting pitchers who throw the slider 50% of the time, or even close to that. Jeremy Bonderman, who threw more sliders than any other major league pitcher, still threw 600 more fastballs than sliders. There are some relievers, however, who do make a living off the slider. The most notable of those in 2007:

1. Justin Speier   378 Sliders   252 Fastballs
2. Jorge Sosa   938 Sliders   668 Fastballs
3. Mike Wuertz   585 Sliders   452 Fastballs
4. Ray King   325 Sliders   252 Fastballs
5. Jamie Walker   359 Sliders   310 Fastballs

Derrick Turnbow
Record of Opposing Batters

Season	AB	R	H	2B	3B	HR	RBI	BB	SO	SB	CS	GIDP	Avg	OBP	Slg	OPS
2003	50	1	7	0	0	0	1	3	15	0	0	2	.140	.189	.140	.329
2004	19	0	2	0	0	0	0	7	3	0	0	2	.105	.346	.105	.451
2005	246	15	49	10	1	5	15	24	64	0	0	8	.199	.270	.309	.579
2006	220	51	56	12	3	8	36	39	69	3	1	4	.255	.367	.446	.812
2007	241	36	44	4	2	4	33	46	84	3	3	6	.183	.314	.266	.579

Derrick Turnbow – 2005
Pitch Type Analysis

Overall

Total Pitches	1049	
Fastball	761	73%
Curveball	81	8%
Changeup	85	8%
Slider	57	5%
Split Finger	5	0%
Pitchout	4	0%
Not Charted	56	5%

	Vs. RHB		Vs. LHB	
Total Pitches	582		467	
Outs Recorded	108		94	
Fastball	437	75%	324	69%
Curveball	48	8%	33	7%
Changeup	18	3%	67	14%
Slider	46	8%	11	2%
Split Finger	2	0%	3	1%
Pitchout	4	1%	0	0%
Not Charted	27	5%	29	6%

What Happened in '06?

Derrick Turnbow was Milwaukee's closer in 2005, but his 6.87 ERA in '06 lost him his job. In 2007, he figured out how to pitch again and opposing batters had the exact same OPS against him in 2007 as they did in '05 (.579). What did he do different? In 2006 he threw far more curveballs than in either of the other two years. In 2007 he replaced the curve with a slider.

Derrick Turnbow – 2006
Pitch Type Analysis

Overall

Total Pitches	1091	
Fastball	733	67%
Curveball	200	18%
Changeup	67	6%
Slider	77	7%
Not Charted	14	1%

	Vs. RHB		Vs. LHB	
Total Pitches	630		461	
Outs Recorded	85		84	
Fastball	418	66%	315	68%
Curveball	134	21%	66	14%
Changeup	13	2%	54	12%
Slider	59	9%	18	4%
Not Charted	6	1%	8	2%

Derrick Turnbow – 2007
Pitch Type Analysis

Overall

Total Pitches	1163	
Fastball	802	69%
Curveball	95	8%
Changeup	49	4%
Slider	206	18%
Split Finger	1	0%
Not Charted	10	1%

	Vs. RHB		Vs. LHB	
Total Pitches	720		443	
Outs Recorded	126		78	
Fastball	499	69%	303	68%
Curveball	65	9%	30	7%
Changeup	16	2%	33	7%
Slider	132	18%	74	17%
Split Finger	0	0%	1	0%
Not Charted	8	1%	2	0%

The 2007 Brewers lost ten games in which they hit three or more homers. No other major league team had more than seven such losses.

Milwaukee Brewers – 2007
Record by Home Runs

Home Runs	W – L
0 homers	10 - 22
1 homer	34 - 30
2 homers	25 - 17
3 or more homers	14 - 10

Measuring Consistency

by Bill James

My previous efforts to measure consistency have consistently come to naught.

How do you measure a player's consistency? Anyone can look over the record of a player, and make an assessment of that player's consistency. These observations are not particularly speculative or arbitrary. You and I and Albert, if asked to rate the consistency of Pete Rose and Dave Hollins and Brett Butler and Rico Carty, would probably all agree that Rose and Butler could be described as "consistent" players, while Hollins and Carty would have to be described as highly inconsistent players.

If something can be impartially observed in this manner, it has long seemed to me, it must be possible to measure it objectively. Nonetheless, my previous efforts to measure consistency have consistently come to naught.

I think I finally have the problem whupped. I believe that I finally have a measure of consistency that is logical enough and sensible enough that it has a chance of being widely accepted.

My measure of consistency starts with the player's year-by-year Win Share totals, and measures the consistency thereof in two different ways. Let's use Gil Hodges, Billy Williams, Pete Reiser and Bob Knepper as test players to explain the system. These are these players Win Shares, given by age:

Player	21	22	23	24	25	26	27	28	29	30	31	32	33	34	35	36	37	38	Total
Hodges, Gil			1	10	21	21	26	26	25	29	23	21	21	12	17	3	5	2	263
Williams, Billy	0	2	15	18	28	28	33	21	28	30	24	29	26	32	20	16	17	7	374
Reiser, Pete	7	34	28				19	18	4	8	2	5	0						125
Knepper, Bob		2	12	22	5	6	13	2	8	13	9	17	0	10	4	1			124

Gil Hodges also played at ages 19 and ages 39, but had zero Win Shares both years, so I have chopped those off in the interests of making the chart fit.

The first thing we do here is to measure the year-to-year changes in performance. If a player is "consistent", what we mean by that, essentially, is that he is the same one year as he is the next. We thus measure the year-to-year changes. Hodges' value was zero at age 22, one at age 23; that's a difference of one. His value was one at age 23, ten at age 24; that's a difference of nine. Adding nine plus one, his total so far is ten.

Figuring Hodges' entire career in this manner, the sum of his year-to-year changes in performance value is 74 points. The sum for Billy Williams is 108 points, for Pete Reiser, 120 points, for Bob Knepper, 118. We will call this number the player's "inconsistency".

We could measure consistency, then, by simply dividing the player's career value by his inconsistency. The less inconsistent a player has been, the more consistent he has been. This would produce, for these four players:

Gil Hodges	74 divided by 263	28%
Billy Williams	108 divided by 374	29%
Pistol Pete	120 divided by 125	96%
Bob Knepper	118 divided by 124	95%

I suspect that no one has any problem with the general conclusion that Gil Hodges and Billy Williams were extremely consistent players, while Reiser and Knepper were inconsistent players. I don't really see how one *could* disagree with this conclusion, and this method essentially is what we will come back to after we dodge through a few hoops. The method so far is a little bit simple, and it has some logical problems. For one thing, it measures every player, no matter how perfectly consistent he might have been, as having a significant degree of inconsistency. It is impossible to get to 30 Win Shares in a season and then to the end of your career with year-to-year changes smaller than 60 points, no matter how consistent the player might actually have been. Also, this system would represent a small number of players as having inconsistency greater than 100%—thus having consistency of less than zero percent. This doesn't seem right.

To avoid that, we measure consistency as *the player's career Win Shares, minus the sum of his season-to-season inconsistency, plus two times his Win Shares in his best season, divided by the player's career Win Shares.* What we're doing, by this adjusting, is removing from the "inconsistency penalty" the number of Win Shares required for the player to go directly to his career peak, and to return from there to zero. If a player's values go 0, 5, 10, 15, 20, 15, 10, 5, 0, there is no inconsistency in that. This makes it theoretically possible for a player to be 100% consistent, while bringing all players or almost all players within the normal range of zero to one.

For Gil Hodges, then, we would measure his consistency as 94%:

$$(263 - 74 + 58) / 263 = .939$$

Billy Williams' consistency measures at 89%, Pete Reiser at 58%, and Bob Knepper at 40%.

So far, so good; I have no real problem with any of those measures. The problem is, we haven't really looked at the whole issue of consistency as yet. So far, what we have been looking at, really, is not consistency, but inconsistency. We have been using, so far, a negative definition of consistency: consistency is the absence of inconsistency.

Well, yes—but there is another meaning of the word. Suppose that there are two players, one of whom has a value pattern of 0-10-15-10-0, and the other of whom has a value pattern of 0-10-15-15-15-15-15-15-10-0. Both players have zero inconsistency in their careers—but one player has had one good season, while the other player has had six seasons equally good.

Part of what we mean when we say that a player has been consistent is that he has not merely done something *once* or done it a couple of times, but that he has performed consistently at that level over a period of years. There are many players in baseball history whose consistency is 100%, as measured by the first test of consistency—because they had only one good year. Mark Fidrych, by this test, was 100% consistent, because his

If a player is "consistent", what we mean by that, essentially, is that he is the same one year as he is the next.

career moved in only one direction. Pete Reiser's best season was better than Billy Williams' best season—but Reiser had two good years, Williams had twelve. So how do we measure the other form of consistency—positive consistency, as opposed to consistency measured as the absence of inconsistency?

Positive consistency is measured by the relationship between the player's best season and his career value. We subtract the player's Win Shares in his best season from his career total, and divide that by his career total:

Gil Hodges $(263 - 29) / 263 = .889$
Billy Williams $(374 - 33) / 374 = .911$
Pete Reiser $(125 - 34) / 125 = .728$
Bob Knepper $(118 - 22) / 118 = .814$

Except that this produces figures which are too high... Pete Reiser is really not 73% consistent, nor is Bob Knepper 81% consistent. Using this method, the "positive consistency" measure doesn't carry nearly as much weight in the calculation as the "negative consistency" measure. To correct for that, we subtract double the player's Win Shares in his best season.

We now have two measures of consistency, a "negative measure" which is:

Consistency = (Career – Inconsistency +
        2 * Max Season) / Career

And a "positive measure" which is:

Consistency = (Career – 2 * Max Season) / Career

Since the denominator in both formulas is the same—Career Win Shares—and since two times the player's best season is added into one formula and taken out of the other, it thus becomes a very simple matter to combine the two into one simple formula. That formula is:

Consistency = (2 * Career – Inconsistency) /
        (2 * Career)

For these four players, this yields:

Player	Total	Inconsistency	Consistency
Hodges, Gil	263	74	.859
Williams, Billy	374	108	.856
Reiser, Pete	125	120	.520
Knepper, Bob	124	118	.524

Williams and Hodges were both very consistent players; Knepper and Reiser were very inconsistent players. Which you knew anyway, but now we have a method to pin it down, a method to state objectively who were the most consistent players of all time, a method to identify the most inconsistent players of all time, a method to study the issue of whether past consistency projects future success, a method to study objectively whether relief pitchers tend to be less consistent than starting pitchers.

The most consistent player of all time was...you probably know this, too...Henry Aaron. The ten most consistent players of all time, among those with 40 or more career Win Shares, were:

Player	Career	Consistency
Aaron, Hank	643	.893
Wagner, Honus	655	.889
Cey, Ron	280	.879
Rose, Pete	547	.876
Boggs, Wade	394	.876
Cramer, Doc	219	.872
Gehrig, Lou	489	.871
Ott, Mel	528	.867
Garvey, Steve	279	.867
Shocker, Urban	225	.867

The ten most *in*consistent players were mostly nineteenth century or early twentieth-century pitchers, many of whom got most of their 40 Win Shares in one big shot:

Player	Career	Consistency
Wilhelm, Kaiser	54	.185
Hudson, Nat	66	.182
Lisenbee, Hod	40	.175
Barr, Bob	48	.125
Spalding, Al	62	.081
Atkinson, Al	50	.080
Burns, Dick	44	.068
Demmitt, Ray	50	.060
Barnes, Ross	41	.049
Sweeney, Bill	59	.000

Hitters are more consistent than pitchers, but actually not as much more consistent as I would have guessed. The average consistency for a non-pitcher with 100 or more career Win Shares is .743. The average consistency for a pitcher with 100 or more career Win Shares is .696.

I have figured the consistency for all players in major league history, and will present here the figures for all players with 100 or more Win Shares whose careers ended prior to the 2004 season. I also assigned them letter grades for career consistency, on the following scale:

.8667 or higher	A+
.8333-.8667	A
.8000-.8333	A-
.7667-.8000	B+
.7333-.7667	B
.7000-.7333	B-
.6667-.7000	C+
.6333-.6667	C
.6000-.6333	C-
.5667-.6000	D+
.5333-.5667	D
.5000-.5333	D-
Less than .5000	F

These are the career figures for every former player with 100 or more Win Shares (data comprehensive through 2003):

Player	Consistency	Player	Consistency	Player	Consistency	Player	Consistency
Aaron, Hank	.89 A+	Andujar, Joaquin	.60 C-	Bannister, Floyd	.68 C+	Bell, Gus	.74 B
Abernathy, Ted	.53 D-	Anson, Cap	.85 A	Barber, Steve	.62 C-	Bell, Jay	.85 A
Adams, Babe	.72 B-	Antonelli, Johnny	.68 C+	Barfield, Jesse	.77 B+	Belle, Albert	.76 B
Adams, Bobby	.79 B+	Aparicio, Luis	.83 A-	Barnes, Jesse	.72 B-	Bench, Johnny	.81 A-
Adams, Sparky	.66 C	Appling, Luke	.71 B-	Barr, Jim	.72 B-	Bender, Chief	.74 B
Adcock, Joe	.73 B-	Armas, Tony	.62 C-	Barrett, Jimmy	.73 B	Benes, Andy	.78 B+
Agee, Tommie	.63 C-	Ashburn, Richie	.84 A	Barry, Jack	.79 B+	Beniquez, Juan	.74 B
Aguilera, Rick	.73 B-	Ashby, Alan	.80 B+	Bartell, Dick	.81 A-	Bennett, Charlie	.78 B+
Aldridge, Vic	.75 B	Auker, Eldon	.63 C-	Bass, Kevin	.78 B+	Benton, Al	.47 F
Alexander, Doyle	.70 C+	Austin, Jimmy	.78 B+	Bassler, Johnny	.78 B+	Benton, Larry	.67 C+
Alexander, Pete	.76 B	Averill, Earl	.84 A	Bates, Johnny	.81 A-	Benton, Rube	.61 C-
Alicea, Luis	.64 C	Avila, Bobby	.79 B+	Battey, Earl	.71 B-	Berger, Wally	.82 A-
Allen, Dick	.77 B+	Backman, Wally	.56 D	Bauer, Hank	.84 A	Bernazard, Tony	.67 C+
Allen, Ethan	.65 C	Bagby, Jim	.63 C-	Baylor, Don	.78 B+	Bernhard, Bill	.61 C-
Allen, Johnny	.74 B	Bahnsen, Stan	.68 C+	Beaumont, Ginger	.75 B	Berra, Yogi	.87 A+
Alley, Gene	.74 B	Bailey, Bob	.79 B+	Beckert, Glenn	.74 B	Berry, Ken	.67 C+
Allison, Bob	.77 B+	Bailey, Ed	.75 B	Beckley, Jake	.86 A	Bescher, Bob	.82 A-
Alomar, Sandy	.74 B	Baines, Harold	.82 A-	Bedrosian, Steve	.75 B	Bichette, Dante	.82 A-
Alou, Felipe	.76 B	Baker, Dusty	.76 B	Belanger, Mark	.70 C+	Bierbauer, Lou	.75 B
Alou, Matty	.77 B+	Baker, Home Run	.75 B	Belcher, Tim	.64 C	Bigbee, Carson	.81 A-
Ames, Red	.80 A-	Baldwin, Mark	.69 C+	Bell, Buddy	.79 B+	Billingham, Jack	.68 C+
Anderson, Brady	.74 B	Bancroft, Dave	.80 B+	Bell, Derek	.64 C	Bishop, Max	.80 B+
Anderson, John	.78 B+	Bando, Sal	.79 B+	Bell, Gary	.74 B	Black, Bud	.70 C+
Andrews, Mike	.76 B	Banks, Ernie	.82 A-	Bell, George	.79 B+	Blackwell, Ewell	.52 D-

Player	Consistency	Player	Consistency	Player	Consistency	Player	Consistency
Blaeholder, George	.84 A	Brunansky, Tom	.79 B+	Casey, Dan	.69 C+	Corcoran, Larry	.68 C+
Blair, Paul	.72 B-	Bruton, Bill	.80 A-	Casey, Doc	.67 C+	Corcoran, Tommy	.82 A-
Blasingame, Don	.69 C+	Buckner, Bill	.72 B-	Cash, Dave	.82 A-	Corkhill, Pop	.78 B+
Blauser, Jeff	.66 C	Buechele, Steve	.70 C+	Cash, Norm	.80 A-	Coveleski, Stan	.81 A-
Blefary, Curt	.72 B-	Buffinton, Charlie	.62 C-	Cater, Danny	.71 B-	Covington, Wes	.73 B-
Blue, Lu	.72 B-	Buford, Don	.79 B+	Cavarretta, Phil	.76 B	Cowens, Al	.66 C
Blue, Vida	.61 C-	Buhl, Bob	.70 B-	Cedeno, Cesar	.77 B+	Cramer, Doc	.87 A+
Bluege, Ossie	.80 A-	Buhner, Jay	.76 B	Cepeda, Orlando	.74 B	Crandall, Del	.72 B-
Blyleven, Bert	.76 B	Bumbry, Al	.60 C-	Cey, Ron	.88 A+	Crandall, Doc	.64 C
Bochte, Bruce	.72 B-	Bunning, Jim	.75 B	Chamberlin, Elton	.71 B-	Crane, Ed	.58 D+
Boddicker, Mike	.72 B-	Burdette, Lew	.71 B-	Chambliss, Chris	.80 A-	Cravath, Gavy	.74 B
Bodie, Ping	.59 D+	Burgess, Smoky	.78 B+	Chance, Dean	.68 C+	Crawford, Sam	.84 A
Boggs, Wade	.88 A+	Burgmeier, Tom	.58 D+	Chance, Frank	.82 A-	Crawford, Willie	.72 B-
Bolin, Bobby	.62 C-	Burkett, Jesse	.82 A-	Chandler, Spud	.49 F	Cree, Birdie	.69 C+
Bolling, Frank	.71 B-	Burkett, John	.74 B	Chapman, Ben	.86 A	Critz, Hughie	.69 C+
Bond, Tommy	.68 C+	Burleson, Rick	.77 B+	Chapman, Ray	.72 B-	Cromartie, Warren	.77 B+
Bonds, Bobby	.84 A	Burns, George	.82 A-	Chapman, Sam	.64 C	Cronin, Joe	.80 A-
Bonham, Tiny	.76 B	Burns, George	.64 C	Charles, Ed	.69 C+	Crosetti, Frankie	.72 B-
Bonilla, Bobby	.80 A-	Burns, Oyster	.70 C+	Chase, Hal	.80 A-	Cross, Lave	.79 B+
Bonura, Zeke	.76 B	Burns, Tom	.73 B	Cheney, Larry	.70 C+	Cross, Monte	.79 B+
Boone, Bob	.75 B	Burroughs, Jeff	.68 C+	Chesbro, Jack	.71 B-	Crowder, General	.72 B-
Boone, Ray	.80 A-	Busby, Jim	.71 B-	Childs, Cupid	.79 B+	Cruz, Jose	.82 A-
Bordick, Mike	.74 B	Bush, Donie	.81 A-	Cicotte, Eddie	.71 B-	Cuccinello, Tony	.72 B-
Borowy, Hank	.71 B-	Bush, Guy	.77 B	Clancy, Jim	.52 D-	Cuellar, Mike	.80 A-
Bottomley, Jim	.76 B	Bush, Joe	.71 B-	Clark, Jack	.73 B-	Cullenbine, Roy	.78 B+
Boudreau, Lou	.79 B+	Butcher, Max	.71 B-	Clark, Watty	.68 C+	Cunningham, Bert	.56 D
Bowa, Larry	.79 B+	Butler, Brett	.85 A	Clark, Will	.77 B+	Cunningham, Joe	.66 C
Boyer, Clete	.73 B-	Byrne, Bobby	.72 B-	Clarke, Fred	.83 A-	Cuppy, Nig	.69 C+
Boyer, Ken	.83 A-	Cabell, Enos	.78 B+	Clarke, Horace	.71 B-	Cutshaw, George	.84 A
Boyle, Henry	.67 C+	Calderon, Ivan	.62 C-	Clarkson, John	.72 B-	Cuyler, Kiki	.73 B-
Bradley, Bill	.82 A-	Caldwell, Mike	.60 D+	Clemente, Roberto	.83 A-	Dahlen, Bill	.82 A-
Bradley, George	.40 F	Caldwell, Ray	.66 C	Clements, Jack	.73 B-	Daily, Ed	.53 D-
Bradley, Phil	.75 B	Callahan, Nixey	.76 B	Clendenon, Donn	.72 B-	Dalrymple, Abner	.73 B-
Brandt, Ed	.63 C-	Callison, Johnny	.84 A	Clift, Harlond	.78 B+	Daly, Tom	.68 C+
Brandt, Jackie	.70 C+	Camilli, Dolph	.84 A	Cobb, Ty	.85 A	Daniels, Kal	.60 D+
Bransfield, Kitty	.66 C	Caminiti, Ken	.75 B	Cochrane, Mickey	.87 A	Danning, Harry	.71 B-
Braun, Steve	.81 A-	Camnitz, Howie	.67 C+	Colavito, Rocky	.78 B+	Dark, Al	.80 B+
Brazle, Al	.66 C	Campanella, Roy	.69 C+	Colbert, Nate	.75 B	Darling, Ron	.69 C+
Brecheen, Harry	.83 A-	Campaneris, Bert	.78 B+	Coleman, Joe	.75 B	Darwin, Danny	.68 C+
Breitenstein, Ted	.77 B+	Campbell, Bill	.65 C	Coleman, Vince	.71 B-	Daubert, Jake	.79 B+
Bresnahan, Roger	.72 B-	Campbell, Bruce	.77 B+	Collins, Dave	.65 C	Daulton, Darren	.58 D+
Bressler, Rube	.65 C	Candelaria, John	.73 B-	Collins, Eddie	.86 A	Dauss, Hooks	.76 B
Bressoud, Eddie	.59 D+	Candiotti, Tom	.70 B-	Collins, Hub	.74 B	Davalillo, Vic	.60 C-
Brett, George	.76 B	Canseco, Jose	.72 B-	Collins, Jimmy	.77 B	Davenport, Jim	.76 B
Brewer, Jim	.80 B+	Carbo, Bernie	.65 C	Collins, Rip	.49 F	Davis, Alvin	.73 B-
Bridges, Tommy	.82 A-	Cardenal, Jose	.76 B	Collins, Ripper	.76 B	Davis, Chili	.76 B
Bridwell, Al	.72 B-	Cardenas, Leo	.73 B	Collins, Shano	.72 B-	Davis, Curt	.70 C+
Briggs, John	.79 B+	Carew, Rod	.83 A-	Combs, Earle	.84 A	Davis, Eric	.67 C
Briles, Nelson	.69 C+	Carey, Max	.84 A	Comiskey, Charlie	.74 B	Davis, George	.81 A-
Brinkman, Ed	.73 B-	Carlson, Hal	.56 D	Concepcion, Dave	.84 A	Davis, Glenn	.67 C+
Brock, Lou	.83 A-	Carlton, Steve	.75 B	Cone, David	.78 B+	Davis, Harry	.79 B+
Brodie, Steve	.74 B	Carpenter, Hick	.74 B	Conigliaro, Tony	.64 C	Davis, Jody	.80 A-
Brooks, Hubie	.75 B	Carrasquel, Chico	.73 B	Connor, Roger	.85 A	Davis, Spud	.76 B
Brosius, Scott	.57 D+	Carroll, Clay	.67 C+	Conroy, Wid	.84 A	Davis, Tommy	.65 C
Brouthers, Dan	.81 A-	Carroll, Cliff	.66 C	Cooley, Duff	.68 C+	Davis, Willie	.84 A
Brown, Clint	.57 D+	Carroll, Fred	.70 C+	Coombs, Jack	.60 C-	Dawson, Andre	.85 A
Brown, Lloyd	.77 B+	Carter, Gary	.78 B+	Cooney, Johnny	.65 C	Dean, Dizzy	.77 B+
Brown, Three Finger	.81 A-	Carter, Joe	.78 B+	Cooper, Cecil	.83 A-	DeCinces, Doug	.75 B
Brown, Tom	.74 B	Carty, Rico	.51 D-	Cooper, Mort	.74 B	Deer, Rob	.77 B+
Browne, George	.78 B+	Caruthers, Bob	.83 A-	Cooper, Walker	.69 C+	DeJesus, Ivan	.72 B-
Browning, Pete	.73 B	Case, George	.73 B-	Cooper, Wilbur	.81 A-	Delahanty, Ed	.80 B+

Player	Consistency	Player	Consistency	Player	Consistency	Player	Consistency
Delahanty, Jim	.70 C+	Elberfeld, Kid	.68 C+	Forster, Terry	.62 C-	Goltz, Dave	.72 B-
Demaree, Frank	.65 C	Elliott, Bob	.81 A-	Foster, Eddie	.73 B-	Gomez, Lefty	.66 C
Demeter, Don	.71 B-	Ellis, Dock	.74 B	Foster, George	.81 A-	Gonzalez, Tony	.75 B
DeMontreville, Gene	.64 C	Ellsworth, Dick	.58 D+	Fothergill, Bob	.70 B-	Gooden, Dwight	.69 C+
Dempsey, Rick	.75 B	Ely, Bones	.67 C+	Fournier, Jack	.65 C	Goodman, Billy	.81 A-
Denny, Jerry	.79 B+	English, Woody	.78 B+	Foutz, Dave	.78 B+	Goodman, Ival	.76 B
Denny, John	.57 D+	Ennis, Del	.75 B	Fox, Nellie	.82 A-	Gordon, Joe	.76 B
Dent, Bucky	.72 B-	Epstein, Mike	.71 B-	Fox, Pete	.68 C+	Gordon, Sid	.76 B
Derringer, Paul	.78 B+	Erskine, Carl	.80 A-	Foxx, Jimmie	.84 A	Gore, George	.76 B
DeShields, Delino	.70 B-	Etten, Nick	.68 C+	Francona, Tito	.73 B-	Goslin, Goose	.86 A
Devlin, Art	.80 B+	Evans, Darrell	.79 B+	Frankhouse, Fred	.69 C+	Gossage, Goose	.72 B-
Devlin, Jim	.47 F	Evans, Dwight	.82 A-	Fraser, Chick	.74 B	Gowdy, Hank	.72 B-
Dickey, Bill	.81 A-	Evans, Steve	.63 C	Frederick, Johnny	.73 B	Grace, Mark	.83 A-
Dickson, Murry	.78 B+	Evers, Hoot	.67 C+	Freehan, Bill	.75 B	Grady, Mike	.59 D+
Dierker, Larry	.63 C-	Evers, Johnny	.76 B	Freeman, Buck	.73 B-	Graney, Jack	.68 C+
DiMaggio, Dom	.73 B-	Ewing, Bob	.80 B+	Fregosi, Jim	.83 A-	Grant, Mudcat	.63 C
DiMaggio, Joe	.75 B	Ewing, Buck	.74 B	French, Larry	.77 B+	Grantham, George	.83 A-
DiMaggio, Vince	.61 C-	Faber, Red	.76 B	Frey, Lonny	.76 B	Gray, Sam	.64 C
Dinneen, Bill	.84 A	Face, Roy	.71 B-	Friberg, Bernie	.68 C+	Green, Danny	.81 A-
Doak, Bill	.68 C+	Fain, Ferris	.79 B+	Friend, Bob	.80 A-	Green, Dick	.51 D-
Dobson, Joe	.70 B-	Fairly, Ron	.79 B+	Frisch, Frankie	.81 A-	Greenberg, Hank	.61 C-
Dobson, Pat	.68 C+	Falk, Bibb	.72 B-	Fryman, Travis	.75 B	Greenwell, Mike	.62 C-
Doby, Larry	.84 A	Falkenberg, Cy	.59 D+	Fryman, Woodie	.62 C-	Greer, Rusty	.79 B+
Doerr, Bobby	.76 B	Farrell, Duke	.80 B+	Fuentes, Tito	.60 D+	Gregg, Vean	.58 D+
Donahue, Red	.67 C+	Farrell, Jack	.75 B	Furillo, Carl	.78 B+	Grich, Bobby	.82 A-
Donlin, Mike	.43 F	Farrell, Turk	.60 C-	Gaetti, Gary	.81 A-	Griffey Sr., Ken	.80 A-
Donohue, Pete	.74 B	Feller, Bob	.72 B-	Gagne, Greg	.75 B	Griffin, Alfredo	.69 C+
Donovan, Dick	.72 B-	Felsch, Happy	.54 D	Galan, Augie	.72 B-	Griffin, Mike	.80 A-
Donovan, Patsy	.78 B+	Fennelly, Frank	.81 A-	Galehouse, Denny	.70 C+	Griffith, Clark	.72 B-
Donovan, Wild Bill	.74 B	Ferguson, Charlie	.65 C	Galvin, Pud	.66 C	Griffith, Tommy	.71 B-
Doolan, Mickey	.75 B	Ferguson, Joe	.62 C-	Gamble, Oscar	.75 B	Grimes, Burleigh	.71 B-
Doran, Bill	.77 B+	Fernandez, Alex	.65 C	Gandil, Chick	.73 B-	Grimm, Charlie	.78 B+
Dougherty, Patsy	.74 B	Fernandez, Sid	.72 B-	Gant, Ron	.60 C-	Groat, Dick	.77 B+
Douglas, Phil	.66 C	Fernandez, Tony	.81 A-	Gantner, Jim	.80 B+	Groh, Heine	.82 A-
Douthit, Taylor	.75 B	Ferrell, Rick	.81 A-	Garber, Gene	.65 C	Gromek, Steve	.60 D+
Downing, Al	.66 C	Ferrell, Wes	.79 B+	Garcia, Mike	.76 B	Groom, Bob	.77 B+
Downing, Brian	.77 B+	Ferris, Hobe	.75 B	Gardner, Larry	.80 B+	Gross, Greg	.70 C+
Doyle, Jack	.72 B-	Fielder, Cecil	.73 B-	Garner, Phil	.80 A-	Gross, Kevin	.80 A-
Doyle, Larry	.82 A-	Fingers, Rollie	.78 B+	Garr, Ralph	.73 B	Gross, Wayne	.65 C
Drabek, Doug	.79 B+	Finley, Chuck	.77 B+	Garrett, Wayne	.67 C+	Grote, Jerry	.65 C
Drabowsky, Moe	.54 D	Fisher, Eddie	.62 C-	Garver, Ned	.66 C	Groth, Johnny	.78 B+
Drago, Dick	.75 B	Fisher, Ray	.54 D	Garvey, Steve	.87 A+	Grove, Lefty	.81 A-
Driessen, Dan	.78 B+	Fisk, Carlton	.70 B-	Gaston, Milt	.63 C-	Grubb, Johnny	.66 C
Drysdale, Don	.81 A-	Fitzsimmons, Freddie	.76 B	Gehrig, Lou	.87 A+	Gubicza, Mark	.72 B-
Duffy, Hugh	.84 A	Flack, Max	.72 B-	Gehringer, Charlie	.84 A	Guerrero, Pedro	.65 C
Dugan, Joe	.79 B+	Flagstead, Ira	.73 B-	Gentile, Jim	.74 B	Guidry, Ron	.70 B-
Duncan, Mariano	.69 C+	Flanagan, Mike	.66 C	Gerber, Wally	.78 B+	Guillen, Ozzie	.70 C+
Dunlap, Fred	.71 B-	Fletcher, Art	.82 A-	Geronimo, Cesar	.74 B	Gullett, Don	.68 C+
Dunston, Shawon	.67 C+	Fletcher, Elbie	.65 C	Gessler, Doc	.64 C	Gullickson, Bill	.73 B-
Durham, Leon	.73 B-	Fletcher, Scott	.70 C+	Getzien, Charlie	.73 B	Gumbert, Ad	.78 B+
Durocher, Leo	.78 B+	Flick, Elmer	.78 B+	Gibson, Bob	.78 B+	Gumbert, Harry	.75 B
Dwyer, Frank	.77 B	Flood, Curt	.82 A-	Gibson, George	.71 B-	Gura, Larry	.71 B-
Dykes, Jimmy	.82 A-	Fogarty, Jim	.78 B+	Gibson, Kirk	.71 B-	Gustine, Frankie	.65 C
Dykstra, Lenny	.69 C+	Foli, Tim	.78 B+	Gilkey, Bernard	.66 C	Gwynn, Tony	.79 B+
Earnshaw, George	.63 C-	Ford, Dan	.67 C+	Gilliam, Jim	.72 B-	Haas, Mule	.79 B+
Easler, Mike	.59 D+	Ford, Hod	.77 B	Giusti, Dave	.70 B-	Hack, Stan	.80 B+
Eckersley, Dennis	.76 B	Ford, Russ	.60 C-	Gladden, Dan	.74 B	Haddix, Harvey	.71 B-
Edwards, Johnny	.78 B+	Ford, Whitey	.79 B+	Glasscock, Jack	.80 B+	Hadley, Bump	.64 C
Ehmke, Howard	.73 B-	Foreman, Frank	.40 F	Gleason, Bill	.81 A-	Hafey, Chick	.72 B-
Ehret, Red	.63 C-	Forsch, Bob	.63 C-	Gleason, Kid	.74 B	Hahn, Noodles	.76 B
Eisenreich, Jim	.65 C	Forsch, Ken	.76 B	Goldsmith, Fred	.75 B	Haines, Jesse	.71 B-

Player	Consistency	Player	Consistency	Player	Consistency	Player	Consistency
Hale, Odell	.79 B+	Hernandez, Willie	.64 C	Hutchison, Bill	.74 B	Kelly, George	.78 B+
Hall, Dick	.71 B-	Herndon, Larry	.75 B	Incaviglia, Pete	.66 C	Kelly, King	.85 A
Hall, Jimmie	.65 C	Herr, Tom	.75 B	Irwin, Arthur	.67 C+	Kelly, Pat	.75 B
Hall, Mel	.64 C	Hershiser, Orel	.73 B	Isbell, Frank	.68 C+	Kelly, Roberto	.80 B+
Hallahan, Wild Bill	.71 B-	Herzog, Buck	.75 B	Jackson, Danny	.56 D	Keltner, Ken	.67 C+
Haller, Tom	.83 A-	Hickman, Charlie	.81 A-	Jackson, Joe	.70 B-	Kemp, Steve	.77 B+
Hallman, Bill	.69 C+	Hickman, Jim	.66 C	Jackson, Larry	.80 A-	Kennedy, Brickyard	.72 B-
Hamilton, Billy	.82 A-	Higbe, Kirby	.71 B-	Jackson, Reggie	.78 B+	Kennedy, Terry	.73 B
Hamilton, Darryl	.72 B-	Higgins, Mike	.75 B	Jackson, Travis	.75 B	Kennedy, Vern	.61 C-
Hamilton, Earl	.70 B-	High, Andy	.62 C-	Jacobson, Baby Doll	.74 B	Kessinger, Don	.81 A-
Hamner, Granny	.81 A-	Higuera, Teddy	.73 B-	Jacoby, Brook	.73 B-	Key, Jimmy	.69 C+
Hands, Bill	.79 B+	Hill, Ken	.65 C	Jamieson, Charlie	.79 B+	Kile, Darryl	.61 C-
Hanlon, Ned	.84 A	Hiller, John	.60 D+	Jansen, Larry	.72 B-	Killebrew, Harmon	.81 A-
Hansen, Ron	.51 D-	Hinchman, Bill	.59 D+	Javier, Julian	.78 B+	Killen, Frank	.62 C-
Harder, Mel	.79 B+	Hines, Paul	.83 A-	Javier, Stan	.66 C	Killian, Ed	.51 D-
Hargrave, Bubbles	.66 C	Hinton, Chuck	.79 B+	Jefferies, Gregg	.75 B	Kilroy, Matt	.48 F
Hargrove, Mike	.83 A	Hisle, Larry	.66 C	Jenkins, Fergie	.79 B+	Kinder, Ellis	.72 B-
Harnisch, Pete	.55 D	Hoak, Don	.70 C+	Jennings, Hughie	.75 B	Kiner, Ralph	.78 B+
Harper, George	.54 D	Hoblitzell, Doc	.81 A-	Jensen, Jackie	.73 B-	King, Jeff	.68 C+
Harper, Tommy	.72 B-	Hodges, Gil	.86 A	John, Tommy	.76 B	King, Silver	.68 C+
Harrah, Toby	.78 B+	Hoeft, Billy	.66 C	Johnson, Alex	.58 D+	Kingman, Dave	.69 C+
Harrelson, Bud	.71 B-	Hoffer, Bill	.57 D+	Johnson, Bill	.56 D	Kitson, Frank	.76 B
Harris, Bucky	.81 A-	Hoffman, Danny	.74 B	Johnson, Bob	.82 A-	Klein, Chuck	.84 A
Harris, Greg	.70 B-	Hofman, Solly	.66 C	Johnson, Cliff	.68 C+	Kline, Ron	.61 C-
Harris, Joe	.57 D+	Hogan, Shanty	.74 B	Johnson, Dave	.78 B+	Kling, Johnny	.65 C
Hart, Jim Ray	.76 B	Hoiles, Chris	.77 B+	Johnson, Deron	.60 D+	Klippstein, Johnny	.59 D+
Hartnett, Gabby	.74 B	Holliday, Bug	.75 B	Johnson, Howard	.76 B	Kluszewski, Ted	.79 B+
Hartsel, Topsy	.80 A-	Hollins, Dave	.63 C-	Johnson, Lance	.74 B	Knabe, Otto	.77 B+
Hartzell, Roy	.77 B+	Hollocher, Charlie	.65 C	Johnson, Roy	.68 C+	Knepper, Bob	.52 D-
Hassey, Ron	.58 D+	Holmes, Ducky	.53 D	Johnson, Syl	.64 C	Knight, Ray	.63 C-
Hatton, Grady	.73 B-	Holmes, Tommy	.83 A-	Johnson, Walter	.81 A-	Knoblauch, Chuck	.81 A-
Hawley, Pink	.72 B-	Holtzman, Ken	.74 B	Johnston, Jimmy	.79 B+	Knowles, Darold	.63 C-
Hayes, Charlie	.72 B-	Honeycutt, Rick	.62 C-	Johnstone, Jay	.58 D+	Koenig, Mark	.76 B
Hayes, Frankie	.73 B-	Hooper, Harry	.82 A-	Jones, Charley	.70 B-	Konetchy, Ed	.83 A-
Hayes, Von	.77 B+	Hooton, Burt	.74 B	Jones, Cleon	.61 C-	Koosman, Jerry	.71 B-
Hearn, Jim	.65 C	Hopp, Johnny	.68 C+	Jones, Davy	.55 D	Koufax, Sandy	.74 B
Heath, Jeff	.72 B-	Horlen, Joe	.71 B-	Jones, Doug	.60 D+	Kranepool, Ed	.66 C
Heath, Mike	.77 B+	Horner, Bob	.68 C+	Jones, Fielder	.84 A	Kreevich, Mike	.71 B-
Heathcote, Cliff	.66 C	Hornsby, Rogers	.75 B	Jones, Mack	.62 C-	Kremer, Ray	.75 B
Hebner, Richie	.84 A	Hornung, Joe	.76 B	Jones, Puddin' Head	.82 A-	Kress, Red	.67 C+
Hecker, Guy	.71 B-	Horton, Willie	.79 B+	Jones, Randy	.56 D	Kruk, John	.79 B+
Hegan, Jim	.78 B+	Hough, Charlie	.78 B+	Jones, Ruppert	.64 C	Krukow, Mike	.69 C+
Heidrick, Emmett	.65 C	Howard, Elston	.71 B-	Jones, Sad Sam	.72 B-	Kubek, Tony	.73 B-
Heilmann, Harry	.83 A-	Howard, Frank	.80 A-	Jones, Sam	.71 B-	Kuehne, Bill	.74 B
Held, Woodie	.75 B	Howell, Harry	.76 B	Joost, Eddie	.67 C	Kuenn, Harvey	.80 A-
Helms, Tommy	.77 B+	Hoy, Dummy	.65 C	Joss, Addie	.79 B+	Kuhel, Joe	.71 B-
Hemphill, Charlie	.54 D	Hoyt, Waite	.81 A-	Joyce, Bill	.64 C	Kurowski, Whitey	.80 A-
Hemsley, Rollie	.72 B-	Hrbek, Kent	.85 A	Joyner, Wally	.79 B+	LaChance, Candy	.68 C+
Hemus, Solly	.59 D+	Hubbard, Glenn	.81 A-	Judge, Joe	.85 A	Lacy, Lee	.66 C
Henderson, Dave	.72 B-	Hubbell, Carl	.85 A	Judnich, Wally	.54 D	Lajoie, Nap	.76 B
Henderson, Hardie	.64 C	Hudlin, Willis	.68 C+	Jurges, Billy	.69 C+	Lamp, Dennis	.64 C
Henderson, Ken	.67 C+	Hudson, Sid	.54 D	Justice, David	.75 B	Landis, Jim	.78 B+
Henderson, Rickey	.84 A	Huggins, Miller	.77 B+	Kaat, Jim	.76 B	Landreaux, Ken	.74 B
Hendrick, George	.79 B+	Hughes, Long Tom	.49 F	Kaline, Al	.82 A-	Lange, Bill	.79 B+
Hendrix, Claude	.70 C+	Hughson, Tex	.51 D-	Kamm, Willie	.76 B	Langston, Mark	.67 C+
Henke, Tom	.76 B	Hummel, John	.80 B+	Kauff, Benny	.71 B-	Lanier, Max	.66 C
Henrich, Tommy	.71 B-	Hundley, Todd	.64 C	Keefe, Tim	.78 B+	Lansford, Carney	.73 B-
Herbert, Ray	.61 C-	Hunt, Ron	.72 B-	Keeler, Willie	.83 A-	Lansing, Mike	.70 B-
Herman, Babe	.82 A-	Hunter, Catfish	.76 B	Kell, George	.78 B+	LaPorte, Frank	.74 B
Herman, Billy	.75 B	Hurst, Bruce	.83 A	Keller, Charlie	.69 C+	Larkin, Henry	.82 A-
Hernandez, Keith	.84 A	Hutchinson, Fred	.72 B-	Kelley, Joe	.83 A-	Larkin, Terry	.61 C-

Player	Consistency	Player	Consistency	Player	Consistency	Player	Consistency
Lary, Frank	.64 C	Lord, Harry	.67 C+	Martinez, Ramon	.71 B-	McIntyre, Matty	.52 D-
Lary, Lyn	.70 B-	Lowe, Bobby	.83 A-	Masi, Phil	.76 B	McKean, Ed	.79 B+
Latham, Arlie	.76 B	Lowenstein, John	.67 C+	Mathews, Bobby	.60 C-	McLain, Denny	.60 C-
Lavagetto, Cookie	.70 C+	Lowrey, Peanuts	.62 C-	Mathews, Eddie	.86 A	McMahon, Don	.64 C
Lavelle, Gary	.74 B	Lucas, Red	.74 B	Mathewson, Christy	.85 A	McMahon, Sadie	.69 C+
Law, Vance	.62 C-	Luderus, Fred	.76 B	Matlack, Jon	.53 D-	McManus, Marty	.79 B+
Law, Vern	.56 D	Lumley, Harry	.63 C-	Matthews, Gary	.78 B+	McMillan, Roy	.80 B+
Lazzeri, Tony	.81 A-	Lumpe, Jerry	.83 A	Mattingly, Don	.81 A-	McMullen, Ken	.74 B
Leach, Tommy	.77 B+	Luque, Dolf	.71 B-	Maxwell, Charlie	.71 B-	McNally, Dave	.70 B-
Lee, Bill	.72 B-	Luzinski, Greg	.77 B+	May, Carlos	.71 B-	McPhee, Bid	.85 A
Lee, Bill	.59 D+	Lyle, Sparky	.74 B	May, Lee	.80 A-	McQuillan, George	.55 D
Lee, Thornton	.67 C+	Lynn, Fred	.73 B-	May, Milt	.69 C+	McQuinn, George	.75 B
Leever, Sam	.77 B+	Lyons, Denny	.71 B-	May, Rudy	.61 C-	McRae, Brian	.73 B-
Lefebvre, Jim	.72 B-	Lyons, Ted	.74 B	Mayberry, John	.73 B-	McRae, Hal	.75 B
LeFlore, Ron	.78 B+	Macfarlane, Mike	.75 B	Maye, Lee	.74 B	McReynolds, Kevin	.75 B
Leiber, Hank	.56 D	MacFayden, Danny	.72 B-	Mays, Carl	.69 C+	McTamany, Jim	.78 B+
Leibold, Nemo	.62 C-	Mack, Shane	.65 C	Mays, Willie	.83 A-	Meadows, Lee	.74 B
Leibrandt, Charlie	.65 C	Maddox, Garry	.81 A-	Mazeroski, Bill	.77 B+	Medich, Doc	.78 B+
Leifield, Lefty	.74 B	Madlock, Bill	.76 B	Mazzilli, Lee	.76 B	Medwick, Joe	.81 A-
Lemon, Bob	.80 B+	Magadan, Dave	.71 B-	McAuliffe, Dick	.83 A	Meekin, Jouett	.61 C-
Lemon, Chet	.83 A-	Magee, Lee	.68 C+	McBride, Bake	.74 B	Melton, Bill	.70 C+
Lemon, Jim	.72 B-	Magee, Sherry	.81 A-	McBride, George	.74 B	Menke, Denis	.69 C+
Leonard, Dennis	.73 B-	Maglie, Sal	.60 C-	McCarthy, Jack	.70 B-	Merced, Orlando	.69 C+
Leonard, Dutch	.70 C+	Majeski, Hank	.64 C	McCarthy, Tommy	.82 A-	Mercer, Win	.71 B-
Leonard, Dutch	.68 C+	Maldonado, Candy	.66 C	McCarver, Tim	.75 B	Merkle, Fred	.79 B+
Leonard, Jeffrey	.71 B-	Malone, Pat	.63 C	McCormick, Frank	.81 A-	Mertes, Sam	.83 A-
Lewis, Buddy	.71 B-	Maloney, Jim	.77 B	McCormick, Jim	.74 B	Messersmith, Andy	.74 B
Lewis, Duffy	.72 B-	Malzone, Frank	.83 A-	McCormick, Mike	.61 C-	Meusel, Bob	.79 B+
Lewis, Ted	.66 C	Mancuso, Gus	.71 B-	McCosky, Barney	.66 C	Meusel, Irish	.83 A-
Lezcano, Sixto	.70 B-	Mann, Les	.75 B	McCovey, Willie	.75 B	Meyers, Chief	.82 A-
Lindell, Johnny	.53 D-	Manning, Rick	.71 B-	McDaniel, Lindy	.55 D	Michaels, Cass	.74 B
Lindstrom, Freddy	.71 B-	Mantle, Mickey	.82 A-	McDougald, Gil	.82 A-	Milan, Clyde	.79 B+
Litwhiler, Danny	.65 C	Manush, Heinie	.75 B	McDowell, Jack	.75 B	Millan, Felix	.76 B
Lobert, Hans	.69 C+	Maranville, Rabbit	.75 B	McDowell, Roger	.69 C+	Miller, Bing	.83 A-
Lockman, Whitey	.74 B	Marberry, Firpo	.73 B-	McDowell, Sam	.67 C+	Miller, Doggie	.69 C+
Logan, Johnny	.77 B+	Marichal, Juan	.77 B+	McFarland, Ed	.66 C	Miller, Dots	.70 C+
Lolich, Mickey	.77 B+	Marion, Marty	.82 A-	McGann, Dan	.78 B+	Miller, Eddie	.70 C+
Lollar, Sherm	.79 B+	Maris, Roger	.75 B	McGee, Willie	.71 B-	Miller, Rick	.72 B-
Lombardi, Ernie	.77 B	Marquard, Rube	.69 C+	McGinnis, Jumbo	.59 D+	Miller, Stu	.64 C
Lonborg, Jim	.55 D	Marshall, Mike (of)	.69 C+	McGinnity, Joe	.79 B+	Milligan, Jocko	.67 C+
Long, Herman	.82 A-	Marshall, Mike (p)	.63 C-	McGraw, John	.73 B-	Milner, John	.71 B-
Lopat, Ed	.78 B+	Marshall, Willard	.64 C	McGraw, Tug	.66 C	Mincher, Don	.74 B
Lopata, Stan	.68 C+	Martin, Al	.69 C+	McGregor, Scott	.73 B-	Minoso, Minnie	.82 A-
Lopes, Davey	.79 B+	Martin, Pepper	.65 C	McGuire, Deacon	.74 B	Minton, Greg	.67 C+
Lopez, Al	.80 A-	Martinez, Dave	.73 B	McGwire, Mark	.75 B	Mitchell, Clarence	.70 C+
Lopez, Hector	.78 B+	Martinez, Dennis	.76 B	McInnis, Stuffy	.84 A	Mitchell, Dale	.80 B+

Now we have a method to pin it down, a method to state objectively who were the most consistent players of all time, a method to identify the most inconsistent players of all time, a method to study the issue of whether past consistency projects future success, a method to study objectively whether relief pitchers tend to be less consistent than starting pitchers.

Player	Consistency	Player	Consistency	Player	Consistency	Player	Consistency
Mitchell, Kevin	.69 C+	Nicholson, Bill	.80 B+	Pearson, Monte	.68 C+	Ramsey, Toad	.49 F
Mitchell, Mike	.72 B-	Niekro, Joe	.67 C+	Peckinpaugh, Roge	.82 A-	Randolph, Willie	.78 B+
Mize, Johnny	.77 B+	Niekro, Phil	.79 B+	Peitz, Heinie	.83 A-	Raschi, Vic	.83 A-
Mogridge, George	.69 C+	Nieman, Bob	.74 B	Pelty, Barney	.65 C	Rawley, Shane	.71 B-
Molitor, Paul	.75 B	Nixon, Otis	.81 A-	Pena, Tony	.74 B	Ray, Johnny	.78 B+
Monbouquette, Bill	.75 B	Nolan, Gary	.58 D+	Pendleton, Terry	.64 C	Reardon, Jeff	.84 A
Monday, Rick	.83 A-	Noren, Irv	.63 C-	Pennock, Herb	.75 B	Redus, Gary	.80 A-
Money, Don	.69 C+	Norman, Fred	.81 A-	Pepitone, Joe	.82 A-	Reed, Jody	.81 A-
Montanez, Willie	.77 B	North, Bill	.70 C+	Perez, Tony	.84 A	Reed, Ron	.78 B+
Montgomery, Jeff	.75 B	Northey, Ron	.65 C	Perranoski, Ron	.64 C	Reese, Pee Wee	.78 B+
Moon, Wally	.66 C	Northrup, Jim	.80 B+	Perry, Gaylord	.80 B+	Regan, Phil	.55 D
Moore, Charlie	.69 C+	Nuxhall, Joe	.71 B-	Perry, Jim	.73 B-	Reichardt, Rick	.75 B
Moore, Earl	.68 C+	Oakes, Rebel	.69 C+	Pesky, Johnny	.62 C-	Reilly, John	.72 B-
Moore, Gene	.58 D+	Oberkfell, Ken	.80 A-	Peters, Gary	.62 C-	Reiser, Pete	.52 D-
Moore, Jo-Jo	.85 A	O'Brien, Darby	.72 B-	Peterson, Fritz	.74 B	Remy, Jerry	.76 B
Moore, Mike	.70 C+	O'Brien, Pete	.72 B-	Petrocelli, Rico	.74 B	Renko, Steve	.66 C
Moore, Terry	.74 B	O'Connell, Danny	.58 D+	Petry, Dan	.73 B-	Rettenmund, Merv	.69 C+
Morandini, Mickey	.75 B	O'Connor, Jack	.69 C+	Pfeffer, Fred	.82 A-	Reulbach, Ed	.75 B
Moreland, Keith	.76 B	O'Dell, Billy	.63 C-	Pfeffer, Jeff	.65 C	Reuschel, Rick	.74 B
Moreno, Omar	.80 B+	O'Doul, Lefty	.69 C+	Philley, Dave	.80 A-	Reuss, Jerry	.65 C
Morgan, Joe	.80 A-	Oester, Ron	.69 C+	Phillippe, Deacon	.70 B-	Reynolds, Allie	.79 B+
Morgan, Mike	.62 C-	O'Farrell, Bob	.63 C	Phillips, Bill	.78 B+	Reynolds, Carl	.67 C+
Morrill, John	.82 A-	Oglivie, Ben	.77 B+	Phillips, Tony	.78 B+	Reynolds, Craig	.69 C+
Morris, Ed	.64 C	Ojeda, Bobby	.63 C-	Pierce, Billy	.81 A-	Reynolds, Harold	.76 B
Morris, Hal	.70 B-	Oldring, Rube	.69 C+	Piersall, Jimmy	.76 B	Rhines, Billy	.51 D-
Morris, Jack	.78 B+	O'Leary, Troy	.78 B+	Pinckney, George	.76 B	Rhoden, Rick	.65 C
Morrison, Johnny	.69 C+	Oliva, Tony	.78 B+	Piniella, Lou	.65 C	Rice, Del	.72 B-
Moseby, Lloyd	.82 A-	Oliver, Al	.85 A	Pinson, Vada	.80 A-	Rice, Harry	.71 B-
Moses, Wally	.79 B+	Olson, Ivy	.74 B	Pipp, Wally	.74 B	Rice, Jim	.78 B+
Mossi, Don	.71 B-	O'Neill, Paul	.84 A	Pittinger, Togie	.74 B	Rice, Sam	.82 A-
Mostil, Johnny	.61 C-	O'Neill, Steve	.77 B+	Pizarro, Juan	.65 C	Richard, J.R.	.74 B
Mota, Manny	.79 B+	O'Neill, Tip	.78 B+	Plank, Eddie	.80 B+	Richards, Gene	.74 B
Mowrey, Mike	.66 C	Orosco, Jesse	.72 B-	Plesac, Dan	.74 B	Richardson, Bobby	.76 B
Mueller, Ray	.47 F	O'Rourke, Jim	.86 A	Podres, Johnny	.71 B-	Richardson, Danny	.71 B-
Mullane, Tony	.72 B-	Orr, Dave	.77 B+	Pollet, Howie	.58 D+	Richardson, Hardy	.78 B+
Mullin, George	.77 B+	Orta, Jorge	.72 B-	Polonia, Luis	.73 B-	Righetti, Dave	.81 A-
Mulliniks, Rance	.73 B-	Orth, Al	.78 B+	Porter, Darrell	.76 B	Rijo, Jose	.70 B-
Mumphrey, Jerry	.75 B	Osteen, Claude	.77 B+	Porter, Henry	.64 C	Ring, Jimmy	.72 B-
Mungo, Van Lingle	.61 C-	Ostermueller, Fritz	.58 D+	Portugal, Mark	.60 C-	Ripken Jr., Cal	.84 A
Munson, Thurman	.81 A-	Otis, Amos	.80 A-	Post, Wally	.73 B-	Ritchey, Claude	.85 A
Murcer, Bobby	.85 A	Ott, Mel	.87 A+	Potter, Nels	.63 C-	Rivera, Jim	.79 B+
Murphy, Dale	.80 B+	Overall, Orval	.59 D+	Powell, Boog	.76 B	Rivers, Mickey	.75 B
Murphy, Danny	.81 A-	Owen, Spike	.72 B-	Powell, Jack	.71 B-	Rixey, Eppa	.74 B
Murphy, Dwayne	.76 B	Paciorek, Tom	.73 B	Power, Vic	.70 B-	Rizzuto, Phil	.69 C+
Murphy, Johnny	.66 C	Pafko, Andy	.75 B	Pratt, Del	.82 A-	Roberts, Bip	.65 C
Murray, Eddie	.86 A	Pagliarulo, Mike	.64 C	Priddy, Jerry	.62 C-	Roberts, Dave	.60 C-
Murray, Red	.76 B	Palmer, Dean	.77 B+	Puckett, Kirby	.84 A	Roberts, Robin	.83 A-
Musial, Stan	.79 B+	Palmer, Jim	.74 B	Puhl, Terry	.76 B	Robinson, Bill	.60 D+
Myer, Buddy	.77 B+	Pappas, Milt	.79 B+	Purcell, Blondie	.70 B-	Robinson, Brooks	.83 A-
Myers, Hi	.76 B	Parent, Freddy	.71 B-	Purkey, Bob	.64 C	Robinson, Don	.61 C-
Myers, Randy	.71 B-	Parker, Dave	.79 B+	Quinn, Jack	.68 C+	Robinson, Eddie	.79 B+
Nagy, Charles	.58 D+	Parker, Wes	.75 B	Quinn, Joe	.66 C	Robinson, Floyd	.76 B
Nash, Billy	.85 A	Parnell, Mel	.65 C	Quisenberry, Dan	.73 B-	Robinson, Frank	.82 A-
Neagle, Denny	.77 B	Parrish, Lance	.79 B+	Radbourn, Old Hos	.71 B-	Robinson, Jackie	.81 A-
Nehf, Art	.73 B-	Parrish, Larry	.69 C+	Radcliff, Rip	.66 C	Robinson, Wilbert	.72 B-
Nen, Robb	.68 C+	Pascual, Camilo	.72 B-	Rader, Doug	.81 A-	Robinson, Yank	.78 B+
Nettles, Graig	.85 A	Paskert, Dode	.70 B-	Radford, Paul	.74 B	Rodriguez, Aurelio	.77 B+
Newcombe, Don	.67 C+	Passeau, Claude	.75 B	Raffensberger, Ken	.58 D+	Roe, Preacher	.70 C+
Newhouser, Hal	.78 B+	Patek, Freddie	.78 B+	Raines, Tim	.85 A	Rogell, Billy	.79 B+
Newsom, Bobo	.75 B	Pattin, Marty	.72 B-	Ramirez, Rafael	.65 C	Rogers, Steve	.71 B-
Nichols, Kid	.78 B+	Pearson, Albie	.51 D-	Ramos, Pedro	.80 B+	Rojas, Cookie	.72 B-

Player	Consistency	Player	Consistency	Player	Consistency	Player	Consistency
Rolfe, Red	.77 B+	Schmitz, Johnny	.65 C	Slagle, Jimmy	.78 B+	Stennett, Rennie	.79 B+
Romano, John	.74 B	Schoendienst, Red	.80 B+	Slaton, Jim	.67 C+	Stenzel, Jake	.76 B
Rommel, Eddie	.83 A-	Schofield, Dick	.74 B	Slaught, Don	.75 B	Stephens, Vern	.82 A-
Rooker, Jim	.66 C	Schulte, Fred	.75 B	Slaughter, Enos	.71 B-	Stephenson, Riggs	.72 B-
Root, Charlie	.77 B+	Schulte, Wildfire	.76 B	Smalley, Roy	.72 B-	Stewart, Dave	.72 B-
Rose, Pete	.88 A+	Schumacher, Hal	.79 B+	Smiley, John	.62 C-	Stewart, Lefty	.75 B
Roseboro, John	.80 A-	Scioscia, Mike	.73 B-	Smith, Al	.81 A-	Stieb, Dave	.79 B+
Rosen, Al	.75 B	Scott, Everett	.77 B+	Smith, Bob	.78 B+	Stirnweiss, Snuffy	.70 C+
Roth, Braggo	.77 B+	Scott, George	.77 B+	Smith, Bryn	.71 B-	Stivetts, Jack	.76 B
Roush, Edd	.71 B-	Scott, Jack	.49 F	Smith, Dave	.70 C+	Stock, Milt	.73 B
Rowe, Jack	.81 A-	Scott, Jim	.58 D+	Smith, Elmer	.64 C	Stone, George	.70 C+
Rowe, Schoolboy	.57 D+	Scott, Mike	.64 C	Smith, Elmer	.60 C-	Stone, John	.78 B+
Rucker, Nap	.79 B+	Seaver, Tom	.78 B+	Smith, Frank	.60 D+	Stottlemyre, Mel	.73 B-
Rudi, Joe	.73 B-	Seery, Emmett	.58 D+	Smith, Germany	.79 B+	Stottlemyre, Todd	.78 B+
Rudolph, Dick	.67 C+	Segui, Diego	.73 B-	Smith, Jack	.66 C	Stovall, George	.70 B-
Ruel, Muddy	.82 A-	Seitzer, Kevin	.76 B	Smith, Lee	.86 A	Stovey, Harry	.82 A-
Ruether, Dutch	.66 C	Selbach, Kip	.79 B+	Smith, Lonnie	.70 B-	Strang, Sammy	.63 C
Ruffing, Red	.83 A-	Selkirk, George	.70 B-	Smith, Ozzie	.76 B	Stratton, Scott	.45 F
Runnels, Pete	.72 B-	Seminick, Andy	.80 A-	Smith, Pop	.72 B-	Strawberry, Darryl	.78 B+
Rush, Bob	.75 B	Severeid, Hank	.79 B+	Smith, Red	.84 A	Stricker, Cub	.71 B-
Rusie, Amos	.68 C+	Seward, Ed	.59 D+	Smith, Reggie	.78 B+	Stripp, Joe	.73 B-
Russell, Bill	.74 B	Sewell, Joe	.82 A-	Smith, Sherry	.67 C+	Strunk, Amos	.80 A-
Russell, Jack	.71 B-	Sewell, Luke	.71 B-	Smith, Zane	.67 C+	Stuart, Dick	.69 C+
Russell, Jeff	.65 C	Sewell, Rip	.78 B+	Snider, Duke	.84 A	Sudhoff, Willie	.68 C+
Russell, Jim	.73 B	Seybold, Socks	.83 A-	Snodgrass, Fred	.70 C+	Suggs, George	.57 D+
Russell, Reb	.56 D	Seymour, Cy	.75 B	Snyder, Frank	.71 B-	Suhr, Gus	.74 B
Ruth, Babe	.84 A	Shaffer, Orator	.58 D+	Soto, Mario	.73 B	Sullivan, Frank	.76 B
Ruthven, Dick	.54 D	Shanks, Howard	.77 B+	Southworth, Billy	.66 C	Sundberg, Jim	.80 A-
Ryan, Connie	.61 C-	Shantz, Bobby	.66 C	Spahn, Warren	.80 A-	Sutcliffe, Rick	.59 D+
Ryan, Jimmy	.77 B+	Shaute, Joe	.62 C-	Sparks, Tully	.68 C+	Sutter, Bruce	.68 C+
Ryan, Nolan	.81 A-	Shaw, Bob	.61 C-	Speaker, Tris	.84 A	Sutton, Don	.82 A-
Saberhagen, Bret	.56 D+	Shawkey, Bob	.69 C+	Speier, Chris	.75 B	Sutton, Ezra	.79 B+
Sabo, Chris	.61 C-	Sheckard, Jimmy	.78 B+	Spence, Stan	.62 C-	Swartwood, Ed	.56 D
Sadecki, Ray	.58 D+	Sheely, Earl	.66 C	Spencer, Daryl	.71 B-	Sweeney, Bill	.78 B+
Saier, Vic	.73 B-	Sherdel, Bill	.76 B	Spencer, Jim	.69 C+	Swift, Bill	.75 B
Sain, Johnny	.65 C	Shindle, Billy	.76 B	Splittorff, Paul	.75 B	Swift, Bill	.73 B-
Sallee, Slim	.78 B+	Shocker, Urban	.87 A+	Stahl, Chick	.69 C+	Swindell, Greg	.74 B
Samuel, Juan	.78 B+	Short, Chris	.71 B-	Stahl, Jake	.55 D	Tanana, Frank	.76 B
Sandberg, Ryne	.79 B+	Shotton, Burt	.75 B	Staley, Gerry	.67 C+	Tannehill, Jesse	.79 B+
Sanders, Ben	.65 C	Siebern, Norm	.77 B	Staley, Harry	.81 A-	Tapani, Kevin	.77 B
Sanderson, Scott	.69 C+	Siebert, Sonny	.77 B+	Stanky, Eddie	.74 B	Tartabull, Danny	.73 B-
Sanford, Jack	.61 C-	Sievers, Roy	.74 B	Stanley, Bob	.76 B	Taylor, Jack	.77 B+
Sanguillen, Manny	.78 B+	Simmons, Al	.84 A	Stanley, Mickey	.79 B+	Taylor, Jack	.70 B-
Santo, Ron	.83 A-	Simmons, Curt	.65 C	Stanley, Mike	.77 B+	Taylor, Luther	.76 B
Sauer, Hank	.70 B-	Simmons, Ted	.77 B+	Stargell, Willie	.79 B+	Taylor, Tony	.71 B-
Sax, Steve	.73 B-	Singer, Bill	.48 F	Start, Joe	.82 A-	Tebbetts, Birdie	.75 B
Schaal, Paul	.59 D+	Singleton, Ken	.78 B+	Staub, Rusty	.81 A-	Tebeau, Patsy	.70 C+
Schaefer, Germany	.63 C-	Sisler, George	.77 B+	Stein, Ed	.63 C-	Tekulve, Kent	.78 B+
Schalk, Ray	.70 B-	Sizemore, Ted	.65 C	Steinbach, Terry	.78 B+	Temple, Johnny	.80 B+
Schang, Wally	.79 B+	Skinner, Bob	.63 C-	Steinfeldt, Harry	.74 B	Templeton, Garry	.78 B+
Schmidt, Mike	.85 A	Skowron, Bill	.72 B-	Stengel, Casey	.68 C+	Tenace, Gene	.81 A-

Pete Reiser's best season was better than Billy Williams' best season—but Reiser had two good years, Williams had twelve.

Player	Consistency	Player	Consistency	Player	Consistency	Player	Consistency
Tenney, Fred	.78 B+	Uhle, George	.68 C+	Washington, Claud	.73 B-	Wilson, Don	.77 B+
Terry, Adonis	.66 C	Unser, Del	.65 C	Watson, Bob	.81 A-	Wilson, Earl	.75 B
Terry, Bill	.80 B+	Upshaw, Willie	.77 B	Weaver, Buck	.67 C+	Wilson, Hack	.74 B
Terry, Ralph	.70 B-	Valentin, John	.71 B-	Webster, Mitch	.70 C+	Wilson, Jimmie	.81 A-
Tesreau, Jeff	.78 B+	Valenzuela, Fernan	.71 B-	Weilman, Carl	.62 C-	Wilson, Mookie	.76 B
Tettleton, Mickey	.79 B+	Valo, Elmer	.68 C+	Weimer, Jake	.71 B-	Wilson, Willie	.76 B
Tewksbury, Bob	.65 C	Van Haltren, Geor	.85 A	Weiss, Walt	.64 C	Wiltse, Hooks	.80 A-
Thomas, Derrel	.67 C+	Van Slyke, Andy	.78 B+	Welch, Bob	.74 B	Winfield, Dave	.80 B+
Thomas, Gorman	.67 C+	Vance, Dazzy	.73 B-	Welch, Curt	.79 B+	Wingo, Ivy	.73 B-
Thomas, Roy	.85 A	Vander Meer, John	.55 D	Welch, Mickey	.74 B	Wise, Rick	.66 C
Thomas, Tommy	.69 C+	Vangilder, Elam	.65 C	Werber, Bill	.75 B	Wise, Sam	.70 B-
Thompson, Hank	.68 C+	Vaughan, Arky	.80 A-	Wertz, Vic	.75 B	Witt, Bobby	.54 D
Thompson, Jason	.73 B	Vaughn, Greg	.69 C+	West, Sammy	.83 A	Witt, Mike	.73 B-
Thompson, Milt	.69 C+	Vaughn, Hippo	.79 B+	Wetteland, John	.79 B+	Witt, Whitey	.64 C
Thompson, Robby	.72 B-	Vaughn, Mo	.76 B	Weyhing, Gus	.80 A-	Wolf, Chicken	.72 B-
Thompson, Sam	.78 B+	Veach, Bobby	.80 A-	Wheat, Zack	.80 A-	Wood, George	.78 B+
Thomson, Bobby	.67 C+	Veale, Bob	.73 B-	Whitaker, Lou	.85 A	Wood, Joe	.57 D+
Thon, Dickie	.61 C-	Velarde, Randy	.60 C-	White, Bill	.77 B+	Wood, Wilbur	.78 B+
Thornton, Andre	.65 C	Vernon, Mickey	.68 C+	White, Deacon	.72 B-	Woodling, Gene	.80 A-
Tiant, Luis	.73 B	Versalles, Zoilo	.73 B-	White, Devon	.70 C+	Worrell, Todd	.60 C-
Tidrow, Dick	.70 C+	Viola, Frank	.74 B	White, Doc	.85 A	Worthington, Al	.72 B-
Tiernan, Mike	.83 A-	Virdon, Bill	.73 B-	White, Frank	.81 A-	Wright, Glenn	.67 C+
Tinker, Joe	.84 A	Vosmik, Joe	.70 C+	White, Roy	.79 B+	Wright, Taffy	.67 C+
Titus, John	.81 A-	Waddell, Rube	.81 A-	White, Will	.64 C	Wyatt, Whit	.56 D
Tobin, Jack	.69 C+	Wagner, Heinie	.64 C	Whitehill, Earl	.78 B+	Wynegar, Butch	.71 B-
Tobin, Jim	.73 B	Wagner, Honus	.89 A+	Whitney, Jim	.74 B	Wynn, Early	.71 B-
Tolan, Bobby	.47 F	Wagner, Leon	.75 B	Whitney, Pinky	.77 B	Wynn, Jimmy	.69 C+
Toney, Fred	.72 B-	Waitkus, Eddie	.68 C+	Whitson, Ed	.59 D+	Wyrostek, Johnny	.70 B-
Torgeson, Earl	.69 C+	Walberg, Rube	.76 B	Whitt, Ernie	.83 A-	Yastrzemski, Carl	.84 A
Torre, Joe	.79 B+	Walker, Curt	.76 B	Whitted, Possum	.69 C+	Yeager, Steve	.76 B
Torrez, Mike	.73 B-	Walker, Dixie	.78 B+	Wiedman, Stump	.58 D+	York, Rudy	.74 B
Tovar, Cesar	.75 B	Walker, Gee	.78 B+	Wilcox, Milt	.75 B	York, Tom	.75 B
Trammell, Alan	.72 B-	Walker, Tilly	.69 C+	Wilhelm, Hoyt	.79 B+	Yost, Eddie	.82 A-
Travis, Cecil	.66 C	Wallace, Bobby	.85 A	Williams, Billy	.86 A	Young, Cy	.85 A
Traynor, Pie	.84 A	Wallach, Tim	.75 B	Williams, Cy	.83 A-	Youngs, Ross	.80 A-
Tresh, Tom	.78 B+	Walsh, Ed	.73 B-	Williams, Jimmy	.78 B+	Yount, Robin	.83 A-
Triandos, Gus	.74 B	Walters, Bucky	.78 B+	Williams, Ken	.79 B+	Zachary, Tom	.70 C+
Trillo, Manny	.80 A-	Wambsganss, Bill	.82 A-	Williams, Matt	.72 B-	Zahn, Geoff	.68 C+
Trosky, Hal	.68 C+	Waner, Lloyd	.76 B	Williams, Stan	.61 C-	Zernial, Gus	.77 B+
Trout, Dizzy	.67 C+	Waner, Paul	.86 A	Williams, Ted	.70 C+	Zimmer, Chief	.78 B+
Trucks, Virgil	.60 C-	Ward, Aaron	.64 C	Williamson, Ned	.81 A-	Zimmerman, Heinie	.79 B+
Tucker, Tommy	.78 B+	Ward, Gary	.73 B-	Willis, Vic	.74 B	Zisk, Richie	.83 A-
Tudor, John	.58 D+	Ward, Monte	.78 B+	Wills, Maury	.79 B+		
Turner, Terry	.70 C+	Ward, Pete	.64 C	Wilmot, Walt	.72 B-		
Tyler, Lefty	.71 B-	Warneke, Lon	.83 A-	Wilson, Chief	.77 B+		

Hitters are more consistent than pitchers, but actually not as much as I would have guessed.

Improving the System

I think that this is a good system, and I am fairly confident that certain elements of it will stand the test of time. However, it is one thing to say that this is a good system, and a very different thing to suggest that it is a perfect system which could never be improved. It is not a perfect system; so let's take a moment to look at how it could be improved.

I see essentially two problems with this method. First, the method looks only at consistency of *value*, rather than consistency of *type*. Wally Moses, for example, scores as a consistent player—a player of "B+" consistency.

Wally Moses had a very odd career in which he did many things well, but usually not at the same time. One year he hit 25 homers; in the rest of his career he never hit more than eight. One year he stole 56 bases; in the rest of his career he never stole more than 21. One year he hit .345; another year, .239.

However, most of these up-and-down swings in Moses' career reflect the context in which he played. The year he hit 25 homers (and also 48 doubles, 13 triples) the league ERA was 5.04, and Moses was playing in a hitter's park. The year Moses hit .245 with 3 homers but 56 stolen bases, the league ERA was 3.30, and he wasn't playing in a hitter's park.

Moses' *value* was fairly consistent, but his performance in specific categories was all over the map. You can call these performance swings what you like, but one thing a lot of people would call them is "inconsistency". A system of evaluating consistency *could* consider not merely the consistency of overall value, but the consistency of performance in specific areas of the game—the consistency of power, the consistency of batting average, etc.

The second problem is the problem of consistency of *performance*, as opposed to consistency of *opportunity*. Pete Reiser, in the example we gave above, takes a huge hit in his consistency number because of the gap in his career caused by World War II. So do Ted Williams, Bob Feller, Hank Greenberg, Stan Musial, etc. Anybody who has a gap in his career gets a bunch of "inconsistency points" which are completely unrelated to his individual performance.

The same is true of injuries…Willie Randolph, who I always think of as the model of consistency, scores as only a "B+" because of a couple of injury-shortened seasons.

You could take out the World War II problem by considering Ted Williams' 1942 and 1946 seasons to be consecutive. The problem is, does this really solve the problem? What about the Korean War? What about the partial seasons—Greenberg playing a few games in 1941 and half a season in 1945? How do you adjust for those things?

I don't know. I'm sure there is a way to do it, but I am uncertain as to whether it should be done. Rico Carty, let's say. Rico had as inconsistent a career as anybody you can name—became of repeated injuries and illnesses. Is it better to say that Rico was a consistent hitter when he was healthy, or is it better to say that, because of miscellaneous health problems, Rico was never able to perform consistently at the best of his ability? It seems to me that the latter statement is better—and thus, that it is better not to adjust for opportunity. But there would be another way to look at the issue.

The most consistent player of all time was…you probably know this, too…Henry Aaron.

Minnesota Twins

Description		Ranking
Won-Lost Record	79-83	
Place	3rd of 5 in American League Central	
Runs Scored	718	25th in the majors
Runs Allowed	725	7th in the majors
Home Runs	118	29th in the majors
Home Runs Allowed	185	25th in the majors
Batting Average	.264	18th in the majors
Batting Average Allowed	.269	19th in the majors
Walks Drawn	512	19th in the majors
Walks Given	420	2nd in the majors
OPS For	.721	27th in the majors
OPS Against	.755	15th in the majors
Stolen Bases	112	9th in the majors
Stolen Bases Allowed	65	2nd in the majors

Key Players

Pos	Player	G	AB	R	H	2B	3B	HR	RBI	SB	CS	BB	SO	Avg	OBP	Slg	OPS	WS
C	Joe Mauer	109	406	62	119	27	3	7	60	7	1	57	51	.293	.382	.426	.808	21
1B	Justin Morneau	157	590	84	160	31	3	31	111	1	1	64	91	.271	.343	.492	.834	18
2B	Luis Castillo	85	349	54	106	11	3	0	18	9	4	29	28	.304	.356	.352	.709	9
3B	Nick Punto	150	472	53	99	18	4	1	25	16	6	55	90	.210	.291	.271	.562	5
SS	Jason Bartlett	140	510	75	135	20	7	5	43	23	3	50	73	.265	.339	.361	.699	16
LF	Jason Kubel	128	418	49	114	31	2	13	65	5	0	41	79	.273	.335	.450	.785	12
CF	Torii Hunter	160	600	94	172	45	1	28	107	18	9	40	101	.287	.334	.505	.839	22
RF	Michael Cuddyer	144	547	87	151	28	5	16	81	5	0	64	107	.276	.356	.433	.790	16
DH	Mike Redmond	82	272	23	80	13	0	1	38	0	0	18	23	.294	.346	.353	.699	11

Key Pitchers

Pos	Player	G	GS	W	L	Sv	IP	H	R	ER	BB	SO	BR/9	ERA	WS
SP	Johan Santana	33	33	15	13	0	219.0	183	88	81	52	235	9.82	3.33	17
SP	Carlos Silva	33	33	13	14	0	202.0	229	99	94	36	89	11.99	4.19	11
SP	Boof Bonser	31	30	8	12	0	173.0	199	108	98	65	136	13.99	5.10	4
SP	Scott Baker	24	23	9	9	0	143.2	162	70	68	29	102	12.28	4.26	8
SP	Matt Garza	16	15	5	7	0	83.0	96	44	34	32	67	14.31	3.69	4
CL	Joe Nathan	68	0	4	2	37	71.2	54	15	15	19	77	9.29	1.88	16
RP	Pat Neshek	74	0	7	2	0	70.1	44	25	23	27	74	9.34	2.94	8
RP	Matt Guerrier	73	0	2	4	1	88.0	71	23	23	21	68	9.92	2.35	9

Runnin' on Empty

Twins' seventh-place hitters had a .662 OPS, second-lowest in the major leagues (ahead of the White Sox at .660).

Their eight-place hitters had a .605 OPS, also second-lowest in the majors (ahead of Toronto at .594).

Their ninth-place hitters had an OPS of .582, lowest in the American League, and lower than the Cardinals in the National League.

As a whole, the bottom third of the Twins' order was by far the weakest in the major leagues.

Minnesota Twins– 2007
Productivity by Batting Order Position

Pos	Players	Avg	OBP	Slg	OPS
1	Castillo (85g), Casilla (28g), Tyner (24g)	.275	.331	.328	.659
2	Bartlett (60g), Punto (37g), Mauer (18g)	.257	.326	.378	.704
3	Mauer (88g), Cuddyer (38g), Hunter (30g)	.283	.365	.421	.787
4	Morneau (80g), Cuddyer (59g), Hunter (23g)	.293	.356	.475	.831
5	Morneau (77g), Hunter (59g), Cuddyer (24g)	.272	.340	.494	.834
6	Hunter (46g), Kubel (41g), Redmond (32g)	.291	.343	.456	.799
7	Kubel (50g), Redmond (27g), White (22g)	.239	.306	.356	.662
8	Rodriguez (28g), Tyner (24g), Punto (20g)	.231	.297	.308	.605
9	Punto (73g), Bartlett (45g), Casilla (20g)	.230	.293	.289	.582
	Total	.264	.330	.391	.721

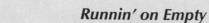

Drop Back Seven and Punto

On balls put in play as a right-handed batter in 2006 Nick Punto hit .362.
In 2007, that dropped to .200.

Nick Punto
Hitting Analysis

	Batting Left-handed			Batting Right-handed		
	Balls in Play	Hits	Avg	Balls in Play	Hits	Avg
2006	253	79	.326	155	54	.362
2007	252	72	.291	139	27	.200

Note: Balls in Play include sacrifice hits and flies which don't count as at-bats.
At-bats are used for batting averages (Avg).

That Magic Moment

The Twins had a great year in 2006, and Justin Morneau won the American League Most Valuable Player Award, in large part because Morneau hit .377 with 39 RBI in clutch situations.

They had a miserable season in 2007 in part because Morneau hit .213 with 9 RBI in clutch situations. Joe Mauer had a similar if less dramatic decline in clutch performance.

For the sake of clarity, we take no position on the issue of whether some players have an ability to come through in the clutch, or whether clutch performance is a random abberation. We simply believe that it can't hurt to define a clutch situation and put the data on record.

Justin Morneau
Clutch Hitting

Season	AB	H	2B	3B	HR	RBI	BB	SO	GIDP	Avg	OBP	Slg
2003	15	4	1	0	1	5	2	5	0	.267	.353	.533
2004	53	14	4	0	3	13	7	13	1	.264	.339	.509
2005	66	18	6	0	0	17	9	10	5	.273	.351	.364
2006	77	29	6	0	6	39	8	14	1	.377	.427	.688
2007	47	10	1	0	3	9	8	10	1	.213	.339	.426
Totals	258	75	18	0	13	83	34	52	8	.291	.369	.512

Joe Mauer
Clutch Hitting

Season	AB	H	2B	3B	HR	RBI	BB	SO	GIDP	Avg	OBP	Slg
2004	12	4	0	0	1	6	2	2	0	.333	.375	.583
2005	58	16	4	0	0	14	16	6	3	.276	.427	.345
2006	53	18	5	0	3	22	9	6	3	.340	.429	.604
2007	41	9	1	0	1	13	8	8	2	.220	.347	.317
Totals	164	47	10	0	5	55	35	22	8	.287	.404	.439

An Off Year

Opposing hitters batted .209 and slugged .310 against Joe Nathan last year. It was the first time in his five years as a closer that they hit over .200 or slugged over .300 against him.

Joe Nathan
Record of Opposing Batters

Season	AB	R	H	2B	3B	HR	RBI	BB	SO	SB	CS	GIDP	Avg	OBP	Slg	OPS
2002	12	0	1	1	0	0	0	0	2	0	0	0	.083	.083	.167	.250
2003	274	26	51	10	0	7	36	33	83	5	1	4	.186	.274	.299	.573
2004	257	14	48	9	0	3	14	23	89	4	3	3	.187	.254	.257	.510
2005	251	22	46	11	0	5	19	22	94	2	1	2	.183	.249	.287	.536
2006	240	12	38	7	2	3	13	16	95	2	0	1	.158	.211	.242	.453
2007	258	15	54	14	0	4	18	19	77	7	0	4	.209	.264	.310	.574

Johan Santana Against a Sub-.400 Team

If that sounds like a mismatch to you, you'd be right—he's won 19 of 20 decisions against sub-.400 teams since the start of 2002. But even Santana's biggest admirers might be surprised to know that he's won seven of eight decisions against .600 teams over that period.

Johan Santana
Career Records Against Quality of Opposition

Opponent	G	IP	W	L	SO	BB	ERA
.600 teams	16	88.1	7	1	106	30	2.04
.500 - .599 teams	86	475.1	28	27	486	123	3.26
.400 - .499 teams	71	435.1	36	12	497	95	3.02
sub .400 teams	33	180.0	19	1	200	46	2.25

Scott Baker hardly threw his slider at all in 2006 (3%), but in 2007 he began using it as his primary complement to his fastball (25%), and his ERA fell by more than two full runs.

Scott Baker – 2006
Pitch Type Analysis

Overall

Total Pitches	1441	
Fastball	940	65%
Curveball	200	14%
Changeup	218	15%
Slider	43	3%
Cut Fastball	18	1%
Pitchout	1	0%
Not Charted	21	1%

	Vs. RHB		Vs. LHB	
Total Pitches	711		730	
Outs Recorded	134		116	
Fastball	452	64%	488	67%
Curveball	100	14%	100	14%
Changeup	99	14%	119	16%
Slider	37	5%	6	1%
Cut Fastball	14	2%	4	1%
Pitchout	0	0%	1	0%
Not Charted	9	1%	12	2%

Scott Baker – 2007
Pitch Type Analysis

Overall

Total Pitches	2097	
Fastball	1232	59%
Curveball	143	7%
Changeup	157	7%
Slider	516	25%
Pitchout	2	0%
Not Charted	47	2%

	Vs. RHB		Vs. LHB	
Total Pitches	1085		1012	
Outs Recorded	248		183	
Fastball	609	56%	623	62%
Curveball	38	4%	105	10%
Changeup	51	5%	106	10%
Slider	362	33%	154	15%
Pitchout	2	0%	0	0%
Not Charted	23	2%	24	2%

The Minnesota Twins were the slowest-starting team in the major leagues in 2007. They were 23 games below .500 at the end of the first inning. Other slow starters included the Cardinals, –20 after the first inning, and the Rangers, at –19.

Minnesota Twins – 2007
Innings Ahead/Behind/Tied

Inning	1	2	3	4	5	6	7	8	9	Extra	Final
Ahead	26	47	61	64	67	68	68	70	74	5	79
Behind	49	59	71	71	73	78	77	74	75	7	83
Tied	87	56	30	27	22	18	16	17	12	12	—

New York Mets

New York Mets – 2007
Team Overview

Description		Ranking
Won-Lost Record	88-74	
Place	2nd of 5 in National League East	
Runs Scored	804	10th in the majors
Runs Allowed	750	12th in the majors
Home Runs	177	10th in the majors
Home Runs Allowed	165	15th in the majors
Batting Average	.275	7th in the majors
Batting Average Allowed	.255	5th in the majors
Walks Drawn	549	8th in the majors
Walks Given	570	23rd in the majors
OPS For	.775	8th in the majors
OPS Against	.737	8th in the majors
Stolen Bases	200	1st in the majors
Stolen Bases Allowed	105	22nd in the majors

Jose Reyes was 78 of 99 in stolen base attempts, a 79% success rate.
The rest of the Mets were successful in 122 of 147 attempts, an 83% success rate.

Key Players

Pos	Player	G	AB	R	H	2B	3B	HR	RBI	SB	CS	BB	SO	Avg	OBP	Slg	OPS	WS
C	Paul Lo Duca	119	445	46	121	18	1	9	54	2	0	24	33	.272	.311	.378	.689	9
1B	Carlos Delgado	139	538	71	139	30	0	24	87	4	0	52	118	.258	.333	.448	.781	13
2B	Luis Castillo	50	199	37	59	8	2	1	20	10	2	24	17	.296	.371	.372	.742	7
3B	David Wright	160	604	113	196	42	1	30	107	34	5	94	115	.325	.416	.546	.963	34
SS	Jose Reyes	160	681	119	191	36	12	12	57	78	21	77	78	.280	.354	.421	.775	24
LF	Moises Alou	87	328	51	112	19	1	13	49	3	0	27	30	.341	.392	.524	.916	12
CF	Carlos Beltran	144	554	93	153	33	3	33	112	23	2	69	111	.276	.353	.525	.878	25
RF	Shawn Green	130	446	62	130	30	1	10	46	11	1	37	62	.291	.352	.430	.782	12

Key Pitchers

Pos	Player	G	GS	W	L	Sv	IP	H	R	ER	BB	SO	BR/9	ERA	WS
SP	Tom Glavine	34	34	13	8	0	200.1	219	102	99	64	89	12.89	4.45	10
SP	John Maine	32	32	15	10	0	191.0	168	90	83	75	180	11.69	3.91	11
SP	Oliver Perez	29	29	15	10	0	177.0	153	90	70	79	174	12.15	3.56	10
SP	Orlando Hernandez	27	24	9	5	0	147.2	109	64	61	64	128	10.85	3.72	9
SP	Jorge Sosa	42	14	9	8	0	112.2	109	58	56	41	69	11.98	4.47	6
CL	Billy Wagner	66	0	2	2	34	68.1	55	22	20	22	80	10.40	2.63	12
RP	Pedro Feliciano	78	0	2	2	2	64.0	47	26	22	31	61	11.67	3.09	6
RP	Aaron Heilman	81	0	7	7	1	86.0	72	36	29	20	63	10.15	3.03	8

Every year that passes, Earned Run Average becomes a little bit more irrelevant. At some point in the past, so far back that the sunlight no longer lingers, a decision was made to charge a run allowed to the pitcher who put the runner on base.

At the time, that was probably a good enough rule. When a pitcher started an inning he finished the inning 99-plus percent of the time. If he didn't, he worked his way well into the inning, and was taken out only after a fair effort to work his way through the mess.

The rule probably needed to be reviewed about 1915, maybe 1920. It was a tiny problem then, the stat being corrupted a little bit more every year. When I became a baseball fan in 1960 ERA was still a pretty good stat. Almost every pitcher, at that time, still worked something vaguely resembling whole innings. If there had been a moment when this decision to charge the run always to the *first* pitcher…if there was just a moment when it stopped working, somebody certainly would have fixed it. Instead the change crept up on us over the course of a century.

In modern baseball, really beginning in the late 1980s, each reliever in the late innings just works to one batter or a few batters. A runs-accounting process which envisions and assumes whole innings doesn't work in a fractured-inning environment.

Who had the *most* misleading ERA of 2007? Probably Joe Smith of the Mets, also winner of the Most Nondescript Name award. Smith was charged with 18 runs allowed—but he gave up 36 RBI.

That would be a fairly simple way to fix the ERA mess; charge the run allowed equally to the pitcher who put the runner on base and the pitcher who allowed the RBI. Logically, if you're just going to do one or the other, which would you do?

For hitters, much more attention is paid to RBI than to runs scored. I'm not saying that's right; it's just the way it is. If you paid no attention to who put the runner on base and charged the run to the pitcher who gave up the RBI, that would be as logical as the way we do it now; not more logical, but not less.

Joe Smith's ERA in 2007 was 3.45. If we had charged runs scored based on RBI, rather than runs scored, it would have been 6.90. If we charged them half and half it would have been 5.18. His component ERA was 5.04.

Cla Meredith of San Diego was charged with 38 runs scored—but allowed 55 RBI. Randy Messenger was charged with 30 runs scored, gave up 46 RBI. Boone Logan was 28 and 43—a good thing, because his ERA was 4.97 anyway. I don't want to know what it would have been if they were charging all the runs he let in to him.

If we had data for 1915, I would predict that every pitcher would have allowed at least as many runs scored as RBI. There could have been a couple of exceptions, but basically, the way the game was then, it was impossible to allow more RBI than runs scored.

Now it's not only possible to allow more RBI than runs scored, it's much more the rule than the exception for relief pitchers. There were 155 major league pitchers in 2007 who worked in 45 or more games—all of those basically relievers, of course. Forty-one of those allowed more Runs than RBI, and eleven more had the same number of each. The other 103 allowed more RBI than runs scored. Two-thirds of relievers allow more RBI than runs scored.

It's not that we can't figure out how well a pitcher "really" pitched; we have component ERA now, and WHIP; we have records spelled out in exhaustive detail, and armies of analysts who are unpaid to make sense of them. It's not that we're losing information. What we're losing is the ERA. The ERA is gradually slipping toward insignificance.

On the other side of the line from Joe Smith were Daniel Cabrera, Edwin Jackson, Jose Contreras, Jeremy Bonderman and others. I'm not suggesting that those pitchers pitched well, but they were charged with full responsibility for runs let in by other pitchers. Edwin Jackson gave up 116 runs, but only 98 RBI. Tyler Yates gave up 44 runs, but only 30 RBI. If the batter who got the RBI deserves some of the credit for that run, doesn't the pitcher who gave up the RBI deserve some of the responsibility?

Joe Smith – NYM – 2007
Record of Opposing Batters

Season	AB	R	H	2B	3B	HR	RBI	BB	SO	SB	CS	GIDP	Avg	OBP	Slg	OPS
2007	175	18	48	10	0	3	36	21	45	5	1	5	.274	.352	.383	.735

Cla Meredith – SD – 2007
Record of Opposing Batters

Season	AB	R	H	2B	3B	HR	RBI	BB	SO	SB	CS	GIDP	Avg	OBP	Slg	OPS
2007	318	38	94	11	0	6	55	17	59	7	2	14	.296	.331	.387	.718

Tyler Yates – Atl – 2007
Record of Opposing Batters

Season	AB	R	H	2B	3B	HR	RBI	BB	SO	SB	CS	GIDP	Avg	OBP	Slg	OPS
2007	255	44	64	14	3	6	30	31	69	7	1	1	.251	.332	.400	.732

At What Point Does That Cease to Be a "Change" And Become Just a Really Slow Pitch?

Tom Glavine last year threw 1,485 changeups, leading the major leagues in changeups used by more than 500. Fausto Carmona was the only major league pitcher who pitched 200 innings without throwing a change.

Tom Glavine – 2007
Pitch Type Analysis

Overall		
Total Pitches	3341	
Fastball	1670	50%
Curveball	83	2%
Changeup	1485	44%
Slider	63	2%
Pitchout	1	0%
Not Charted	39	1%

	Vs. RHB		Vs. LHB	
Total Pitches	2508		833	
Outs Recorded	460		139	
Fastball	1212	48%	458	55%
Curveball	60	2%	23	3%
Changeup	1168	47%	317	38%
Slider	40	2%	23	3%
Pitchout	1	0%	0	0%
Not Charted	27	1%	12	1%

Carlos Beltran – 2005
Pitch Analysis

Overall		
Pitches Seen	2443	
Taken	1383	57%
Swung At	1060	43%
Pitches Taken		
Taken for a Strike	445	32%
Called a ball	938	68%
Pitches Taken by Pitch Location		
In Strike Zone	445	32%
High	123	9%
Low	348	25%
Inside	175	13%
Outside	292	21%
Swung At		
Missed	174	16%
Fouled Off	390	37%
Put in Play	496	47%
Swung At by Pitch Location		
In Strike Zone	876	83%
High	42	4%
Low	60	6%
Inside	27	3%
Outside	55	5%

Opening Up

In each of 2005 and 2006, 16% of the pitches Carlos Beltran swung at were outside of strike zones.
In 2007, 26% were not in the strike zone.

Carlos Beltran – 2006
Pitch Analysis

Overall		
Pitches Seen	2572	
Taken	1611	63%
Swung At	961	37%
Pitches Taken		
Taken for a Strike	512	32%
Called a ball	1099	68%
Pitches Taken by Pitch Location		
In Strike Zone	512	32%
High	188	12%
Low	386	24%
Inside	182	11%
Outside	343	21%
Swung At		
Missed	151	16%
Fouled Of	391	41%
Put in Play	419	44%
Swung At by Pitch Location		
In Strike Zone	749	78%
High	43	4%
Low	78	8%
Inside	21	2%
Outside	70	7%

Carlos Beltran – 2007
Pitch Analysis

Overall		
Pitches Seen	2368	
Taken	1334	56%
Swung At	1034	44%
Pitches Taken		
Taken for a Strike	426	32%
Called a ball	908	68%
Pitches Taken by Pitch Location		
In Strike Zone	426	32%
High	133	10%
Low	343	26%
Inside	151	11%
Outside	281	21%
Swung At		
Missed	197	19%
Fouled Off	383	37%
Put in Play	454	44%
Swung At by Pitch Location		
In Strike Zone	717	69%
High	67	6%
Low	110	11%
Inside	37	4%
Outside	103	10%

Luis Castillo swung and missed only 45 times all year. That represented only 5% of his swings, the lowest figure in the majors among hitters who saw 500 pitches.

Leaning In

Lastings Milledge was thrown 50 inside pitches and chased only one of them. He was thrown 132 outside pitches and chased more than half of them.

Luis Castillo – 2007
Pitch Analysis

Overall		
Pitches Seen	2439	
Taken	1536	63%
Swung At	903	37%
Pitches Taken		
Taken for a Strike	619	40%
Called a ball	917	60%
Pitches Taken by Pitch Location		
In Strike Zone	619	40%
High	209	14%
Low	345	22%
Inside	114	7%
Outside	249	16%
Swung At		
Missed	45	5%
Fouled Of	341	38%
Put in Play	517	57%
Swung At by Pitch Location		
In Strike Zone	757	84%
High	57	6%
Low	39	4%
Inside	24	3%
Outside	26	3%

Lastings Milledge – 2007
Pitch Analysis

Overall		
Pitches Seen	778	
Taken	400	51%
Swung At	378	49%
Pitches Taken		
Taken for a Strike	117	29%
Called a ball	283	71%
Pitches Taken by Pitch Location		
In Strike Zone	117	29%
High	52	13%
Low	118	30%
Inside	49	12%
Outside	64	16%
Swung At		
Missed	92	24%
Fouled Off	142	38%
Put in Play	144	38%
Swung At by Pitch Location		
In Strike Zone	247	65%
High	23	6%
Low	39	10%
Inside	1	0%
Outside	68	18%

In the 22 games where they had starts with a Game Score of 70 or better the New York Mets were 22-0.

New York Mets – 2007
Performance by Quality of Start

Game Score	#	ERA	W	-	L
80 and above	1	0.00	1	-	0
70 to 79	21	0.72	21	-	0
60 to 69	37	2.32	29	-	8
50 to 59	31	3.38	18	-	13
40 to 49	27	4.54	16	-	11
30 to 39	20	6.76	2	-	18
20 to 29	14	9.05	0	-	14
Below 20	11	10.23	1	-	10

On the morning of September 7, the Mets led the Phillies in the standings by 5 games. Each team had 23 games to go with two homestands and one road trip remaining on the schedule.

The Phillies pitching was struggling. They just came off two road trips and a homestand in which their team ERAs were 5.65, 5.44 and 6.57—and it didn't get much better in their second-to-last homestand of the season beginning on the 7th. They did manage a 4-3 record, but the pitching still struggled, posting a 5.34 ERA.

The Mets pitching was better by more than a run per game. In their two road trips and homestand before September 7th, their ERAs were 4.58, 4.91 and 4.80. In their second-to-last homestand they pitched well (3.84 ERA) and also were one game over .500 (5-4).

Then the disaster that all Mets fans will remember for years hit. And it was the pitching that did it. The Mets hit .302 and .299 in their last road trip and last homestand, but the pitchers were rocked, to the tune of 6.14 and 6.86 ERAs. The Phillies pitching completely turned it around and pitched better by a full three runs per game than the Mets (3.63 and 3.17 ERAs).

New York Mets – 2007 – Last 6 Segments
Tracking the Season by Segments

	W-L	R	PG	Avg	OR	PG	ERA	W-L
Road Trip, August 14 to 19	5-1	43	7.2	.321	30	5.0	4.58	70-53
Homestand, August 21 to 26	3-3	31	5.2	.266	33	5.5	4.91	73-56
Road Trip, August 27 to September 5	5-5	52	5.2	.276	49	4.9	4.80	78-61
Homestand, September 7 to 16	5-4	41	4.6	.250	41	4.6	3.84	83-65
Road Trip, September 17 to 23	4-3	50	7.1	.302	47	6.7	6.14	87-68
Homestand, September 24 to 30	1-6	37	5.3	.299	50	7.1	6.86	88-74

Philadelphia Phillies – 2007 – Last 6 Segments
Tracking the Season by Segments

	W-L	R	PG	Avg	OR	PG	ERA	W-L
Road Trip, August 14 to 19	3-3	30	5.0	.251	35	5.8	5.65	65-58
Homestand, August 21 to 30	6-4	57	5.7	.314	60	6.0	5.44	71-62
Road Trip, August 31 to September 5	2-4	35	5.8	.298	37	6.2	6.57	73-66
Homestand, September 7 to 13	4-3	40	5.7	.263	41	5.9	5.34	77-69
Road Trip, September 14 to 23	8-2	59	5.9	.238	43	4.3	3.63	85-71
Homestand, September 25 to 30	4-2	31	5.2	.236	21	3.5	3.17	89-73

End Game

by Bill James

How do you know when a team is *virtually* eliminated? There is a point in a pennant race at which a team has not been technically eliminated, but they're just not going to win. They're not dead, they're as good as dead. Twenty games out in late August...you're not theoretically eliminated, because in theory you could go 40-0 in the closing weeks and the first-place team could go 10-30 and you could beat them by ten games, but it ain't going to happen. There is a point of no return. What is that point?

I think we all use this phrase sometimes, "virtually eliminated", but what *specifically* does it mean? Let's say that a team is 17 games behind on July 28. Have they been virtually eliminated, or not?

• • •

Personal digression....

When I was in college sometime in the middle of the last century I developed a formula in my head to determine when the lead in a basketball game was safe and the game was essentially over. It's been 40 years, and I have never published this, but I still use it. I'll be watching a game with my wife or my wife and kids, and the Jayhawks will be ahead by 25 points with seven minutes to go, and I'll turn to my wife and say, "The lead is safe." Or the game will be close, and somebody will hit a 3-pointer with 14 seconds to go, and, in the din of Allen Fieldhouse, I will signal to my wife, "That's it. The lead is safe." This has a sort of life of its own, its own rituals. Every close game, there will be a point where the Jayhawks get 2 points ahead with eleven minutes to go or something, and I say "The lead is not safe." This is a kind of stupid little joke, because it is obvious to anybody that the lead is not safe, so I'm sort of pretending to offer some mock expert insight into the game, when I'm really just stating the obvious. Eventually it gets serious, and we'll be nine points ahead (or, occasionally, nine points behind) with two minutes to go, and Susie will ask "Is that it?", meaning, "Is the lead safe?" Which it wouldn't be, but there is a point there. I'm always figuring...the lead is 28% safe, or the lead is 71% safe.

A "safe" lead is a point of no return. Once a lead is safe, it's permanently safe, even though it is common for the losing team to struggle back over the "safe lead" line for one or two possessions, occasionally more. In a basketball game there are actual consequences to the lead being safe. When the lead is safe...normally about 20 seconds after the lead becomes safe...the bench players come in, usually on both sides. I have never been to a game at which a team lost a "safe" lead, but I have been to games at which a coach miscalculated when the lead was safe, put in his bench players, and found himself in serious danger of losing the game. If a team gets ten points ahead with 12 minutes to go and then just hangs there, eight to twelve points ahead, then when the clock runs down to about

There is a point of no return. What is that point?

three minutes it *feels* like it is over, but it isn't. Ten points ahead with even two minutes to go is nowhere near a safe lead. You hit a couple of threes, it's 70-66 with 1:40 to go.

I have seen games on TV in which the announcer miscalculated when the lead was safe and started talking about the consequences of the game's outcome, only to see the outcome reverse itself. And I did once see a game on television in which a team lost a game after having a safe lead...the famous Indiana Pacers game a few years ago in which the Pacers, down by 8 points with about ten seconds to go, rallied to win. Reggie Miller hit a three, the Pacers stole the in-bounds pass, Miller drained another three, they stole the in-bounds pass again, tied it up and won the game in overtime. That's the only game I've ever heard of in which a team lost after having a safe lead, and one of the most memorable things I've ever seen on TV. A series of events so improbable that one would think it couldn't happen, but it did.

Anyway, my son has been urging me for years to publish this thing, and I guess I will, during the basketball season. This is a baseball book.

We're trying to identify the moment at which it ain't over, but it's over.

• • •

I have wanted to have a "safe lead" formula in baseball for 35 years, but until now I have never been able to put the elements together in my head. Now I think I've got it...you ready?

A baseball team is virtually eliminated if the number of games they are behind, squared, is greater than four times their number of games remaining.

Our formula is the counterpoint to the ultimate Yogiism: It ain't over 'til it's over. We're trying to identify the moment at which it ain't over, but it's over. To the best of my knowledge, no major league team has ever won the pennant after having been virtually eliminated. There are a number of teams which have walked right up to the line, and come back to win. There are a number of teams which got into a position where if they dropped another two games back, maybe even another one game back, it would have been too late. Let's review a few of those:

The 1914 Boston Braves, the Miracle Braves, were in last place on July 5. They were 26-40, 15 games out, but rallied to win.

15 squared is 225. The Braves had 88 games left; 88 times 4 is 352. So the Braves were 64% eliminated (225/352) at their worst point, but came back to win. They would have been over the virtual elimination line if they had dropped another 3½ back.

The 1934 St. Louis Cardinals were seven games behind on September 6. They were 77-53, while the Giants were 85-47. This was the year that Giants manager Bill Terry made the ultimate bulletin-board crack about the Dodgers, "Brooklyn? Is Brooklyn still in the league?" In the closing weeks the Dodgers made it a point to remind Terry that they were still in the league.

The Cardinals (the Gas House Gang, led by 30-game winner Dizzy Dean) were 7 games behind by early August and just hung there for a month, barely moving. At their worst point they were 7 back with 24 to play, which is 51% eliminated (49/96). They would have been virtually eliminated had they dropped another two and a half games behind.

The 1938 Chicago Cubs were 9 games back on August 20, with 44 games to play, and 8½ back on August 24, with 39 games to play. That's a very serious situation for a baseball team, but it's 46% eliminated. If they

had dropped another 3½ back, that would have virtually eliminated them.

This was the year of the Homer in the Gloaming. Gabby Hartnett hit an 0-2 pitch into the fog and darkness at Wrigley Field. The umpire ruled it a home run, which put the Cubs in first place on September 28.

The 1951 New York Giants were 13 games out on August 11; they were 59-51. That's 96% dead (169/176). One more game, one more half-game even, it was time to send flowers. But they won fifteen straight games beginning August 12, went 12-1 in their last 13 regular-season games, caught the Dodgers at the wire and won the play-off on Bobby Thomson's home run off of Ralph Branca.

The 1962 San Francisco Giants, although it pales by comparison, were 4 games behind on September 22, four games back with seven to play. That's 57% eliminated (16/28), and one game away from the virtual elimination tripwire. They also caught the Dodgers at the last moment, and won the playoff.

The 1964 St. Louis Cardinals, the first Cardinal team post-Musial, were 39-41 on July 9, eleven games back. That's only 37% eliminated, but it would get much worse. Although the Cardinals played competitive baseball over the second half they were still 6½ games back on September 20, thirteen games remaining to be played. That's 81% eliminated (42.25/52). A half-game further back would have put them over the virtual elimination line (49/48). Instead, they won 10 of their last 13 games while the Phillies collapsed, and the Cardinals won the World Championship.

The 1969 New York Mets were 10 games behind on August 14, in third place. They were 62-51, while the Cubs were 74-43, the Cardinals 65-52. That's 51% eliminated (100/196), but the Cardinals were under .500 the rest of the way, while the Cubs almost completely collapsed (18-27 finish), and the Mets wound up beating them by eight full games.

• • •

Brief digression...the '69 Cardinals are also a very interesting team. The Cardinal front office historically overreacted to their poor performance down the stretch, and blew up the team, trading away several key performers. They had a nucleus of talent that should have carried them through the 1970s in good shape. Bob Gibson remained a great pitcher until '72; Steve Carlton became a great pitcher in '71. Mike Torrez, then 22, and Jerry Reuss, then 20, were both on the team; they would go on to win about 400 games between them, and Reggie Cleveland would have added a few. Joe Torre, who was on the '69 team, was the MVP in '71, and was a good player for several years after that. Lou Brock remained a great player until '76, Tim McCarver played until 1980. Curt Flood retired, but almost certainly would not have retired had he not been traded that winter. The 19-year-old Ted Simmons was on the '69 team; he would be an outstanding player throughout the 1970s. Willie Montanez and Jose Cruz, both excellent players later on, were then at the higher levels of the Cardinal farm system.

If the Cardinals had just kept their wits about them they probably could have been competitive if not dominant throughout the 1970s. Instead, they misjudged their minor league talent, bet on Joe Hague and Leron Lee to play key roles on the team, tried to move Joe Torre back to catcher, traded away Flood and Montanez that winter and Torrez, Reuss and Steve Carlton over the next couple of years, and just drifted away, spending much of the 1970s arguing with their players about haircuts and travel policies.

Continuing on with our list....

• • •

The 1978 New York Yankees were 14 games behind on July 19, with 72 games left on the schedule. That's 68% eliminated (196/288); they could have been written off at that point if they had dropped another three games behind.

The 2006 Minnesota Twins were 10½ games behind Detroit on August 7, 51 games left on the schedule. They were 54% eliminated, and were 3½ games from touching the third rail. They rallied to win the division.

We come, then, to the wild ending of the 2007 National League schedule, when the Mets lost a race that many of their fans had already taken to the bank, and the Rockies rallied from a seemingly impossible position to win the National League West. How close were these teams to virtual elimination, and how does that stack up with the other storybook finishes of baseball history?

The 2007 Philadelphia Phillies were, at their worst position, 7 games back with 17 to play. That was their position after the games of September 12. That's 72% eliminated, one and a half games from virtual elimination. If they had gotten to 8 back with 15 to play, the race would have been virtually over.

Instead, the Phillies cut it to 6.5 back on September 13, then cut the lead by a game every day until Septem-

ber 18. By that point—1½ back with eleven games still to be played—virtual elimination was no longer a factor for them. It was, at that point, apparent that they were going to be in the race until they were mathematically eliminated.

Whle things were getting better for Philadelphia, they were getting worse for Colorado. **The 2007 Rockies** had been six games out on September 1—34% eliminated. By September 12 they had cut that to 2½ games back, less than 10% (virtually) eliminated. They slipped a game back on the 14th, another on the 15th, a half-game further on the 17th; they were at 25/52, 48% eliminated. Although they picked up a half-game on the 18th, they held steady on the 19th and 20th. Their progress was running slower than the calendar; they were 4½ back with 9 to play, which is 56% eliminated.

In a sense, the Rockies' position was more precarious than this estimate reflects, in that they were behind not one team, but three, and basically even with two more. It was foreseeable that they would have to win virtually every game from then on to make the playoffs, as they did. But the closest they got to the virtual elimination line was the same as the Phillies—one and a half games.

It has become the thing to say, about the 2007 Mets, that this was the greatest collapse of all time. There has been research quoted widely arguing that no team before ever lost after being as certain to win as the 2007 Mets were certain to win.

There are different ways to look at it, and maybe that's the right way. I don't see it that way. The 2007 Phillies were 7 games back with 17 to play:

September 12, 2007

Team	W	L	Pct	GB
New York Mets	83	62	.572	...
Philadelphia Phillies	76	69	.524	7

But the 1964 Phillies were 6½ games ahead with 12 to play:

September 20, 1964

Team	W	L	Pct	GB
Philadelphia Phillies	90	60	.600	...
Cincinnati Reds	83	66	.557	6½
St. Louis Cardinals	83	66	.557	6½

It is really hard to see how seven games ahead with seventeen to play is a stronger position than six and half

We come, then, to the wild ending of the 2007 National League schedule, when the Mets lost a race that many of their fans had already taken to the bank, and the Rockies rallied from a seemingly impossible position to win the National League West.

up with twelve to play. The calculation that the Mets were more certain to make *the playoffs* is apparently based on the calculation that, even if they failed to hold their lead, they still could make the playoffs as the wild card. OK; if you want to see it that way, go ahead. I think it is a Met-centric view of the universe. If anybody ever asks me what the greatest collapse in the history of baseball was, I'm sticking with the 1964 Phillies.

My list of the greatest in-season comebacks ever,

ranked by the percentage of "virtually eliminated" the team had reached:

1. 1951 New York Giants   96%
2. 1964 St. Louis Cardinals   81%
3. 2007 Philadelphia Phillies 72%
4. 1978 New York Yankees   68%
5. 1914 Boston Braves   64%

If anybody ever asks me what the greatest collapse in the history of baseball was, I'm sticking with the 1964 Phillies.

New York Yankees

New York Yankees – 2007
Team Overview

Description		Ranking
Won-Lost Record	94-68	
Place	2nd of 5 in American League East	
Runs Scored	968	1st in the majors
Runs Allowed	777	16th in the majors
Home Runs	201	4th in the majors
Home Runs Allowed	150	7th in the majors
Batting Average	.290	1st in the majors
Batting Average Allowed	.268	14th in the majors
Walks Drawn	637	4th in the majors
Walks Given	578	25th in the majors
OPS For	.829	1st in the majors
OPS Against	.757	16th in the majors
Stolen Bases	123	7th in the majors
Stolen Bases Allowed	136	29th in the majors

Key Players

Pos	Player	G	AB	R	H	2B	3B	HR	RBI	SB	CS	BB	SO	Avg	OBP	Slg	OPS	WS
C	Jorge Posada	144	506	91	171	42	1	20	90	2	0	74	98	.338	.426	.543	.970	24
1B	Andy Phillips	61	185	27	54	7	1	2	25	0	3	12	26	.292	.338	.373	.711	3
2B	Robinson Cano	160	617	93	189	41	7	19	97	4	5	39	85	.306	.353	.488	.841	21
3B	Alex Rodriguez	158	583	143	183	31	0	54	156	24	4	95	120	.314	.422	.645	1.067	37
SS	Derek Jeter	156	639	102	206	39	4	12	73	15	8	56	100	.322	.388	.452	.840	24
LF	Hideki Matsui	143	547	100	156	28	4	25	103	4	2	73	73	.285	.367	.488	.855	16
CF	Melky Cabrera	150	545	66	149	24	8	8	73	13	5	43	68	.273	.327	.391	.718	12
RF	Bobby Abreu	158	605	123	171	40	5	16	101	25	8	84	115	.283	.369	.445	.814	18
DH	Johnny Damon	141	533	93	144	27	2	12	63	27	3	66	79	.270	.351	.396	.747	15

Key Pitchers

Pos	Player	G	GS	W	L	Sv	IP	H	R	ER	BB	SO	BR/9	ERA	WS
SP	Chien-Ming Wang	30	30	19	7	0	199.1	199	84	82	59	104	12.01	3.70	15
SP	Andy Pettitte	36	34	15	9	0	215.1	238	106	97	69	141	12.87	4.05	13
SP	Mike Mussina	28	27	11	10	0	152.0	188	90	87	35	91	13.44	5.15	6
SP	Roger Clemens	18	17	6	6	0	99.0	99	52	46	31	68	12.27	4.18	5
SP	Phil Hughes	13	13	5	3	0	72.2	64	39	36	29	58	11.77	4.46	4
CL	Mariano Rivera	67	0	3	4	30	71.1	68	25	25	12	74	10.85	3.15	12
RP	Luis Vizcaino	77	0	8	2	0	75.1	66	37	36	43	62	13.26	4.30	6
RP	Kyle Farnsworth	64	0	2	1	0	60.0	60	35	32	27	48	13.35	4.80	3

The Yankees last year had SEVEN players who scored 90 or more runs. That's only the second time since 1900 that has happened. The 1950 Red Sox also had seven.

101 of Alex Rodriguez' 156 RBI in 2007 came from his home runs. Bobby Abreu had more RBI singles, more RBI doubles, more RBI triples and more miscellaneous RBI from things like walks and groundouts than did A-Rod.

Bobby Abreu – 2007
RBI Analysis

Hits		RBI Hits		RBI Total		Drove In	
Home Runs:	16			RBI on Home Runs:	24	Melky Cabrera	10
Triples	5	RBI Triples:	4	RBI on Triples:	4	Robinson Cano	1
Doubles:	40	RBI Doubles:	18	RBI on Doubles:	25	Johnny Damon	31
Singles:	110	RBI Singles:	27	RBI on Singles:	31	Alberto Gonzalez	1
				Sacrifice Flies:	7	Derek Jeter	19
		Other RBI: Walks	2			Hideki Matsui	3
		Other RBI: Ground Outs	2	Total Other:	10	Doug Mientkiewicz	5
						Jose Molina	3
				Total RBI:	101	Wil Nieves	1
						Andy Phillips	4
						Jorge Posada	2
						Alex Rodriguez	4
						Kevin Thompson	1
						His Own Bad Self	16
						Total	101

Alex Rodriguez – 2007
RBI Analysis

Hits		RBI Hits		RBI Total		Drove In	
Home Runs:	54			RBI on Home Runs:	101	Bobby Abreu	33
Triples:	0	RBI Triples:	0	RBI on Triples:	0	Melky Cabrera	9
Doubles:	31	RBI Doubles:	11	RBI on Doubles:	15	Robinson Cano	2
Singles:	98	RBI Singles:	23	RBI on Singles:	24	Johnny Damon	19
				Sacrifice Flies:	9	Jason Giambi	1
		Other RBI: Walks	1			Derek Jeter	32
		Other RBI: Ground Outs	4	Total Other:	7	Hideki Matsui	1
						Doug Mientkiewicz	2
				Total RBI:	156	Jose Molina	1
						Andy Phillips	2
						His Own Bad Self	54
						Total	156

In 2002-2003, Jason Giambi hit .339 and .327 in clutch situations, with an OPS both years over 1.000.

Since 2004 he has hit .217, .229, .203 and .222 in clutch situations.

Jason Giambi
Clutch Hitting

Season	AB	H	2B	3B	HR	RBI	BB	SO	GIDP	Avg	OBP	Slg
2002	56	19	1	0	7	24	10	17	3	.339	.465	.732
2003	52	17	3	0	3	14	18	15	0	.327	.514	.558
2004	23	5	1	0	1	9	3	7	1	.217	.286	.391
2005	48	11	2	0	5	16	11	15	1	.229	.383	.583
2006	59	12	3	0	7	30	20	22	1	.203	.417	.610
2007	27	6	1	0	1	3	7	7	0	.222	.382	.370
Totals	265	70	11	0	24	96	69	83	6	.264	.427	.577

Since joining the Yankees in 2001 Mike Mussina has posted a winning record every season. He was able to keep the streak intact in 2007 although the league's batting average against him jumped from .242 to .311, the slugging percentage against him jumped by almost 100 points, and the OPS against him jumped by more than 150. Also check out the stolen bases allowed (below); his data in that column has slipped gradually from "great" to "problematic". Of course, Posada's throwing arm isn't what it used to be.

Mike Mussina
Record of Opposing Batters

Season	AB	R	H	2B	3B	HR	RBI	BB	SO	SB	CS	GIDP	Avg	OBP	Slg	OPS
2002	823	103	208	39	6	27	93	48	182	6	10	14	.253	.294	.413	.707
2003	807	86	192	41	2	21	80	40	195	9	10	11	.238	.274	.372	.646
2004	646	91	178	33	4	22	79	40	132	10	3	13	.276	.318	.441	.759
2005	701	93	199	36	1	23	89	47	142	15	7	21	.284	.329	.437	.765
2006	762	88	184	33	1	22	82	35	172	15	4	19	.242	.275	.374	.649
2007	605	90	188	49	1	14	83	35	91	24	3	18	.311	.348	.465	.813

A Contrast in Styles

The Red Sox only lost three games when they scored 6 or more runs. The Yankees lost 14. When scoring exactly six runs, New York went 10-8 compared to Boston's 9-0.

Boston Red Sox – 2007
Record by Runs Scored and Allowed

	Scored	Allowed
10 runs or more	25 - 0	2 - 5
9 runs	6 - 0	1 - 6
8 runs	8 - 1	0 - 5
7 runs	16 - 2	1 - 6
6 runs	9 - 0	10 - 13
5 runs	7 - 9	7 - 10
4 runs	12 - 12	13 - 5
3 runs	4 - 11	16 - 6
2 runs	6 - 10	16 - 8
1 run	3 - 14	17 - 2
0 runs	0 - 7	13 - 0
Total	96 - 66	96 - 66

New York Yankees – 2007
Record by Runs Scored and Allowed

	Scored	Allowed
10 runs or more	24 - 1	2 - 16
9 runs	10 - 3	1 - 2
8 runs	14 - 1	2 - 2
7 runs	14 - 1	3 - 14
6 runs	10 - 8	7 - 10
5 runs	10 - 5	9 - 6
4 runs	6 - 13	8 - 6
3 runs	4 - 5	18 - 8
2 runs	2 - 11	20 - 4
1 run	0 - 12	19 - 0
0 runs	0 - 8	5 - 0
Total	94 - 68	94 - 68

New York Yankees – 2007
Performance by Starting Pitcher

In 2005, the Astros were 15-17 in games started by Roger Clemens. In 2006, they were 9-10. In 2007, the Yankees were 8-9 in Clemens' starts.

Games Started By	G	RS	RA	Won	Lost
Pettitte, Andy	34	200	148	21	13
Wang, Chien-Ming	30	193	125	21	9
Mussina, Mike	27	154	153	13	14
Clemens, Roger	17	80	71	8	9
Hughes, Phil	13	88	64	8	5
Igawa, Kei	12	75	76	6	6
Rasner, Darrell	6	28	28	3	3
DeSalvo, Matt	6	33	27	2	4
Clippard, Tyler	6	53	34	5	1
Karstens, Jeff	3	8	20	1	2
Kennedy, Ian	3	13	10	2	1
Pavano, Carl	2	17	7	2	0
Wright, Chase	2	16	10	1	1
Henn, Sean	1	10	4	1	0
Team Totals	162	968	777	94	68

Alex Rodriguez in 2007 hit only one ground ball single through the right side of the infield.

Alex Rodriguez – 2007
Hitting Analysis

Batting Right-Handed								1B	2B	3B	HR
Ground Balls to Left	140	Outs	107	Hits	33	Average	.236	Hit Type	32 - 1 - 0 - 0
Ground Balls to Center	42	Outs	28	Hits	14	Average	.333	Hit Type	14 - 0 - 0 - 0
Ground Balls to Right	12	Outs	11	Hits	1	Average	.083	Hit Type	1 - 0 - 0 - 0
Line Drives to Left	42	Outs	6	Hits	36	Average	.857	Hit Type	17 - 16 - 0 - 3
Line Drives to Center	23	Outs	3	Hits	20	Average	.870	Hit Type	17 - 3 - 0 - 0
Line Drives to Right	15	Outs	4	Hits	11	Average	.733	Hit Type	8 - 3 - 0 - 0
Fly Balls to Left	66	Outs	26	Hits	40	Average	.615	Hit Type	2 - 4 - 0 - 34
Fly Balls to Center	70	Outs	54	Hits	16	Average	.242	Hit Type	4 - 2 - 0 - 10
Fly Balls to Right	62	Outs	50	Hits	12	Average	.207	Hit Type	3 - 2 - 0 - 7
Total on Ground Balls	194	Outs	146	Hits	48	Average	.247	Hit Type	47 - 1 - 0 - 0
Total on Line Drives	80	Outs	13	Hits	67	Average	.838	Hit Type	42 - 22 - 0 - 3
Total on Fly Balls	198	Outs	130	Hits	68	Average	.360	Hit Type	9 - 8 - 0 - 51
Total Hit to Left	248	Outs	139	Hits	109	Average	.441	Hit Type	51 - 21 - 0 - 37
Total Hit to Center	135	Outs	85	Hits	50	Average	.382	Hit Type	35 - 5 - 0 - 10
Total Hit to Right	89	Outs	65	Hits	24	Average	.282	Hit Type	12 - 5 - 0 - 7
All Balls in Play	472	Outs	289	Hits	183	Average	.395	Hit Type	98 - 31 - 0 - 54

Mariano Rivera last year threw 99% fastballs and cut fastballs. No other major league pitcher (pitching 50 or more games or 100 or more innings) threw more than 86% fastballs.

Mariano Rivera – 2007
Pitch Type Analysis

Overall		
Total Pitches	1125	
Fastball	297	26%
Changeup	1	0%
Cut Fastball	816	73%
Not Charted	11	1%

	Vs. RHB		Vs. LHB	
Total Pitches	604		521	
Outs Recorded	108		106	
Fastball	210	35%	87	17%
Changeup	0	0%	1	0%
Cut Fastball	385	64%	431	83%
Not Charted	9	1%	2	0%

Closer Fatigue

by Bill James

Every morning I roll out of bed, look at who the Red Sox are playing, look at who the Yankees are playing, and do a little mental calculation of the odds. Let's see…we're playing a pretty good team, they're playing a bad team, but we're at home, they're on the road, and then,

Rivera pitched an inning and gave up a run last night, so he's probably not available…looks like it could be a decent day.

But wait a minute. I realized that I was *assuming*, as I was doing this, that the Yankees were less likely to win the game if Rivera was tired, the Red Sox were less likely to win if Papelbon was tired, the Angels less likely to win if K-Rod was tired, etc. What if it's not true? Is there actual evidence that the fatigue level of the closer is a factor predicting success for the team? Or is that just something that seems like it might be true, but in fact gets lost in the laundry among the hundreds of things that might be used to predict the outcome of a game?

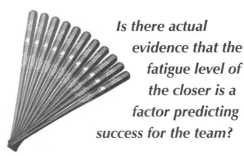

Is there actual evidence that the fatigue level of the closer is a factor predicting success for the team?

The obvious way to study this issue is to study the Yankees and their Henry Fonda looka-like closer, Mariano Rivera. Rivera had been the Yankees closer for ten years before this year in mid-summer, 2007. More important than that,

1) he's been good every year,

2) the Yankees have been good every year,

3) his role hasn't changed very much over the years, and

4) he's generally been healthy.

Those things eliminate a lot of problems. The ten years give us 1,620 games to study, which gives us fairly meaningful data…not perfect data, but pretty good data. If we studied, let's say, Bruce Sutter…sometimes he's healthy, sometimes he's not, sometimes he's great, sometimes he's mediocre, sometimes he's pitching just the ninth, sometimes he's getting two- and even three-inning saves, sometimes his team is good, sometimes they're bloody awful. These things screw up the data, so that when you get done you don't know what you have.

So we're studying Mariano and the Yankees. How do we decide whether Rivera is tired?

I want to be careful about saying he is "tired". A pitcher can be tired, after all, for any of a thousand reasons; for all I know Mariano is spending his off hours hunting caribou, as so many of the players do now. We only measure that part of his fatigue that results from his major league workload. I developed a "Closer Workload Fatigue Store", which is as follows:

5 times the number of batters faced yesterday,

Plus 4 times the number of batters faced the day before,

Plus 3 times the number of batters faced the day before that,

Plus 2 times the number of batters faced the day before that,

Plus the number of batters faced the day before that.

Twice during the ten-year study, in August of 1997 and again in August of 2005, Mo's Workload Fatigue Score reached a peak of 89.

On August 10, 2005, Rivera pitched two innings, facing 7 batters.

On August 11 he pitched an inning and a third, facing 5 batters.

On August 12 he didn't pitch, but on August 13, 2005, he again pitched two innings, giving up 5 hits and facing 12 batters.

Thus, on the morning of August 14, 2005, Rivera's Closer Workload Fatigue Score was 89:

60 points for his 12 batters faced on August 13,

15 points for his 5 batters faced on August 11,

14 points for his 7 batters faced on August 10.

I got the data for this, obviously, from Retrosheet, and once more, let me express my deep appreciation to the volunteers of Retrosheet for making real baseball research possible.

I figured Rivera's Workload for every day of the regular season during the ten years, and then for every regu-

So we're studying Mariano and the Yankees.
How do we decide whether Rivera is tired?

lar-season game the Yankees played. When the Yankees played a double header and he pitched in the first game, I added six times the batters faced in the first game to his score going into the second game. The peak point was 89, and sometimes he was at zero—after the all-star break, for example, and on opening day.

When Rivera was on the Disabled List—meaning that he was *totally* unavailable for the game—I entered that as "100", indicating that he was 100% out of action for that day. If you were doing a different pitcher—Dick Radatz, for example, or Goose Gossage, or (God forbid) Mike Marshall, his workload would no doubt peak over 100; in fact, I would suppose that it would peak over 200. Anyway, you couldn't use "100" as a top end of the scale. But I was just figuring Mariano, so 100 works for the days when he is "beyond fatigued", so to speak.

The essential conclusions of this study are as follows:

1) Rivera pitched less often when his Workload Fatigue Score was high,

2) Rivera was less effective when his Workload Fatigue Score was high, and

3) The Yankees' winning percentage dipped quite significantly when Rivera was tired.

I sorted the data in several different ways to ward against conclusions suggested by random groupings in the data. Perhaps the most useful split was the split dividing the Yankee games over the ten years into four groups:

1) High Fatigue
2) Fatigue Fairly High
3) Fatigue Fairly Low
4) Low Fatigue

These are Mariano's Games Appearances and ERA by the four groups:

	Games	ERA
1) High Fatigue	90	2.71
2) Fatigue Fairly High	164	2.18
3) Fatigue Fairly Low	185	2.00
4) Low Fatigue	201	1.60

There are 405 Yankee games in each group (more or less…a couple of games were cancelled, so I cut a couple of the groups to 404.) When he was most rested Rivera pitched in essentially one-half the games, and posted a

1.60 ERA. As his Closer Workload Fatigue Score increased he pitched less, and his ERA ascended.

In the top group Rivera pitched in only 90 games of 405, but this is a little bit misleading because the top group includes the games for which Rivera was on the Disabled List. There were 98 Yankee games over the ten years for which Rivera was on the Disabled List, so actually Rivera pitched in 29% of the Yankee games (90 of 307) even when his fatigue score was highest, a rate of 48 appearances per 162 games.

This was one thing that surprised me in the study—that the slope of the line indicating likelihood of appearing in the game was not more steep than it is. What I take from that realization is this: *in modern baseball the closer's role is so limited and defined that the closer is almost always available for one inning of work.* I would have thought that there would be days when Rivera's recent workload was so high that he was simply not available for this game, and no doubt there are some such days. But there aren't very many of them. The point of the modern "closer usage" rules is, in a sense, to make the closer always available if you really need him.

In this data sort the Yankee winning percentage also declines as Rivera becomes less available and less effective:

	Games	ERA	Yankee WPct
1) High Fatigue	90	2.71	.602
2) Fatigue Fairly High	164	2.18	.588
3) Fatigue Fairly Low	185	2.00	.633
4) Low Fatigue	201	1.60	.620

The Yankee winning percentage is higher when Rivera is more rested. However, there is a "random sort glitch" in this one that causes me to suspect that we are actually understating the effect of the fatigue. The .602 percentage in the top group there includes the 98 games for which Rivera was on the Disabled List, and the Yankees actually played extremely well (67-31) when Rivera was on the DL. If you take those games out of it, the "high fatigue" winning percentage drops to .577—the lowest point on the chart. This becomes even more clear when we split the data into five groups of 324 Yankee games, rather than four groups of 405:

	Games	ERA	Yankee WPct
1) High Fatigue	63	2.57	.608
High Fatigue *(not including DL)*	63	2.57	.575
2) Fatigue Fairly High	123	2.36	.586
3) Middle group	137	2.16	.594
4) Fatigue Fairly Low	152	1.67	.630
5) Low Fatigue	165	1.77	.635

In the bottom group in this sort, when Rivera is most rested, Rivera appears in 82 games per season and the Yankees win 103 per season. In the top group, when he is least rested, Rivera appears in 45 games per season and the Yankees win 93 per season. (There's a tie game in there screwing up the calculations, if you're trying to extrapolate from this.)

I am not a gambler, I don't write to gamblers specifically, and I don't claim to know the things that gamblers can profit from knowing. However, it would seem to me that if you have a gambler's focus this would be an extremely important "razor" to sort the data, to decide whether to bet for or against the Yankees. Fifty, sixty points of winning percentage is a huge edge.

Of course, at this point we can't say with confidence that that's the real size of the advantage. We would need to study this repeatedly, studying different pitchers, before we could definitively reach a conclusion that a tired closer reduces the winning percentage of his team by 50 or 60 points. There could also be biases in the data which have not yet been called to our attention. I'm just saying…that's what this study shows, and it seems reasonable. I thought it was interesting enough that I decided to add the daily "closer workload fatigue score" to the statistics section of Bill James Online.

The study also reached the following incidental conclusions, which I will pass along for what they are worth:

1) Rivera's strikeout rate declined significantly as his fatigue went up. In the quartile study his strikeouts per nine innings were 8.47 in the bottom group, 6.82 when he was most fatigued, and in the sevens in the middle two groups (albeit it in the wrong order.)

2) Rivera's double play rate also dropped sharply when his fatigue score was high. Rivera received the support of 40 double plays in 437.2 innings in the bottom two groups of the quartile study, when he was most rested. This is .82 double plays per nine innings. When his fatigue score was higher he received only 14 double plays in 269.1 innings, or .47 double plays per nine innings.

3) Rivera also allowed more home runs when he was tired, his rate per nine innings increasing from .37 to .50. When he was more rested Rivera had 40 double plays against 18 home runs allowed. When he was more tired he had 14 double plays and 15 homers.

4) However, Rivera's WALK rate improved sharply when he was more tired. Of course, Rivera's walk rate is always fantastic. Even when he was most rested, Rivera allowed only 2.00 walks per nine innings (not including intentional walks). But when he was most tired this figure was essentially cut in half, down to 1.10 walks per nine innings. In the quintile split (split into five groups) Rivera allowed 1.08 and 1.11 un-intentional walks in the two "highest fatigue" groups.

Presumably, Rivera's control "improves" when he is more tired because

1) there is more early contact, and

2) his ball doesn't move as much, meaning that it doesn't jump out of the strike zone as often.

When he was most rested Rivera pitched in essentially one-half the games, and posted a 1.60 ERA. As his Closer Workload Fatigue Score increased he pitched less, and his ERA ascended.

Oakland Athletics

Oakland Athletics – 2007
Team Overview

Description		Ranking
Won-Lost Record	76-86	
Place	3rd of 4 in American League West	
Runs Scored	741	19th in the majors
Runs Allowed	758	13th in the majors
Home Runs	171	13th in the majors
Home Runs Allowed	138	3rd in the majors
Batting Average	.256	25th in the majors
Batting Average Allowed	.263	10th in the majors
Walks Drawn	664	2nd in the majors
Walks Given	530	16th in the majors
OPS For	.745	19th in the majors
OPS Against	.733	7th in the majors
Stolen Bases	52	30th in the majors
Stolen Bases Allowed	101	21st in the majors

Key Players

Pos	Player	G	AB	R	H	2B	3B	HR	RBI	SB	CS	BB	SO	Avg	OBP	Slg	OPS	WS
C	Jason Kendall	80	292	24	66	10	0	2	22	3	1	12	27	.226	.261	.281	.542	3
1B	Dan Johnson	117	416	53	98	20	1	18	62	0	0	72	77	.236	.349	.418	.768	10
2B	Mark Ellis	150	583	84	161	33	3	19	76	9	4	44	94	.276	.336	.441	.777	20
3B	Eric Chavez	90	341	43	82	21	2	15	46	4	2	34	76	.240	.306	.446	.752	6
SS	Bobby Crosby	93	349	40	79	16	0	8	31	10	2	23	62	.226	.278	.341	.619	4
LF	Shannon Stewart	146	576	79	167	22	1	12	48	11	3	47	60	.290	.345	.394	.739	13
CF	Nick Swisher	150	539	84	141	36	1	22	78	3	2	100	131	.262	.381	.455	.836	18
RF	Jack Cust	124	395	61	101	18	1	26	82	0	2	105	164	.256	.408	.504	.912	19
DH	Mike Piazza	83	309	33	85	17	1	8	44	0	0	18	61	.275	.313	.414	.727	5

Key Pitchers

Pos	Player	G	GS	W	L	Sv	IP	H	R	ER	BB	SO	BR/9	ERA	WS
SP	Dan Haren	34	34	15	9	0	222.2	214	91	76	55	192	10.99	3.07	17
SP	Joe Blanton	34	34	14	10	0	230.0	240	106	101	40	140	11.11	3.95	13
SP	Chad Gaudin	34	34	11	13	0	199.1	205	108	98	100	154	14.13	4.42	9
SP	Lenny DiNardo	35	20	8	10	0	131.1	136	74	60	50	59	12.95	4.11	6
SP	Joe Kennedy	27	16	3	9	0	101.0	109	53	49	48	42	14.44	4.37	4
CL	Alan Embree	68	0	1	2	17	68.0	67	30	30	19	51	11.38	3.97	8
RP	Huston Street	48	0	5	2	16	50.0	35	20	16	12	63	8.46	2.88	10
RP	Jay Marshall	51	0	1	2	0	42.0	50	33	30	22	18	16.29	6.43	0

Odd Man Out

Taking up the old concept of secondary average, which is the sum of the other things that a player does to create runs, other than hit for average. Occasionally you get a player who is so extreme that baseball doesn't quite know what to do with him. Gene Tenace was such a player. He hit just .241 in his career, but he had 20-30 home run power, was a decent defensive catcher and drew walks with ridiculous frequency. Nobody quite knew what to make of him, so he sat on the bench for a couple of years while the league tried to figure him out. Finally he hit four homers in a World Series, and then he got to play, but he was always tremendously undervalued.

Later on we had Mickey Tettleton, who was a similar player, not quite as extreme, and then Darren Daulton. A player like this will typically waste three or four years at the start of his career waiting for somebody to work up the nerve to put him in the lineup. Howard Johnson was like that, and Don Mincher, although not quite in the class with Tenace.

And now there is Jack Cust, who is…well, out-Tenacing Tenace, out Gormaning-Thomas, and out-Deering Rob Deer. Like Nolan Ryan and Vladimir Guerrero, Jack Cust is a player who makes no compromises and offers no apologies. Here it is, buddy; you or me is going down in flames, one or the other. He strikes out at a rate that, projected to 600 at bats, would obliterate the major league strikeout record. He struck out 164 times last year in 395 at bats. On the other hand:

a) a fourth of his hits were home runs, and
b) he had more walks than he did hits.

He hit .256, which isn't too bad, but with a secondary average of .514. He drove in more runs per plate appearance than Nick Markakis, Manny Ramirez, Jorge Posada, Lance Berkman, Albert Pujols, Jeff Francoeur, David Wright, Ken Griffey, Troy Tulowitzki, Robinson Cano, Bobby Abreu, Carlos Delgado, Paul Konerko, Adrian Gonzalez or Todd Helton. He also scored more runs per plate appearance than Freddy Sanchez or Michael Young or Orlando Hudson or Jerry Owens or Melky Cabrera.

Still, because he does strike out with frightening frequency, nobody seems to know quite what to make of him. He hit .256 last year, but it's hard to sustain even a .256 batting average when you strike out one and a half times a game, and I wouldn't bet on him to hit .250 this year. It's real easy for a guy like that to go into a slump and hit .170 for half a season, frankly. He's unique, the far side of a spectrum, and I'm glad to see him in the league.

Major League Leaders
Secondary Average
2007

1.	Barry Bonds	.691
2.	Carlos Pena	.557
3.	Alex Rodriguez	.535
4.	Ryan Howard	.520
5.	Jack Cust	514
6.	Jim Thome	.507
7.	Adam Dunn	.500
8.	David Ortiz	497
9.	Prince Fielder	.490
10.	Pat Burrell	.487

The formula
for secondary average is
Total Bases Minus Hits
Plus Walks, plus Stolen Bases
Divided by At Bats

Getting to 15-9 from two different directions:

Dan Haren – Oak – 2007
Decision Analysis

Group	G	IP	W	L	Pct	H	R	SO	BB	ERA
Wins	15	101.1	15	0	1.000	83	33	84	20	2.66
Losses	9	56.1	0	9	.000	66	34	44	13	3.83
No Decisions	10	65.0	0	0	—	65	24	64	22	3.05
Quality Starts: 13 in Wins, 7 in Losses, 8 in no-decisions										

Russ Ortiz – SF – 2004
Decision Analysis

Group	G	IP	W	L	Pct	H	R	SO	BB	ERA
Wins	15	106.0	15	0	1.000	77	18	69	43	1.53
Losses	9	48.1	0	9	.000	68	45	37	24	7.82
No Decisions	10	50.1	0	0	—	52	35	37	45	6.08
Quality Starts: 13 in Wins, 2 in Losses, 5 in no-decisions										

Alan Embree has been remarkably consistent, allowing opponents an OPS in the 600's in each of the last six years. Except one. He went off the chart during the 2005 season when he allowed an .891 OPS and posted ERAs of 7.65 for the Red Sox and 7.53 for the Yankees.

Alan Embree
Record of Opposing Batters

Season	AB	R	H	2B	3B	HR	RBI	BB	SO	SB	CS	GIDP	Avg	OBP	Slg	OPS
2002	227	19	47	7	2	6	27	20	81	11	1	3	.207	.271	.335	.606
2003	203	26	49	9	1	5	27	16	45	5	3	7	.241	.297	.370	.666
2004	201	28	49	9	2	7	26	11	37	7	2	5	.244	.283	.413	.696
2005	209	47	62	21	1	10	43	14	38	6	1	4	.297	.341	.550	.891
2006	201	21	50	9	2	4	29	15	53	12	1	2	.249	.301	.373	.674
2007	260	30	67	12	2	5	33	19	51	4	1	4	.258	.308	.377	.685

Marco Scutaro chased outside pitches less often than any other hitter last year (minimum 500 pitches seen). He was thrown 189 outside pitches and swung at only 13 of them.

Marco Scutaro – 2007
Pitch Analysis

Overall		
Pitches Seen	1339	
Taken	794	59%
Swung At	545	41%
Pitches Taken		
Taken for a Strike	265	33%
Called a ball	529	67%
Pitches Taken by Pitch Location		
In Strike Zone	265	33%
High	119	15%
Low	193	24%
Inside	39	5%
Outside	176	22%
Swung At		
Missed	41	8%
Fouled Off	202	37%
Put in Play	302	55%
Swung At by Pitch Location		
In Strike Zone	447	83%
High	25	5%
Low	38	7%
Inside	18	3%
Outside	13	2%

Oakland Athletics – 2007
Games Played by Opening Day Starter At Each Position

Pos	Player	Starts
C	Kendall	80
1B	Swisher	147
2B	Ellis	149
3B	Chavez	87
SS	Crosby	92
LF	Stewart	131
CF	Bradley	18
RF	Buck	75
DH	Piazza	71
	Total	850

Oakland's opening-day starters accounted for only 58% of their regular season starting lineup.

Bobby Crosby's offensive downturn over the last two years has coincided with a steady loss of his patience at the plate. He took 61% of the pitches he saw in 2005 (which ranked among the top 10 percent in the majors), but only 57% in 2006 and 54% last year.

Bobby Crosby – 2005
Pitch Analysis

Overall		
Pitches Seen	1555	
Taken	946	61%
Swung At	609	39%

Pitches Taken		
Taken for a Strike	329	35%
Called a ball	617	65%

Pitches Taken by Pitch Location		
In Strike Zone	329	36%
High	82	9%
Low	241	27%
Inside	96	11%
Outside	161	18%

Swung At		
Missed	123	20%
Fouled Off	205	34%
Put in Play	281	46%

Swung At by Pitch Location		
In Strike Zone	461	80%
High	22	4%
Low	28	5%
Inside	15	3%
Outside	53	9%

Bobby Crosby – 2007
Pitch Analysis

Overall		
Pitches Seen	1358	
Taken	732	54%
Swung At	626	46%

Pitches Taken		
Taken for a Strike	268	37%
Called a ball	464	63%

Pitches Taken by Pitch Location		
In Strike Zone	268	37%
High	74	10%
Low	204	28%
Inside	65	9%
Outside	121	17%

Swung At		
Missed	139	22%
Fouled Off	200	32%
Put in Play	287	46%

Swung At by Pitch Location		
In Strike Zone	481	77%
High	37	6%
Low	52	8%
Inside	12	2%
Outside	44	7%

Suppose that you identified the 300 best pitcher's seasons since the year 2000. Since there are 30 teams, that would be ten per team, right? But how many of those seasons would be Oakland A's pitchers? The answer, surprisingly, is "only 19"; I thought it would be more, but it's only 19. Every one of the 30 teams has at least one of the "top 300" seasons, and Oakland is actually second on the list:

Number of "Top 300" Seasons

Yankees	24	White Sox	16	Seattle	11	San Diego	8	Detroit	3
Oakland	19	Houston	15	Indians	10	Toronto	8	Tampa Bay	3
Atlanta	18	Angels	13	Mets	9	Mon-Wash	6	Texas	3
Dodgers	17	Arizona	12	Phillies	9	Cincinnati	5	Pittsburgh	2
Twins	17	St. Louis	12	Giants	9	Brewers	4	Colorado	1
Boston	16	Cubs	11	Marlins	8	Baltimore	3	Kansas City	1

That totals 293; the other seven were traded in midseason. The Oakland pitchers are:

Oakland's "Top 300" Pitchers

First	Last	Year	G	W - L	WPct	IP	SO	BB	GS	GF	Sv	ERA
Tim	Hudson	2000	32	20 - 6	.769	202	169	82	32	0	0	4.14
Mark	Mulder	2001	34	21 - 8	.724	229	153	51	34	0	0	3.45
Tim	Hudson	2001	35	18 - 9	.667	235	181	71	35	0	0	3.37
Barry	Zito	2001	35	17 - 8	.680	214	205	80	35	0	0	3.49
Jason	Isringhausen	2001	65	4 - 3	.571	71	74	23	0	54	34	2.65
Cory	Lidle	2001	29	13 - 6	.684	188	118	47	29	0	0	3.59
Barry	Zito	2002	35	23 - 5	.821	229	182	78	35	0	0	2.75
Billy	Koch	2002	84	11 - 4	.733	94	93	46	0	79	44	3.27
Mark	Mulder	2002	30	19 - 7	.731	207	159	55	30	0	0	3.47
Tim	Hudson	2002	34	15 - 9	.625	238	152	62	34	0	0	2.98
Keith	Foulke	2003	72	9 - 1	.900	87	88	20	0	67	43	2.08
Tim	Hudson	2003	34	16 - 7	.696	240	162	61	34	0	0	2.70
Mark	Mulder	2003	26	15 - 9	.625	187	128	40	26	0	0	3.13
Danny	Haren	2005	34	14 - 12	.538	217	163	53	34	0	0	3.73
Huston	Street	2005	67	5 - 1	.833	78	72	26	0	47	23	1.72
Huston	Street	2006	69	4 - 4	.500	71	67	13	0	55	37	3.31
Danny	Haren	2006	34	14 - 13	.519	223	176	45	34	0	0	4.12
Danny	Haren	2007	34	15 - 9	.625	223	192	55	34	0	0	3.07
Joe	Blanton	2007	34	14 - 10	.583	230	140	40	34	0	0	3.95

How many of those men were established pitchers before they came to Oakland? Answer: zero. Well…Koch had had a good year with Toronto in 2000 and a bad year in 2001, and Keith Foulke had pitched very well for the White Sox for several years but the White Sox lost confidence in him in his final season with them.

My general point is, the Oakland A's have this ability to kind of manufacture top-end pitching. It's a pitcher's park, and the A's usually score some runs. A 4.50 ERA in Kansas City might be a 3.90 ERA here; a pitcher who goes 9-15 with the Royals might go 14-11 here—and pitching success feeds on itself, since pitching requires confidence.

The trade of Danny Haren, then, can be interpreted in two ways. One is, the A's have decided to coast for two or three years, and focus on having a powerhouse in place when they open the new stadium in 2011. But another is, the A's can trade Haren because they know they can make somebody else into a number one starter. When they got Danny Haren, he was just a kid with a good arm. They can find another kid with a good arm, and make the magic of the Oakland Coliseum work for him.

Philadelphia Phillies

Philadelphia Phillies – 2007
Team Overview

Description		Ranking
Won-Lost Record	89-73	
Place	1st of 5 in National League East	
Runs Scored	892	2nd in the majors
Runs Allowed	821	22nd in the majors
Home Runs	213	2nd in the majors
Home Runs Allowed	198	27th in the majors
Batting Average	.274	10th in the majors
Batting Average Allowed	.276	23rd in the majors
Walks Drawn	641	3rd in the majors
Walks Given	558	20th in the majors
OPS For	.812	2nd in the majors
OPS Against	.797	26th in the majors
Stolen Bases	138	4th in the majors
Stolen Bases Allowed	84	8th in the majors

Key Players

Pos	Player	G	AB	R	H	2B	3B	HR	RBI	SB	CS	BB	SO	Avg	OBP	Slg	OPS	WS
C	Carlos Ruiz	115	374	42	97	29	2	6	54	6	1	42	49	.259	.340	.396	.735	13
1B	Ryan Howard	144	529	94	142	26	0	47	136	1	0	107	199	.268	.392	.584	.976	26
2B	Chase Utley	132	530	104	176	48	5	22	103	9	1	50	89	.332	.410	.566	.976	28
3B	Greg Dobbs	142	324	45	88	20	4	10	55	3	0	29	67	.272	.330	.451	.780	7
SS	Jimmy Rollins	162	716	139	212	38	20	30	94	41	6	49	85	.296	.344	.531	.875	28
LF	Pat Burrell	155	472	77	121	26	0	30	97	0	0	114	120	.256	.400	.502	.902	20
CF	Aaron Rowand	161	612	105	189	45	0	27	89	6	3	47	119	.309	.374	.515	.889	21
RF	Shane Victorino	131	456	78	128	23	3	12	46	37	4	37	62	.281	.347	.423	.770	11

Key Pitchers

Pos	Player	G	GS	W	L	Sv	IP	H	R	ER	BB	SO	BR/9	ERA	WS
SP	Cole Hamels	28	28	15	5	0	183.1	163	72	69	43	177	10.26	3.39	15
SP	Jamie Moyer	33	33	14	12	0	199.1	222	118	111	66	133	13.23	5.01	8
SP	Adam Eaton	30	30	10	10	0	161.2	192	117	113	71	97	15.25	6.29	2
SP	Kyle Kendrick	20	20	10	4	0	121.0	129	53	52	25	49	11.98	3.87	9
SP	Jon Lieber	14	12	3	6	0	78.0	91	44	41	22	54	13.38	4.73	3
CL	Brett Myers	51	3	5	7	21	68.2	61	33	33	27	83	11.67	4.33	9
RP	Antonio Alfonseca	61	0	5	2	8	49.2	65	31	30	27	24	16.85	5.44	3
RP	Geoff Geary	57	0	3	2	0	67.1	72	44	33	25	38	14.17	4.41	3

MVPs

The Philadelphia Phillies have won two MVP Awards in the last two years, which is two more than the New York Mets have won in their 46-year-history. I was happy to see Jimmy Rollins win the MVP Award because

a) He seems like a good guy, and

b) He's an outstanding player every year.

I wouldn't have voted for him, because I can't see that he was the best player in the league, but on the other hand, who do you vote for? Pujols? Holliday? Cabrera? There are problems with all of these.

In my view, the MVP in the National League was probably David Wright, but it's hard to vote for him because:

1) The Mets did a pratfall at show time,

2) His best years are still ahead of him, and

3) I think there is a rule that Mets players are not allowed to win the Award.

Rollins established a record for outs made by an MVP, by the way:

1. Rollins, 2007	527
2. Maury Wills, 1962	518
3. Zoilo Versalles, 1965	510

Rollins, Wills and Versalles have much in common. Shortstops. Very small. About the same age. Extremely durable. Fast. A little erratic in the field. Don't walk, but bat leadoff and score a lot of runs. Miguel Tejada (2002) is sort of in the same group; he made 486 outs, too, but Tejada was never exceptionally fast and didn't bat leadoff. Rollins is probably closer to Versalles than to any other MVP.

One thing I always enjoy about the MVP debate is those guys who say "It's an award for the most Val-u-a-ble player," elongating all four syllabels of "valuable" as if somehow this would illuminate the debate.

This was the fifth time that Rollins has made 500 outs in a season, tying him with Cal Ripken and Juan Pierre for the most 500-out seasons ever:

Ripken, Pierre and Rollins	5
Bobby Richardson and Dave Cash	4
Juan Samuel and Larry Bowa	3
Omar Moreno and Rick Burleson	3

Speaking of Cal Ripken…has anybody else noticed that he now bears an uncanny resemblence to Uncle Fester from the Addams Family?

It has been fifteen years since a pitcher won the MVP Award (Eckersley in '92), giving us a list of 30 MVPs since there has been a flinger in there. Both 1993 MVPs, Frank Thomas and Barry Bonds, were still active in 2007. I wonder when the last time both MVPs were still active 14 years later? Probably 1960; both MVPs from 1946 (Williams and Musial) were still playing in 1960. May have happened since then, I'm not sure.

Among the last 30 MVPs, Rollins ranks:

- tied for first in games played (162)
- first in at bats (obviously, since his 716 at bats were a major league record)
- third in runs scored (139)
- second in hits (212—30 behind Ichiro in 2001)
- sixth in doubles (38)
- first in triples (20). In fact, no other MVP since 1993 has hit more than eight triples.
- tied for sixth in extra base hits (88)
- third in stolen bases (41).

However, he ranks:

- dead last in batting average (.296)
- last in on-base percentage (.344)
- fourth-lowest in slugging percentage (.531)
- third-lowest in OPS (.875).
- third from the bottom in home runs (30).
- fourth from the bottom in RBI (94)

The most interesting thing in there is the realization that virtually all MVPs now are power hitters. Among the last 30 MVPs, 93% have hit 30 homers, 90% have driven in 100 runs, and 93% have hit .300. Most—63%—have hit 40 homers. Most—67%—have had an OPS over 1.000.

However, only one-third have drawn 100 walks. And half of those seasons are accounted for by Barry Bonds. More MVPs have hit over .350 than have hit under .300.

As a starter in 2006, Brett Myers threw a significant number of cut fastballs (182, about 6% of his pitches). In 2007 he eliminated the cut fastball and instead threw more curveballs (up to 26% from 21%) and more changeups (12%, up from 6%).

Brett Myers – 2006
Pitch Type Analysis

Overall		
Total Pitches	3216	
Fastball	1583	49%
Curveball	665	21%
Changeup	209	6%
Slider	486	15%
Split Finger	12	0%
Cut Fastball	182	6%
Pitchout	2	0%
Not Charted	77	2%

	Vs. RHB		Vs. LHB	
Total Pitches	1643		1573	
Outs Recorded	326		268	
Fastball	819	50%	764	49%
Curveball	322	20%	343	22%
Changeup	28	2%	181	12%
Slider	312	19%	174	11%
Split Finger	6	0%	6	0%
Cut Fastball	127	8%	55	3%
Pitchout	2	0%	0	0%
Not Charted	27	2%	50	3%

Brett Myers – 2007
Pitch Type Analysis

Overall		
Total Pitches	1193	
Fastball	560	47%
Curveball	314	26%
Changeup	148	12%
Slider	148	12%
Split Finger	5	0%
Cut Fastball	5	0%
Pitchout	1	0%
Not Charted	12	1%

	Vs. RHB		Vs. LHB	
Total Pitches	654		539	
Outs Recorded	110		96	
Fastball	328	50%	232	43%
Curveball	153	23%	161	30%
Changeup	46	7%	102	19%
Slider	117	18%	31	6%
Split Finger	3	0%	2	0%
Cut Fastball	3	0%	2	0%
Pitchout	1	0%	0	0%
Not Charted	3	0%	9	2%

From 2003 to 2007 Pat Burrell's flies were equally distributed:

271 to Left
284 to Center
284 to Right

His Home Runs on flies were not as equally split:

99 to Left
23 to Center
2 to Right

Pat Burrell – 2007
Hitting Analysis

Batting Left-Handed							1B	2B	3B	HR
Ground Balls to Left	61	Outs 48	Hits 13	Average .213	Hit Type		11	- 2	- 0	- 0
Ground Balls to Center	38	Outs 30	Hits 8	Average .211	Hit Type		8	- 0	- 0	- 0
Ground Balls to Right	11	Outs 6	Hits 5	Average .455	Hit Type		4	- 1	- 0	- 0
Line Drives to Left	38	Outs 11	Hits 27	Average .711	Hit Type		14	- 13	- 0	- 0
Line Drives to Center	15	Outs 4	Hits 11	Average .733	Hit Type		9	- 2	- 0	- 0
Line Drives to Right	12	Outs 2	Hits 10	Average .833	Hit Type		10	- 0	- 0	- 0
Fly Balls to Left	62	Outs 33	Hits 29	Average .483	Hit Type		3	- 4	- 0	- 22
Fly Balls to Center	64	Outs 50	Hits 14	Average .226	Hit Type		2	- 4	- 0	- 8
Fly Balls to Right	59	Outs 55	Hits 4	Average .073	Hit Type		4	- 0	- 0	- 0
Total on Ground Balls	110	Outs 84	Hits 26	Average .236	Hit Type		23	- 3	- 0	- 0
Total on Line Drives	65	Outs 17	Hits 48	Average .738	Hit Type		33	- 15	- 0	- 0
Total on Fly Balls	185	Outs 138	Hits 47	Average .266	Hit Type		9	- 8	- 0	- 30
Total Hit to Left	161	Outs 92	Hits 69	Average .434	Hit Type		28	- 19	- 0	- 22
Total Hit to Center	117	Outs 84	Hits 33	Average .287	Hit Type		19	- 6	- 0	8
Total Hit to Right	82	Outs 63	Hits 19	Average .244	Hit Type		18	- 1	- 0	- 0
All Balls in Play	360	Outs 239	Hits 121	Average .344	Hit Type		65	- 26	- 0	- 30

If I Had a Hamel

I have a friend who is a Phillies fan. He is optimistic about the 2008 season because, he says, "we finally have an ace. We haven't had an ace of the staff since we traded Schilling."

He is referring, of course, to Cole Hamels—and yes, that is the worst title in the book; thank you for noticing. (The Spoonerism for Cole Hamels, by the way, would be Whole Camels, whereas the Spoonerism for Curt Schilling would be Shirt Killing.) Anyway, I have this system, Season Scores, which is just a way of getting a reasonable answer to a question like "Who was the Phillies' best pitcher in 2003?" without doing a lot of complicated math. Cole Hamels' Season Score was 233, which was the highest by a Phillies pitcher since 1998. Schilling was at 327 in 1997, 271 in 1998.

While I was figuring this, however, I struck across something else really striking. *The Phillies best pitcher, over the last twenty years, has usually been their relief ace.* This is my list of the Phillies best pitchers, 1986-2007, with the RELIEVERS in all caps:

1986: STEVE BEDROSIAN	1997: Curt Schilling
1987: STEVE BEDROSIAN	1998: Curt Schilling
1988: STEVE BEDROSIAN	1999: Curt Schilling
1989: JEFF PARRETT	2000: Curt Schilling
1990: ROGER MC DOWELL	2001: JOSE MESA
1991: MITCH WILLIAMS	2002: JOSE MESA
1992: Curt Schilling	2003: Randy Wolf
1993: Tommy Greene	2004: BILLY WAGNER
1994: Danny Jackson	2005: BILLY WAGNER
1995: HEATHCLIFF SLOCUMB	2006: Bret Myers
1996: RICKY BOTTALICO	2007: Cole Hamels

Jeff Parrett (1989) was not the team's closer; Bedrosian was still the closer, but Parrett had a better year.

The Phillies in 2003 had what looked like a top-flight rotation shaping up: 22-year-old Bret Myers (14-9), 25-year-old Vicente Padilla (14-12), 26-year-old Randy Wolf (16-10) and 28-year-old Kevin Millwood (14-12). Free agency and injuries decimated that effort, but setting that aside, what do we make of the curious decision to make their best starting pitcher of 2006, Brett Myers, into a reliever?

Has their ever, in the history of baseball, been any other team that moved their best starting pitcher to the bullpen? I doubt it. There are very, very few teams in baseball history who have moved a healthy and successful starting pitcher to the bullpen, period—certainly less than ten such teams, and I haven't been able to identify five.

People like to talk about the importance of the Closer, and certainly it is a wonderful thing to have a good Closer. But I don't think it is a normal thing, in building a pitching staff, to start with the closer and build back from there. If you look at the teams that made the playoffs last year, the number one pitchers (by Season Score) were Brandon Webb, Ted Lilly, Jeff Francis and Cole Hamels in the National League, and Josh Beckett, C. C. Sabathia, John Lackey and Chien-Ming Wang in the American League—all starting pitchers. On half of those teams, their number two pitcher was another starter—Zambrano, Carmona, Escobar and Pettitte.

Myers is supposedly going back to the starting rotation, which should give the Phillies their strongest rotation in years: Hamels, Kendrick, Moyer, Myers and somebody. Whether Hamels' arm will stand up to the pounding of throwing 3,000 pitches a season is an open question. If he can carry the load, the Phillies would have an ace for the first time in years.

In 2006 Ryan Howard hit an astonishing 23 home runs to the opposite field. This is the highest number I have ever seen, I believe, although I haven't seen data for Bonds in his best years.

Last year, establishing a major league record for strikeouts, Howard hit just as many home runs to center and to right as he had in 2007—but his opposite field home runs dropped to 10, which is still a very large number for opposite field home runs. Obviously, while Howard remains a formidable hitter, he did, to an extent, get into a pattern of trying to pull everything, more than he had in 2006, resulting in more strikeouts and fewer opposite-field home runs.

I believe that study will show that this is a common pattern—that young power hitters, when they come to the major leagues, OFTEN hit a good number of opposite-field home runs, but that after they have been in the league a year or two the opposite-field power tends to disappear. I certainly have seen numerous other cases in which this has happened. David Ortiz is an exceptionally similar player to Howard in a skills profile—a left-handed hitter with phenomenal power, limited defense and mobility. When he first came to the majors Ortiz hit with a lot of power to left field, but, while he remains a fantastic player, he rarely does anymore.

We often think about young players as LACKING abilities that veterans acquire, but I wonder if "negative learning" in this area doesn't outweigh positive learning. Hitters "learn" to look for a pitch they can pull, when sometimes they might be better off if they didn't.

Ryan Howard – 2006
Hitting Analysis

Batting Left-Handed								1B	2B	3B	HR
Ground Balls to Left	10	Outs 4	Hits 6	Average .600	Hit Type	6 -	0 -	0 -	0
Ground Balls to Center	41	Outs 25	Hits 16	Average .390	Hit Type	16 -	0 -	0 -	0
Ground Balls to Right	119	Outs 98	Hits 21	Average .176	Hit Type	19 -	2 -	0 -	0
Line Drives to Left	15	Outs 2	Hits 13	Average .867	Hit Type	9 -	2 -	0 -	2
Line Drives to Center	31	Outs 5	Hits 26	Average .839	Hit Type	24 -	2 -	0 -	0
Line Drives to Right	43	Outs 12	Hits 31	Average .721	Hit Type	23 -	7 -	0 -	1
Fly Balls to Left	67	Outs 41	Hits 26	Average .394	Hit Type	0 -	3 -	0 -	23
Fly Balls to Center	53	Outs 29	Hits 24	Average .500	Hit Type	1 -	7 -	0 -	16
Fly Balls to Right	27	Outs 8	Hits 19	Average .704	Hit Type	0 -	2 -	1 -	16
Total on Ground Balls	170	Outs 127	Hits 43	Average .253	Hit Type	41 -	2 -	0 -	0
Total on Line Drives	89	Outs 19	Hits 70	Average .787	Hit Type	56 -	11 -	0 -	3
Total on Fly Balls	147	Outs 78	Hits 69	Average .489	Hit Type	1 -	12 -	1 -	55
Total Hit to Left	92	Outs 47	Hits 45	Average .495	Hit Type	15 -	5 -	0 -	25
Total Hit to Center	125	Outs 59	Hits 66	Average .550	Hit Type	41 -	9 -	0 -	16
Total Hit to Right	189	Outs 118	Hits 71	Average .376	Hit Type	42 -	11 -	1 -	17
All Balls in Play	406	Outs 224	Hits 182	Average .455	Hit Type	98 -	25 -	1 -	58

Ryan Howard – 2007
Hitting Analysis

Batting Left-Handed								1B	2B	3B	HR
Ground Balls to Left	5	Outs 3	Hits 2	Average .400	Hit Type	2 -	0 -	0 -	0
Ground Balls to Center	27	Outs 20	Hits 7	Average .259	Hit Type	7 -	0 -	0 -	0
Ground Balls to Right	74	Outs 64	Hits 10	Average .135	Hit Type	9 -	1 -	0 -	0
Line Drives to Left	13	Outs 4	Hits 9	Average .692	Hit Type	5 -	3 -	0 -	1
Line Drives to Center	21	Outs 7	Hits 14	Average .700	Hit Type	14 -	0 -	0 -	0
Line Drives to Right	48	Outs 10	Hits 38	Average .792	Hit Type	26 -	10 -	0 -	2
Fly Balls to Left	52	Outs 39	Hits 13	Average .260	Hit Type	1 -	2 -	0 -	10
Fly Balls to Center	60	Outs 36	Hits 24	Average .429	Hit Type	3 -	5 -	0 -	16
Fly Balls to Right	37	Outs 12	Hits 25	Average .676	Hit Type	2 -	5 -	0 -	18
Total on Ground Balls	106	Outs 87	Hits 19	Average .179	Hit Type	18 -	1 -	0 -	0
Total on Line Drives	82	Outs 21	Hits 61	Average .753	Hit Type	45 -	13 -	0 -	3
Total on Fly Balls	149	Outs 87	Hits 62	Average .434	Hit Type	6 -	12 -	0 -	44
Total Hit to Left	70	Outs 46	Hits 24	Average .353	Hit Type	8 -	5 -	0 -	11
Total Hit to Center	108	Outs 63	Hits 45	Average .437	Hit Type	24 -	5 -	0 -	16
Total Hit to Right	159	Outs 86	Hits 73	Average .459	Hit Type	37 -	16 -	0 -	20
All Balls in Play	337	Outs 195	Hits 142	Average .430	Hit Type	69 -	26 -	0 -	47

Howard's Mark

In 1884 the Boston Red Stockings short-stop, Sam Wise, struck out 104 times. For many years Wise was the only player documented to have reached the century mark in strikeouts, although it is unlikely that there was anyone on earth who knew this, given the state of record-keeping at that time. A lot of leagues weren't keeping any strikeout records.

In 1913 Washington outfielder Danny Moeller struck out 103 times, and in 1914 St. Louis Browns outfielder Gus Williams struck out 120, shattering the record. Wise, Moeller and Williams weren't big-swinging power hitters; they were just lousy hitters.

No one struck out 100 times in a season again until 1932, when Bruce Campbell struck out 104. That was the first time somebody who could actually hit had struck out 100 times in a season. After that sometimes the triple-digit level would be reached by selective hitters who were looking for a pitch to hit out of the park. Many of the players who first joined the growing 100-strikeout club were very good hitters—Jimmie Foxx, Dolph Camilli, Harlond Clift. Gus Williams, however, held the strikeout mark until 1938, when it was broken by Vince DiMaggio.

Vince was the lesser DiMaggio. He was a very good defensive outfielder with a big, big swing and some power. He drove in 100 runs once. He was pretty close, as a player, to Preston Wilson or Mike Cameron. He was ahead of his time. With 134 strikeouts in 1938, Vince DiMaggio held the record for almost twenty years—an irony that a DiMaggio would hold the record, since his younger brother almost never struck out.

Anyway, the record was finally broken in 1956 by Jim Lemon, who struck out 138 times. Lemon was the Pat Burrell of his time, a tall right-handed hitter who had real power and was actually a fairly productive hitter, but who had a poor reputation because he struck out a lot, was slow and a terrible outfielder.

From 1884 to 1956 the strikeout record had been held by only three players—Sam Wise for 30 years, Gus Williams for 24, and Vince DiMaggio for 18. That was about to change. Jake Wood, a second baseman, broke the record in '61 with 141 strikeouts. Harmon Killebrew broke it again in '62, with 142 strikeouts. Dave Nicholson broke in '63, with 175 strikeouts.

Nicholson was a strikeout prodigy. He struck out 175 times in '63 in only 449 at bats. If he had been able to stay in the lineup he would have struck out 230+ times. He'd still hold the record today. He couldn't stay in the lineup.

He held the record only six years. In 1969 Bobby Bonds, Barry's father, struck out 187 times. In 1970 he upped the ante to 189.

And then, improbably, Bonds held the record for 34 years. This was really an astonishing thing. During much of that time strikeout rates were climbing steadily. The record had been broken six times in fifteen years—by Lemon, Wood, Killebrew, Nicholson, and twice by Bonds. In 1956 Lemon had set the record with 138 strikeouts. By 1970 this was a commonplace accomplishment. In 1970 alone, six players struck out more than 138 times. We all assumed, at the time, that Bonds' would hold the record for only a couple of years, and then pass it on to the next slugger.

It didn't happen that way. It didn't happen that way for four reasons:

1) Strikeout rates did go down sometimes…up and down, but there were down periods, so the overall upward slope of the line was limited.

2) Bobby Bonds, though nowhere near as great a player as his son, was a tremendous player—a much better player than Lemon, or Wood, of Nicholson, or Vince DiMaggio. His speed, defense, power and his surprising .302 batting average kept him in the lineup despite his strikeouts. Many of the people who chased him couldn't stay in the lineup.

3) Bonds had a huge number of at bats—663 in 1970. Bonds was a leadoff man most of his career, a leadoff man that season. Most of the people who "tried" to break his record, over the next 30 years, were not leadoff men, and so did not have the same number of at bats.

4) Just luck. Mike Schmidt struck out 180 times in 1975. Gorman Thomas got close, and Rob Deer. There *could* well have been a player who had the right combination of playing time, strikeout tendency and bad luck, but there just never was.

No one struck out 100 times in the 1920s.

10 players did in the 1930s.

12 players did in the 1940s.

28 players did in the 1950s.

195 did it in the 1960s.

221 did it in the 1970s.

280 did it in the 1980s.

478 made it in the 1990s.

In this decade the number will be something over 700. Through the 1950s there were 54 players in history with one hundred strikeouts. Now there are more than 70 a year. History would suggest that a thousand-plus players will strike out 100 times in a season between 2010 and 2019.

Meanwhile, despite the explosive popularity of the strikeout concept, Bonds' 189- and 187-strikeout seasons rested improbably at the top of the list for 30-plus years. This finally began to crack up in 2002, when Jose Hernandez struck out 188 times, and then Adam Dunn broke through with 195 strikeouts in 2004, 194 more in 2006. Ryan Howard re-broke the record last year with 199. It probably wasn't exactly the way he had dreamed of entering the record book.

We have finally burst through the Bobby Bonds logjam, and gotten back to the pre-Bonds normalcy in which the record is broken every couple of years. Therefore, assuming that this continues to hold, somebody within two or three years should enjoy the ignominy of being the first to get 200 strikeouts in a season.

Ryan Howard? Could be. More likely not. Often player's career strikeout highs come in their first two or three seasons as a regular. Vince DiMaggio set the record in his second season as a regular in 1938. Although he was a regular several more years and led his league in strikeout four more times, he never pushed past 134.

Jim Lemon broke his record in 1956 in Lemon's first year as a regular. Although he led the league in strikeout the next two seasons, he never got past 138.

Jake Wood broke the record in 1961 in his rookie season.

Harmon Killebrew broke the record in 1962 in his fourth season as a regular, but he was younger then than Ryan Howard was in 2007.

Dave Nicholson broke the record in 1963 in his first (and only) year as a sort-of regular player.

Bobby Bonds broke the record in 1969, his first season as a regular, and re-broke it in 1970, his second season as a regular.

Adam Dunn broke the record in 2004 in his second season as a regular, aged 24.

By the way, did you realize that Harmon Killebrew is the only player in major league history whose first name was "Harmon"? He is.

It could be Howard or Dunn who gets the record to 200, but my money would be on the next guy down the line—Jack Cust, perhaps, or B. J. Upton or Wily Mo Pena or Richie Robnett or Chip Cannon or Justin Ruggiano or Ryan Royster or Travis Snyder. Baseball has been a game increasingly of power against power, for 130 years almost always more power against more power. I'm not betting on that to go on forever, but I'm not betting on it to end in March, either.

A Game Score of 50 or above is roughly equivalent to a Quality Start. It is a game in which the starting pitcher has delivered a creditable performance.

Of the eight teams that made the playoffs, all except the Phillies had more Game Scores over 50 than under. The Phillies had 83 games under 50.

Philadelphia Phillies – 2007
Performance by Quality of Start

Game Score	#	ERA	W	-	L
80 and above	4	0.75	4	-	0
70 to 79	9	1.31	6	-	3
60 to 69	26	2.37	21	-	5
50 to 59	40	3.69	25	-	15
40 to 49	35	5.11	21	-	14
30 to 39	26	6.46	8	-	18
20 to 29	12	8.83	3	-	9
Below 20	10	10.05	1	-	9

Strength Up the Middle

by Bill James

Perhaps the first lick of old baseball wisdom that I ever encountered was that championship teams are strong up the middle. This was 1960, 1961; the fifties were still echoing in the wind, and it was still the general practice to look first, in selecting the MVP, at the

catchers, the center fielders, the shortstops and the second basemen. The first principle of baseball analysis, I suppose, was that baseball is 75% pitching, but the second was that championship teams are strong up the middle.

With the development of Win Shares, it occurred to me that I was in a stronger position to evaluate this theory. In 2004 I had Matthew Namee construct a spreadsheet, Win Shares by Teams, which has all of the Win Shares in history stored in a meaningful pattern—for example, the Win Shares earned by Jason Giambi in 2003 (28) are stored on the row set aside for the New York Yankees, 2003, and in the column set aside for the regular first basemen. The Win Shares earned by Mike Piazza in 1993 (31) are stored on the row set aside for the Los Angeles Dodgers, 1993, and in the column reserved for the regular catcher, and the Win Shares earned by Wade Boggs in 1983 (34) are stored on the row marked for the Boston Red Sox, 1983, and in the column which is indicated for the team's regular third baseman.

This spreadsheet makes it possible to test in a fairly simple, direct, and convincing manner whether it is or is not true that championship teams are strong up the middle. First, however, I would like to ask you to do something. I would like to ask you to set this aside for a moment, close your eyes, and think as deeply as you can about this question: is it true that championship teams are strong up the middle?

I have done studies of this issue before, I am sure—not as good as this study—and I have expressed my opinion before. That opinion was that I thought it was probably true that championship teams were strong up the middle. I was saying this, as much as anything, to avoid the argument. The assertion requires the student,

Meaning no disrespect to whatever sportswriter or manager first came up with this idea, this seems to me to be asking a great deal of the human mind.

requires the person defending the assertion, to form a mental image of all of the championship teams within his knowledge, form a general impression of their strength at catcher, at second base, at short and in center, form a general impression of their overall strength, relate the general impression of the strength up the middle to the general impression of the overall strength, and then mentally weigh that against the comparable ratio on non-championship teams. Meaning no disrespect to whatever sportswriter or manager first came up with this idea, this seems to me to be asking a great deal of the human mind. Human beings are really not very good at this kind of mental exercise, which requires us to draw together a wide range of memories and associations, and balance one against another. That's why I ask you to try to think deeply about the issue; if you actually try to think it through, you should realize how nearly impossible it is to do this.

Using this spreadsheet, Win Shares by Teams, I sorted out three groups of teams. Group One was championship teams, Group Two was average teams, and Group Three was bad teams. I used all major leagues, 1900-2003, including the Federal League and the strike-shortened 1981 and 1994 seasons. Each league was represented by one team in each group—thus, there were 209 teams in each group, two per season from 1901 to 2003, plus the National League in 1900, plus the two seasons of the Federal League.

For the "championship" teams, I used

a) whatever team represented the league in the World Series, if there was such a team (which there was for 200 of the 209 leagues), or

b) whichever team had the highest winning percentage (for the other nine leagues).

For the "average" teams, I used

a) whichever team had a winning percentage closest to .500,

b) with ties broken by the ratio of runs scored to runs allowed. If two or three teams were equally close to .500, I used whichever team was closest to scoring exactly as many runs as they allowed.

For the "bad" teams,

a) whichever team had the worst winning percentage,

b) with ties broken by the worst ratio of runs scored to runs allowed.

The "championship" teams in the study had an overall winning percentage of .622 (101-61 in a 162-games season). The "average" teams had an overall winning percentage of .500, and the "bad" teams had an overall winning percentage of .359 (58 wins in a 162-game schedule). The "bad" teams were further from .500 than good teams because, since 1969, the "championship" team has sometimes not been the team with the best won-lost record.

We are then in a position to compare the 209 regular first basemen on championship teams to 209 first basemen on average teams, representing the same leagues, and 209 first basemen on lousy teams, representing the same leagues. If it is true that championship teams are strong up the middle, then it should be true that the advantage of the championship teams is larger at the "up the middle" positions than it is at the "corner" positions (first and third base, left and right field).

The conclusion of our study is that it appears to be unquestionably true that championship teams are strong up the middle. Unless there is something wrong with my study, unless there is some hidden bias in the Win Shares system toward up the middle players on championship teams, then it is clearly true that championship teams are strong up the middle.

The 209 regular catchers on championship teams, in this study, earned a total of 3,424 Win Shares. The regular catchers on average teams earned 2,417 Win Shares, and the regular catchers on bad teams earned 1,614 Win Shares. The ratio of good teams to average teams was 1.42 to 1; average teams to bad teams had a ratio of 1.50 to 1, and good teams to bad teams, a ratio of 2.12 to 1.

This chart summarizes the parallel data for all the eight regular positions:

	Champions	Average Teams	Bad Teams	Ratio Top to Bottom
Catcher	3424	2417	1614	2.12
First Base	4069	3422	2446	1.66
Second Base	4022	3037	2023	1.99
Third Base	3857	3149	2226	1.73
Shortstop	3762	2806	1847	2.04
Left Field	4385	3409	2595	1.69
Center Field	4673	3659	2539	1.84
Right Field	4531	3471	2453	1.85

The ratios are obviously tied to the defensive spectrum. The ratio between good and bad teams, at first base, is 1.66 to 1; at shortstop, it is 2.04 to 1. Both the ratios and the actual differences between the good teams and the bad teams are markedly higher at the "up-the-middle" positions than at the corner positions. Sorting the chart above:

The first principle of baseball analysis, I suppose, was that baseball is 75% pitching, but the second was that championship teams are strong up the middle.

The championship teams were 98% better than the bad teams at the "up the middle" positions, 73% better at the corner positions.

	Champions	Average Teams	Bad Teams	Ratio Top to Bottom
Catcher	3424	2417	1614	2.12
Second Base	4022	3037	2023	1.99
Shortstop	3762	2806	1847	2.04
Center Field	4673	3659	2539	1.84
Total	**15881**	**11919**	**8023**	**1.98**
First Base	4069	3422	2446	1.66
Third Base	3857	3149	2226	1.73
Left Field	4385	3409	2595	1.69
Right Field	4531	3471	2453	1.85
Total	**16842**	**13451**	**9720**	**1.73**

The championship teams were 98% better than the bad teams at the "up the middle" positions, 73% better at the corner positions. The largest values are at the "corner" positions, the positions played by Lou Gehrig, Albert Pujols, Ted Williams and Barry Bonds. But the largest differences are at the up-the-middle positions.

Although only one-seventh of the teams had Designated Hitters, the ratio between good and bad teams at DH, as we would expect, is even flatter than the ratio at first base:

	Champions	Average Teams	Bad Teams	Ratio Top to Bottom
DH	426	380	295	1.44

While at pitcher, the difference between good and bad teams is more notable in pitching depth than in front-line starting quality:

	Champions	Average Teams	Bad Teams	Ratio Top to Bottom
First Starters	5072	4116	2970	1.71
Second Starters	3924	3103	2069	1.90
Third Starters	3076	2350	1578	1.95
Fourth Starters	2254	1739	1137	1.98
Fifth Starters	1472	1158	733	2.01
Relief Aces	2091	1697	1180	1.77

However, this effect is not to be taken as reliable, due to the fact that the pitchers are sorted by quality after the fact…the man who starts the season as the team's third starting pitcher often winds up the year as the number one starting pitcher, etc. If we sorted infielders after the season as "first infielder", "second infielder", etc., best to worst, we would probably get a similar "depth effect" among infielders. Also, the relief ace data cannot be compared directly to the data at other positions, since the time line is different for relief aces than for players at other positions. Many of the early teams didn't have relief aces, and the overall ratio of wins by good teams to wins by bad teams has changed significantly over time.

In a sense…returning to the main topic here, which is strength up the middle. . .in a sense, it is more true that bad teams are weak up the middle than that good teams are strong up the middle. Good teams are strong up the middle, but they are equally strong—even stronger, perhaps, at the corner positions. But as you go down in the standings, the weakness becomes more apparent at the "up the middle" positions than it is at the corner positions.

In a sense, it is more true that bad teams are weak up the middle than that good teams are strong up the middle.

The strongest team in the study, up the middle, was the 1956 Yankees. They were in fact, not merely the strongest team in the study, but the strongest team of all time up the middle. Their catcher, Yogi Berra, hit .298 with 30 homers, 105 RBI, while their center fielder, Mickey Mantle, won the Triple Crown and the Most Valuable Player Award. But the Yankee double play combination, which often was not good in those years, was also pretty decent in 1956. Shortstop Gil McDougald hit .311 with 13 homers and a .405 on-base percentage, while second baseman Billy Martin hit .264 with 9 homers. All four were also good defensive players, and the '56 Yankees led the league in double plays by a wide margin. While the second-place Cleveland Indians turned 130 double plays, the Yankees turned 214.

These are the ten strongest teams of all time, up the middle:

1. 1956 Yankees (C—Berra, 2B—Martin, SS—McDougald, CF—Mantle)
2. (tie) 1909 Pirates (C-G. Gibson, 2B-Dots Miller, SS—H. Wagner, CF—Tommy Leach)
2. (tie) 1953 Dodgers (C—Campanella, 2B—Jr. Gilliam, SS—Reese, CF—Snider)
2. (tie) 1949 Dodgers (C—Campanella, 2B—J. Robinson, SS—Reese, CF—Snider)
5. (tie) 1950 Yankees (C—Berra, 2B—Jer. Coleman, SS—Rizzuto, CF—DiMaggio)
5   (tie) 1950 Dodgers (Campanella, Robinson, Reese and Snider, again)
7. 1974 Reds (C—Bench, 2B—Morgan, SS—Concepcion, CF—Geronimo)
8. 1908 Pirates (C—Gibson, 2B—Abbaticchio, SS—Wagner, CF—Roy Thomas)
9. 1961 Yankees (C—E. Howard, 2B—Richardson, SS—Kubek, CF—Mantle)
10. 1975 Reds (C—Bench, 2B—Morgan, SS—Concepcion, CF—Geronimo)

Just outside the top ten you have the same teams, only in different years…the '57 Yankees, 1952 Dodgers, 1962 Yankees, etc. A few teams you might not immediately think of as extremely strong up the middle: the 1952 Cardinals, 1920 White Sox, 1929 Cubs, and 1946 Red Sox. The 1949-1952 Dodgers had four Hall of Famers up the middle.

This study was done several years ago, and I don't have completely organized data for the last four years. However, I don't *believe* that any recent team would make

this list or be within hailing distance of the list. The 2006-2007 Tigers are strong up the middle (Ivan Rodriguez, Placido Polanco, Carlos Guillen and Curtis Granderson), but miss the top ten by a whopping 26 Win Shares. The 2007 Phillies were stronger up the middle than the Tigers (Carlos Ruiz, Chase Utley, Jimmy Rollins and Aaron Rowand), but they, again, are not in the top fifty, let alone the top ten.

The '56 Yankees are also the "most imbalanced" team of all time in terms of the comparison between their strength up the middle and their strength at the corner positions. Up the middle they were formidable; at the corners they were unimpressive. Their first baseman, Bill Skowron, was a good player—.308 with 23 homers—but on the other hand, he was a first baseman who did not hit as well as the catcher or the center fielder on the team. The third baseman, Andy Carey, was a glove man who hit .237, the right fielder, Hank Bauer, was a power hitter who hit .241, and the left fielders were a collection of out-of-position guys like Elston Howard and Norm Siebern, both of whom became outstanding players, but about six years later and not playing left field.

The other end of that spectrum is interesting. Of the three teams in history which were weakest up the middle compared to their strength at the corners, two were managed by the same man, Frankie Frisch. Frisch was one of those guys who liked to say about his shortstop that he didn't care what he hit as long as he did the job in the field, which is a real useful theory if you're trying to get the crap beat out of you. Frisch's up-the-middle guys were *such* weak hitters that they dragged the team down. His 1937 Cardinals had fantastic players in left field (Joe Medwick, who won the triple crown, also leading the league in hits, doubles and runs scored) and Johnny Mize (who was second in the league in batting average, on base percentage, slugging percentage, doubles and total bases, third in RBI, fourth in home runs). Up the middle, however, he had one good player (Terry Moore) and three glove guys who didn't hit. Given the league's two best hitters, they finished fourth. Frisch's '44 Pirates were the same— very strong at the corners, but so punchless through the middle that they fell short overall.

Of the "average" teams in our study—the 209 teams that finished at or near .500—not a single one was of anything like comparable strength up the middle to the strongest of the championship teams.

How many championship teams are strong up the middle? Using the standard of 60 Win Shares at the four up the middle positions to indicate strength up the middle, 84% of the championship teams in this study were strong up the middle, whereas only 43% of the average teams were strong up the middle, and only 2% of the bad teams were strong up the middle. This fact, however, is potentially misleading, because there is a similar breakdown if you use 60 Win Shares at the four corner positions to represent strength at the corners.

Good teams are strong everywhere; we all know this. However, we are asking the simple question: is it true that good teams are strong up the middle? Certainly it is true that good teams are strong up the middle, and this appears to be distinctly *more* true than saying that good teams are strong at the corners, or even that good teams have strong pitching staffs. One could romanticize this fact inappropriately, and use it as an excuse to vote for Curtis Granderson and Carlos Beltran as the 2008 MVPs, even if Miguel Cabrera and David Wright have better years. It is not a universal, sweeping truth. It is not a magic bullet that explains why all winners succeed. But the best answer to the question is: Yes. Championship teams are strong up the middle.

Frisch was one of those guys who liked to say about his shortstop that he didn't care what he hit as long as he did the job in the field, which is a real useful theory if you're trying to get the crap beat out of you.

Pittsburgh Pirates

Pittsburgh Pirates – 2007
Team Overview

Description		Ranking
Won-Lost Record	68-94	
Place	6th of 6 in National League Central	
Runs Scored	724	23rd in the majors
Runs Allowed	846	26th in the majors
Home Runs	148	22nd in the majors
Home Runs Allowed	174	21st in the majors
Batting Average	.263	20th in the majors
Batting Average Allowed	.288	29th in the majors
Walks Drawn	463	28th in the majors
Walks Given	518	13th in the majors
OPS For	.736	23rd in the majors
OPS Against	.799	27th in the majors
Stolen Bases	68	24th in the majors
Stolen Bases Allowed	110	26th in the majors

Key Players

Pos	Player	G	AB	R	H	2B	3B	HR	RBI	SB	CS	BB	SO	Avg	OBP	Slg	OPS	WS
C	Ronny Paulino	133	457	56	120	25	0	11	55	2	2	33	79	.263	.314	.389	.703	10
1B	Adam LaRoche	152	563	71	153	42	0	21	88	1	1	62	131	.272	.345	.458	.803	16
2B	Freddy Sanchez	147	602	77	183	42	4	11	81	0	1	32	76	.304	.343	.442	.784	21
3B	Jose Bautista	142	532	75	135	36	2	15	63	6	3	68	101	.254	.339	.414	.753	12
SS	Jack Wilson	135	477	67	141	29	2	12	56	2	5	38	46	.296	.350	.440	.791	19
LF	Jason Bay	145	538	78	133	25	2	21	84	4	1	59	141	.247	.327	.418	.746	12
CF	Chris Duffy	70	241	31	60	11	3	3	22	13	4	21	43	.249	.313	.357	.670	5
RF	Xavier Nady	125	431	55	120	23	1	20	72	3	1	23	101	.278	.330	.476	.805	10

Key Pitchers

Pos	Player	G	GS	W	L	Sv	IP	H	R	ER	BB	SO	BR/9	ERA	WS
SP	Tom Gorzelanny	32	32	14	10	0	201.2	214	90	87	68	135	13.08	3.88	11
SP	Ian Snell	32	32	9	12	0	208.0	209	94	87	68	177	12.33	3.76	11
SP	Paul Maholm	29	29	10	15	0	177.2	204	110	99	49	105	13.12	5.02	5
SP	Zach Duke	20	19	3	8	0	107.1	161	74	66	25	41	15.85	5.53	2
SP	Tony Armas Jr.	31	15	4	5	0	97.0	111	68	65	38	73	14.57	6.03	1
CL	Matt Capps	76	0	4	7	18	79.0	64	22	20	16	64	9.46	2.28	14
RP	Damaso Marte	65	0	2	0	0	45.1	32	14	12	18	51	10.32	2.38	5
RP	John Grabow	63	0	3	2	1	51.2	56	27	26	19	42	13.24	4.53	3

In games where the Pirates got an above-average start, Game Score above 50, they were 51-24. But when they didn't they were 17-70, a league-worst .195 winning percentage.

Pittsburgh Pirates – 2007
Performance by Quality of Start

Game Score	#	ERA	W	-	L
80 and above	4	1.18	3	-	1
70 to 79	7	1.09	5	-	2
60 to 69	25	2.06	20	-	5
50 to 59	39	3.75	23	-	16
40 to 49	36	4.99	11	-	25
30 to 39	22	6.76	5	-	17
20 to 29	15	9.07	1	-	14
Below 20	14	10.35	0	-	14

Jason Bay hit essentially as many fly balls in 2007 (184) as he had in 2006 (186) or 2005 (188). But whereas 56 of these were extra-base hits in 2005 and again in 2006, only 34 of them were extra-base hits in 2007.

Jason Bay
Hitting Analysis

	Total Fly Balls	Extra-Base Hits	2B	-	3B	-	HR
2005	188	56	21	-	5	-	30
2006	186	56	20	-	3	-	33
2007	184	34	11	-	2	-	21

In each of the past two seasons, the same three players have been the Pirates' three most commonly-used leadoff men: Nate McLouth, Chris Duffy and Jose Bautista. Over the two-year span, they've shared the role fairly equally, with McLouth getting 88 starts at leadoff, Duffy getting 110, and Bautista getting 72. There doesn't appear to be a lot to choose between with Nate McLouth and Chris Duffy. They're both left-handed hitters, and their skills are similar. Both in 2006 and 2007, the team scored substantially more runs per inning when McLouth led off.

	06	07
McLouth	.79	.77
Duffy	.46	.55
Bautista	.55	.54

Nate McLouth – 2007
Impact by Position in Inning

Position	Innings	Runs	Runs/Inning	Runs/RBI
Leading Off	123	95	.77	30/5
Batting Second	90	62	.69	15/4
Batting Third	72	25	.35	4/10
Batting Fourth	47	26	.55	4/3
Batting 5th or later	50	133	2.66	7/16

Chris Duffy – 2007
Impact by Position in Inning

Position	Innings	Runs	Runs/Inning	Runs/RBI
Leading Off	97	53	.55	16/0
Batting Second	69	40	.58	7/2
Batting Third	41	17	.41	4/4
Batting Fourth	27	21	.78	1/5
Batting 5th or later	36	60	1.67	3/11

The Pirates in 2007 had an .800 OPS from their number eight hitters, mostly Jack Wilson. Among the nine positions, Pirate number eight hitters finished first in slugging percentage (.452) and tied for first in on base percentage (.348).

Pittsburgh Piratces – 2007
Productivity by Batting Order Position

Pos	Players	Avg	OBP	Slg	OPS
1	McLouth (45g), Duffy (38g), Bautista (28g)	.262	.341	.406	.748
2	Bautista (48g), Wilson (39g), Sanchez (30g)	.257	.320	.398	.718
3	Sanchez (111g), LaRoche (25g), Bay (23g)	.281	.328	.406	.734
4	LaRoche (72g), Bay (57g), Nady (25g)	.265	.348	.444	.792
5	Nady (49g), Bay (43g), LaRoche (28g)	.272	.333	.450	.784
6	Doumit (33g), Nady (28g), LaRoche (21g)	.260	.327	.442	.769
7	Paulino (89g), Bautista (19g)	.271	.317	.404	.721
8	Wilson (82g), Castillo (19g), Paulino (17g)	.296	.348	.452	.800
9	Snell (31g), Gorzelanny (29g), Maholm (27g)	.191	.245	.287	.532
	Total	.263	.325	.411	.736

While Paul Maholm was no more effective in 2007 than he had been in 2006, he was notably more efficient, retiring the side on 10 pitches or less 63% more often, and incurring 25% fewer long innings.

Paul Maholm – 2006
Inning Analysis

Innings Pitched	176.0
Runs Allowed	98
Innings Started	182
Runs in Those Innings	99
Shutout Innings	130
One-Run Innings	26
Two-Run Innings	14
Three-Run Inning	5
Four-Run Innings	6
Five-Run Innings	1
Got First Man Out	116
Runs Scored in Those Innings	41
Runs/9 Innings	3.18
First Man Reached	66
Runs Scored in Those Innings	58
Runs/9 Innings	7.91
1-2-3 Innings	60
10-pitch Innings (or less)	35
Long Innings (20 or more pitches)	48
Failed to Finish Inning	10

Paul Maholm – 2007
Inning Analysis

Innings Pitched	177.2
Runs Allowed	110
Innings Started	184
Runs in Those Innings	115
Shutout Innings	124
One-Run Innings	30
Two-Run Innings	17
Three-Run Inning	5
Four-Run Innings	4
Five-Run Innings	4
Got First Man Out	107
Runs Scored in Those Innings	20
Runs/9 Innings	1.68
First Man Reached	77
Runs Scored in Those Innings	95
Runs/9 Innings	11.10
1-2-3 Innings	77
10-pitch Innings (or less)	57
Long Innings (20 or more pitches)	36
Failed to Finish Inning	11

And He Lived to Tell

Ian Snell last year threw 1,108 sliders—the most of any major league pitcher.

Ian Snell – 2007
Pitch Type Analysis

Overall		
Total Pitches	3125	
Fastball	1561	50%
Changeup	303	10%
Slider	1108	35%
Pitchout	4	0%
Not Charted	149	5%

	Vs. RHB		Vs. LHB	
Total Pitches	1577		1548	
Outs Recorded	333		291	
Fastball	723	46%	838	54%
Changeup	85	5%	218	14%
Slider	699	44%	409	26%
Pitchout	0	0%	4	0%
Not Charted	70	4%	79	5%

The two Pennsylvania teams scored 2 or fewer runs in 66 of their games.
In those games their combined record was 0-66.
The only other team without a win in a game where they scored 2 or fewer runs was the Marlins.

Pittsburgh Pirates – 2007
Record by Runs Scored and Allowed

	Scored	Allowed
10 runs or more	11 - 0	1 - 16
9 runs	2 - 0	0 - 13
8 runs	9 - 6	0 - 8
7 runs	9 - 2	3 - 9
6 runs	9 - 3	2 - 15
5 runs	8 - 9	7 - 16
4 runs	9 - 15	9 - 6
3 runs	11 - 18	12 - 8
2 runs	0 - 12	18 - 1
1 run	0 - 16	11 - 2
0 runs	0 - 13	5 - 0
Total	68 - 94	68 - 94

Philadelphia Phillies – 2007
Record by Runs Scored and Allowed

	Scored	Allowed
10 runs or more	17 - 0	2 - 17
9 runs	10 - 0	0 - 4
8 runs	13 - 2	2 - 9
7 runs	6 - 0	4 - 7
6 runs	15 - 9	7 - 6
5 runs	13 - 9	7 - 14
4 runs	11 - 12	14 - 9
3 runs	4 - 16	20 - 3
2 runs	0 - 14	18 - 3
1 run	0 - 8	10 - 1
0 runs	0 - 3	5 - 0
Total	89 - 73	89 - 73

St. Louis Cardinals

St. Louis Cardinals – 2007
Team Overview

Description		Ranking
Won-Lost Record	78-84	
Place	3rd of 6 in National League Central	
Runs Scored	725	22nd in the majors
Runs Allowed	829	23rd in the majors
Home Runs	141	24th in the majors
Home Runs Allowed	168	17th in the majors
Batting Average	.274	11th in the majors
Batting Average Allowed	.271	20th in the majors
Walks Drawn	506	22nd in the majors
Walks Given	509	11th in the majors
OPS For	.743	20th in the majors
OPS Against	.768	19th in the majors
Stolen Bases	56	28th in the majors
Stolen Bases Allowed	58	1st in the majors

Key Players

Pos	Player	G	AB	R	H	2B	3B	HR	RBI	SB	CS	BB	SO	Avg	OBP	Slg	OPS	WS
C	Yadier Molina	111	353	30	97	15	0	6	40	1	1	34	43	.275	.340	.368	.708	12
1B	Albert Pujols	158	565	99	185	38	1	32	103	2	6	99	58	.327	.429	.568	.997	32
2B	Adam Kennedy	87	279	27	61	9	1	3	18	6	2	22	33	.219	.282	.290	.572	2
3B	Scott Rolen	112	392	55	104	24	2	8	58	5	3	37	56	.265	.331	.398	.729	11
SS	David Eckstein	117	434	58	134	23	0	3	31	10	1	24	22	.309	.356	.382	.739	12
LF	Chris Duncan	127	375	51	97	20	0	21	70	2	1	55	123	.259	.354	.480	.834	17
CF	Jim Edmonds	117	365	39	92	15	2	12	53	0	2	41	75	.252	.325	.403	.728	9
RF	Juan Encarnacion	78	283	43	80	17	1	9	47	2	2	18	43	.283	.324	.445	.769	5

Key Pitchers

Pos	Player	G	GS	W	L	Sv	IP	H	R	ER	BB	SO	BR/9	ERA	WS
SP	Adam Wainwright	32	32	14	12	0	202.0	212	93	83	70	136	12.97	3.70	13
SP	Braden Looper	31	30	12	12	0	175.0	183	100	96	51	87	12.24	4.94	6
SP	Brad Thompson	44	17	8	6	0	129.1	157	76	68	40	53	14.61	4.73	4
SP	Kip Wells	34	26	7	17	0	162.2	186	116	103	78	122	15.10	5.70	2
SP	Anthony Reyes	22	20	2	14	0	107.1	108	77	72	43	74	13.42	6.04	0
CL	Jason Isringhausen	63	0	4	0	32	65.1	42	21	18	28	54	9.92	2.48	12
RP	Russ Springer	76	0	8	1	0	66.0	41	18	16	19	66	8.59	2.18	8
RP	Randy Flores	70	0	3	0	1	55.0	71	31	26	15	47	14.56	4.25	3

2 For Tony
1 For Tradition

Sometime last summer Tony La Russa broke with tradition, and started putting his pitcher batting eighth. With respect to this, four points:

1) There is no research and no logic that shows that this is a bad idea. It's just tradition. What the research shows is that where the hitters hit, within reason, makes almost no difference.

Look at the Runs and RBI by batting order position of the Cardinals, let's say, and the Houston Astros. Their team OPS was the same, their runs scored were almost the same (725-723, Cardinals). Yes, the Cardinals had fewer runs scored from the 7-8 spots in the lineup, but just a few less, and they had many more runs scored from the #9 hitters. What really is the evidence that it doesn't work just as well?

2) What a lot of people say, in arguing against this move, is that it embarrasses the #9 hitter to bat him below the pitcher.

Well, if that's the argument against it, mark me down in favor of it. You can't manage a baseball team based on what makes million-dollar athletes feel good about themselves. A good manager has to worry about the self-image of his players, but the egos of the players are not supposed to be barriers that you have to tip-toe around. And if they *are*, then you need to work on breaking down those barriers.

3) On the other hand, what's the point of creating RBI opportunities for David Eckstein? I mean, I love David Eckstein, but the little guy almost never gets the ball out of the infield. If the leadoff man was Biggio or Grady Sizemore or Curtis Granderson, somebody who could actually drive in some runs, I could see why you would worry about getting runners on ahead of him. But David Eckstein? Why would you worry about getting runners on base for David Eckstein?

4) Innovation in baseball almost never accompanies talent. Innovations in baseball usually arise from those 75-85 win teams that are desperately trying to find a way to scratch out two more wins. We all know that what wins baseball games is good baseball players. When you have the players, you're going to stick to proven strategies because you're more afraid of screwing it up than you are anxious to gain a small advantage.

St. Louis Cardinals – 2007
Runs and RBI by Batting Order Position

Pos	Players	Runs	RBI
1	Eckstein (95g), Taguchi (23g), Miles (20g)	88	51
2	Duncan (45g), Ankiel (32g), Taguchi (26g)	118	96
3	Pujols (153g)	102	101
4	Edmonds (53g), Encarnacion (35g), Rolen (25g)	77	103
5	Rolen (74g), Edmonds (25g)	77	81
6	Encarnacion (27g), Ludwick (23g), Molina (23g)	73	93
7	Molina (60g), Kennedy (27g), Miles (24g)	59	67
8	Miles (19g), Kennedy (18g)	61	49
9	Ryan (29g), Wainwright (20g), Miles (19g)	70	49
	Total	725	690

St. Louis Cardinals – 2007
Productivity by Batting Order Position

Pos	Players	Avg	OBP	Slg	OPS
1	Eckstein (95g), Taguchi (23g), Miles (20g)	.283	.323	.346	.670
2	Duncan (45g), Ankiel (32g), Taguchi (26g)	.309	.372	.498	.870
3	Pujols (153g)	.326	.425	.557	.982
4	Edmonds (53g), Encarnacion (35g), Rolen (25g)	.246	.320	.386	.706
5	Rolen (74g), Edmonds (25g)	.246	.317	.357	.675
6	Encarnacion (27g), Ludwick (23g), Molina (23g)	.266	.320	.441	.762
7	Molina (60g), Kennedy (27g), Miles (24g)	.267	.332	.367	.699
8	Miles (19g), Kennedy (18g)	.265	.316	.338	.654
9	Ryan (29g), Wainwright (20g), Miles (19g)	.249	.298	.345	.643
	Total	.274	.337	.405	.743

St. Louis Cardinals – 2007
Games Played by Opening Day Starter
At Each Position

Pos	Player	Starts
C	Molina	101
1B	Pujols	153
2B	Kennedy	74
3B	Rolen	108
SS	Eckstein	112
LF	Taguchi	64
CF	Edmonds	99
RF	Wilson	14
	Total	725

St. Louis's opening-day starters accounted for only 56% of their regular season starting lineup.

The Cardinals are classic...they lost 30 games in 2007 because the starting pitcher was pounded (3-30 with Game Score below 29). As long as they got an OK start from the starting pitcher they were fine. They were 22-10 with a starter Game Score of 50 to 59, but 11-20 at 40 to 49. Most teams divide there, but not as sharply.

St. Louis Cardinals – 2007
Performance by Quality of Start

Game Score	#	ERA	W	-	L
80 and above	4	1.00	4	-	0
70 to 79	10	0.98	7	-	3
60 to 69	27	2.20	22	-	5
50 to 59	32	2.83	22	-	10
40 to 49	31	4.35	11	-	20
30 to 39	25	6.01	9	-	16
20 to 29	21	8.55	3	-	18
Below 20	12	11.73	0	-	12

Jim Edmonds
Striking Out Less
Producing Less

When he was an MVP candidate in 2004 Jim Edmonds struck out in just over 30% of his at bats, in 2007, only 21%.

But when he DIDN'T strike out, Edmonds' slugging percentage was:

.920 in 2004
.759 in 2005
.663 in 2006
.507 in 2007

Jim Edmonds – 2004
Pitch Analysis

Overall		
Pitches Seen	2552	
Taken	1438	57%
Swung At	1114	43%
Pitches Taken		
Taken for a Strike	382	26%
Called a ball	1056	74%
Pitches Taken by Pitch Location		
In Strike Zone	382	27%
High	159	11%
Low	300	22%
Inside	221	16%
Outside	331	24%
Swung At		
Missed	328	29%
Fouled Off	430	39%
Put in Play	356	32%
Swung At by Pitch Location		
In Strike Zone	910	86%
High	46	4%
Low	38	4%
Inside	35	3%
Outside	33	3%

Jim Edmonds – 2007
Pitch Analysis

Overall		
Pitches Seen	1594	
Taken	874	55%
Swung At	720	45%
Pitches Taken		
Taken for a Strike	262	30%
Called a ball	612	70%
Pitches Taken by Pitch Location		
In Strike Zone	262	30%
High	113	13%
Low	206	24%
Inside	91	10%
Outside	200	23%
Swung At		
Missed	148	21%
Fouled Of	277	38%
Put in Play	295	41%
Swung At by Pitch Location		
In Strike Zone	564	79%
High	53	7%
Low	45	6%
Inside	22	3%
Outside	31	4%

How did Russ Springer post the lowest ERA of his career last year, at age 38 no less? He started throwing his cutter a lot more. It gave him a third pitch to show righthanded hitters besides his fastball and slider, and it became one of his more important weapons against lefthanded hitters.

Russ Springer – 2006
Pitch Type Analysis

Overall		
Total Pitches	1008	
Fastball	623	62%
Curveball	101	10%
Changeup	14	1%
Slider	217	22%
Cut Fastball	40	4%
Pitchout	1	0%
Not Charted	12	1%

	Vs. RHB		Vs. LHB	
Total Pitches	630		378	
Outs Recorded	120		59	
Fastball	396	63%	227	60%
Curveball	50	8%	51	13%
Changeup	3	0%	11	3%
Slider	155	25%	62	16%
Cut Fastball	17	3%	23	6%
Pitchout	0	0%	1	0%
Not Charted	9	1%	3	1%

Russ Springer – 2007
Pitch Type Analysis

Overall		
Total Pitches	1070	
Fastball	635	59%
Curveball	77	7%
Changeup	21	2%
Slider	159	15%
Cut Fastball	167	16%
Pitchout	2	0%
Not Charted	9	1%

	Vs. RHB		Vs. LHB	
Total Pitches	750		320	
Outs Recorded	142		56	
Fastball	449	60%	186	58%
Curveball	36	5%	41	13%
Changeup	13	2%	8	3%
Slider	136	18%	23	7%
Cut Fastball	113	15%	54	17%
Pitchout	1	0%	1	0%
Not Charted	2	0%	7	2%

The best overall skills assessment in baseball is probably not a surprise to anyone, Albert Pujols. Still, to be in the 90th percentile in your worst category while being at 95 to 100 in the others is very impressive.

The other players you might suspect as a contender for having the best skills have one hole or another.

Alex Rodriguez isn't above the 90th percentile in Hitting for Average. The guy that plays third at Shea is about as good.

Chase Utley is in the 69th percentile in plate discipline at second.

Joe Mauer's hitting for power is 37th percentile at catcher.

Albert Pujols – 2007
Skills Assessment

Hitting for Average:	100th percentile	100th percentile among first basemen
Hitting for Power:	99th percentile	100th percentile among first basemen
Plate Discipline:	95th percentile	90th percentile among first basemen
Running:	61st percentile	95th percentile among first basemen

Wells Enough

Kip Wells led the National League in losses in 2007 for the second time in three years—2005 with Pittsburgh, 2007 with the Cardinals. The Cardinals were outscored in Wells' starts 165 to 91. This was the worst ratio of runs/runs allowed in the starts of any major league pitcher (20 or more starts) since *at least* 2002.

Wells has made 156 starts since 2002, resulting in a won-lost record for his teams of 59-97. This is by far the worst record of any pitcher with 150 or more starts in that period, although in all fairness this is not entirely his fault; his offensive support has been very poor. Still, the next man up on the list is Mark Redman at 69-89—nine full games ahead of Wells.

St. Louis Cardinals – 2007
Performance by Starting Pitcher

Games Started By	G	RS	RA	Won	Lost
Wainwright, Adam	32	154	130	19	13
Looper, Braden	30	139	176	16	14
Wells, Kip	26	91	165	6	20
Reyes, Anthony	20	65	95	4	16
Thompson, Brad	17	95	77	12	5
Pineiro, Joel	11	45	48	7	4
Wellemeyer, Todd	11	70	46	9	2
Maroth, Mike	7	38	49	2	5
Keisler, Randy	3	15	13	2	1
Mulder, Mark	3	6	19	0	3
Carpenter, Chris	1	1	6	0	1
Percival, Troy	1	6	5	1	0
Team Totals	162	725	829	78	84

Throwing Pythagoras for a Looper

The St. Louis Cardinals were outscored by 37 runs in the games started by Braden Looper—yet finished 16-14 in those games. They were four games better than their Pythagorean expectation with Looper on the mound—the biggest over-achievement in that area since 2004.

With Kip Wells, on the other hand, the Cardinals had a Pythagorean record of 6 and 20—and an actual record of 6 and 20.

The Cardinals claimed Todd Wellemeyer off waivers from the Royals on May 15. Just over two weeks later, they gave him his first major league start, which he won. The club went on to win each of his first six starts. He sprained his elbow in early July and missed seven weeks, but returned to make three more starts in late September. The club won two of those three games to push their record in his starts to 9-2.

Bullpens and Crunches

by Bill James

I. Introduction

The goal of this research, this paper, is to provide definitive or as near as possible to definitive answers to two questions:

1) Do teams with outstanding bullpens tend to do well in close games?

2) Do teams with outstanding bullpens tend to do well in post-season play?

These are questions, of course, to which the average sports broadcaster already has quite definitive answers: *Of course they do.* We are involved in the familiar and treacherous process of documenting what seems obvious to those who are wise enough to be less skeptical. Also, there may be…I believe there is…previously published research in this area by other writers, but I don't know because I don't know how to find that stuff.

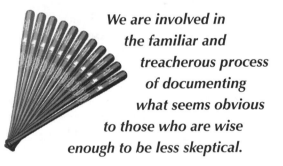

We are involved in the familiar and treacherous process of documenting what seems obvious to those who are wise enough to be less skeptical.

To figure out whether teams with good bullpens do well in close games, we first have to establish by some systematic process whether a particular team does or does not have a good bullpen. In order to address *that* question, we have to back up to a yet more elementary question: How good is this reliever? How good is Keith Foulke, 2004, compared to Dick Radatz, 1964, or compared to Bill Campbell in 1977, or, for that matter, compared to Dick Drago in 1978 or Luis Aponte in 1982?

Let me stress this up front: I am not here to debate those issues. I am not here to debate who was the greatest relief pitcher of all time, or how good was Dennis Eckersley in 1991 compared to Goose Gossage in 1977. What I am really trying to do is not to debate those issues, but to get past the debate on those issues so that I can engage a couple of questions that lie further down the battlefield.

However, neither can we afford, if we are to develop convincing answers to the target questions, to dodge these earlier questions. We have to deal with the entry-level questions in a satisfactory manner, so that we are then in a position to deal with the subsequent questions which are our real purpose. It is my view that it is impossible to give completely convincing or satisfying answers to these entry-level questions about specific pitchers in specific seasons. No matter what values we place on Dennis Eckersley in 1991 and Goose Gossage in 1977, somebody is going to be unsatisfied, and he or she will always have a valid point to make in support of his or her position. Our answers will not be perfect, because no answers to those questions are perfect.

What our answers to those questions must be is *consistently reasonable*, more or less without exception. We thus need to begin by assigning consistently reasonable values to every relief pitcher in baseball, in every season in baseball history.

II. Method

The method I have chosen here is essentially to ask, "How many standards of performance does this relief pitcher meet?" What we're really doing is asking ten yes-or-no questions about each reliever's season, although we are asking those questions through mathematical equations. If the pitcher has a "yes" answer to all 10 questions, that's a 10-point season; if he has yes answers to none of them, that's a 0-point or "non-contributing" season.

These standards are not set so that every relief pitcher is automatically included. You have to do something sort of marginally note-worthy to make the list, even if it is only show up all season. If a pitcher pitches 40 games in relief, league-average ERA, three wins and three saves...that's a zero-point season. He would be near the top of the non-contributing range, but he'd still be in it. 50 games, league-average ERA, five wins and five saves—that's a three-point season. But if a pitcher's season is so unremarkable that you would assume every team has some guys like that...he could be a zero.

The first two standards are easy to count:

1) If the pitcher pitches 50 games in relief, 1 point.

2) If the pitcher pitches 65 games in relief, 1 additional point.

The next three standards depend on a combination of wins and saves, with each win counting two points, each save one point:

3) If a pitcher has 15 saves (with each win counting as two saves), add one point.

4) If a pitcher has 30 saves (with each win counting as two saves), add an additional point.

5) If a pitcher has 45 saves (with each win counting as two saves), add an additional point.

We added wins to saves in an effort to make the scores of the earlier pitchers balance better with those of pitchers today. When I first laid out the system I had points for saves, then wins + saves, but the system created too-low values for relievers before Bruce Sutter. Rollie Fingers had only two seasons in his career with 30 saves, Hoyt Wilhelm had none—but they won more games than modern relievers, since they were often brought into the game with the score tied. Fingers won 11 games in 1972, 10 in '75, 13 in '76. Double-counting wins puts Fingers and Wilhelm (and Perranoski and Konstanty and others) on a more equal footing with modern relievers.

Standards 6-9 are based on the pitcher's Games in Relief, multiplied by 1.30 minus his relative ERA...let's call it a gorilla number (GIR-ERA). Suppose a pitcher has an ERA of 3.00, and the league ERA is 4.00. That's a relative ERA of 0.75. Subtract that from 1.30, to get a measure of how much better he is than a useless pitcher, a pitcher 30% worse-than-league. If he has pitched in 40 games in relief with a 0.75 relative ERA, that makes a gorilla number of 22 [(1.30 – 0.75) * 40 = 22]. If he pitches 50 games, that's a gorilla number of 27.50; 60 games, a gorilla number of 33.00. The highest gorilla number in the history of baseball is 79.4, by Paul Quantrill in 2003 (89 games pitched with an ERA of 1.75. Remarkably enough, a teammate of Quantrill's in the same season, Eric Gagne, also posted the third-highest gorilla number in history, 78.6.) Here are

the next four standards:

6) Add one point if the pitcher has a gorilla number above 13.

7) Add an additional point if the pitcher has a gorilla number above 26.

8) Add an additional point if the pitcher has a gorilla number above 39.

9) Add an additional point if the pitcher has a gorilla number above 52.

The final point is based on strikeout/walk ratio...actually, not EXACTLY strikeout/walk ratio. Strikeout/walk ratio, but

a) not counting intentional walks, and

b) counting hit batsmen as walks.

Call it "adjusted KW":

10) Add one point if a pitcher has an adjusted KW rate of 3-1 or better with 10 or more strikeouts and 10 or more games in relief.

That's the system...very simple, very straightforward. Essentially, what we're saying is that a pitcher is a contributing member of the bullpen if he stays healthy and pitches all year, if he piles up saves and/or wins, if he pitches a good number of games with a good ERA, and, to a small extent, if he has a good strikeout/walk ratio.

It is a not a precise system. It is a solid, reliable system. It reliably places each relief pitcher in a group with other relievers of essentially comparable value, so that the overall credentials of a *group* of relievers can be compared to another group. This is all we're asking it to do.

III. Evolution of Scores over Time

In all of 19th-century baseball, only one pitcher receives a point for his contributions to his team as a reliever. Monte Ward in 1879 pitched 10 times in relief, and had a strikeout/walk ratio (for the season) better than three to one...that's a point. Otherwise, the nineteenth century was shut out.

The first twentieth-century pitcher to earn a point was Doc White in 1907, then three pitchers contributed in 1908—Christy Mathewson, Ed Walsh, and Jake Boultes. (This is, by the way, the first time in 99 years that Jake Boultes has been placed in a group with Christy Mathewson and Ed Walsh.) Doc Crandall in 1911 earned two points, and two points (by Crandall and others) remained the record until 1925.

These standards are not set so that every relief pitcher is automatically included. You have to do something sort of marginally note-worthy to make the list, even if it is only show up all season.

In 1925 and again in 1926, Firpo Marberry is credited with a five-point season by our simple method...a breakthrough season for a reliever, as is generally known. A long series of other pitchers then had fives, and Ace Adams finally pushed the record to six in 1945. Joe Page recorded a seven in 1949, Jim Konstanty an eight in 1950, and Ellis Kinder recorded a nine in 1953. Sevens, eights and nines became common in the late 1950s, and finally, in 1964, Dick Radatz and Hoyt Wilhelm recorded the first ten-point seasons for relief aces.

Along the same time-line, the standard for a team in a season wriggled slowly up from zero. In 1900, of course, the average total for a team in a season was zero. By 1920 the average was 0.13 per season; by 1940 it was 1.00, and by 1950 still only 1.56. As late as 1950, seven of the 16 major league teams were still at zero. Essentially, those teams simply did not have bullpens. They had starters, and they had spot starters, and they had extra pitchers, but they had no pitcher who met any significant standard of quality or quantity as a reliever.

The point was finally reached at which every team had some bullpen of some kind in 1957. Excluding the strike-fractured 1981 season, the last team in major league history which had essentially no bullpen, no points going to the bullpen, was the California Angels of 1974. The Angels had two terrific starting pitchers, Nolan Ryan and Frank Tanana; as long as Bill Singer was healthy they had three terrific starting pitchers. The team leader in saves was the 40-year-old Orlando Pena, who pitched in only four games for the Angels at the end of the season, saving three of them. The leader in relief appearances was Skip Lockwood, who appeared in relief 35 times, but apparently almost always when the team was losing; he finished 23 of his 35 games, but had only one save and two wins. With an ERA far worse than the league norm, he was nowhere near qualifying for a point in our system. No one else on the team appeared in relief more than 20 times, and all of the leaders in relief appearances had bad ERAs.

There is no indication that the '74 Angels ever tried to develop a bullpen. It doesn't appear that they were worried about it. The team's manager at the start of the year was Bobby Winkles, who had been a highly successful college manager. I hope I'm not reading too much into it, but college baseball in many respects trails the evolution of major league ball. Winkles may have simply figured that with Ryan, Tanana, Singer and Chuck Dobson, he could win games with his starters and use his bullpen to mop up, as had been done in the major leagues up until 1956. Singer and Dobson went out early with injuries, and he found himself trying to stagger through games with Andy Hassler and Dick Lange. They finished last. Winkles was fired in late June.

With the exceptions of the Angels, the '62 Mets and two teams from 1959 and two from 1981 (which involves a data and standards problem), every major league team since 1957 has had at least some bullpen, although of-

ten, until the mid-1970s, it was a very limited bullpen. In 1948 major league teams had an average of one contributing reliever apiece. In 1957 the average reached 2.00, and in 1964 it reached 3.00.

Bullpens reached a peak of usage in 1965 and then *declined* for almost ten years. We have two measures here—the number of contributing relievers per team, and the average "bullpen score" for a team. In 1965 the average major league team had 3.25 relievers and a bullpen score of 9.50. Both of these numbers went *down* almost every year from 1965 to 1974, reaching lows of 2.13 relievers per team (1974) and a bullpen score of 6.33 (1972). That, of course, was the era of abundant twenty-game winners. In the early 1970s there were historic numbers of twenty-game winners, and of starting pitchers pitching huge numbers of innings, up to 376 innings in a season by Wilbur Wood and Mickey Lolich. As starting pitchers worked harder and harder, the bullpens, for a few years, were asked to do less.

Beginning in 1975, however, the trend lines went back in their normal direction—fewer innings for starters, fewer complete games, deeper and deeper bullpens. The average number of contributing relievers per team was back up to 2.85 in 1980, back over 3.00 in 1982, over 4.00 in 1987, and over 5.00 in 1996. The trend toward higher and higher numbers continues to this day. The average bullpen score in 2007 was an all-time record 22.90, while the number of contributing relievers per team was 6.57 per team—just a hair below the record set in 2006. Both measures of bullpen use have increased more than 20% since the year 2000.

Through 2007 there have been 53 perfect or ten-point seasons by relief pitchers—four each by Mariano Rivera and Robb Nen, three each by Billy Wagner, Eric Gagne, and Trevor Hoffman, two by Dan Quisenberry, and one apiece by Dennis Eckersley, Keith Foulke, Tom Gordon, Goose Gossage, Willie Hernandez, Joe Nathan, Al Hrabosky, Brad Lidge, Bruce Sutter, John Wetteland, Donnie Moore, Phil Regan and twenty-three other pitchers. Again, we're not trying to sort among them and say which of these is the greatest season ever by a reliever; we're just recognizing that these pitchers all had really good years as a reliever—as, for that matter, did the guys who rank at "9" or "8" or even "7". Anything over six is a heck of a year.

IV. Off-topic Conclusions

We are now in a position to state objectively whether a team did or did not have a good bullpen, relative to the league. Let's take 1983, for example...I always like to back away 20 years or so to get away from the controversial present and take advantage of our more settled view of the past. In 1983 the Chicago Cubs had Lee Smith, who had a 1.85 ERA and led the National League in Saves, backed by Warren Brusstar, who pitched 59 times with a 2.35 ERA, backed by Bill Campbell, Craig Lefferts and Mike Proly, who pitched 56 to 82 times apiece and were mostly pretty good. We credit Lee Smith with a 9-point season, Campbell with 4 points, Brusstar with 3, Lefferts with 2, Proly with 2 and Willie Hernandez with 1…altogether, 21 points for the Cub bullpen:

Lee Smith	9
Bill Campbell	4
Warren Brusstar	3
Craig Lefferts	2
Mike Proly	2
Willie Hernandez	1
Cub bullpen, 1983	21

The Cleveland Indians that year, on the other end, had a bullpen score of 2—one point for Dan Spillner, one for Jamie Easterly. The Cubs had a very strong bullpen; the Indians had a weak bullpen.

Again, I will re-iterate that it is not our purpose here to make a list of the best and worst bullpens. We are trying to get beyond that issue. However, we do at this point have an evaluation of every bullpen every season, and it is required for our purpose that this be a reasonable evaluation. If you don't accept that our method works, you won't accept our conclusions later on. It may be appropriate to ask, then, who had the best bullpens of all time?

The greatest bullpen of all time, in terms of bullpen points, belonged to the St. Louis Cardinals of 2004. These are their stats:

Name	W	L	PCT	G	SV	GF	IP	BB	SO	ERA	Points
Jason Isringhausen	4	2	.667	74	47	66	75.1	23	71	2.87	9
Julian Tavarez	7	4	.636	77	4	27	64.1	19	48	2.38	7
Ray King	5	2	.714	86	0	9	62.0	24	40	2.61	6
Steve Kline	2	2	.500	67	3	22	50.1	17	35	1.79	6
Cal Eldred	4	2	.667	52	1	10	67.0	17	54	3.76	3
Kiko Calero	3	1	.750	41	2	4	45.1	10	47	2.78	3
Al Reyes	0	0	.000	12	0	4	12.0	2	11	0.75	1

That is, I think you will admit, one hell of a bullpen. The closer, Jason Isringhausen, did not have a historic season, but he wasn't chopped spinach, either, with 47 saves, a 2.87 ERA, and a strikeout/walk ratio better than three to one. Behind him you've got two left-handers and a right-hander pitching 67 to 86 times apiece with ERAs between 1.79 and 2.61, and behind them you have two more very good relievers in Cal Eldred and Kiko Calero. I credit them with 35 points as a bullpen—three more than any other team in the history of baseball. It's just a shame they never got to pitch in the World Series.

These are the top ten bullpens in baseball history:

1. St. Louis, 2004	35
2t. Florida, 2006	33
2t. Pittsburgh, 2006	33
4t. Atlanta, 2002	32
4t. San Diego, 2006	32
4t. San Diego, 2007	32
7t. LA Dodgers, 2003	31
7t. New York Mets, 2006	31
9t. Texas, 1999	30
9t. Minnesota Twins, 2006	30

If we re-drew the list in five years it would look entirely different. Bullpens are simply much deeper than they were just a few years ago. As bullpens continue to get deeper and deeper, teams will occasionally put together outstanding six- and seven-man combinations, and these teams are likely to be pushed off the top of the list.

By this method, of course, there is no "worst bullpen ever", because there were hundreds of teams pre-1957 which had bullpen scores of zero. There is another way to look at the issue. Since the standards in this area change so dramatically over time, perhaps a more accurate way of looking at the issue is to compare each team to the league average in that season.

By that method, the greatest bullpen of all time was that of the Chicago White Sox of 1968. The White Sox in 1968 had only four contributing relievers—Wilbur Wood, Hoyt Wilhelm, Bob Locker and Don McMahon. Wood pitched 88 times, 159 innings, with an ERA of 1.87. Wilhelm pitched 72 times with an ERA of 1.72. Locker pitched 70 times with an ERA of 2.30, and McMahon, traded away at mid-season, pitched 25 times with an ERA of 1.96. Among the four of them they pitched 265 times, just short of 400 innings, with an ERA in the ones (1.95). I credit the team with 24 bullpen points, in a season in which the American League average was 7.5. The White Sox were +16.5.

The worst bullpen of all time, relative to the league, was the bullpen of the 2006 Cleveland Indians—a bullpen widely blamed for keeping the Indians out of a pennant race that they very possibly might have won. They worked hard over the winter, and re-built the bullpen for 2007.

Maybe it is time to get to one general conclusion. Teams with very strong bullpens tend to be good teams. These are the ten best bullpens of all time, relative to the league averages, with the won-lost records of those teams:

Team	Lg	Year	Tm Total	Lg Avg	Tm V Avg	Won	Lost
Chicago White Sox	AL	1968	24	7.5	16.5	67	95
St. Louis Cardinals	NL	2004	35	20.4	14.6	105	57
Texas Rangers	AL	1999	30	16.8	13.2	95	67
Minnesota Twins	AL	2002	29	16.0	13.0	94	67
Oakland A's	AL	1975	18	5.6	12.4	98	64
St. Louis Cardinals	NL	1992	28	16.0	12.0	83	79
Atlanta Braves	NL	2002	32	20.1	11.9	101	59
Los Angeles Dodgers	NL	2003	31	19.4	11.6	85	77
Cleveland Indians	AL	1995	22	10.7	11.3	100	44
Pittsburgh Pirates	NL	1979	21	9.8	11.3	98	64
Average Won-Lost						93	67

All of these were good teams except the 1968 White Sox. These were the teams with the ten weakest or thinnest bullpens of all time, relative to the league:

Team	Lg	Year	Tm Total	Lg Avg	Tm V Avg	Won	Lost
Cleveland Indians	AL	2006	8	20.6	-12.6	78	84
Tampa Bay Rays	AL	2002	4	16.0	-12.0	55	106
San Francisco Giants	NL	2006	11	23.0	-12.0	76	85
Milwaukee Brewers	NL	2006	11	23.0	-12.0	75	87
Arizona Diamondbacks	NL	2004	9	20.4	-11.4	51	111
Chicago Cubs	NL	1988	3	14.3	-11.3	77	85
Kansas City Royals	AL	2000	7	18.1	-11.1	77	85
Cincinnati Reds	NL	2007	14	25.1	-11.1	72	90
Texas Rangers	AL	2005	9	20.0	-11.0	89	73
Arizona Diamondbacks	NL	1998	6	16.7	-10.7	65	97
Average Won-Lost						71	91

Of course, teams which are outstanding in *any* area tend to be good teams overall, so we don't want to get ahead of ourselves in talking about the importance of the bullpen. But, in general, teams with outstanding bullpens are good teams, and vice versa.

The greatest bullpen of all time, in terms of bullpen points, belonged to the St. Louis Cardinals of 2004.

Another thing we can do with the data we have so far is to compare relievers' careers. What we are essentially asking here is not "who was the greatest relief pitcher of all time?" but rather "which relief pitcher, over the course of his career, met the most standards of performance for a season's work?"—defining standards as we have in this study. But the two questions may be taken to be related, and perhaps the pedantic count we have to offer here may be considered a contribution to the larger discussion.

The first generation of career relievers retired in the very early 1970s. Elroy Face had a career total of 66 points for his bullpen work, Ron Perranoski 65, Lindy McDaniel 60, Don McMahon 57, Stu Miller 51—and Hoyt Wilhelm 94. Wilhelm was clearly the best of the first generation of career relievers, and he was the only one of that generation elected to the Hall of Fame.

Wilhelm's record total of 94 bullpen points was surpassed by Lee Smith, and Smith has been passed by Trevor Hoffman and Mariano Rivera, who are sort of dueling for the spot as the greatest reliever of all time. Lee Smith is an interesting figure. I don't know that he left a great many friends behind him in baseball, and I don't know that he was ever regarded, while active, as a towering figure. His records are more notable for endurance and consistency than for dominance. He didn't dominate hitters the way Sutter did, or Gossage, or Eckersley, but in his own way he was a powerful and impressive pitcher. He wasn't out there throwing tricky stuff, like Doug Jones or Stu Miller, Quisenberry or Hoyt Wilhelm. He was throwing gas.

Until recently, Lee Smith held the career record for Saves. Perhaps more impressively than that, Smith had an ERA better than league average (park adjusted) every season from the beginning of his career in 1980 through 1992—thirteen consecutive years. In 1993 he was average (four runs worse than average in the National League, but then four runs better than average in the American League)—and then he began another run of three seasons of better-than-league performance. Seventeen straight seasons, 1980 through 1996, he was average or better every single season, and better than average 16 out of 17. Only in his final season, 1997, did the league get the best of him. Compare that to a handful of Hall of Famers. It's pretty hard to find another pitcher who had 17 consecutive seasons without a bad one—and Smith was pitching 65, 70 games every year, and he was pitching most of the time with the game on the line.

Relief pitchers are being selected to the Hall of Fame with some regularity now—Eckersley, now Sutter. The

standards for outstanding performance as a relief pitcher have been in constant upheaval since 1924. There are no historic norms by which to evaluate relievers, no magic numbers hallowed by time. It's harder to focus on who the right relievers are, because we just don't have the reference points that we have in other areas. The oft-cited corruption of the numbers of the steroid era is trivial compared to the seismic shifts that occur every few years in save totals and in how those saves are earned.

Dennis Eckersley, I think, is a Hall of Fame selection that will stand the test of time. Eckersley's career total is "only" 76 bullpen points, but

a) 76 points is 14th on the all-time list, and

b) Eckersley also made very substantial contributions as a starting pitcher.

But Bruce Sutter, I think, was frankly a mistake. Sutter was very impressive on the mound. His best seasons, half seasons, he was unhittable. His career, taken as a whole, is really not all that impressive. What did he do that Sparky Lyle didn't?

I have in the past been critical of Rollie Fingers' selection to the Hall of Fame, and I guess I still would be at a certain level. Compared to Bruce Sutter, Rollie was awesome. To me, Bruce Sutter should have been in line behind Goose Gossage and behind Lee Smith. In any case, these are the top career bullpen totals, through 2007:

1.	Trevor Hoffman	105
2.	Mariano Rivera	101
3.	Lee Smith	96
4.	Hoyt Wilhelm	94
5.	Rollie Fingers	92
6.	John Franco	90
7.	Jesse Orosco	86
	Roberto Hernandez	86
9.	Doug Jones	83
10.	Kent Tekulve	82
	Billy Wagner	82

After them: Goose Gossage, 79, Jeff Reardon, 78, Dennis Eckersley, 76, Sparky Lyle, 74, Robb Nen, 74, Todd Jones, 72, Jose Mesa, 72, Mike Timlin, 71, Bob Wickman, 71, Gene Garber, 70, John Wetteland, 70, Mike Stanton, 69, Tom Henke, 68, Armando Benitez, 67. This list is entirely different than it was when I first figured it in 2004, and if I figure it again in 2013, it will be all different again. There are many other ways to compare bullpen careers, and in any case that is not what we are here to discuss.

V. Conclusion in re Close Games

It appears to be unquestionably true that teams with good bullpens tend to exceed expectations in one-run games and in close games in general, and even more true that teams with bad bullpens tend to under-achieve in these games. The effects measured are not large in terms of the 30- or 40-game separation between a first-place team and a last-place team, but they are quite large when compared to the relatively few runs saved by a bullpen or the relatively small differences between teams in terms of one-run victories.

The "direct" or "normal" benefit of having a good bullpen, in terms of runs saved, could be estimated at about 8-10 games per season. (Let's assume that the bullpen pitches 540 innings or 60 games per season, and that the difference between a good bullpen and a poor bullpen is 1.50 runs per 9 innings. The difference in runs over the course of a season would be about 90 runs, or about 9 games.) Beyond that, however, there is an additional benefit of about 3 ½ games due to the fact that these runs saved (or not saved) tend to come at critical moments of the game.

I identified the teams with the 50 best bullpens of all time relative to league norms (through 2004; this study was done in the off season 2004-2005), and the 50 worst bullpens. All of these tend to be recent teams; the first teams chronologically on the "good bullpen" list are the 1959 White Sox and the 1959 Cubs, and the first team chronologically on the "bad bullpen" list is the 1965 Mets. 84 of the 100 teams in this portion of the study are post-1980 teams.

I looked at two measures of performance in close games:

1) The team's record in one-run games.

2) The team's actual won-lost record contrasted with their pythagorean expectation.

The 50 teams which had strong bullpens had an expected average, based on their runs scored and runs allowed, or 88.95. They actually won an average of 90.34 games, exceeding expectations by 1.39 wins.

Previous research, which may be unpublished, shows that a team's expected ratio of wins to losses in one-run games is the same as the ratio of their runs scored to runs allowed. The teams with strong bullpens had an expected won-lost record in one-run games of 26-23 on average, a .526 winning percentage. Their actual winning percent-

age in one-run games was .550. These teams exceeded their expected one-run wins by 1.19 games.

The data on teams with bad bullpens is more dramatic. The teams with weak bullpens under-achieved by 2.06 wins overall, and by 1.95 wins in one-run games. The teams with poor bullpens had an expected winning percentage of .475 in one-run games—but an actual winning percentage of .433.

Most of you probably know that winning percentages in one-run games tend to be nearer to .500 than overall winning percentages. .600 teams tend to play about .550 ball in one-run games, and .400 teams tend to play about .450 ball. But the teams with bad bullpens actually had a worse winning percentage in one-run games (.433) than overall (.439). The data seems to leave no doubt that a weak bullpen means trouble in one-run games.

VI. Since You Asked

Are the standards of bullpen performance different between the leagues, you asked? I knew you would.

The norms for bullpen performance were essentially the same between the leagues prior to the adoption of the DH rule in 1973. The DH Rule did create a separation of standards between the leagues. This separation reached its widest point in 1977, when the average National League bullpen score was 13.2, the American League, 6.7.

By 1990, however, the American League had largely caught up, and since 1990 the norms have been in the same range in both leagues. Bullpen usage in modern baseball is controlled by pitch limits for starters, the use of closers and left/right matchups versus hitters. The DH rule sometimes affects *when* a substitution occurs, but, in modern baseball, it has little to do with how much the bullpen is used.

VII. Conclusion in re Post-Season Play

With regard to the issue of whether teams with strong bullpens tend to do well in post-season play, we encounter our old friend "no definitive evidence".

I looked at all post-season matchups in history, trying to find cases in which a team with a strong bullpen played a team with a much weaker bullpen. In 1979, for example, the Pittsburgh Pirates (we-are-fam-a-lee), who had a strong bullpen by the standards of the time (Kent

It appears to be unquestionably true that teams with good bullpens tend to exceed expectations in one-run games and in close games in general, and even more true that teams with bad bullpens tend to under-achieve in these games.

Tekulve, Enrique Romo and Grant Jackson) played the Baltimore Orioles in the World Series. The Oriole bullpen, led by Don (Full Pack) Stanhouse, was of nowhere near the same quality, even adjusting for the difference in league norms. The Pirate bullpen was credited with 21 points vs. a league norm of 9.8, while the Orioles were credited with 9 points vs. a norm of 7.0.

My standard was that the stronger bullpen had to have an advantage of at least eight points in raw terms and also of at least eight points vs. league norms. The Pirates were +12 in raw terms and +9.3 vs. league norms, so this qualifies.

I found 38 qualifying post-season matchups in baseball history—and the team with the stronger bullpen did in fact win 24 of the 38 series. This certainly suggests the possibility that a strong bullpen does become especially important in post-season play.

But we can't reach that conclusion, for two reasons. First, the teams with good bullpens were almost always better teams in other regards—they had better offenses, for example—and thus very probably would have won more than half of these series even if the bullpens were even. The 1979 example, in which the Orioles were otherwise probably a better team, is atypical. A more typical example would be the 1988 Oakland A's vs. the Red Sox in the league championship series, or the 1989 A's vs. the Giants in the World Series. The A's *did* have a much stronger bullpen than the Red Sox in '88 or the Giants in '89—but they also had much stronger teams in other respects. My best estimate is that the teams with better bullpens could have been expected to win 21.5 of these 38 series based on their overall strength, without suggesting that there was any special importance to the bullpen.

The "good bullpen teams" *did* exceed expectations in these 38 series—24 wins versus 21.5 expected wins—but that is nowhere near a statistically significant separation of the data. The chance that the same separation would occur as a random event is 26%.

In fact—this is the second problem—even if there were no bias in the data, a 24-14 record is still nowhere near statistically significant. Even if the teams were even overall, there would still be a 7% chance that the teams with better bullpens would go 24-14 or better in 38 matchups. So…sorry to have led you on, but we just can't reach any conclusion on that one. It is possible that there is such a special significance to bullpens in post-season play; it is possible that there is not.

The worst bullpen of all time, relative to the league, was the bullpen of the 2006 Cleveland Indians—a bullpen widely blamed for keeping the Indians out of a pennant race that they very possibly might have won.

San Diego Padres

San Diego Padres – 2007
Team Overview

Description		Ranking
Won-Lost Record	89-74	
Place	3rd of 5 in National League West	
Runs Scored	741	19th in the majors
Runs Allowed	666	2nd in the majors
Home Runs	171	13th in the majors
Home Runs Allowed	119	1st in the majors
Batting Average	.251	28th in the majors
Batting Average Allowed	.250	3rd in the majors
Walks Drawn	557	7th in the majors
Walks Given	474	3rd in the majors
OPS For	.732	25th in the majors
OPS Against	.686	1st in the majors
Stolen Bases	55	29th in the majors
Stolen Bases Allowed	189	30th in the majors

Key Players

Pos	Player	G	AB	R	H	2B	3B	HR	RBI	SB	CS	BB	SO	Avg	OBP	Slg	OPS	WS
C	Josh Bard	118	389	42	111	27	2	5	51	0	1	50	58	.285	.364	.404	.768	16
1B	Adrian Gonzalez	161	646	101	182	46	3	30	100	0	0	65	140	.282	.347	.502	.849	25
2B	Marcus Giles	116	420	52	96	19	3	4	39	10	3	44	82	.229	.304	.317	.621	12
3B	Kevin Kouzmanoff	145	484	57	133	30	2	18	74	1	0	32	94	.275	.329	.457	.786	15
SS	Khalil Greene	153	611	89	155	44	3	27	97	4	0	32	128	.254	.291	.468	.759	19
LF	Terrmel Sledge	100	200	22	42	9	0	7	23	1	2	27	60	.210	.310	.360	.670	3
CF	Mike Cameron	151	571	88	138	33	6	21	78	18	5	67	160	.242	.328	.431	.759	20
RF	Brian Giles	121	483	72	131	27	2	13	51	4	6	64	61	.271	.361	.416	.777	17

Key Pitchers

Pos	Player	G	GS	W	L	Sv	IP	H	R	ER	BB	SO	BR/9	ERA	WS
SP	Jake Peavy	34	34	19	6	0	223.1	169	67	63	68	240	9.79	2.54	21
SP	Greg Maddux	34	34	14	11	0	198.0	221	92	91	25	104	11.45	4.14	9
SP	Chris Young	30	30	9	8	0	173.0	118	66	60	72	167	10.25	3.12	12
SP	Justin Germano	26	23	7	10	0	133.1	133	72	66	40	78	12.22	4.46	4
SP	David Wells	22	22	5	8	0	118.2	156	74	73	33	63	14.56	5.54	1
CL	Trevor Hoffman	61	0	4	5	42	57.1	49	21	19	15	44	10.05	2.98	11
RP	Heath Bell	81	0	6	4	2	93.2	60	21	21	30	102	8.84	2.02	13
RP	Cla Meredith	80	0	5	6	0	79.2	94	38	31	17	59	12.88	3.50	5

Khalil Greene hit 47 homers in the first four years of his career (2003-2006), including only 5 home runs to center field.

In 2007 he hit 10 home runs to center field.

Khalil Greene – 2007
Hitting Analysis

Batting Left-Handed								1B	2B	3B	HR
Ground Balls to Left	130	Outs	109	Hits	21	Average	.162	Hit Type	17 - 4 - 0 - 0
Ground Balls to Center	36	Outs	29	Hits	7	Average	.194	Hit Type	7 - 0 - 0 - 0
Ground Balls to Right	7	Outs	7	Hits	0	Average	.000	Hit Type	0 - 0 - 0 - 0
Line Drives to Left	54	Outs	12	Hits	42	Average	.778	Hit Type	24 - 18 - 0 - 0
Line Drives to Center	23	Outs	4	Hits	19	Average	.826	Hit Type	16 - 3 - 0 - 0
Line Drives to Right	11	Outs	5	Hits	6	Average	.545	Hit Type	5 - 1 - 0 - 0
Fly Balls to Left	57	Outs	31	Hits	26	Average	.481	Hit Type	2 - 7 - 0 - 17
Fly Balls to Center	96	Outs	73	Hits	23	Average	.247	Hit Type	4 - 7 - 2 - 10
Fly Balls to Right	80	Outs	69	Hits	11	Average	.147	Hit Type	6 - 4 - 1 - 0
Total on Ground Balls	173	Outs	145	Hits	28	Average	.162	Hit Type	24 - 4 - 0 - 0
Total on Line Drives	88	Outs	21	Hits	67	Average	.761	Hit Type	45 - 22 - 0 - 0
Total on Fly Balls	233	Outs	173	Hits	60	Average	.270	Hit Type	12 - 18 - 3 - 27
Total Hit to Left	241	Outs	152	Hits	89	Average	.374	Hit Type	43 - 29 - 0 - 17
Total Hit to Center	155	Outs	106	Hits	49	Average	.322	Hit Type	27 - 10 - 2 - 10
Total Hit to Right	98	Outs	81	Hits	17	Average	.183	Hit Type	11 - 5 - 1 - 0
All Balls in Play	494	Outs	339	Hits	155	Average	.321	Hit Type	81 - 44 - 3 - 27

Take That, Parker Brothers

Milton Bradley was a terror in the clutch for the fourth straight season, batting .385 with four homers and 15 RBI in 26 at-bats. Over those four years he's batted .330 and slugged .600 in 185 clutch at-bats.

Milton Bradley
Clutch Hitting

Season	AB	H	2B	3B	HR	RBI	BB	SO	GIDP	Avg	OBP	Slg
2002	30	4	1	0	1	7	2	3	2	.133	.188	.267
2003	36	8	2	0	0	8	5	9	1	.222	.317	.278
2004	76	23	3	0	4	13	12	13	1	.303	.404	.500
2005	27	9	3	0	2	13	0	5	2	.333	.333	.667
2006	56	19	0	1	4	10	8	13	2	.339	.422	.589
2007	26	10	0	0	4	15	3	6	2	.385	.433	.846
Totals	251	73	9	1	15	66	30	49	10	.291	.367	.514

Chris Young's 2006 and 2007 data is in many respects almost the same, and in some respects remarkably different. Whereas his innings, strikeouts, walks, ERA and won-lost record are pretty much the same, his home runs allowed dropped from 28 to 10, and he stopped throwing his curve ball almost entirely—presumably because that was what was leaving the yard.

Chris Young – 2006
Pitch Type Analysis

Overall		
Total Pitches	3028	
Fastball	2213	73%
Curveball	191	6%
Changeup	253	8%
Slider	306	10%
Pitchout	2	0%
Not Charted	63	2%

	Vs. RHB		Vs. LHB	
Total Pitches	1592		1436	
Outs Recorded	277		261	
Fastball	1132	71%	1081	75%
Curveball	109	7%	82	6%
Changeup	97	6%	156	11%
Slider	228	14%	78	5%
Pitchout	0	0%	2	0%
Not Charted	26	2%	37	3%

Chris Young – 2007
Pitch Type Analysis

Overall		
Total Pitches	2884	
Fastball	2128	74%
Curveball	48	2%
Changeup	151	5%
Slider	522	18%
Pitchout	13	0%
Not Charted	22	1%

	Vs. RHB		Vs. LHB	
Total Pitches	1481		1403	
Outs Recorded	283		234	
Fastball	933	63%	1195	85%
Curveball	17	1%	31	2%
Changeup	86	6%	65	5%
Slider	425	29%	97	7%
Pitchout	6	0%	7	0%
Not Charted	14	1%	8	1%

Chris Young
Record of Opposing Batters

Season	AB	R	H	2B	3B	HR	RBI	BB	SO	SB	CS	GIDP	Avg	OBP	Slg	OPS
2004	144	21	36	2	0	7	21	10	27	4	1	2	.250	.299	.410	.708
2005	642	84	162	36	3	19	75	45	137	13	6	6	.252	.301	.407	.708
2006	649	72	134	20	5	28	62	69	164	41	4	8	.207	.283	.382	.665
2007	616	66	118	19	8	10	57	72	167	44	0	9	.192	.276	.297	.573

Among the most
remarkable stats of 2007

Chris Young had 44 stolen bases allowed, with no one caught stealing. That's hard to do; you'd think somebody would fall down or something. But the data suggests that this cost him only five or six runs:

Chris Young – 2007
Runs Allowed Analysis

Reached by Single:	81	Scored:	20	25%
Reached by Double:	19	Scored:	5	26%
Reached by Triple:	8	Scored:	4	50%
Reached by Homer:	10			
Reached by Walk:	72	Scored:	19	26%
Reached by HBP:	7	Scored:	4	57%
Reached by Error:	4	Scored:	1	25%
Reached by FC - Out:	8	Scored:	1	13%
Reached by Other:	1	Scored:	1	100%
Total On Base	210	Scored:	97	46%
Stolen Bases Allowed:	44	Scored:	16	36%
Steal Attempts:	44	Scored:	16	36%

Do you suppose it could be true that strikeout/walk ratio indicates a player's ability to cope with better pitching?

This seems like a plausible theory. A hitter who doesn't control the strike zone might be able to compete against inferior pitching, but might be vulnerable to good pitching. I don't know; it just seems reasonable.

I was thinking about this in connection to the Padres, and, while of course it is a ridiculously small sample, it works here. Khalil Greene, a good hitter with a bad strikeout/walk ratio (128-32) was very vulnerable to good pitching:

Khalil Greene – 2007
Batting Performance by Quality of Opposing Pitcher

	AB	H	HR	RBI	Avg	OPS
Pitcher with ERA <= 3.50	118	23	2	10	.195	.548
Pitcher with ERA 3.51 to 4.25	177	36	4	19	.203	.598
Pitcher with ERA 4.26 to 5.25	176	51	10	30	.290	.861
Pitcher with ERA over 5.25	140	45	11	38	.321	1.014

He hit 27 homers, but 21 of them against weaker pitching. On the other hand Josh Bard—not as much power as Greene, but a better strikeout/walk ratio—did very well against good pitchers:

Josh Bard – 2007
Batting Performance by Quality of Opposing Pitcher

	AB	H	HR	RBI	Avg	OPS
Pitcher with ERA <= 3.50	64	23	1	9	.359	.917
Pitcher with ERA 3.51 to 4.25	120	33	0	13	.275	.716
Pitcher with ERA 4.26 to 5.25	115	28	3	14	.243	.742
Pitcher with ERA over 5.25	90	27	1	15	.300	.764

The Giles brothers…one of them has a good K/W ratio; the other one not so good. Brian, with the good K/W, did well against good pitchers:

Brian Giles – 2007
Batting Performance by Quality of Opposing Pitcher

	AB	H	HR	RBI	Avg	OPS
Pitcher with ERA <= 3.50	107	35	1	11	.327	.834
Pitcher with ERA 3.51 to 4.25	128	29	2	9	.227	.611
Pitcher with ERA 4.26 to 5.25	143	37	5	11	.259	.776
Pitcher with ERA over 5.25	105	30	5	20	.286	.914

While Marcus did not, although he also did not do well against bad pitching.

Marcus Giles – 2007
Batting Performance by Quality of Opposing Pitcher

	AB	H	HR	RBI	Avg	OPS
Pitcher with ERA <= 3.50	77	15	0	3	.195	.470
Pitcher with ERA 3.51 to 4.25	122	30	1	11	.246	.655
Pitcher with ERA 4.26 to 5.25	129	33	3	19	.256	.743
Pitcher with ERA over 5.25	92	18	0	6	.196	.529

I don't…just a theory. To me, the fun part of putting this information on record is to allow us to pick through and see what we can figure out. In two years, we'll know the answer to that question.

Best Career Herbie Scores
Active Pitchers with 500 or More Innings

Pitcher	Herbie
Mariano Rivera	4.43
Greg Maddux	4.54
Chien-Ming Wang	4.71
Roy Oswalt	5.22
Roy Halladay	5.46
Pedro Martinez	5.69
John Smoltz	5.71
Trevor Hoffman	5.74
Joe Blanton	5.81
Roger Clemens	5.84

Best Herbie Scores of 2007
(minimum 100 innings pitched)
All had winning records with at least 14 wins.

Pitcher (W-L)	Herbie
Greg Maddux (14-11)	3.95
Tim Hudson (16-10)	4.05
Joe Blanton (14-10)	4.23
Roy Halladay (16-7)	4.43
Chien-Ming Wang (19-7)	4.65
C. C. Sabathia (19-7)	4.67
Brandon Webb (18-10)	4.76
Brad Penny (16-4)	4.93
Josh Beckett (20-7)	5.07
Jake Peavy (19-6)	5.08
Kelvim Escobar (18-7)	5.20
Roy Oswalt (14-7)	5.22

(See Herbie article, page 287)

Greg Maddux has thrown 2,495 pitches to left-handed batters in the last two seasons, and only 50 of them have been breaking balls (curves and sliders).

Greg Maddux – 2006
Pitch Type Analysis

Overall		
Total Pitches	2802	
Fastball	1813	65%
Curveball	51	2%
Changeup	747	27%
Slider	67	2%
Cut Fastball	35	1%
Pitchout	14	0%
Not Charted	75	3%

	Vs. RHB		Vs. LHB	
Total Pitches	1512		1290	
Outs Recorded	337		292	
Fastball	998	66%	815	63%
Curveball	48	3%	3	0%
Changeup	364	24%	383	30%
Slider	39	3%	28	2%
Cut Fastball	10	1%	25	2%
Pitchout	11	1%	3	0%
Not Charted	42	3%	33	3%

Greg Maddux – 2007
Pitch Type Analysis

Overall		
Total Pitches	2703	
Fastball	1890	70%
Curveball	24	1%
Changeup	542	20%
Slider	40	1%
Cut Fastball	112	4%
Pitchout	20	1%
Not Charted	75	3%

	Vs. RHB		Vs. LHB	
Total Pitches	1498		1205	
Outs Recorded	326		268	
Fastball	1081	72%	809	67%
Curveball	19	1%	5	0%
Changeup	269	18%	273	23%
Slider	26	2%	14	1%
Cut Fastball	44	3%	68	6%
Pitchout	11	1%	9	1%
Not Charted	48	3%	27	2%

Scott Hairston hit five home runs in clutch situations for the Padres. That's pretty remarkable, considering that he wasn't acquired until July 27 and later spent four weeks on the DL. All told, he was on their active roster for only 36 games. Even so, his five clutch homers would have been enough to lead most other teams—only six other clubs had someone who hit more. The White Sox's entire power-laden lineup produced a combined total of only five clutch home runs *all season*. The only thing more impressive than Hairston's productivity was his timing. Consider the details of each of the five:

- #1 and #2: August 3 vs. San Francisco. Hits a game-tying three-run homer with two out in the bottom of the eighth, then hits a game-winning solo shot in the bottom of the 10th.

- #3: September 14 vs. San Francisco. Leads off the bottom of the ninth with his team trailing by two, and homers to make it a one-run game. The Padres tie it up later in the inning and go on to win in extra innings.

- #4: September 19 vs. Pittsburgh. Trailing 3-2 with two out and two on in the bottom of the ninth, Hairston hits a game-winning three-run homer off Pirates' closer Matt Capps.

- #5: October 1 at Colorado. In a one-game playoff for the NL wild card, Hairston hits a two-run homer in the top of the 13th to put the Padres three outs away from a playoff berth.

Of course, the Rockies pulled out a dramatic win in the bottom of the inning, rendering a mere footnote the role Hairston had played that night and over the previous eight weeks.

San Diego Padres – 2007
Clutch Hitting

Hitter	AB	H	2B	3B	HR	RBI	BB	SO	GIDP	Avg	OBP	Slg
Bard, Josh	57	17	4	0	0	11	7	6	3	.298	.375	.368
Barrett, Michael	32	7	2	0	0	5	1	6	2	.219	.235	.281
Blum, Geoff	56	12	3	0	1	10	4	8	1	.214	.270	.321
Bocachica, Hiram	6	1	0	0	0	0	1	1	0	.167	.286	.167
Bowen, Rob	9	0	0	0	0	0	1	5	0	.000	.100	.000
Bradley, Milton	20	8	0	0	3	12	3	5	2	.400	.478	.850
Branyan, Russell	14	3	0	0	1	2	5	6	1	.214	.450	.429
Cameron, Mike	75	16	4	1	5	23	11	21	1	.213	.318	.493
Cassel, Jack	1	1	0	0	0	0	0	0	0	1.000	1.000	1.000
Clark, Brady	17	6	0	0	0	3	1	2	1	.353	.389	.353
Cruz, Jose	21	4	2	0	0	2	1	6	0	.190	.227	.286
Ensberg, Morgan	10	1	0	0	0	0	3	3	0	.100	.308	.100
Germano, Justin	5	0	0	0	0	0	0	2	0	.000	.000	.000
Giles, Brian	74	22	6	0	2	12	9	6	1	.297	.373	.459
Giles, Marcus	33	10	0	1	0	8	4	5	1	.303	.368	.364
Gonzalez, Adrian	97	28	9	1	6	27	13	23	1	.289	.369	.588
Greene, Khalil	87	24	9	1	1	19	6	17	2	.276	.333	.437
Hairston, Scott	26	8	2	0	5	13	1	6	0	.308	.333	.962
Hampson, Justin	3	0	0	0	0	0	0	1	1	.000	.000	.000
Headley, Chase	2	1	0	0	0	0	0	0	0	.500	.500	.500
Hensley, Clay	1	0	0	0	0	0	0	1	0	.000	.000	.000
Kouzmanoff, Kevin	66	22	3	0	4	20	6	12	1	.333	.382	.561
LaForest, Pete	3	1	0	0	0	0	0	0	0	.333	.333	.333
Lane, Jason	1	0	0	0	0	0	0	0	0	.000	.000	.000
Mackowiak, Rob	10	1	0	0	0	1	0	5	0	.100	.100	.100
Maddux, Greg	6	1	0	0	0	0	1	3	1	.167	.286	.167
McAnulty, Paul	3	1	0	0	0	0	0	0	0	.333	.333	.333
Morton, Colt	1	0	0	0	0	0	0	0	0	.000	.000	.000
Myrow, Brian	6	1	1	0	0	1	0	2	1	.167	.167	.333
Peavy, Jake	12	4	1	0	0	2	0	1	0	.333	.333	.417
Robles, Oscar	3	2	0	0	0	1	2	0	0	.667	.800	.667
Sledge, Terrmel	23	4	3	0	0	7	8	4	3	.174	.364	.304
Stansberry, Craig	2	2	0	0	0	1	0	0	0	1.000	1.000	1.000
Stauffer, Tim	1	0	0	0	0	0	0	0	0	.000	.000	.000
Wells, David	2	0	0	0	0	0	0	0	0	.000	.000	.000
Young, Chris	7	2	1	0	0	0	0	2	0	.286	.286	.429
Totals	792	210	50	4	28	180	88	159	23	.265	.339	.444

Marcus Giles over the last five seasons has hit .316, .311, .291, .262 and .229.

His on-base percentages have marched downward in lockstep, and, while his slugging percentage did go up once, on the whole his slugging percentage has suffered rather more than the rest of his record, dropping a whopping 209 points:

Marcus Giles – 2003 - 2007

Year	Team	Lg	G	AB	H	2B	3B	HR	TB	R	RBI	TBB	SO	Avg	OBP	Slg
2003	ATL	NL	145	551	174	49	2	21	290	101	69	59	80	.316	.390	.526
2004	ATL	NL	102	379	118	22	2	8	168	61	48	36	70	.311	.378	.443
2005	ATL	NL	152	577	168	45	4	15	266	104	63	64	108	.291	.365	.461
2006	ATL	NL	141	550	144	32	2	11	213	87	60	62	105	.262	.341	.387
2007	SD	NL	116	420	96	19	3	4	133	52	39	44	82	.229	.304	.317

This got me interested in the question of historically sustained declines in performance. How long would you think you could keep a thing like that going? Hall of Famer Edd Roush, from 1921 to 1928, managed this:

Edd Roush

Year	Avg	OBP	Slg
1921	.352	.403	.502
1922	.352	.428	.461
1923	.351	.406	.531
1924	.348	.376	.501
1925	.339	.383	.494
1926	.323	.366	.462
1927	.304	.335	.402
1928	.252	.315	.356

Roush had a higher .352 average in 1921 than in 1922, so he gets credit for that. He bounced back to hit .324 in 1929. Brooks Robinson, after his his MVP year in 1964, had five straight seasons of declining batting, on-base and slugging:

Brooks Robinson

Year	Avg	OBP	Slg
1964	.317	.368	.521
1965	.297	.351	.445
1966	.269	.333	.444
1967	.269	.328	.434
1968	.253	.304	.416
1969	.234	.298	.395

But he lasted eight years after that. Jose Cruz matched him after the 1983 season:

Jose Cruz

Year	Avg	OBP	Slg
1983	.318	.385	.463
1984	.312	.381	.462
1985	.300	.366	.426
1986	.278	.351	.403
1987	.241	.307	.400
1988	.200	.284	.262

But that ended his career. Oh well; we can't all be Brooks Robinson. Shawn Wooten from 2000 to 2005 went from .556 to zero:

Shawn Wooten

Year	Avg	OBP	Slg
2000	.556	.556	.667
2001	.312	.332	.466
2002	.292	.331	.442
2003	.243	.303	.349
2004	.170	.228	.226
2005	.000	.000	.000

But of course he was only batting a few times a year. Bill White had declining batting averages from 1962 to 1969, although his other numbers bounced around a little.

It turns out there are hundreds of players who have had four straight seasons of declining batting and on-base percentages, many of whom held on to play for several more years. Al Dark had declining batting and on-base averages from 1951 to 1956, but played until 1960. Andres Galarraga had declines from 1987 to 1991, but played until 2004. Bert Campaneris had declines from 1974 to 1978, but played until 1983. Hang in there, Mark. Perhaps the end is near. Better yet, perhaps the end is not near.

Tightrope

Padres' reliever Kevin Cameron in 2007 allowed the leadoff man to reach base in 46% of the innings he started, the highest percentage in baseball for a pitcher starting 50 or more innings, but escaped with a sterling 2.79 ERA for two reasons:

1) He allowed no homers, no triples and only 5 doubles on the season.

2) Six of the 24 runs that he allowed were scored as unearned.

Kevin Cameron – 2007
Inning Analysis

Innings Pitched	58.0
Runs Allowed	24
Innings Started	56
Runs in Those Innings	24
Shutout Innings	46
One-Run Innings	4
Two-Run Innings	1
Three-Run Inning	3
Four-Run Innings	1
Five-Run Innings	1
Got First Man Out	30
Runs Scored in Those Innings	8
Runs/9 Innings	2.40
First Man Reached	26
Runs Scored in Those Innings	16
Runs/9 Innings	5.54
1-2-3 Innings	14
10-pitch Innings (or less)	6
Long Innings (20 or more pitches)	15
Failed to Finish Inning	9

The Padres won 5 games when they managed to score only one run.

No other team in the majors won more than three 1-0 games.

The rest of the NL West had four 1-0 wins combined.

San Diego Padres – 2007
Record by Runs Scored and Allowed

	Scored	Allowed
10 runs or more	14 - 0	1 - 8
9 runs	6 - 0	1 - 8
8 runs	4 - 1	1 - 3
7 runs	12 - 1	1 - 10
6 runs	9 - 3	5 - 9
5 runs	12 - 7	5 - 11
4 runs	9 - 13	9 - 11
3 runs	15 - 14	18 - 10
2 runs	3 - 13	11 - 4
1 run	5 - 14	17 - 0
0 runs	0 - 8	20 - 0
Total	89 - 74	89 - 74

San Francisco Giants

San Francisco Giants – 2007
Team Overview

Description		Ranking
Won-Lost Record	71-91	
Place	5th of 5 in National League West	
Runs Scored	683	29th in the majors
Runs Allowed	720	6th in the majors
Home Runs	131	25th in the majors
Home Runs Allowed	133	2nd in the majors
Batting Average	.254	27th in the majors
Batting Average Allowed	.261	7th in the majors
Walks Drawn	532	14th in the majors
Walks Given	593	27th in the majors
OPS For	.708	30th in the majors
OPS Against	.740	10th in the majors
Stolen Bases	119	8th in the majors
Stolen Bases Allowed	77	6th in the majors

Key Players

Pos	Player	G	AB	R	H	2B	3B	HR	RBI	SB	CS	BB	SO	Avg	OBP	Slg	OPS	WS
C	Bengie Molina	134	497	38	137	19	1	19	81	0	0	15	53	.276	.298	.433	.731	13
1B	Ryan Klesko	116	362	51	94	27	3	6	44	5	1	46	68	.260	.344	.401	.744	7
2B	Ray Durham	138	464	56	101	21	2	11	71	10	2	53	75	.218	.295	.343	.638	6
3B	Pedro Feliz	150	557	61	141	28	2	20	72	2	2	29	70	.253	.290	.418	.708	12
SS	Omar Vizquel	145	513	54	126	18	3	4	51	14	6	44	48	.246	.305	.316	.621	12
LF	Barry Bonds	126	340	75	94	14	0	28	66	5	0	132	54	.276	.480	.565	1.045	19
CF	Dave Roberts	114	396	61	103	17	9	2	23	31	5	42	66	.260	.331	.364	.695	10
RF	Randy Winn	155	593	73	178	42	1	14	65	15	3	44	85	.300	.353	.445	.798	16

Key Pitchers

Pos	Player	G	GS	W	L	Sv	IP	H	R	ER	BB	SO	BR/9	ERA	WS
SP	Noah Lowry	26	26	14	8	0	156.0	155	76	68	87	87	14.25	3.92	10
SP	Barry Zito	34	33	11	13	0	196.2	182	105	99	83	131	12.31	4.53	8
SP	Tim Lincecum	24	24	7	5	0	146.1	122	70	65	65	150	11.62	4.00	8
SP	Matt Cain	32	32	7	16	0	200.0	173	84	81	79	163	11.57	3.65	12
SP	Matt Morris	21	21	7	7	0	136.2	162	79	66	39	73	13.57	4.35	6
CL	Brad Hennessey	69	0	4	5	19	68.1	66	26	26	23	40	12.12	3.42	10
RP	Jack Taschner	63	0	3	1	0	50.0	44	31	30	29	51	13.32	5.40	2
RP	Steve Kline	68	0	1	2	2	46.0	58	25	24	18	17	15.26	4.70	2

Full Speed Behind

The two key questions that face the San Francisco Giants as they open the 2008 season are:

1) Have they hit bottom yet? and
2) Will they be able to bounce back?

I *suspected*, before I researched the subject, that the degeneration of the San Francisco Giants over the last three or four years might be of historic magnitude. It seems like just yesterday that the Giants were really good. The Giants won 100 games in 2003, 91 in 2004. How did they get into the mess they're in now?

But when I checked it out, it's *not* a turnaround of historic proportions. The Giants have degenerated more than any other major league franchise over the last two years or three years or four years, but if you compare them to Seattle (2002-2006), Arizona (2002-2006), the Mets (2000-2004), the Rangers (1999-2003), the Orioles (1998-2002), the Expos (1996-2000), you find that there are a lot of teams that have gone through equally rapid or worse degenerations.

Some of those teams—about half of them—bounced right back. The Diamondbacks went south from 2002 through 2006, but they're obviously on the way back now. The Mets fell apart just after the turn of the century, but they're back in competition now, Seattle appears to be on the way back. The Tigers went through a terrible down phase, but they're back.

On the other hand, the Rangers, the Orioles, the Expos…those teams got knocked down, and have not been able to get back up. The Blue Jays were knocked way back from 1993 to 1997, and have come back part way but it's been a long time and they haven't been able to get all the way back. The Royals and the Pirates got knocked flat in the mid-nineties, and then got run over by the 21st century.

It's not a historic degeneration *yet*, but if the Giants continue to go backward for two or three more seasons, it's going to be one. My point is, this is a very serious event—and there appears to be *no* reason to think that the Giants have hit bottom yet. They do have some good young pitchers, and their farm teams at the lower levels have had very good records the last two years. But if you look at their regular players from 2007, it is likely that only one of those players will even be in the major leagues in three years. Catcher Bengie Molina will probably still be around in three years, as a backup catcher somewhere, but every other regular for the 2007 Giants will probably be out of the majors by…well, in most cases, sometime tomorrow afternoon. There is *nothing* there to build on. Their young players for 2008, Kevin Frandsen and Dan Ortmeier, have very little or no star potential. Aaron Rowand seems more likely to make Giants fans remember Ron Cey than to make them forget Willie Mays.

I can't foresee the future, and I'm not saying that the Giants will take another step backward in 2008. But I *really* can't foresee them getting any better.

In 2004, when Barry Bonds was one of the first three hitters up for San Francisco, the Giants scored .723 runs per inning, or 6.50 runs per nine innings.

In 2007, when Bonds was one of the first three hitters, the Giants scored only .463 runs per inning, or 4.17 runs per nine innings.

Barry Bonds – 2004
Impact by Position in Inning

Position	Innings	Runs	Runs/Inning	Runs/RBI
Leading Off	144	79	.55	38/12
Batting Second	96	79	.82	27/11
Batting Third	106	92	.87	27/20
Batting Fourth	194	205	1.06	24/38
Batting 5th or later	77	178	2.31	13/20

Barry Bonds – 2007
Impact by Position in Inning

Position	Innings	Runs	Runs/Inning	Runs/RBI
Leading Off	120	50	.42	27/8
Batting Second	85	30	.35	9/6
Batting Third	95	59	.62	12/12
Batting Fourth	135	132	.98	21/27
Batting 5th or later	42	103	2.45	6/13

What If the Games Were Only One Inning Long?

San Francisco led after the first inning 50 times and trailed only 39 times.
Every other NL West team trailed after the first inning more often than they led.

San Francisco Giants – 2007
Innings Ahead/Behind/Tied

Inning	1	2	3	4	5	6	7	8	9	Extra	Final
Ahead	50	60	60	58	58	66	70	69	65	6	71
Behind	39	48	64	73	68	70	74	73	76	15	91
Tied	73	54	38	31	36	26	18	20	21	20	—

Barry Bonds swung at only 13% of the non-strikes he saw last year, the lowest percentage in baseball among players who saw 1000 pitches.

Barry Bonds – 2007
Pitch Analysis

Overall		
Pitches Seen	1741	
Taken	1118	64%
Swung At	623	36%
Pitches Taken		
Taken for a Strike	293	26%
Called a ball	825	74%
Pitches Taken by Pitch Location		
In Strike Zone	293	26%
High	84	8%
Low	313	28%
Inside	102	9%
Outside	326	29%
Swung At		
Missed	84	13%
Fouled Off	251	40%
Put in Play	288	46%
Swung At by Pitch Location		
In Strike Zone	497	80%
High	28	4%
Low	27	4%
Inside	21	3%
Outside	50	8%

Barry Bonds has drawn 2,558 walks in his major league career. In order to accumulate that number of walks at the rate at which they are going:

- Omar Vizquel would have to play for another 33 years,

- Ray Durham would have to play for another 35 years,

- Randy Winn would have to play for another 47 years,

- Ryan Klesko and Dave Roberts would have to play another 49 years each,

- Pedro Feliz would have to play for another 76 years, and

- Bengie Molina would have to play for another 132 years.

In their first seasons with 300 or more at bats, Bengie Molina, Dave Roberts, Omar Vizquel and Ryan Klesko all had better strikeout/walk ratios than Barry Bonds. However, Bonds established a new career-best K/W rate in 1988, in 1989, 1990, 1991, 1992, 1996, 2002 and 2004—a total of eight times. Molina never improved his, Roberts improved only once, Vizquel established a new career high twice and Klesko twice.

Giant Pain

The last major league pitcher to receive offensive support as bad as Matt Cain (20 or more team starts) was Nate Cornejo in Detroit in 2003. Each pitcher made 32 starts, in which his team scored 101 runs. The Tigers' record with Cornejo on the mound was 8-24. Cain beat him by one game, at 9-23.

The 23 losses in Cain's starts tied Edwin Jackson of Tampa Bay for the most in the majors. The Rays were 8-23 with Jackson as the starter.

San Francisco Giants – 2007
Performance by Starting Pitcher

Games Started By	G	RS	RA	Won	Lost
Zito, Barry	33	137	154	14	19
Cain, Matt	32	101	133	9	23
Lowry, Noah	26	119	94	16	10
Lincecum, Tim	24	112	109	11	13
Morris, Matt	21	104	101	9	12
Correia, Kevin	8	33	26	6	2
Ortiz, Russ	8	43	45	4	4
Misch, Pat	4	14	26	0	4
Sanchez, Jonathan	4	10	22	1	3
Blackley, Travis	2	10	10	1	1
Team Totals	162	683	720	71	91

Ray Durham had only 19 multi-hit games, the fewest of any batting title qualifier. All 19 of them were two-hit games—he didn't notch a single three-hit game all year. All other big-league regulars had at least two three-hit games.

Ray Durham – 2007
Games with X Hits

	G	AB	R	H	2B	3B	HR	RBI	Avg
0 Hits	56	166	4	0	0	0	0	8	.000
1 Hits	63	219	36	63	11	1	5	39	.288
2 Hits	19	79	16	38	10	1	6	24	.481

Well, What Did You Walk Them for if You Didn't Intend to Let Them Score?

There were ten major league pitchers in 2007 who walked 85 or more batters.

On average, 25% of the batters they walked came around to score.

The most effective pitcher at stranding the runners he had put on base was Noah Lowry, who stranded 85% of his gift runners (74 of 87).

The least effect was Edwin Jackson, who stranded only 67% (59 of 88), and allowed the other 29 to fulfill their mission.

Noah Lowry – 2007
Runs Allowed Analysis

Reached by Single:	112	Scored:	27	24%
Reached by Double:	23	Scored:	11	48%
Reached by Triple:	8	Scored:	6	75%
Reached by Homer:	12			
Reached by Walk:	87	Scored:	13	15%
Reached by HBP:	5	Scored:	3	60%
Reached by Error:	8	Scored:	2	25%
Reached by FC - All Safe:	2	Scored:	0	0%
Reached by FC - Out:	22	Scored:	2	9%
Reached by Other:	1	Scored:	0	0%
Total On Base	280	Scored:	82	29%
Stolen Bases Allowed:	7	Scored:	3	43%
Caught Stealing:	4	Scored:	0	0%
Steal Attempts:	11	Scored:	3	27%
Intentional Walks:	2	Scored:	0	0%

Edwin Jackson – TB – 2007
Runs Allowed Analysis

Reached by Single:	137	Scored:	43	31%
Reached by Double:	34	Scored:	14	41%
Reached by Triple:	5	Scored:	3	60%
Reached by Homer:	19			
Reached by Walk:	88	Scored:	29	33%
Reached by HBP:	4	Scored:	2	50%
Reached by Error:	6	Scored:	3	50%
Reached by FC - All Safe:	1	Scored:	1	100%
Reached by FC - Out:	21	Scored:	2	9%
Total On Base	315	Scored:	132	41%
Stolen Bases Allowed:	17	Scored:	8	47%
Caught Stealing:	5	Scored:	0	0%
Steal Attempts:	22	Scored:	8	36%
Intentional Walks:	3	Scored:	0	0%

Field Day at the Retirement Home...

The notoriously old Giants starting lineup weren't as poor on the bases as you might guess. Here are their baserunning +/- ratings:

Giants 2007 Starting Lineup Baserunning +/- Ratings

B Molina	-20
Klesko	-4
Durham	+10
Feliz	-13
Vizquel	-2
Bonds	+1
Roberts	+29
Winn	+8
Total	+9

Astros 2007 Starting Lineup Baserunning +/- Ratings

Ausmus	-5
Berkman	-8
Biggio	-6
Ensberg	-8
Loretta	-15
Lee	-28
Pence	-1
Scott	+3
Total	-68

The starting lineup for the Astros was much worse:

In the year 2000 the eight players who were regulars for the 2007 San Francisco Giants hit an overall .285, with a .378 on-base percentage, .471 slugging, .849 OPS. This stayed in the same range until 2004:

San Francisco Giants
Eight Regulars

Year	Avg.	OBA	Slg	OPS
2000	.285	.378	.471	.849
2001	.275	.367	.485	.852
2002	.291	.382	.469	.851
2003	.279	.364	.459	.824
2004	.290	.385	.472	.857
2005	.277	.343	.431	.774
2006	.277	.349	.444	.794
2007	.262	.335	.407	.742

Hall of Famers Among Us

by Bill James

I have to begin here by making a very fundamental admission. To a large extent, the way that I have always looked at the Hall of Fame debate no longer works, or no longer can be expected to work.

The way that I have always analyzed who is likely to go into the Hall of Fame is to assume that Hall of Fame selections in the future will follow the patterns of selections in the past. My first effort along these lines, published sometime in the late 1970s, was something called the Hall of Fame monitor. Each accomplishment has a certain "weight" in that system toward putting the player in the Hall of Fame. The player gets five points for 200 hits in a season, three points for driving in 100 runs, etc.; if you get over 100 points in your career you are likely to go into the Hall of Fame. The system was structured so that it worked for players from the past, thus could be presumed to work for players of the future.

What I am talking about here is a much more fundamental change. Expansion.

Later, when I developed similarity scores, I would study whether a player was likely to be a Hall of Famer by looking for similar players from the past. In the 1990s I developed the Hall of Fame Career Standards test, which was a way of estimating how many Hall of Fame standards a player met based on his career totals. About 2000, when I developed Win Shares, I tried to match Hall of Fame selection to career Win Shares, and after that, when I developed the system of Season Scores (which are described briefly in the "Medley" article in this book, and described in more detail in the Bill James Online), I tried to use Season Scores to retroactively "predict" Hall of Fame selections. All of these are manifestations of a common approach to the problem.

On a certain fundamental level this approach either
a) no longer works, or
b) never actually worked, or
c) will need to be radically re-calibrated.

I am not concerned here with the inflation of batting numbers that began in the early 1990s; that's a fairly trivial problem, and it's pretty easy to adjust it out of ex-

istence. I am not talking, either, about the Hall of Fame's restructuring of the Veterans' Committee; the Hall of Fame, after all, has changed its rules one way or another every few years since they opened their doors. Check that; history shows that they actually started changing their rules *before* they opened the doors. Whatever the Hall of Fame does in one decade, they will undo two decades later, or at least they always have.

What I am talking about here is a much more fundamental change.

Expansion.

In 1960 there were sixteen major league teams. Now there are nearly twice as many. When you have twice as many teams, you have twice as many players hitting .300, twice as many players driving in 100 runs, twice as many players getting to 3,000 hits, twice as many players hitting 500 homers, twice as many 20-game winners, twice as many pitchers striking out 3,000 batters, twice as many pitchers winning 300 games. Maybe it is more than 2X in some of those categories, because of other changes in the game, and less than 2X in others. Fundamentally, it's twice as many.

That means that, when you compare the records of the retiring players today to the records of players retiring years earlier, you have twice as many players meeting Hall of Fame standards, or what have traditionally been Hall of Fame standards.

Well, what do we do about that?

What we *could* do is start inducting twice as many players into the Hall of Fame. That could happen. As I've said, the Hall of Fame changes its induction procedures pretty much on a regular schedule, and they could re-constitute their selection procedures so that the turnstiles click twice as fast.

But I don't think that will happen. It won't happen, because the fact is, most people never liked the old standards anyway.

The real standards for Hall of Fame election—the de facto standards—have always been much, much more liberal than the public thought they were or wanted them to be. People have always had the idea that the standard for selection to the Hall of Fame was Willie Mays or Mickey Mantle. In reality, almost from the day the institution was built, the real standard was more like Johnny Damon or Bernie Williams. Richie Ashburn is in the Hall of Fame, as are Larry Doby, Earle Combs, Earl Averill, Kiki Cuyler, Edd Rousch and Lloyd Waner. Those guys are much closer to Johnny Damon, Bernie Williams and Steve Finley than they are to Willie, Mickey and the Clipper.

In order to carry the past standards forward, the Hall of Fame would have to start inducting twice as many people, or its not going to get around to Damon and Bernie. My opinion is that there will not be sufficient pressure to open the doors wider, because

1) most of the public doesn't really understand what the historic standard has been, and

2) those people who do understand it by and large don't like it.

Absent a massive adjustment by the selection process, which I don't think will happen, there is going to be a very significant shift in the standards for selection to the Hall of Fame. There's a new sheriff in Cooperstown. Most sportswriters will interpret that shift as resulting from the inflated scoring numbers of the modern era, but that's really not what is causing it; it's actually expansion.

Baseball began expanding in 1961. This is 2008. Why is this change only hitting us now?

It's a change with a very, very long fuse. Albert Pujols has been in the majors for seven years. It will probably be another twenty years before he goes into the Hall of Fame. The change results from the systematic re-shaping of the candidate pool over time. The first expansion, in 1961-1962, probably didn't begin to measurably re-shape the candidate pool until the mid-1980s, and the first expansion was just four teams, from 16 to 20. The real effects of expansion on the Hall of Fame candidates didn't hit until about the year 2000. I was slow to pick up on it. I could have realized that this change was coming in the 1970s, should have realized it when I wrote a book about the Hall of Fame in the 1990s, but I was kind of in denial about this issue, perhaps wanting to believe that my old approach would continue to work. I am now facing the fact that it won't.

OK, well…who will get into the Hall of Fame, then? What standard do we use?

To an extent, my old work remains valid, in the sense that the same things that impressed Hall of Fame voters in the past will probably impress them in the future, albeit at a different level. Beyond that I don't really know, honestly, but for purposes of this article I'm going to use the standard of "two or three players per year." Let's assume that the Hall of Fame in the future will continue to induct two or three players per year. That means that there will be room for two or three players from each year of birth—five in one year, none in the next, but two or three on average. The standard I will use in this article, to try to figure out which active players have a chance to go into the Hall of Fame, is "is this player one of the two or three best-qualified players from a typical birth year?" We can also use the old tools—similarity scores, the Hall of Fame monitor, the Hall of Fame standards—but we just have to remember: those tools implicitly assume that the future will resemble the past, and that's probably not exactly true.

Hall of Fame Chances for Active Players

Sorry for the long preamble. This, then, is my take on the Hall of Fame prospects for players active in 2007. I'll estimate each player's chance of going into the Hall of Fame on two bases

a) if he retired today (present accomplishments), and

b) eventually, based on a projection of what he might accomplish.

Bobby Abreu (0% present, 20% eventual)

Only 34, but his game has slipped steadily for several years, and he certainly doesn't have Hall of Fame credentials yet.

Moises Alou (10% present, 15% eventual)

He now has the best career totals of anybody in the Alou family, none of whom are Hall of Famers but several of whom have been fine players. Career numbers are comparable to Edgar Martinez, Ellis Burks and Reggie Smith.

Garret Anderson (2% present, 25% eventual)

Anderson can still hit, and it is not impossible, if he can stay healthy, for him to make a run at 3,000 career hits.

Jason Bay (0% present, 10% eventual)

Erik Bedard (0% present, 5% eventual)

With only 40 career wins he is far behind the best pitchers of the same age, but if he stays healthy he will soon be universally recognized as one of the best pitchers in baseball.

Josh Beckett (0% present, 33% eventual)

Four of the best starting pitchers of 2007—Sabathia, Beckett, Peavy and Zambrano—are all near the same age, all born in 1980 or 1981. All won 18 to 20 games in 2007, and all have comparable career won-lost records, although Sabathia is maybe one year ahead. All are big men except Peavy, and all four are power pitchers, with 177 to 240 strikeouts each in 2007.

The real standards for Hall of Fame election—the de facto standards—have always been much, much more liberal than the public thought they were or wanted them to be.

Whereas there were very few top-rank pitchers born in the years 1970-75, there were a large number born in the years 1977-1982, including Oswalt, Buerhle, Santana, these four men and others.

Among those four, history suggests that one or two will continue to be dominant pitchers and rivals for pre-eminence until they are 40 and beyond, like Clemens, Maddux and Randy Johnson, while two or three are likely to drop out of the chase due to injuries, as did Dwight Gooden, Bret Saberhagen and David Cone, who were in the same age range as Clemens and Randy Johnson. There probably is no reliable way of predicting which will hang in and which will drop out, and thus we should probably assess all of their Hall of Fame chances as being about the same.

Beckett, with his four post-season wins in 2007 and World Series heroics of 2003, is ahead of the others in what could be called Building His Legend, and Legend Building is certainly important in a Hall of Fame career; that's why Don Drysdale is in the Hall of Fame and Billy Pierce is not, Catfish Hunter is in and Bert Blyleven is not. Still, it will be nearly 20 years until any of these men will be inducted into anything, and it's hard to know how that stuff will play out over time.

Lance Berkman *(0% present, 35% eventual)*

Through age 31 he has 259 homers, 855 RBI, a .300 career average. He is very unlikely to wind up a career .300 hitter, since batting averages almost always fade as a player ages. The 259 homers, 855 RBI are numbers already similar to some Hall of Famers (Larry Doby, Hack Wilson, Roy Campanella, Bobby Doerr) but that's not really relevant because those players had things to sell that Berkman doesn't.

Doing research here because I don't really know what to think otherwise…there are 96 players in history who had 200 to 300 home runs through age 31. Fifteen of those are players who are in the Hall of Fame now and several more are players who will be, but that analysis has the same problem. Berkman is not really similar to Stan Musial and Ryne Sandberg. Let's trim the list to players who had averages at that time between .290 and .310.

That leaves us 21 players, but ten of them are active or recently retired. The other 11 are, chronologically, Wally Berger, Hal Trosky, Ted Kluszewski, Yogi Berra, Al Kaline, Billy Williams, Vada Pinson, Carl Yastrzemski, Joe Torre, Dick Allen and Will Clark.

Berra, Kaline, Williams and Yastrzemski are in the Hall of Fame. Berra is obviously not relevant because he's a catcher and a three-time MVP. Kaline and Yastrzemski got to 3,000 hits, but Kaline was 800 hits ahead of Berkman at the same age, Yastrzemski 550 ahead. Billy Williams was 400 hits ahead of Berkman, plus Williams was different in that his "up to age 31" stats were compiled in the run-starved 1960s; his best statistical seasons, 1970 and 1972, were still ahead of him.

Essentially, it seems unlikely that Berkman will make the Hall of Fame, based on players who had comparable stats at the same age. He seems most comparable to Berger and Kluszewski, within this group, and to Kent Hrbek, Del Ennis, George Foster, Jim Rice, Albert Belle and Rocky Colavito outside this group. But…he's a big-time hitter, and if he ages well he clearly has a shot.

Carlos Beltran *(0% present, 70% eventual)*

Through age 30 he has seven 100-RBI seasons, and he is no more an RBI man than he is everything else…a base stealer, a center fielder, a player who gets on base and scores runs. I would guess that his Hall of Fame chances were measurably impacted by the Mets' collapse in 2007. He needs championships to be seen as a winner.

But he is

1) an exceptionally well-rounded player, and

2) unnaturally graceful.

I would bet, based on those things, that he will age well—that he will be essentially the same player three or four years from now that he is now. He may have ten years left to win a World Championship, and, with Reyes and Wright, he's got a lot of help.

Adrian Beltre *(0% present, 10% eventual)*

His early start gives him the opportunity to pile up big bulk numbers by the time he is through. His Gold Glove last year was deserved, albeit probably not last year; he deserved it several years earlier, but it takes time for the voters to latch onto those things. He has Hall of Fame ability, and has only wasted about half of it so far.

Craig Biggio *(98% present, 98% eventual)*

Barry Bonds *(85% present, 85% eventual)*

No one was ever a more certain Hall of Famer than Pete Rose, who

a) broke the all-time record for hits, and

b) was more beloved by sportswriters, before his fall, than any other athlete of the late twentieth century.

He was a lock for the Hall, but the lock popped open. We can't question Barry Bonds' accomplishments; he has been the greatest player in baseball since Babe Ruth. He is also the residue and expression of the game's illness. No one really knows how that will shake out within the next few years, and, until we know, I think it is an open question whether Bonds will be accepted into the Hall of Fame fraternity, or whether a significant number of people will refuse to vote for him because they regard him as a cheater and a disgrace.

Mark Buehrle (0% present, 10% eventual)

A plodder, he has plodded along to 100+ wins already, and he won't be 30 years old until 2009. His credentials include a no-hitter, a 19-win season and a World Championship. He needs a lot more.

Miguel Cabrera (0% present, 40% eventual)

The 40% is conservative. Certainly, more than 40% of players who accomplish what Cabrera has accomplished through age 24 are eventually Hall of Famers. I'm just trying to avoid getting carried away.

Birthdays are unkind to .250 hitters.

Orlando Cabrera (0% present, 5% eventual)

33 years old but aging well, he is coming off his first .300 season, his first 100 runs scored season, and a career high in hits, 192. He was very good in 2006. He has a cheering section in the media, and if the White Sox have a big comeback season he'll get a lot of the credit for it.

Chris Carpenter (0% present, 1% eventual)

Would require a complete comeback and a sustained sequence of outstanding seasons.

Eric Chavez (0% present, 5% eventual)

Looked great a couple of years ago, but the back trouble has really shot him down.

Roger Clemens (99% present, 99% eventual)

I think Clemens is the greatest pitcher who ever lived. There may not be a consensus for that, but there doesn't need to be.

Bartolo Colon (0% present, 4% eventual)

Jason Schmidt and Bartolo Colon have had the best careers among the pitchers who will be 35 years old in 2008 (1. Colon, 2. Schmidt, 3. Armando Benitez, 4. Derek Lowe, 5. Jason Isringhausen). There doesn't appear to be a Hall of Famer in the group—but they certainly look like Hall of Famers if you compare them to the pitchers who will 34 years old in 2008 (1. Octavio Dotel, 2. Russ Ortiz, 3. Bobby Howry, 4. Justin Speier, 5. John Thompson).

Carl Crawford (0% present, 20% eventual)

Simply noting that he has ability.

Johnny Damon (2% present, 30% eventual)

Damon lost his streak of consecutive 100-run seasons last year due to an early-season injury, but he played extremely well the second half, and remains a strong candidate to make a run at 3,000 career hits.

Carlos Delgado (5% present, 30% eventual)

Carlos is not the player he once was, but these kind of players often have a late-in-life comeback season, as McCovey did in '77, Stargell in '79, Frank Thomas in 2006. If the comeback is big enough he could ride it out to 550 homers or thereabouts. He was an impact player for many years.

Jermaine Dye (0% present, 1% eventual)

Too much up and down time.

Adam Dunn (0% present, 2% eventual)

Could be the first player to hit 600 home runs and not be elected to the Hall of Fame.

Jim Edmonds (10% present, 15% eventual)

The Freddy Lynn of the steroid age...a truly great player, but time has run out on him before he got the numbers where they needed to be.

Kelvim Escobar (0% present, 2% eventual)

I have always liked Kelvim Escobar, and I have always felt that he was going to break through to a higher level of performance. He finally did break through in 2007 (18-7), and, if he sustains that level of performance, could conceivably emerge as a Hall of Fame candidate.

Steve Finley (20% present, 20% eventual)

Let's see...Finley has 2500 career hits, 300 home runs...is there anybody who has that combination and has been left out of the Hall of Fame?

Andre Dawson, Harold Baines, Dave Parker, plus some guys who are active or recently retired.

He also has 300 steals...let's add that in.

2500 hits, 300 homers and 300 steals turns out to be a class of four men: Barry Bonds, Willie Mays, Steve Finley and Andre Dawson. Only one of the four is in the Hall of Fame as of now, so...that doesn't seem to create a case for him.

He has some impressive career totals, but I don't see Finley as a Hall of Famer. His career on-base percentage is just .332, his slugging percentage just .442—essentially the same numbers as Troy O'Leary (.332/.448), Casey

Blake (.332/.444), Sean Berry (.334/.445), Rich Aurilia (.330/.439), Ivan Calderon (.333/.442) and Jay Payton (.325/.432). He never led the league in anything except triples and games played, and, interestingly enough, never hit .300—.298 and .297, but not .300. His career is unusual, but not *great*.

Julio Franco (25% present, 25% eventual)

With 2,586 career hits and a very unique identity, he would have been a strong Hall of Fame candidate before expansion expanded the candidate pool. I doubt that he will qualify in the Brave New World.

Rafael Furcal (0% present, 1% eventual)

Eric Gagne (0% present, 3% eventual)

Had some monster seasons before his injury, but not nearly enough at this point.

Freddy Garcia (0% present, 1% eventual)

Would have to have a complete comeback and at least six-seven years of sustained performance.

Nomar Garciaparra (5% present, 15% eventual)

Troy Glaus (0% present, 3% eventual)

Birthdays are unkind to .250 hitters.

Tom Glavine (99% present, 99% eventual)

Jason Giambi (20% present, 35% eventual)

Comparing Jason Giambi to Jim Thome…very similar players, same age, but Thome is far ahead in "counting stats", based on playing time, and slightly ahead in "production stats", relative to playing time.

People always think that playing in New York helps you win the MVP Award or the Cy Young, but actually, if you study the issue, it is very clear that there is no such benefit. The BBWAA balances the ballots so that each city is fairly represented, and, if anything, playing in New York hurts you a little bit in MVP voting. But the Hall of Fame ballots aren't balanced, and playing in New York does help you in Hall of Fame voting.

Brian Giles (1% present, 10% eventual)

I'd compare him to Jim Edmonds, as a Hall of Fame candidate…a wonderful player, but time is running out on him and the numbers just aren't where they need to be.

Luis Gonzalez (20% present, 20% eventual)

See comments on Steve Finley. Gonzalez is a little better hitter than Finley, but represents essentially the same problem.

Tom Gordon (1% present, 1% eventual)

A memorable career and a memorable player, but not enough high-impact seasons to make a Hall of Famer.

Shawn Green (0% present, 4% eventual)

Would need an exceptional comeback.

Ken Griffey Jr. (99% present, 99% eventual)

Vladimir Guerrero (70% present, 95% eventual)

Travis Hafner (0% present, 5% eventual)

His late start and narrow base of skills make an unpromising foundation for a Hall of Fame career. Jim Thome has overcome those things to forge a good run, but the margin for error is slim.

Roy Halladay (0% present, 25% eventual)

The only issue with Halladay is health. He's a Hall of Fame caliber pitcher; he just needs to stay healthy for several more seasons, and it doesn't seem likely that he will.

Aaron Harang (0% present, 7% eventual)

Among the best pitchers in baseball the last two years, but would have to replicate that at least ten more times.

Todd Helton (25% present, 70% eventual)

Hasn't driven in 100 runs in four years, hasn't scored 100 the last three. A player as good as Helton was at his peak is almost always a Hall of Famer, and it's not like Helton is a cripple. He led the National League in on-base percentage in 2007. He is a tough out in the middle of one of the best lineups in baseball, incessantly fouling off the pitches he used to drive into the gap. The Rockies' humidor has emphasized his real and rather hasty decline, but his .332 career batting average…let's say it fades to .325 before he retires…might be enough to get him into the Hall of Fame even if he retires short of 400 homers and short of 2500 hits.

Orlando Hernandez (5% present, 5% eventual)

El Duque has no chance to go into the Hall of Fame based on the way that people think about his career now, but could emerge as a candidate if there is a minor paradigm shift. At the time that Satchel Paige left the majors in 1953, based on his career won-lost record of 28-31, most people would have assumed that there was absolutely no chance that he would ever be in the Hall of Fame. As time passed the way that people thought about the Negro Leagues changed, and Satchel went into the Hall of Fame in 1971. El Duque could emerge as a Hall of Fame candidate if there is a similar change in the way that people think about his Cuban career and/or his dramatic life story.

Roberto Hernandez (1% present, 1% eventual)

With 1000 career appearances and 326 saves he has had a distinguished career.

Trevor Hoffman *(75% present, 85% eventual)*

He holds the career record for saves, and he may well hold it for several years, in that Mariano is just two years younger and 81 saves behind. I also think that 500 Saves is likely to emerge as a magic-number standard for Hall of Fame selection.

Ryan Howard *(0% present, 25% eventual)*

A late start and a big swing may prevent him from hitting 600 career homers, and I wouldn't think he would be a Hall of Famer unless he does.

Matt Holliday *(0% present, 35% eventual)*

I thought he would win the MVP Award. Perhaps I was influenced by the Colorado scoreboards flashing "MVP! MVP! MVP!" every time he did anything during the World Series. He has had two straight MVP-candidate seasons, anyway, and if he keeps doing that, that's what makes a Hall of Famer.

Tim Hudson *(0% present, 18% eventual)*

With 135 career wins through age 31, Hudson certainly is ahead of the pace of innumerable Hall of Fame pitchers. He's 135-70; Whitey Ford was 133-59, Bob Gibson was 125-88, and several Hall of Famers really were just hitting their stride at that age. Warren Spahn was 122-91.

Hudson has been in the majors for nine years and has nine straight winning seasons with double-figure wins. It's an impressive resume, but he has a 1-3 record in postseason play, no Cy Young Awards and no seasons of Cy Young caliber. Absent a breakthrough in one of those categories, the only way he gets into the Hall of Fame is to win 280+ games, and that would be expecting a lot from here on out.

Raul Ibanez *(0% present, 1% eventual)*

Started too late.

Derek Jeter *(95% present, 99% eventual)*

Randy Johnson *(98% present, 99% eventual)*

Chipper Jones *(40% present, 85% eventual)*

Most of the star players Chipper's age—Ivan Rodriguez, Manny Ramirez, Carlos Delgado, Garret Anderson—most of them are fading. Chipper's OPS over the last four seasons reads .847, .968, 1.005, 1.029. This, combined with his notably improved defense last year, suggests that Jones is not fading fast, and, at 36, he has some time left to pass the markers that would represent certain selection.

Andruw Jones *(0% present, 40% eventual)*

Andruw is five years younger than Chipper, but you wouldn't know it by looking at their batting records. If Andruw in 2007 had duplicated his 2005 season, when

he hit 51 homers, that "40%" above would read "75%". Perhaps I'm over-reacting to his subpar 2007, but Hall of Famers shouldn't be hitting .222 in a walk year in the middle of their careers.

Scott Kazmir *(0% present, 8% eventual)*

Could be the next Randy Johnson—or the next Mark Prior.

Jeff Kent *(50% present, 50% eventual)*

In some ways Kent is similar to Steve Finley and Luis Gonzalez—a player who has met some standards that are historically indicative of a second-tier Hall of Famer, but has done this by kind of hanging around and piling up numbers, not really impressing anybody. He is different from Finley and Gonzalez in that

a) he is a middle infielder, and

b) he did win an MVP Award.

The sportswriters don't really *like* him, but I doubt that that is much of a factor. If the sportswriters like you it can put you over the top in Hall of Fame voting, but if they actively dislike you it doesn't really influence the voting; they elect people all the time that they actively disliked.

If I were voting, I think I would have to vote for a middle infielder who has great consistency and drives in 100 runs a year. But I think it's a very close case, and I can easily see it going either way.

John Lackey *(0% present, 6% eventual)*

A competent professional pitcher, he has five winning seasons in six years, and appears to be getting better.

Carlos Lee *(0% present, 10% eventual)*

Derek Lee *(0% present, 10% eventual)*

Kenny Lofton *(1% present, 8% eventual)*

Lofton in many ways is an amazing player. He'll be 41 in May, but he must be the youngest 41-year-old since…I don't know, Davey Lopes maybe. He's four years away from 3,000 hits, and obviously you have to bet against him, but don't put your house on it.

Mike Lowell *(0% present, 2% eventual)*

Lowell played like a Hall of Famer in 2007, and it's not the first time he has done this; he has had 100-RBI seasons periodically since 2001, and hit 32 homers to help the Marlins win the World Championship in 2003. It's a long shot that he would sustain this more than another year or two.

Greg Maddux *(99% present, 99% eventual)*

Pedro Martinez *(80% present, 90% eventual)*

I would think that his combination of 200+ career wins, with a series of brilliant seasons, would easily be enough to make him a Hall of Famer.

Victor Martinez (0% present, 35% eventual)

Long praised as a great-hitting catcher whose defense needed work, he has done the work and improved his D. He's probably more comparable to Ted Simmons than to any other player in history. Simmons pulled up short of the Hall of Fame, but

a) it's not clear that that's a fair judgment about Simmons, and

b) even if it is, it's not clear that the same will happen to Martinez.

Hideki Matsui (0% present, 1% eventual)

Joe Mauer (0% present, 15% eventual)

Kevin Millwood (0% present, 2% eventual)

It would take a near-miraculous turn in his career, but he does have 133 career wins as a platform for what he will do in the future.

Justin Morneau (0% present, 25% eventual)

A relevant fact is that, while MVP voting is very friendly to slugging first basemen and RBI men, Hall of Fame voting is not. Hall of Fame voting is much more friendly to high batting averages, speed and defense. Few RBI men have been elected to the Hall of Fame with marginal credentials, while many have been left out—Jim Rice, Joe Torre, Gil Hodges, Ted Kluszewski, Rocky Colavito, Babe Herman, Dolph Camilli, Sherry Magee, most recently Mark McGwire, although we don't know whether that's going to stick.

Matt Morris (0% present, 1% eventual)

Jamie Moyer (8% present, 13% eventual)

With 230 career wins you certainly have to respect what he has accomplished, and he is still producing. There are less-qualified pitchers in the Hall of Fame.

Mark Mulder (0% present, 1% eventual)

You never know who might come back strong from an injury.

Mike Mussina (70% present, 80% eventual)

Mussina's career won-lost record, 250-144, is comparable to the final records of Bob Gibson (251-174), Juan Marichal (243-142), Iron Man McGinnity (246-142) and Bob Feller (266-162), all of whom were obvious Hall of Famers.

There are 23 pitchers in history who
a) have 220 wins, and
b) are 100 games over .500.

Five of those are still active—Clemens, Maddux, Randy Johnson, Glavine and Mussina. The other 18 are in the Hall of Fame.

Joe Nathan (0% present, 2% eventual)

It is hard to see that there were any Hall of Fame pitchers born between Pedro Martinez (October, 1971) and Tim Hudson (July, 1975). However, Nathan is one of the few pitchers in that age range who is regularly clocking in with impressive seasons.

Magglio Ordonez (0% present, 30% eventual)

Digressing for a moment...I see absolutely nothing wrong or remarkable in the two MVP votes for Magglio Ordonez in 2007, and I think the sportswriters/TV commentators who jumped on the Detroit writers for voting for Ordonez were showing a remarkable level of intolerance. Yes, A-Rod had a fantastic season, but Ordonez' season is...well, Al Kaline was the same kind of hitter, and Kaline never came close to those numbers: 139 RBI, .363 average, 54 doubles and 28 homers. It is well above the standard of your average MVP season.

Yes, A-Rod created more runs than Ordonez, but not that many more (159 to 146). Since when did a 13-run separation in offensive performance become a prohibitive barrier to sportswriters taking a broader view of the issue? David Ortiz created 11 to 27 more runs than Justin Morneau in 2006, depending on how you figure runs created, yet Morneau won the MVP Award. That's alright; we didn't complain about it. I didn't hear anybody complain about it. I'm more puzzled that Ordonez didn't receive more MVP support than I am that his hometown sportswriters would vote for him.

David Ortiz (10% present, 51% eventual)

Roy Oswalt (0% present, 15% eventual)

Oswalt turned 30 last August. His career in his twenties was very impressive—a winning record every year, a couple of 20-win seasons, 112-54 career record. He is among the five best starting pitchers in baseball.

Certainly this is a solid foundation for a Hall of Fame run, but it's not Hall of Fame performance in and of itself. It's not Randy Johnson/Greg Maddux/Roger Clemens/ Pedro Martinez/Johan Santana type stuff. Like Tim Hudson, he will need to continue to win for a long, long time in order to emerge as someone that people think of as a Hall of Famer.

Jonathon Papelbon (0% present, 7% eventual)

Like Chien-Ming Wang and J. J. Putz, he has two great seasons, and it is hard to extrapolate two super seasons into a Hall of Fame career.

Jake Peavy (0% present, 32% eventual)

Brad Penny (0% present, 5% eventual)

We haven't seen a Hall of Famer here yet, but he's a top flight pitcher.

Andy Pettitte (1% present, 40% eventual)

Andy Pettitte's career record (201-113) is much better than many Hall of Famers at the same age (Bob Lemon, 201-116, Early Wynn, 201-161, Eppa Rixey, 201-182,

Herb Pennock, 200-140, Gaylord Perry 198-157, Stan Coveleski 194-129, Jim Bunning 192-133, Rube Marquard 187-153, Ted Lyons 186-178, Red Faber 174-122, Randy Johnson 160-88. Many left out; strings on down to Phil Niekro, 130-107, and Dazzy Vance, 95-56). At this writing he is talking about retiring, but if he stays in the game and continues to win he could certainly emerge as a Hall of Fame candidate or even a 300-win candidate.

Mike Piazza (85% present, 85% eventual)

The best-hitting, worst-throwing catcher of all time.

Jorge Posada (25% present, 55% eventual)

I think of Posada as a Hall of Fame player. In my view, he has meant as much to the Yankees over the years as Mariano. He doesn't really have Hall of Fame numbers, and unless his arm comes back, his days behind the plate may be numbered. But he's lost nothing so far as a hitter, it's hard to say for sure what Hall of Fame numbers are for a catcher, and he is certainly a player who has made a huge impact on a large number of pennant races.

Albert Pujols (0% present, 95% eventual)

J. J. Putz (0% present, 3% eventual)

Impressive, but started late.

Manny Ramirez (50% present, 80% eventual)

In a sense, Manny lost his best Hall of Fame argument last year, as his streak of consecutive 100-RBI seasons ended at nine (eleven total). These are the players with the longest streaks of consecutive 100-RBI seasons:

Jimmie Foxx, 1929-1941	13
Lou Gehrig, 1926-1938	13
Al Simmons, 1924-1934	11
Alex Rodriguez, 1998-2007	10
Albert Belle, 1992-2000	9
Manny Ramirez, 1998-2006	9
Rafael Palmeiro, 1995-2003	9
Sammy Sosa, 1995-2003	9
Babe Ruth, 1926-1933	8
Chipper Jones, 1996-2003	8
Frank Thomas, 1991-1998	8
Mel Ott, 1929-1936	8
Ted Williams, 1939-1949	8
Willie Mays, 1959-1966	8

Ten or twelve consecutive 100-RBI seasons might have taken the issue out of play, whereas nine leaves him even with a couple of guys (Albert Belle and Rafael Palmeiro) who may struggle to achieve immortality.

Edgar Renteria (0% present, 35% eventual)

Extremely well positioned to make a run at 3,000 career hits.

Jose Reyes (0% present, 30% eventual)

Mariano Rivera (98% present, 98% eventual)

I don't have any doubt that Mariano is a Hall of Famer, based on his post-season performance and his long series of outstanding seasons.

Alex Rodriguez (99% present, 99% eventual)

Francisco Rodriguez (0% present, 15% eventual)

Ivan Rodriguez (98% present, 98% eventual)

Kenny Rogers (4% present, 5% eventual)

His career won-lost record is comparable to Don Drysdale, Stan Coveleski, Jesse Haines, Rube Marquard and Hal Newhouser, who are in the Hall of Fame. But with no 20-win seasons and few star-type accomplishments, I don't see it happening.

Scott Rolen (0% present, 1% eventual)

At his best, he was a candidate.

Jimmy Rollins (0% present, 50% eventual)

The 2007 MVP Award certainly enters his name in the Hall of Fame sweepstakes. At this point he is more of the level of Dick Groat/Zoilo Versalles/Barry Larkin than on the level of Ripken, Yount and Joe Morgan.

C. C. Sabathia (0% present, 35% eventual)

Sabathia turned 27 last July, which means that he is considered to be 26 years old for the 2007 season by the conventions of statistical analysis. As such, he is the first pitcher to win 100 games by age 26 since Doc Gooden in 1991. But on the other hand, the last seven pitchers to win 100 games by age 26 were:

Dwight Gooden	1991
Fernando Valenzuela	1987
Frank Tanana	1980
Don Gullett	1977
Bert Blyleven	1977
Vida Blue	1976
Joe Coleman Jr.	1973

None of whom is in the Hall of Fame yet.

Freddy Sanchez (0% present, 1% eventual)

Probably started too late, probably doesn't do enough different things.

Johan Santana (0% present, 45% eventual)

Taking in all phases of his performance, rather than just career wins, Santana has had the best career of any pitcher in baseball under the age of 30, and I doubt that his 2007 "downturn" was meaningful. Beyond any question Santana is on a Hall of Fame glide path; it's simply a question of whether he can sustain altitude long enough to reach the target. With a 93-44 career record he is probably ahead of 60% of the Hall of Famers of the last 50 years. But on the other hand, Mike Hampton at the same age was 99-66, Freddy Garcia 99-62, Mark Mulder was 103-57, Bret Saberhagen 113-83, Jim Maloney 122-75. More pitchers get hurt than stay healthy.

Jason Schmidt (0% present, 3% eventual)
See comment on Bartolo Colon.

Curt Schilling (60% present, 65% eventual)
See comment on John Smoltz.

Richie Sexson (0% present, 1% eventual)
Not "no", but "hell no".

Ben Sheets (0% present, 3% eventual)
Health is a major issue, and his career record is 73-74. But he's pretty good, the Brewers are putting a team around him that could well push them into future World Series, and there have been several Hall of Fame pitchers who were under .500 at his age.

Gary Sheffield (70% present, 80% eventual)
I hate to admit this, but for the first fifteen years of Gary Sheffield's career I had absolutely no understanding of him as a player. I thought he was like Jose Canseco or Greg Vaughn or Juan Gonzalez or somebody…a guy who put up big numbers sometimes and had a visual image because of that weird stuff he does with the bat, but who was kind of unreliable and inattentive to the other parts of the game.

When Sheffield came to the Yankees in 2004, and I started watching him as one watches the Yankees if you're rooting for the Red Sox, I was just amazed; I was never more wrong on a player. He's not *less* of a player than his numbers suggest; he is much, much *more* of a player. His throwing arm is off the charts. He throws like Vladimir Guerrero, except accurately. I'm joking, but his arm was functionally much better than Guerrero's famous arm… quick release, low, flat trajectory on his throws, tremendous power and just phenomenal accuracy. An aggressive thrower; a guy who is not afraid to try to make a play.

I thought he was an OK outfielder. He was an outstanding outfielder, ran well, read the ball well, threw outstanding. Sometimes a little too aggressive. He was—and is now, at 39—an outstanding baserunner.

You guys remember Carl Everett? Carl Everett was crazy, but he played with a kind of crazy intensity which, at his best, made him a frightening opponent—at bat, on the bases or in the field. But the problem with Carl Everett is that he was really crazy; he was crazy all the time, on the field or in the locker room, and most of what we mean when we say "crazy" is "erratic and unpredictable". At a high level. Carl Everett would be an MVP for two months, and useless and a gigantic pain in the ass for the next two months.

You get the feeling, watching Sheffield play against you, that what he really wants is to hurt you, but it's just a game so he'll accept beating you badly as a substitute.

Sheffield plays the game with that same crazy intensity as Carl Everett, but he's not *really* crazy; he's just super-intense, and sometimes he says things you wish he wouldn't.

I've had friends in the media tell me that Sheffield wasn't the same player against Texas and Seattle that he was against the Red Sox. I don't know; I didn't see him every day. Whenever I saw him play, he seemed to be doing everything possible to take over the game—and very often he did.

I don't have any doubt, for myself, that Gary Sheffield is a Hall of Famer. He has broken up his career by bouncing from team to team, not necessarily picking up a lot of fans on the way out the door. Maybe I am generalizing from my own failure to form a clear image of him until he was 34 years old, but I think that some sportswriters don't really have any sharp image of him, other than the bouncing bat, and I do have some doubt, because of that, how the voting will go for him.

Grady Sizemore (0% present, 40% eventual)
Historically, I don't think we could find very many players who
  a) had Sizemore's breadth of skills, and
  b) had three good seasons by age 24, but
  c) didn't go on to Hall of Fame careers.
Vada Pinson, certainly, and Cesar Cedeno. Sizemore does strike out an awful lot, and he hasn't come real close to hitting .300 yet.

John Smoltz (70% present, 80% eventual)
Whenever I do a search for pitchers comparable to Curt Schilling, John Smoltz always comes up as number one on the list, so I decided to write about the two as one. The two men are essentially the same age—41 in 2008—and both have career won-lost records which are in the weak part of the Hall of Fame's range—207-145 for Smoltz, 216-146 for Schilling. Schilling has 3,116 strikeouts in his career, a 3.46 ERA; Smoltz has 2,975 Ks and

*I'm more puzzled that Ordonez didn't receive **more MVP support** than I am that his hometown sportswriters would vote for him.*

a 3.26 ERA. Both men are still producing some wins—25 over the last two years for Schilling, 30 for Smoltz. Both men were traded away by their original teams before reaching the major leagues.

It would seem to me that both men are more likely than not to be in the Hall of Fame at some point. A pitcher with 200-230 wins only goes into the Hall of Fame if he has a lot to sell otherwise, but it seems to me that both men do. Their strikeout totals and winning percentages are Hall of Fame caliber. Both men have outstanding records in post-season play, 11-2, 2.23 ERA for Schilling, 15-4 with a 2.65 ERA for Smoltz.

Smoltz had three outstanding seasons as a reliever, not earning many wins, which I think will put him over the top in most sportswriters' calculation, plus he had a Cy Young season in 1996. Schilling has never won the Cy Young Award, but has had more Cy Young-type seasons in which he didn't win the award than anyone except Marichal (since the Cy Young Award started in '56). The average season score of a Cy Young Award winner is 319 points if you include the strike-shortened '81 and '94 seasons, 324 if you don't include those years. But the best Cy Young-era seasons that didn't win an award were:

Pitcher, Year	W - L	K - W	ERA	Score
Juan Marichal, 1966	25 - 6	222 - 36	2.23	427
Curt Schilling, 2002	23 - 7	316 - 33	3.23	424
Juan Marichal, 1968	26 - 9	218 - 46	2.43	407
Juan Marichal, 1963	25 - 8	248 - 61	2.41	407
Curt Schilling, 2001	22 - 6	293 - 39	2.98	404

None of these five deserved the Cy Young Award, by the way; they just happened to be matched against historic seasons by Sandy Koufax ('63 and '66), Bob Gibson ('68) and Randy Johnson (2001-2002)—all of those among the 11 highest-scoring seasons of the post-1956 era. Anyway, in addition to those two, Schilling has had two other seasons, 1997 and 2004, which score at 327 and 324—about the same as an average Cy Young Award season.

There are only 63 300-strikeout seasons in baseball history, most of them by pitchers who either are in the Hall of Fame or will be. With three such seasons, Schilling has more than anyone except Randy Johnson (6), Nolan Ryan (6), Tim Keefe (also 3) and Sandy Koufax (also 3). It would be one thing if his three 300-strikeout seasons and his three 20-win seasons were redundant counts, but they're not; only one of the 300-strikeout seasons was also a 20-win season. The other two were years when he pitched great, but didn't get the run support to win 20.

Smoltz won a Cy Young Award, but

a) the season scores at 387—the 15th-best Cy Young season of all time, by the way, and

b) Smoltz' best non-Cy Young season (1998) scores at 265.

What I am saying is that, although Smoltz won a Cy Young Award and Schilling hasn't, Schilling probably wins

the Big Seasons comparison with Smoltz, and I think most sportswriters would be perceptive enough to see that. Smoltz has more consistency, but Schilling has more impressive highlights.

We come then to the elusive equalizer, which we can call impact on the culture of the game. Schilling has played on three World Championship teams. He was the co-MVP of the 2001 World Series, which I think was one of the most exciting and dramatic World Series of recent times. The Bloody Sock episode from 2004 was a central storyline in what I would take to be one of the biggest sports stories of the decade, the Red Sox' first world championship in 86 years. It is difficult to say what lasting impact these things will have on the perceptions of sportswriters, but my intuition is that Schilling is more likely than not to draw strong support in Hall of Fame voting.

Alfonso Soriano (0% present, 30% eventual)

Huston Street (0% present, 10% eventual)
Chance of having a street named after him: 100%.

Ichiro Suzuki (0% present, 85% eventual)
I think Ichiro is a Hall of Famer. The record for consecutive 200-hit seasons is 8. Suzuki has been in the US for seven years, and he's at 7. He'll break the record unless he breaks a leg. If he breaks a leg, it's a tossup.

Yes, Suzuki doesn't do all of the things that I like a player to do, but then, neither does David Ortiz or Derek Jeter. Players aren't perfect, and that's not the standard of greatness. He has speed and defense, and he scores 110 runs a year, usually 111. It's enough. And, to me, his accomplishments in Japanese baseball are certainly relevant.

Mike Sweeney (0% present, 1% eventual)
Without the injuries he would have been a Hall of Famer.

Nick Swisher (0% present, 1% eventual)
Has done a couple of things which are suggestive of Hall of Fame ability.

Mark Teixeira (0% present, 20% eventual)
He'll go in the Hall of Fame before I learn to spell his name. Teixeira would be my pre-season pick for the NL MVP. With four straight 100-RBI seasons (including last year, when he missed a month with an injury) he certainly has the ability. At age 28 he is in the prime age range for MVP seasons, and he is expected to be a free agent at the end of the season. The Braves probably still have enough resources to pull together a competitive team, although that is less clear than the other issues.

Miguel Tejada (10% present, 65% eventual)
The Lance Berkman analysis also applies to Miguel Tejada, who is the same age and has comparable career bat-

ting stats. Obviously Tejada is ahead of Berkman because he is a shortstop and has an MVP Award in his ledger, but he also appears to be fading more quickly with the bat.

Frank Thomas (80% present, 80% eventual)

Through the year 2000 Thomas had been in the major leagues eleven seasons and had played 1,530 games, with a career batting average of .321, OPS of 1.018. His .277 batting average last year was his highest batting average since then. His career average has slipped to .303, his OPS to .982. More remarkably: in the last seven years Thomas has hit only 49 home runs (7 per year) on the road. He has hit 120 (17 per year) at home.

It's not exactly true that Thomas hasn't done *anything* since 2000; he hit 42 homers in 2003, and won a Comeback Player of the Year Award for hitting 39 homers, driving in 114 runs for Oakland in 2006. But his low batting averages and long absences with injuries have certainly weakened his Hall of Fame position.

What we are talking about, really, is how people in the future will remember Frank Thomas. A long, slow decline phase doesn't help how you are remembered. Thomas is agonizingly slow, a horrific fielder, and not especially well liked. When you throw in the perception that Thomas' batting numbers are from an era of phony numbers and the realization that he does have a very unusual home/road split in his power numbers, I think some people are not going to see Thomas as a Hall of Famer.

This may be offset to some small extent by the growing acceptance of the importance of on-base percentage. Thomas' on-base percentage as a young player was in the Ted Williams range, and, even though his on-base percentages have been below .390 in six of the last seven years, his career figure remains .421. He should have been in the top ten all time, and he won't be, but he remains in the top 25.

One way to see Thomas' career is simply that his skills matured too early. He was a great player when he was 24, but with no speed, no throwing arm and his on-base and power skills maxed out, there was simply nowhere for him to go.

Bottom line: there is no precedent for leaving a player with his batting totals out of the Hall of Fame, and if that precedent was established on Frank Thomas, I would regard that as a poor choice. Rafael Palmeiro, maybe, and we'll have to see what happens with Mark McGwire. I think Frank Thomas was a genuinely great player when he was young, albeit operating off a narrow base of skills. I think he should be a Hall of Famer, and I think that he most likely will be.

Jim Thome (75% present, 85% eventual)

Comparing Thome to Thomas…Thome got a little bit of a later start, and his batting average was 50 points lower his first few years. Thome strikes out much more than Thomas. As he has aged he has been more healthy and consistent, and his numbers by now have essentially

caught up with Frank's, plus, being two years younger, he has more time left to build his portfolio. But I don't think he's a clear and absolute Hall of Famer just yet.

Chase Utley (0% present, 15% eventual)

One of the best hitters in baseball.

Jason Varitek (1% present, 3% eventual)

There is some precedent for electing players like this to the Hall of Fame—Ray Schalk, Phil Rizzuto, Rick Ferrell. There is precedent for giving special consideration to leadership and defense, in some cases. It might require that people re-evaluate how they think about greatness in a player, but those kind of re-considerations DO happen, over time, and it's not out of the question that it might happen here.

Javier Vazquez (0% present, 5% eventual)

Having a fine career pitching for a lot of not-very-good baseball teams, but his disappointing season with the Yankees in 2004 has colored the way he is perceived, and will almost certainly keep him out of Hall of Fame range.

Omar Vizquel (80% present, 80% eventual)

Ozzie Smith, to whom Omar has always been compared, was a visually very impressive defensive shortstop who also had stunning defensive statistics. Omar is a visually very impressive defensive shortstop who has never had especially good defensive statistics, unless you are one of the slow group who is still impressed by fielding percentage. It is certainly beyond the scope of the present essay to sort out who is right and who is wrong about Omar's defense, but the majority is clearly on the pro-Omar side of the aisle, and I expect this to carry him to a fairly quick berth in the Hall of Fame.

Billy Wagner (0% present, 10% eventual)

Wagner is hard to evaluate as a Hall of Fame candidate because the Hall of Fame standard for a reliever is not clear. But he has 358 career Saves, is still throwing smoke and still producing Saves. He has had an ERA as high as 3.00 only once in his thirteen-year career. If he winds up on a World Championship team, he could become somebody that people talk about.

Chien-Ming Wang (0% present, 9% eventual)

No quantity yet.

Tim Wakefield (0% present, 2% eventual)

Has 168 career wins, would emerge as a Hall of Fame candidate if he had his best years in his 40s, as a couple of knuckle-ballers have had.

Brandon Webb (0% present, 6% eventual)

Followed up a Cy Young season in 2006 with a better one in 2007, but he's 40 wins behind Mark Buehrle, who is the same age, and only ten games over .500 in his career. He would have to be tremendously consistent from here on to emerge as a candidate.

David Wells *(15% present, 17% eventual)*

By historic standards, David Wells is not a bad Hall of Fame candidate. He has 239 career wins, and he is 82 games over .500 in his career. There are 16 Hall of Fame starting pitchers who can't match either of those accomplishments (Jim Bunning, Jack Chesbro, Stan Coveleski, Dizzy Dean, Don Drysdale, Jesse Haines, Waite Hoyt, Catfish Hunter, Addie Joss, Sandy Koufax, Bob Lemon, Rube Marquard, Hal Newhouser, Dazzy Vance, Rube Waddell and Ed Walsh) plus 19 more who can match one but not the other.

By historic standards he might go in, but, in the immortal words of Marty McFly, history is gonna change, and I don't think Wells has made enough of an impact on the public imagination to qualify by the standards of the future, or at least enough of a positive impact. There are some points in his favor. He's been in some World Series, and his affection for Babe Ruth and baseball memorabilia is somewhat endearing.

Vernon Wells *(0% present, 5% eventual)*

Andruw Jones lite…he looks like Andruw in the uniform, in the field, similar player, doesn't strike out as much as Jones and hits for a little higher average, not quite as much power. It's weird that they both had horrible seasons at the same time. Has anyone ever seen them together?

David Wright *(0% present, 45% eventual)*

Michael Young *(0% present, 40% eventual)*

If you keep getting 200 hits every year, sooner or later people have to notice.

Carlos Zambrano *(0% present, 30% eventual)*

Career records for the four horsemen grouped together in the Josh Beckett comment: Sabathia, 100-63, Zambrano, 82-55, Beckett, 77-52, Peavy, 76-51.

Barry Zito *(0% present, 15% eventual)*

A Cy Young season highlights what is otherwise a workmanlike career. If he took everything he has done so far and did it all again, it wouldn't be quite enough.

Not included because it is just too soon to make any meaningful estimate: Chad Billingsley, Ryan Braun, Matt Cain, Fausto Carmona, Prince Fielder, Jeff Francoeur, Adrian Gonzalez, Tom Gorzellany, Curtis Granderson, Cole Hamels, Felix Hernandez, Nick Markakis, Russell Martin, Dustin Pedroia, Hanley Ramirez, Alex Rios, James Shields, Troy Tulowitzki, B. J. Upton, Justin Verlander, Chris Young, Ryan Zimmerman.

It is difficult to say what lasting impact these things will have on the perceptions of sportswriters, but my intuition is that Schilling is more likely than not to draw strong support in Hall of Fame voting.

Seattle Mariners

Seattle Mariners – 2007
Team Overview

Description		Ranking
Won-Lost Record	88-74	
Place	2nd of 4 in American League West	
Runs Scored	794	12th in the majors
Runs Allowed	813	20th in the majors
Home Runs	153	20th in the majors
Home Runs Allowed	147	6th in the majors
Batting Average	.287	3rd in the majors
Batting Average Allowed	.281	26th in the majors
Walks Drawn	389	30th in the majors
Walks Given	546	18th in the majors
OPS For	.762	13th in the majors
OPS Against	.780	23rd in the majors
Stolen Bases	81	19th in the majors
Stolen Bases Allowed	69	3rd in the majors

Key Players

Pos	Player	G	AB	R	H	2B	3B	HR	RBI	SB	CS	BB	SO	Avg	OBP	Slg	OPS	WS
C	Kenji Johjima	135	485	52	139	29	0	14	61	0	2	15	41	.287	.322	.433	.755	17
1B	Richie Sexson	121	434	58	89	21	0	21	63	1	0	51	100	.205	.295	.399	.694	7
2B	Jose Lopez	149	524	58	132	17	2	11	62	2	3	20	64	.252	.284	.355	.639	10
3B	Adrian Beltre	149	595	87	164	41	2	26	99	14	2	38	104	.276	.319	.482	.802	16
SS	Y Betancourt	155	536	72	155	38	2	9	67	5	4	15	48	.289	.308	.418	.725	19
LF	Raul Ibanez	149	573	80	167	35	5	21	105	0	0	53	97	.291	.351	.480	.831	23
CF	Ichiro Suzuki	161	678	111	238	22	7	6	68	37	8	49	77	.351	.396	.431	.827	33
RF	Jose Guillen	153	593	84	172	28	2	23	99	5	1	41	118	.290	.353	.460	.813	18
DH	Jose Vidro	147	548	78	172	26	0	6	59	0	0	63	57	.314	.381	.394	.775	16

Key Pitchers

Pos	Player	G	GS	W	L	Sv	IP	H	R	ER	BB	SO	BR/9	ERA	WS
SP	Miguel Batista	33	32	16	11	0	193.0	209	101	92	85	133	14.08	4.29	12
SP	Felix Hernandez	30	30	14	7	0	190.1	209	88	83	53	165	12.53	3.92	14
SP	Jarrod Washburn	32	32	10	15	0	193.2	201	102	93	67	114	12.83	4.32	10
SP	Horacio Ramirez	20	20	8	7	0	98.0	139	86	78	42	40	16.81	7.16	0
SP	Jeff Weaver	27	27	7	13	0	146.2	190	105	101	35	80	14.30	6.20	1
CL	J.J. Putz	68	0	6	1	40	71.2	37	11	11	13	82	6.53	1.38	20
RP	Sean Green	64	0	5	2	0	68.0	77	31	29	34	53	15.09	3.84	5
RP	George Sherrill	73	0	2	0	3	45.2	28	12	12	17	56	9.07	2.36	8

Seattle Mariners – 2007
Games Played by Opening Day Starter
at Each Position

Pos	Player	Starts
C	Johjima	128
1B	Sexson	118
2B	Lopez	141
3B	Beltre	148
SS	Betancourt	147
LF	Ibanez	144
CF	Suzuki	161
RF	Guillen	152
DH	Vidro	137
	Total	1276

Seattle's opening-day starters made 1,276 starts in 2007, 56 more than any other major league team.

Kenji Johjima in 2007 hit better against good pitchers than he did against weaker ones, with a .323 average against pitchers with ERAs under 4.25 and a .256 average on the other side of the line. Adrian Beltre was at the other extreme; he didn't do much of anything against good pitching. Although the 2007 data was stronger than it has usually been, Beltre has always struggled against good pitching.

Kenji Johjima – 2007
Batting Performance by Quality of Opposing Pitcher

	AB	H	HR	RBI	Avg	OPS
Pitcher with ERA <= 3.50	102	33	2	11	.324	.797
Pitcher with ERA 3.51 to 4.25	121	39	6	19	.322	.892
Pitcher with ERA 4.26 to 5.25	137	34	3	16	.248	.659
Pitcher with ERA over 5.25	125	33	3	15	.264	.690

Adrian Beltre – 2007
Batting Performance by Quality of Opposing Pitcher

	AB	H	HR	RBI	Avg	OPS
Pitcher with ERA <= 3.50	127	26	4	16	.205	.610
Pitcher with ERA 3.51 to 4.25	152	41	6	19	.270	.736
Pitcher with ERA 4.26 to 5.25	161	47	6	25	.292	.843
Pitcher with ERA over 5.25	155	50	10	39	.323	.979

In his historic 2004 season, when he set a major league record with 262 hits, Ichiro had 80 multi-hit games with 208 hits in multi-hit games. In 2007 he had almost as many multi-hit games (76) but the opposition did a better job of stopping him at two hits, and he had "only" 181 hits in multi-hit contests.

Ichiro Suzuki – 2004
Games with X Hits

	G	AB	R	H	2B	3B	HR	RBI	Avg
0 Hits	27	99	4	0	0	0	0	1	.000
1 Hits	54	228	19	54	6	1	2	22	.237
2 Hits	46	204	31	92	10	1	0	12	.451
3 Hits	24	119	29	72	4	1	4	14	.605
4 Hits	6	32	10	24	3	1	2	10	.750
5 Hits	4	22	8	20	1	1	0	1	.909

Ichiro Suzuki – 2007
Games with X Hits

	G	AB	R	H	2B	3B	HR	RBI	Avg
0 Hits	28	108	6	0	0	0	0	1	.000
1 Hits	57	233	27	57	6	0	1	15	.245
2 Hits	52	218	43	104	12	3	1	22	.477
3 Hits	20	98	29	60	4	4	3	25	.612
4 Hits	3	16	5	12	0	0	1	4	.750
5 Hits	1	5	1	5	0	0	0	1	1.000

Ichiro hit 120 ground balls that went for hits, 41% more than any other major league hitter.

Ichiro Suzuki – 2007
Hitting Analysis

Batting Left-Handed						1B	2B	3B	HR
Ground Balls to Left	86	Outs 51	Hits 35	Average .407	Hit Type	35 -	0 -	0 -	0
Ground Balls to Center	121	Outs 76	Hits 45	Average .372	Hit Type	45 -	0 -	0 -	0
Ground Balls to Right	127	Outs 87	Hits 40	Average .315	Hit Type	35 -	4 -	1 -	0
Line Drives to Left	47	Outs 14	Hits 33	Average .702	Hit Type	26 -	7 -	0 -	0
Line Drives to Center	50	Outs 10	Hits 40	Average .800	Hit Type	34 -	3 -	3 -	0
Line Drives to Right	22	Outs 6	Hits 16	Average .727	Hit Type	10 -	4 -	1 -	1
Fly Balls to Left	62	Outs 59	Hits 3	Average .048	Hit Type	2 -	1 -	0 -	0
Fly Balls to Center	54	Outs 40	Hits 14	Average .269	Hit Type	9 -	3 -	1 -	1
Fly Balls to Right	24	Outs 19	Hits 5	Average .208	Hit Type	0 -	0 -	1 -	4
Total on Ground Balls	334	Outs 214	Hits 120	Average .359	Hit Type	115 -	4 -	1 -	0
Total on Line Drives	119	Outs 30	Hits 89	Average .748	Hit Type	70 -	14 -	4 -	1
Total on Fly Balls	140	Outs 118	Hits 22	Average .159	Hit Type	11 -	4 -	2 -	5
Total Hit to Left	195	Outs 124	Hits 71	Average .364	Hit Type	63 -	8 -	0 -	0
Total Hit to Center	225	Outs 126	Hits 99	Average .444	Hit Type	88 -	6 -	4 -	1
Total Hit to Right	173	Outs 112	Hits 61	Average .353	Hit Type	45 -	8 -	3 -	5
Bunts	14	Outs 7	Hits 7	Average .700	Hit Type	7 -	0 -	0 -	0
All Balls in Play	607	Outs 369	Hits 238	Average .396	Hit Type	203 -	22 -	7 -	6

The Mariners' Map

The Seattle Mariners outperformed their starting pitching last year by an almost fantastic margin. Jeff Weaver had a 6.20 ERA—yet the Mariners were 12-15 in the games that he went to the post. Horacio Ramirez had a 7.16 ERA with more walks than strikeouts and a batting average allowed of .337, OPS allowed of .911—yet the Mariners were 9-11 in the games that he started. Cha Seung Baek had an ERA over five, yet the Mariners won nine of his twelve starts. I don't even want to talk about Ryan Feierabend.

Most teams' won-lost record is about the same as their split of Good Games and Bad Games by starting pitchers (Game Score of 50 or above equals a Good Game). The Angels had 92 Game Scores over 50; they won 94. The Mets had 90 Good Games; they won 88. San Diego had 92 Good Games; they won 89. Kansas City had 71 and 69. Obviously there is a lot that goes into winning other than starting pitching, but…a lot of times they go hand in hand.

But the Mariners had only 71 Good Games—yet they won 88. They over-achieved their starting pitching by 17 games, the largest margin in the majors. They chased the Angels almost to the wire because their offense was pretty good and J. J. Putz was a god.

It would be interesting to know whether this is predictive of anything. Do teams that over-achieve their starting pitching in one year discover the next season that they need starting pitching after all? Do they tend to grind their relief aces into the dust? Or does the opposite happen: Do teams whose starting pitching lags behind the rest of the team tend to catch up once they can pick up a couple of good starters?

I'll try to get a minute to study that, and if I don't, I'm sure somebody will. But my instinct is that imbalance is always a trouble sign.

Seattle Mariners– 2007
Performance by Starting Pitcher

Games Started By	G	RS	RA	Won	Lost
Washburn, Jarrod	32	144	152	15	17
Batista, Miguel	32	127	134	19	13
Hernandez, Felix	30	157	110	21	9
Weaver, Jeff	27	131	161	12	15
Ramirez, Horacio	20	125	130	9	11
Baek, Cha Seung	12	75	56	9	3
Feierabend, Ryan	9	35	70	3	6
Team Totals	162	794	813	88	74

When Seattle got an above average starting pitching performance, Game Score of 50 or better, they had the league's best winning percentage, .817, 58-13.

Seattle Mariners – 2007
Performance by Quality of Start

Game Score	#	ERA	W	-	L
80 and above	5	0.00	5	-	0
70 to 79	12	0.50	11	-	1
60 to 69	18	2.27	15	-	3
50 to 59	36	3.47	27	-	9
40 to 49	32	4.17	16	-	16
30 to 39	24	6.60	8	-	16
20 to 29	20	8.27	5	-	15
Below 20	15	10.37	1	-	14

Seattle starters Felix Hernandez and Jarrod Washburn pitched essentially the same number of innings in 2007—within four innings of one another.
Washburn got 255 outs on balls hit in the air (pop outs, fly outs and line drives caught). Hernandez got 107.

Felix Hernandez – 2007
Batters Faced Analysis

Batters Faced	808
Reached Base	299
Retired	509
Reached Base by:	
Single	149
Double	36
Triple	4
Home Run	20
Walk	53
Hit Batsman	3
Error	5
Fielder's Choice - All Safe	1
(Fielder's Choice - Out Recorded)	(28)
Retired by:	
Strikeout	165
Ground Out	237
Line Out	15
Fly Out	68
Pop Out	24

Jarrod Washburn – 2007
Batters Faced Analysis

Batters Faced	839
Reached Base	311
Retired	528
Reached Base by:	
Single	133
Double	41
Triple	4
Home Run	23
Walk	67
Hit Batsman	8
Error	9
Fielder's Choice - All Safe	0
(Fielder's Choice - Out Recorded)	(26)
Retired by:	
Strikeout	114
Ground Out	159
Line Out	17
Fly Out	164
Pop Out	74

Last year the Mariners finally allowed young Felix Hernandez to begin throwing his slider as often as he wanted to. He threw it 20% of the time, roughly twice as often as his curveball and changeup —each of which are fine pitches in their own right. The year before, he'd thrown only 7% sliders.

Felix Hernandez – 2006
Pitch Type Analysis

Overall

Total Pitches	3061	
Fastball	1696	55%
Curveball	611	20%
Changeup	454	15%
Slider	207	7%
Pitchout	3	0%
Not Charted	90	3%

	Vs. RHB		Vs. LHB	
Total Pitches	1434		1627	
Outs Recorded	289		283	
Fastball	812	57%	884	54%
Curveball	318	22%	293	18%
Changeup	87	6%	367	23%
Slider	179	12%	28	2%
Pitchout	1	0%	2	0%
Not Charted	37	3%	53	3%

Felix Hernandez – 2007
Pitch Type Analysis

Overall

Total Pitches	3005	
Fastball	1667	55%
Curveball	364	12%
Changeup	291	10%
Slider	605	20%
Pitchout	2	0%
Not Charted	76	3%

	Vs. RHB		Vs. LHB	
Total Pitches	1441		1564	
Outs Recorded	296		275	
Fastball	888	62%	779	50%
Curveball	145	10%	219	14%
Changeup	44	3%	247	16%
Slider	339	24%	266	17%
Pitchout	2	0%	0	0%
Not Charted	23	2%	53	3%

Tampa Bay Rays

Tampa Bay Rays – 2007
Team Overview

Description		Ranking
Won-Lost Record	66-96	
Place	5th of 5 in American League East	
Runs Scored	782	15th in the majors
Runs Allowed	944	30th in the majors
Home Runs	187	7th in the majors
Home Runs Allowed	199	29th in the majors
Batting Average	.268	15th in the majors
Batting Average Allowed	.290	30th in the majors
Walks Drawn	545	10th in the majors
Walks Given	568	22nd in the majors
OPS For	.769	12th in the majors
OPS Against	.826	30th in the majors
Stolen Bases	131	6th in the majors
Stolen Bases Allowed	96	14th in the majors

Key Players

Pos	Player	G	AB	R	H	2B	3B	HR	RBI	SB	CS	BB	SO	Avg	OBP	Slg	OPS	WS
C	Dioner Navarro	119	388	46	88	19	2	9	44	3	1	33	67	.227	.286	.356	.641	6
1B	Carlos Pena	148	490	99	138	29	1	46	121	1	0	103	142	.282	.411	.627	1.037	28
2B	Ty Wigginton	98	378	47	104	21	0	16	49	1	4	28	73	.275	.329	.458	.786	6
3B	Akinori Iwamura	123	491	82	140	21	10	7	34	12	8	58	114	.285	.359	.411	.770	13
SS	Brendan Harris	137	521	72	149	35	3	12	59	4	1	42	96	.286	.343	.434	.777	13
LF	Carl Crawford	143	584	93	184	37	9	11	80	50	10	32	112	.315	.355	.466	.820	20
CF	B.J. Upton	129	474	86	142	25	1	24	82	22	8	65	154	.300	.386	.508	.894	22
RF	Delmon Young	162	645	65	186	38	0	13	93	10	3	26	127	.288	.316	.408	.723	17
DH	Jonny Gomes	107	348	48	85	20	2	17	49	12	4	35	126	.244	.322	.460	.782	8

Key Pitchers

Pos	Player	G	GS	W	L	Sv	IP	H	R	ER	BB	SO	BR/9	ERA	WS
SP	Scott Kazmir	34	34	13	9	0	206.2	196	91	80	89	239	12.72	3.48	13
SP	James Shields	31	31	12	8	0	215.0	202	98	92	36	184	10.38	3.85	12
SP	Edwin Jackson	32	31	5	15	0	161.0	195	116	103	88	128	16.04	5.76	2
SP	Andy Sonnanstine	22	22	6	10	0	130.2	151	87	85	26	97	12.54	5.85	3
SP	Jason Hammel	24	14	3	5	0	85.0	100	58	58	40	64	15.04	6.14	2
CL	Al Reyes	61	0	2	4	26	60.2	49	35	33	21	70	10.68	4.90	6
RP	Gary Glover	67	0	6	5	2	77.1	87	44	42	27	51	13.38	4.89	4
RP	Brian Stokes	59	0	2	7	0	62.1	90	49	49	25	35	17.04	7.07	0

What Happened Last Year to Carlos Pena?

I am sure there are many different ways to explain it; one friend of ours insists that it is simply a matter of his hot streaks being longer and his slumps shorter than in the past. But another way is:

1) He hit more of his fly balls to right field, and
2) The percentage of his flies to right that went out increased.

From 2003 to 2006, Pena hit more flies to left field than he did to right. Last year he got ahead of the pitch more often.

From 2003 to 2006, 32% of Pena's flies to right were Big Flies to right. Last year it was 47%.

What will happen to Pena in 2008? Pena's season is reminiscent of the season that Jim Gentile had in 1961—a 46-homer outburst, coming out of nowhere, by a left-handed hitting first baseman. Gentile, like Pena, had pretty soft hands and wasn't a bad first baseman, although Pena is better. He was about the same size as Pena, and the seasons are very similar.

Gentile followed up with a season of 33 homers, 87 RBI, and was never able to do better than that, so that's a starting point. But Diamond Jim was a hothead with so-so work habits, and he put on some weight pretty quickly. Pena is more of a solid citizen type, and he's been fighting for a long time to get things going his way. I don't think anybody now is expecting him to have a 1.000-plus OPS every year, but I would expect him to come closer to holding onto his gains than Gentile did.

Carlos Pena – 2007
Hitting Analysis

Batting Left-Handed									1B	2B	3B	HR
Ground Balls to Left	3	Outs	3	Hits	0	Average	.000	Hit Type	0	- 0	- 0	- 0
Ground Balls to Center	28	Outs	21	Hits	7	Average	.250	Hit Type	7	- 0	- 0	- 0
Ground Balls to Right	102	Outs	82	Hits	20	Average	.196	Hit Type	18	- 2	- 0	- 0
Line Drives to Left	3	Outs	0	Hits	3	Average	1.000	Hit Type	2	- 1	- 0	- 0
Line Drives to Center	13	Outs	5	Hits	8	Average	.615	Hit Type	7	- 1	- 0	- 0
Line Drives to Right	48	Outs	12	Hits	36	Average	.750	Hit Type	24	- 12	- 0	- 0
Fly Balls to Left	53	Outs	47	Hits	6	Average	.125	Hit Type	0	- 1	- 1	- 4
Fly Balls to Center	50	Outs	31	Hits	19	Average	.396	Hit Type	0	- 3	- 0	- 16
Fly Balls to Right	55	Outs	17	Hits	38	Average	.704	Hit Type	3	- 9	- 0	- 26
Total on Ground Balls	133	Outs	106	Hits	27	Average	.203	Hit Type	25	- 2	- 0	- 0
Total on Line Drives	64	Outs	17	Hits	47	Average	.734	Hit Type	33	- 14	- 0	- 0
Total on Fly Balls	158	Outs	95	Hits	63	Average	.420	Hit Type	3	- 13	- 1	- 46
Total Hit to Left	59	Outs	50	Hits	9	Average	.167	Hit Type	2	- 2	- 1	- 4
Total Hit to Center	91	Outs	57	Hits	34	Average	.382	Hit Type	14	- 4	- 0	- 16
Total Hit to Right	205	Outs	111	Hits	94	Average	.461	Hit Type	45	- 23	- 0	- 26
Bunts	2	Outs	1	Hits	1	Average	1.000	Hit Type	1	- 0	- 0	- 0
All Balls in Play	357	Outs	219	Hits	138	Average	.397	Hit Type	62	- 29	- 1	- 46

Carl Crawford's batting averages when he hits a fly ball:

2002	.075
2003	.098
2004	.162
2005	.190
2006	.262
2007	.307

Carl Crawford – 2007
Hitting Analysis

Batting Left-Handed										1B	2B	3B	HR
Ground Balls to Left	33	Outs	27	Hits	6	Average	.182	Hit Type		5	1	0	0
Ground Balls to Center	79	Outs	50	Hits	29	Average	.367	Hit Type		29	0	0	0
Ground Balls to Right	114	Outs	87	Hits	27	Average	.237	Hit Type		26	0	1	0
Line Drives to Left	31	Outs	7	Hits	24	Average	.774	Hit Type		17	6	1	0
Line Drives to Center	36	Outs	4	Hits	32	Average	.889	Hit Type		29	2	1	0
Line Drives to Right	28	Outs	8	Hits	20	Average	.714	Hit Type		14	5	1	0
Fly Balls to Left	78	Outs	61	Hits	17	Average	.221	Hit Type		2	12	0	3
Fly Balls to Center	54	Outs	36	Hits	18	Average	.340	Hit Type		4	10	3	1
Fly Balls to Right	20	Outs	9	Hits	11	Average	.550	Hit Type		1	1	2	7
Total on Ground Balls	226	Outs	164	Hits	62	Average	.274	Hit Type		60	1	1	0
Total on Line Drives	95	Outs	19	Hits	76	Average	.800	Hit Type		60	13	3	0
Total on Fly Balls	152	Outs	106	Hits	46	Average	.307	Hit Type		7	23	5	11
Total Hit to Left	142	Outs	95	Hits	47	Average	.333	Hit Type		24	19	1	3
Total Hit to Center	169	Outs	90	Hits	79	Average	.470	Hit Type		62	12	4	1
Total Hit to Right	162	Outs	104	Hits	58	Average	.358	Hit Type		41	6	4	7
Bunts	2	Outs	2	Hits	0	Average	.000	Hit Type		0	0	0	0
All Balls in Play	475	Outs	291	Hits	184	Average	.390	Hit Type		127	37	9	11

Over the last three seasons, Carl Crawford has the largest stolen base gain of any major league player— +100. Crawford is fourth in stolen bases over those three years, behind Jose Reyes, Juan Pierre and Chone Figgins, but has a better stolen base percentage (85%) than those other players.

Carl Crawford – Career
Baserunning Analysis

Year	1st to 3rd Adv	1st to 3rd Opp	2nd to Home Adv	2nd to Home Opp	1st to Home Adv	1st to Home Opp	DP Opp	GIDP	Bases Taken	BR Outs	BR Gain	SB Gain	Net Gain
2002	1	7	3	5	1	1	44	0	15	1	13	-1	+12
2003	6	20	18	24	2	6	105	5	23	4	12	35	+47
2004	4	11	17	25	4	8	91	2	32	5	24	29	+53
2005	8	18	15	28	5	7	122	11	27	9	3	30	+33
2006	3	19	16	18	4	7	123	8	24	7	9	40	+49
2007	5	20	14	23	4	8	122	11	26	5	10	30	+40
Totals	27	95	83	123	20	37	607	37	147	31	72	163	+235
		28%		67%		54%		6%					

Reyes v. Bradford

Al Reyes last year recorded only 23 ground-ball outs, and there were NO forceouts while he was on the mound. Chad Bradford, in essentially the same number of innings, had 101 groundouts plus 9 forceouts. Two pitchers more different from one another would be hard to imagine:

<table>
<tr><td colspan="2">Al Reyes – 2007
Batters Faced Analysis</td><td colspan="2">Chad Bradford – 2007
Batters Faced Analysis</td></tr>
<tr><td>Batters Faced</td><td>254</td><td>Batters Faced</td><td>289</td></tr>
<tr><td>Reached Base</td><td>74</td><td>Reached Base</td><td>112</td></tr>
<tr><td>Retired</td><td>180</td><td>Retired</td><td>177</td></tr>
<tr><td>Reached Base by:</td><td></td><td>Reached Base by:</td><td></td></tr>
<tr><td>Single</td><td>26</td><td>Single</td><td>67</td></tr>
<tr><td>Double</td><td>10</td><td>Double</td><td>9</td></tr>
<tr><td>Triple</td><td>0</td><td>Triple</td><td>0</td></tr>
<tr><td>Home Run</td><td>13</td><td>Home Run</td><td>1</td></tr>
<tr><td>Walk</td><td>21</td><td>Walk</td><td>16</td></tr>
<tr><td>Hit Batsman</td><td>2</td><td>Hit Batsman</td><td>6</td></tr>
<tr><td>Error</td><td>2</td><td>Error</td><td>3</td></tr>
<tr><td>Fielder's Choice - All Safe</td><td>0</td><td>Fielder's Choice - All Safe</td><td>1</td></tr>
<tr><td>(Fielder's Choice - Out Recorded)</td><td>(0)</td><td>(Fielder's Choice - Out Recorded)</td><td>(9)</td></tr>
<tr><td>Retired by:</td><td></td><td>Retired by:</td><td></td></tr>
<tr><td>Strikeout</td><td>70</td><td>Strikeout</td><td>29</td></tr>
<tr><td>Ground Out</td><td>23</td><td>Ground Out</td><td>101</td></tr>
<tr><td>Line Out</td><td>3</td><td>Line Out</td><td>4</td></tr>
<tr><td>Fly Out</td><td>61</td><td>Fly Out</td><td>29</td></tr>
<tr><td>Pop Out</td><td>23</td><td>Pop Out</td><td>14</td></tr>
<tr><td>Other</td><td>0</td><td>Other</td><td>0</td></tr>
</table>

The better the team the better he pitches.
Take a look at Scott Kazmir's ERA by quality of opposition:

Scott Kazmir
Career Records Against Quality of Opposition

Opponent	G	IP	W	L	SO	BB	ERA
.600 teams	4	16.1	1	0	24	10	1.65
.500 - .599 teams	50	298.1	18	16	315	134	3.20
.400 - .499 teams	40	234.0	14	13	253	103	4.23
sub .400 teams	4	22.0	2	0	25	15	4.91

The Rays engineered a six-player swap with the Minnesota Twins last November. The two key players were outfielder Delmon Young, going to the Twins, and starting pitcher Matt Garza, now with Tampa Bay. Both players are highly regarded young players. The trade makes sense because:

1) If Rocco Baldelli ever gets healthy the Rays have an extra outfielder,

2) The Rays have proven that they can produce outfielders with skills, but

3) They need pitching.

How badly do they need pitching? Since 2003 twenty starting pitchers have had 10 or more decisions for the Rays. The Rays have winning records with only two of those twenty on the mound, Rob Bell 21-19 and Victor Zambrano 26-24.

The Rays' record when the other 18 pitchers start the game on the hill is 263-403, a .395 winning percentage.

In the 44 games started by pitchers who did not reach a total of ten decisions the Rays were 16-28 (.364) in 2007.

Tampa Bay Record in Games Started – Last Five Years

	Wins	Losses	Win Pct
Bell, Rob	21	19	.525
Zambrano, Victor	26	24	.520
Kazmir, Scott	48	49	.495
Shields, James	24	28	.462
Hendrickson, Mark	34	40	.459
Fossum, Casey	26	34	.433
Halama, John	6	8	.429
Nomo, Hideo	8	11	.421
Hammel, Jason	9	14	.391
Waechter, Doug	21	33	.389
McClung, Seth	14	23	.387
Sosa, Jorge	10	17	.370
Kennedy, Joe	8	14	.364
Seo, Jae	9	17	.346
Brazelton, Dewon	13	26	.333
Sonnanstine, Andy	7	15	.318
Corcoran, Tim	5	12	.294
Gonzalez, Geremi	9	24	.273
Jackson, Edwin	8	24	.250
Howell, J.P.	4	14	.222

Some Days You Beat the Devil, Some Days the Devil Beats You

All major league teams other than the Devil Rays in 2007 had a won-lost record of 84-4 when the starting pitcher produced a Game Score of 80 or above.

The Devil Rays were 2-2.

Tampa Bay Rays– 2007 Performance by Quality of Start

Game Score	#	ERA	W	-	L
80 and above	4	1.73	2	-	2
70 to 79	11	1.46	9	-	2
60 to 69	26	2.91	15	-	11
50 to 59	35	3.84	20	-	15
40 to 49	34	5.42	13	-	21
30 to 39	22	7.80	4	-	18
20 to 29	19	10.01	2	-	17
Below 20	11	11.61	1	-	10

James Shields retired the first hitter in 74% of the innings he started,
tops in baseball among ERA qualifiers.

James Shields – 2007
Inning Analysis

Innings Pitched	215.0
Runs Allowed	98
Innings Started	220
Runs in Those Innings	105
Shutout Innings	168
One-Run Innings	27
Two-Run Innings	10
Three-Run Inning	9
Four-Run Innings	4
Five-Run Innings	1
Ten+ Run Innings	1
Got First Man Out	162
Runs Scored in Those Innings	42
Runs/9 Innings	2.33
First Man Reached	58
Runs Scored in Those Innings	63
Runs/9 Innings	9.78
1-2-3 Innings	101
10-pitch Innings (or less)	48
Long Innings (20 or more pitches)	32
Failed to Finish Inning	9

Scott Kazmir – 2007
Inning Analysis

Innings Pitched	206.2
Runs Allowed	91
Innings Started	212
Runs in Those Innings	92
Shutout Innings	158
One-Run Innings	26
Two-Run Innings	19
Three-Run Inning	8
Four-Run Innings	1
Got First Man Out	131
Runs Scored in Those Innings	39
Runs/9 Innings	2.68
First Man Reached	81
Runs Scored in Those Innings	53
Runs/9 Innings	5.89
1-2-3 Innings	75
10-pitch Innings (or less)	32
Long Innings (20 or more pitches)	67
Failed to Finish Inning	8

Of all major league pitchers, Scott Kazmir had the most innings where he threw 20 or more pitches (67). That's especially remarkable in light of how well he pitched overall. To run up a lot of high-pitch innings, you generally have to be both 1) wild, and 2) ineffective, as illustrated by the guys who followed Kazmir on the list: Daniel Cabrera, Dontrelle Willis and Edwin Jackson. Somehow Kazmir was able to top those guys despite allowing many fewer inning-extending hits. One thing that likely had something to do with it was his tendency to allow the first batter of an inning to reach base—he put them on 38% of the time, which nearly cracked the bottom 10 among ERA qualifiers.

Texas Rangers

Texas Rangers – 2007
Team Overview

Description		Ranking
Won-Lost Record	75-87	
Place	4th of 4 in American League West	
Runs Scored	816	7th in the majors
Runs Allowed	844	25th in the majors
Home Runs	179	8th in the majors
Home Runs Allowed	155	10th in the majors
Batting Average	.263	19th in the majors
Batting Average Allowed	.274	22nd in the majors
Walks Drawn	503	23rd in the majors
Walks Given	668	29th in the majors
OPS For	.754	16th in the majors
OPS Against	.780	22nd in the majors
Stolen Bases	88	17th in the majors
Stolen Bases Allowed	98	17th in the majors

Key Players

Pos	Player	G	AB	R	H	2B	3B	HR	RBI	SB	CS	BB	SO	Avg	OBP	Slg	OPS	WS
C	Gerald Laird	120	407	48	91	18	3	9	47	6	2	30	103	.224	.278	.349	.627	10
1B	Mark Teixeira	78	286	48	85	24	1	13	49	0	0	45	66	.297	.397	.524	.921	11
2B	Ian Kinsler	130	483	96	127	22	2	20	61	23	2	62	83	.263	.355	.441	.796	17
3B	Ramon Vazquez	104	300	42	69	13	3	8	28	1	0	29	72	.230	.300	.373	.674	6
SS	Michael Young	156	639	80	201	37	1	9	94	13	3	47	107	.315	.366	.418	.783	23
LF	Frank Catalanotto	103	331	52	86	20	4	11	44	2	1	28	37	.260	.337	.444	.781	9
CF	Kenny Lofton	84	317	62	96	16	3	7	23	21	4	39	28	.303	.380	.438	.818	11
RF	Nelson Cruz	96	307	35	72	15	2	9	34	2	4	21	87	.235	.287	.384	.671	4
DH	Sammy Sosa	114	412	53	104	24	1	21	92	0	0	34	112	.252	.311	.468	.779	11

Key Pitchers

Pos	Player	G	GS	W	L	Sv	IP	H	R	ER	BB	SO	BR/9	ERA	WS
SP	Kevin Millwood	31	31	10	14	0	172.2	213	111	99	67	123	15.01	5.16	5
SP	Vicente Padilla	23	23	6	10	0	120.1	146	88	77	50	71	15.33	5.76	2
SP	Kameron Loe	28	23	6	11	0	136.0	162	96	81	56	78	14.69	5.36	3
SP	Brandon McCarthy	23	22	5	10	0	101.2	111	62	55	48	59	14.34	4.87	3
SP	Robinson Tejeda	19	19	5	9	0	95.1	110	78	70	60	69	16.62	6.61	0
CL	Eric Gagne	34	0	2	0	16	33.1	23	8	8	12	29	9.72	2.16	7
RP	Joaquin Benoit	70	0	7	4	6	82.0	68	28	26	28	87	10.76	2.85	10
RP	C.J. Wilson	66	0	2	1	12	68.1	50	25	23	33	63	11.72	3.03	9

You know what was odd about the Texas Rangers in 2007? They hit 179 home runs, as a team—and yet no one on the team hit more than 21. If you had nine positions and everybody hit the same number of home runs, that would be a ratio of 9-to-1…your home run total would be nine times your team leader. The Rangers were at 8.52 to 1.

This is a very high ratio; in fact, it may be the highest of all time, I don't know. I don't have the programming skills or the data base to check out every team, but I checked out every team from the years 1901, 1910, 1920, 1930, 1940, 1950, 1960, 1970, 1980, 1990, 2000 and 2007. No other team that I found has a ratio between the team home runs and the team leader in home runs as high as the 2007 Rangers.

This ratio has stretched out over time—or, actually, since 1920. In 1920 no team had a ratio higher than 4.5 to 1, and the major league norm was 3.3 to 1. This ratio stretched out to 3.5 to 1 in 1930, 3.9 to 1 in 1940, 4.5 to 1 in 1950, and 4.7 to 1 in 1960. It contracted to 4.6 to 1 in 1970, but then began stretching out again: 4.9 to 1 in 1980, down to 4.8 in 1990, but 5.3 to 1 in 2000, and 5.5 to 1 in 2007.

Hitting for power has increasingly become something that *everybody* does. In 1920, 1930, even in 1950, each team had one or two or three power hitters. A team might have, typically,

- a superstar who hit .320 with 30 or more home runs
- a power hitter who struck out and hit .260 but with 30 home runs
- a corner player who hit .280 but with 25 home runs
- an outfielder who hit .320 but with 15 home runs

- a singles hitter who hit .300 but with 5 home runs
- a speed player who hit .270 with 5 home runs but with stolen bases
- a shortstop who hit less than .250 with less than 5 home runs, and
- a catcher who hit less than .250 but with 12-15 home runs.

An offense had a traditional structure with a power core, a leadoff unit, and a back of the order of defensive players who didn't do much with the bat.

Increasingly over time, baseball has become a game in which even the shortstops and second basemen hit for power; everybody hits for power, everybody strikes out, and everybody steals a few bases—like the Rangers, who got 20 home runs from their second baseman, 94 RBI from their shortstop, but who also got 100+ strikeouts from every position in the batting order except the leadoff men and 100+ strikeouts from every lineup position except center field. They got 14 to 28 home runs from each batting order position, and 10 to 30 home runs from each lineup position.

The question could be asked: Does this lack of specialization make sense? Or would teams score more runs if there was more specialization in skills, like in the old days?

It is my view that it doesn't make sense, and that teams would score more runs if they would go back toward more specialized offensive roles. I believe that you can score more runs with two really good power hitters and six guys who get on base than you can with eight guys hitting bases-empty homers. But you have to play the game the way it's played; you can't really make up your universe.

The most starts by a Rangers opening day outfielder in 2006 and 2007 were Sammy Sosa's 103 starts in rightfield last year.

Texas Rangers – 2006
Games Played by Opening Day Starter
at Each Position

Pos	Player	Starts
C	Barajas	95
1B	Teixeira	162
2B	Kinsler	117
3B	Blalock	149
SS	Young	162
LF	Wilkerson	90
CF	Nix	9
RF	Mench	86
DH	Nevin	45
	Total	915

Texas' opening-day starters accounted for 63% of their regular season starting lineup

Texas Rangers – 2007
Games Played by Opening Day Starter
at Each Position

Pos	Player	Starts
C	Laird	114
1B	Teixeira	78
2B	Kinsler	129
3B	Blalock	56
SS	Young	156
LF	Wilkerson	93
CF	Lofton	79
RF	Sosa	103
DH	Catalanotto	89
	Total	897

Texas' opening-day starters accounted for 62% of their regular season starting lineup

The Rangers' first five starting pitchers of the year have made no more than 106 starts in a season since 2003. In 2007, 24 of the 30 teams in Major League Baseball had more than 106.

Starts Made by First Five Starters
Texas Rangers
2003 – 2007

Year	Apr	May	June	July	Aug	Sept	Total
2003	26	16	15	12	16	16	101
2004	18	15	9	7	9	14	72
2005	25	25	20	15	10	10	105
2006	23	23	20	15	13	12	106
2007	23	17	19	19	13	13	104

Michael Young hit the most line drives in the majors (145) in 2007. 99 of them went for hits, also the highest number in the major leagues. Young's 128 line-drive hits in 2003 is the high mark over the last six years since we've been recording hit-type in our database.

Michael Young – 2007
Hitting Analysis

Batting Right-Handed								1B	2B	3B	HR
Ground Balls to Left	93	Outs	69	Hits	24	Average	.258	Hit Type	22 - 2	- 0	- 0
Ground Balls to Center	116	Outs	82	Hits	34	Average	.293	Hit Type	33 - 1	- 0	- 0
Ground Balls to Right	49	Outs	39	Hits	10	Average	.204	Hit Type	9 - 1	- 0	- 0
Line Drives to Left	24	Outs	7	Hits	17	Average	.708	Hit Type	14 - 3	- 0	- 0
Line Drives to Center	59	Outs	21	Hits	38	Average	.655	Hit Type	31 - 7	- 0	- 0
Line Drives to Right	62	Outs	18	Hits	44	Average	.710	Hit Type	35 - 9	- 0	- 0
Fly Balls to Left	11	Outs	8	Hits	3	Average	.273	Hit Type	1 - 1	- 0	- 1
Fly Balls to Center	50	Outs	35	Hits	15	Average	.300	Hit Type	3 - 6	- 1	- 5
Fly Balls to Right	69	Outs	53	Hits	16	Average	.232	Hit Type	6 - 7	- 0	- 3
Total on Ground Balls	258	Outs	190	Hits	68	Average	.264	Hit Type	64 - 4	- 0	- 0
Total on Line Drives	145	Outs	46	Hits	99	Average	.688	Hit Type	80 - 19	- 0	- 0
Total on Fly Balls	130	Outs	96	Hits	34	Average	.262	Hit Type	10 - 14	- 1	- 9
Total Hit to Left	128	Outs	84	Hits	44	Average	.344	Hit Type	37 - 6	- 0	- 1
Total Hit to Center	225	Outs	138	Hits	87	Average	.388	Hit Type	67 - 14	- 1	- 5
Total Hit to Right	180	Outs	110	Hits	70	Average	.389	Hit Type	50 - 17	- 0	- 3
All Balls in Play	533	Outs	332	Hits	201	Average	.378	Hit Type	154 - 37	- 1	- 9

Joaquin Benoit's opponent batting lines show that he's been extremely consistent over the last three seasons, even though his ERAs over those three years have been 3.72, 4.86 and 2.85:

Joaquin Benoit
Record of Opposing Batters

Season	AB	R	H	2B	3B	HR	RBI	BB	SO	SB	CS	GIDP	Avg	OBP	Slg	OPS
2002	335	51	91	18	4	6	46	58	59	7	1	3	.272	.379	.403	.782
2003	403	67	99	21	8	23	64	51	87	4	5	3	.246	.330	.509	.839
2004	405	67	113	18	5	19	63	31	95	4	1	6	.279	.330	.489	.819
2005	326	39	69	9	1	9	34	38	78	5	2	2	.212	.294	.328	.622
2006	303	49	68	11	0	5	44	38	85	1	0	4	.224	.311	.310	.621
2007	302	28	68	17	1	6	30	28	87	2	2	5	.225	.291	.348	.639

Duh

The problems of the 2007 Texas Rangers were serious but not difficult to diagnose. They had two problems exactly: their starting pitching was weak and their outfield was just terrible.

Two charts about the starting pitching.

1) The Rangers had 62 starts with Game Scores of 50 or above, 100 starts below 50. 62-100. They actually were able to win 30 games with a below-average performance from their starting pitcher—not an easy thing to do. As a team, they outperformed their starting pitching by 13 games—and still finished well under .500.

2) The Rangers were 19 games under .500 after the first inning (ahead 25 times, behind 44 times). Again, as was true of the season, they started out behind and spent the season playing catch-up. They were catching up after the first inning, but the poor starting pitching put them in a hole so often that it was really a hopeless cause.

Texas Rangers– 2007
Performance by Quality of Start

Game Score	#	ERA	W	-	L
70 to 79	4	1.00	4	-	0
60 to 69	24	1.88	19	-	5
50 to 59	34	2.83	22	-	12
40 to 49	34	4.72	15	-	19
30 to 39	32	6.27	9	-	23
20 to 29	26	7.46	6	-	20
Below 20	8	9.40	0	-	8

Texas Rangers – 2007
Innings Ahead/Behind/Tied

Inning	1	2	3	4	5	6	7	8	9	Extra	Final
Ahead	25	42	52	54	58	63	66	68	70	5	75
Behind	44	65	74	81	82	86	81	81	78	9	87
Tied	93	55	36	27	22	13	15	13	14	8	—

How Slow Was He?

An average major league player in 2007 went from first to third on a single 27% of the time. For a catcher, the average was 19% (averages based on players catching 400 or more innings.)

An average player scored from second on a single 59% of the time. For catchers, the average was 48%.

An average player scored from first on a double 44% of the time. For catchers, the average was just 26%.

Major league players as a whole grounded into a double play in 11% of the at-bats in which they had a runner on first and less than two out. For catchers, the average was 14%.

How many catchers *do* run well? Among the 40 catchers with the most playing time, five rated as above-average baserunners, two rated at +/- zero, and the other 33 rated as negative runners.

If asked to name the best baserunning catcher in the majors, now that Jason Kendall doesn't get around much anymore, most people would say either "Joe Mauer" or "Russell Martin". Actually, the best baserunning catcher in the majors in 2007 was Texas' Gerald

Laird. Yes, Martin stole 21 bases, which is an unusual number for a catcher, but many of his other baserunning numbers were not too good. He was 6-for-30 going first-to-third on a single, whereas Laird was 4-for-10 and Mauer was 8-for-18. Martin batted in 122 double play situations and grounded into 16 double plays, whereas Laird grounded into only 3 in 84 situations, and Martin ran into eight outs on the bases, the most of any National League catcher, whereas Laird made only one baserunning out.

Mauer, now; Joe Mauer is a good baserunner, about as good as Laird. Kenji Johjima rated as the worst baserunning catcher in the majors, although that's probably misleading because pinch running for Bengie Molina keeps his stats down. Bengie was 0-for-12 going first-to-third on a single, 0-for-9 scoring from second on a single, and 0-for-4 scoring from first on a double—the famous Triple Doughnut. But he made only four outs on the bases, whereas Johjima made 12, and, in our book, running into outs is worse than moving station to station.

Gerald Laird – Career
Baserunning Analysis

Year	1st to 3rd Adv	Opp	2nd to Home Adv	Opp	1st to Home Adv	Opp	DP Opp	GIDP	Bases Taken	BR Outs	BR Gain	SB Gain	Net Gain
2003	1	6	1	2	0	0	8	2	1	0	-2	0	-2
2004	2	6	3	6	4	5	30	5	3	1	-1	-2	-3
2005	0	1	2	3	0	1	9	1	1	0	0	0	0
2006	3	12	7	10	2	6	50	7	11	2	2	1	+3
2007	4	10	4	7	0	0	84	3	7	1	10	2	+12
Totals	10	35	17	28	6	12	181	18	23	4	9	1	+10
		29%		61%		50%		9%					

Bengie Molina – 2002 - 2007
Baserunning Analysis

Year	1st to 3rd Adv	Opp	2nd to Home Adv	Opp	1st to Home Adv	Opp	DP Opp	GIDP	Bases Taken	BR Outs	BR Gain	SB Gain	Net Gain
2002	3	18	3	16	0	5	97	15	6	3	-24	0	-24
2003	0	13	6	13	1	4	78	17	7	0	-12	-1	-13
2004	0	16	1	7	1	3	81	18	9	1	-13	-2	-15
2005	1	19	2	16	0	2	81	14	4	0	-15	-4	-19
2006	1	15	0	7	0	8	75	15	10	6	-28	-1	-29
2007	0	12	0	9	0	4	98	13	4	3	-20	0	-20
Totals	5	93	12	68	2	26	510	92	40	13	-112	-8	-120
		5%		18%		8%		18%					

Copasetic Offense

The Texas Rangers' offense in 2007 was kind of inexplicably good. Their team batting average, .263, was eight points below the league average and fifth-lowest in the league, and their walks drawn were also below average, driving their on-base percentage ten points under the league. Their power was good not great; they were 8th in the majors with 179 team home runs. They were just 16th in the majors in team OPS. They were below average in doubles and stolen bases.

Yet where it counts—producing runs—they were really good. Their offense was above average from 21 of the 24 inning states. They hit .285 with runners in scoring position, and homered 32% more often with men on base than with the bases empty. They finished 8th in the major leagues in runs scored.

Texas Rangers – 2007
24 States Analysis

Situation	Occurred	Runs	Average	MLB Avg.
None on, none out	1504	877	.583	.535
None on, one out	1069	316	.296	.284
None on, two out	863	109	.126	.109
Man on first, none out	342	360	1.053	.926
Man on first, one out	372	202	.543	.543
Man on first, two out	360	87	.242	.235
Man on second, none out	126	154	1.222	1.190
Man on second, one out	216	165	.764	.728
Man on second, two out	232	88	.379	.354
Man on third, none out	16	24	1.500	1.411
Man on third, one out	71	78	1.099	.987
Man on third, two out	112	47	.420	.392
Men on first and second, none out	104	196	1.885	1.510
Men on first and second, one out	164	201	1.226	.914
Men on first and second, two out	206	100	.485	.465
Men on first and third, none out	27	59	2.185	1.794
Men on first and third, one out	69	74	1.072	1.219
Men on first and third, two out	103	69	.670	.505
Men on second and third, none out	21	50	2.381	2.119
Men on second and third, one out	49	83	1.694	1.443
Men on second and third, two out	40	40	1.000	.637
Bases Loaded, none out	21	64	3.048	2.354
Bases Loaded, one out	56	88	1.571	1.611
Bases Loaded, two out	71	82	1.155	.787

You Gotta Have a Fiddle in the Band

The Rangers' 2007 season included thirteen homestands.

In the first six they had only one winning homestand—a 4-2 homestand from April 6 to April 11. The last seven, they won every homestand (4-2, 4-2, 5-3, 5-4, 5-2, 5-1, 5-2). They were 33-16 over their final seven homestands.

As the season went on the Rangers dealt away Mark Teixiera, Eric Gagne and Kenny Lofton and lost Hank Blalock to injury—and got steadily stronger without them. They started the season 20-37, seventeen games under .500. They were 55-50 from June 5 to the end of the season.

Texas Rangers – 2007
Tracking the Season by Segments

	W-L	R	PG	Avg	OR	PG	ERA	W-L
Road Trip, April 2 to 4	0-3	7	2.3	.161	17	5.7	5.63	0-3
Homestand, April 6 to 11	4-2	37	6.2	.270	26	4.3	3.83	4-5
Road Trip, April 13 to 19	2-4	26	4.3	.190	37	6.2	5.94	6-9
Homestand, April 20 to 23	2-2	19	4.8	.274	24	6.0	6.00	8-11
Road Trip, April 25 to 30	2-4	29	4.8	.250	41	6.8	6.08	10-15
Homestand, May 1 to 6	3-3	27	4.5	.267	26	4.3	3.50	13-18
Road Trip, May 8 to 10	1-2	18	6.0	.290	16	5.3	4.68	14-20
Homestand, May 11 to 14	1-3	15	3.8	.227	25	6.3	5.50	15-23
Road Trip, May 15 to 20	2-4	39	6.5	.276	34	5.7	5.68	17-27
Homestand, May 21 to 27	1-5	33	5.5	.271	39	6.5	6.00	18-32
Road Trip, May 28 to June 3	2-5	32	4.6	.235	44	6.3	6.05	20-37
Homestand, June 5 to 10	3-3	30	5.0	.289	43	7.2	6.63	23-40
Road Trip, June 12 to 17	3-3	34	5.7	.280	33	5.5	5.47	26-43
Homestand, June 19 to 24	4-2	44	7.3	.286	30	5.0	4.25	30-45
Road Trip, June 25 to July 2	4-3	30	4.3	.261	28	4.0	4.05	34-48
Homestand, July 3 to 8	4-2	20	3.3	.231	17	2.8	2.62	38-50
Road Trip, July 13 to 18	3-3	26	4.3	.245	26	4.3	3.38	41-53
Homestand, July 19 to 25	5-3	39	4.9	.286	40	5.0	4.38	46-56
Road Trip, July 27 to August 5	2-7	28	3.1	.241	53	5.9	6.12	48-63
Homestand, August 6 to 16	5-4	45	5.0	.269	41	4.6	3.60	53-67
Road Trip, August 17 to 22	3-3	47	7.8	.282	19	3.2	2.94	56-70
Homestand, August 23 to 30	5-2	30	4.3	.262	27	3.9	2.77	61-72
Road Trip, August 31 to September 2	2-1	21	7.0	.295	20	6.7	6.51	63-73
Homestand, September 3 to 9	5-1	37	6.2	.330	33	5.5	4.50	68-74
Road Trip, September 11 to 19	2-8	51	5.1	.256	61	6.1	5.88	70-82
Homestand, September 20 to 26	5-2	45	6.4	.311	29	4.1	3.94	75-84
Road Trip, September 28 to 30	0-3	7	2.3	.175	15	5.0	4.74	75-87

Deep Sixed

This is one of those numbers that seems hardly possible, but we double-checked it and it's true. The Texas Rangers in 2007 got 49 RBI from the sixth spot in their batting order. 49. Middle of the order, almost; 49 RBI. They got 123 RBI from the third spot, 120 from the fourth, 103 from the fifth, 94 RBI from the eighth spot. Their number six hitters hit a respectable .263 with 14 homers; you would guess they would drive in 80, 85 runs.

How is that possible? Well, for one thing, their #4 and #5 hitters specialized in not getting on base and not getting into scoring position. Sammy Sosa, the most-used cleanup hitter, had a .311 on-base percentage and no stolen bases. Their number five hitters collectively had a .313 on-base percentage.

That doesn't really explain it, and, in fact, I can't really explain it. The two men who hit sixth most often, Blalock and Byrd, both hit over .300 with runners in scoring position. Botts, Wilkerson and Nelson Cruz were not outstanding with runners in scoring position, but neither were they horrific. It's just kind of a weird batting order malfunction, sort of like having Bartleby the Scrivener hitting sixth.

Texas Rangers – 2007
Runs and RBI by Batting Order Position

Pos	Players	Runs	RBI
1	Lofton (79g), Catalanotto (37g), Kinsler (26g)	114	56
2	Young (52g), Kinsler (48g), Catalanotto (18g)	114	85
3	Young (104g), Teixeira (55g)	88	123
4	Sosa (83g), Byrd (42g), Teixeira (23g)	92	120
5	Byrd (36g), Blalock (29g), Catalanotto (26g)	87	103
6	Blalock (23g), Byrd (21g), Cruz (20g)	80	49
7	Wilkerson (43g), Cruz (25g), Kinsler (24g)	83	80
8	Laird (39g), Saltalamacchia (28g), Cruz (22g)	74	94
9	Vazquez (51g), Metcalf (35g), Laird (24g)	84	58
	Total	816	768

Herbie

by Bill James

The main things that a pitcher really gives up are home runs and walks. The rest of it depends on the defense, right? The pitcher gives up some runs—when he gives up a home run and when he walks people—but for the rest, it's up to the defense.

Yeah, I know about strikeouts and hit batsmen; we'll get there. I'm just saying…real simple idea. What if we ranked pitchers by how many walks and home runs they give up? How well would that match with more sophisticated performance measures?

Pretty well, it turns out…you can be the judge of that, but I was kind of astonished at how well it did. I ranked pitchers by this simple metric:

Walks
+ Hit Batsmen
+ 4 Times Home Runs
Per 9 innings

This is SUCH a simple concept that somebody must have done this before, but…it's new to me.

I call it Herbie, for HR BB. This is SUCH a simple concept that somebody must have done this before, but… it's new to me. When I was thinking about this, walking home from the park, I assumed that it probably wouldn't work because it would either discriminate against pitchers like Robin Roberts, Catfish Hunter, Ferguson Jenkins, Eric Milton and Bartolo Colon, who give up lots of home runs but win by not walking people, or it would discriminate against pitchers like Whitey Ford, Dave Stewart, Fernando Valenzuela and Kerry Wood, who give up some walks but stay away from the long ball.

And it does discriminate, but not too badly. Robin Roberts led the National League in Herbie in '51 and '52, was close his other good years, while Whitey Ford led the League in Herbie in '64, and was third in the AL in '56 and '58. Actually, it does real well…obviously there are limits to what you're going to get out of a formula like this, but it seems like the pitchers Herbie identifies as the best in the league are the best in the league fairly often.

I compared the Herbie leader to the ERA leaders for the years 1930-1959—a total of 60 competitions. In those years there were ten pitchers who led their league

in both ERA and Herbie (Dazzy Vance, 1930, Carl Hubbell, 1933, 1934 and 1936, Cy Blanton, 1935, Spud Chandler, 1943, Harry Brecheen, 1948, Warren Spahn, 1953, Mike Garcia, 1954 and Bob Friend, 1955.) There were ten more seasons in which the league leader in ERA was second in Herbie, and (oddly enough) ten more in which he was third. Altogether, the league leader in ERA finished 1-3 in Herbie in 30 of the 60 leagues, finished 1-5 in Herbie in 37 of the 60 leagues, and finished 1-10 in Herbie in 53 of the 60 leagues. Many times the pitcher who led the league in Herbie seems like a more reasonable candidate for the league's best pitcher than the actual ERA leader. In 1959, for example, Hoyt Wilhelm was the ERA leader in the American League (15-11, 2.19), whereas Camilo Pascual was the Herbie leader (17-10, 2.64). I think most people would look at those seasons and conclude that Pascual was actually the better pitcher. In 1951 the National League ERA leader was Chuck Nichols (11-8, 2.88), but the Herbie leader was Robin Roberts (21-15, 3.03); and in 1952, combining those two, the NL ERA leader was Wilhelm (15-3, 2.43), but the Herbie leader was again Roberts (28-7, 2.59).

As the leagues have gotten larger, of course, the likelihood of the Herbie leader and the ERA leader being the same person has gotten less, but the relationship doesn't seem any less close. I looked at all pitchers pitching 180 innings from 1950 to 2006. The four best Herbie scores in that group were by Greg Maddux in 1994, 1995, 1996 and 1997. (That last sentence is astonishing, but it's an astonishing statement about Greg Maddux, rather than about Herbie, and I'm writing about Herbie, so I don't have anywhere to go with that.) The worst was by Jose Lima in 2000; Lima had decent control but was lit up for 48 home runs in 196 innings, and finished 7-16 with a 6.65 ERA.

The next question I asked was whether Herbie could be translated into ERA. I was trying to keep it simple. The simple formula for translating Herbie into ERA is:

(Herbie – 1) / 2 + 1 = ERA

In other words, a Herbie score of 8 equals an ERA of 4.50: (8 – 1) / 2 + 1 = 4.50. And a Herbie score of 7 equals an ERA of 4.00.

The best Herbie score of 1950-2006 was 2.36, by Maddux in 1994. A Herbie of 2.36 equals an ERA of 1.68. His actual ERA was 1.56.

The worst Herbie score of that era was 12.01+, by Lima. A Herbie of 12.01+ is equivalent to an ERA of 6.51. His actual ERA was 6.65.

If this translation always worked this well, Herbie would become an important sabermetric tool. Unfortunately it doesn't. It works very well for groups.

A Herbie score of 6 translates to an ERA of 3.50. If you take all pitchers with 180 innings, 1950-2006, there are 205 pitchers with Herbie Scores of 5.90 to 6.10. Their average Herbie score is 6.00, and their average ERA is 3.51—almost exactly what the translation would predict.

The translation works well for many, many pitchers—for example, Bret Saberhagen, 1989, had a Herbie ERA of 2.16, and an actual ERA of 2.16. Fernando Valenzuela in 1986 had a Herbie ERA of 3.14, and an actual ERA of 3.14. Don Cardwell, 1960, and Cliff Chambers, 1951, both had Herbie ERAs of 4.38, and actual ERAs of 4.38. Kevin Gross, 1995, had a Herbie ERA of 5.52, and an actual ERA of 5.54.

But there are also many pitchers whose actual ERA is *not* near their Herbie ERA, and these discrepancies are neither random, meaningless, nor transient. Take, for example, those 205 pitchers who have Herbie scores between 5.90 and 6.10. They include:

Steve Carlton, 1969	Herbie Score: 5.98	Herbie ERA: 3.49	Actual ERA: 2.17
Tom Seaver, 1969	Herbie Score: 6.09	Herbie ERA: 3.55	Actual ERA: 2.21
Joe Horlen, 1968	Herbie Score: 5.95	Herbie ERA: 3.47	Actual ERA: 2.37
Camilo Pascual, 1963	Herbie Score: 6.10	Herbie ERA: 3.55	Actual ERA: 2.47
Randy Johnson, 2001	Herbie Score: 5.95	Herbie ERA: 3.47	Actual ERA: 2.49
John Burkett, 1998	Herbie Score: 6.00	Herbie ERA: 3.50	Actual ERA: 5.68
Mark Clark, 1998	Herbie Score: 6.07	Herbie ERA: 3.53	Actual ERA: 4.84
Joe Blanton, 2006	Herbie Score: 6.07	Herbie ERA: 3.53	Actual ERA: 4.82
Bart Johnson, 1976	Herbie Score: 6.10	Herbie ERA: 3.55	Actual ERA: 4.73
Allan Anderson, 1990	Herbie Score: 5.92	Herbie ERA: 3.46	Actual ERA: 4.53

Obviously, the main thing we haven't considered yet is strikeouts. Most of the pitchers who had better actual ERAs than Herbie ERAs were power pitchers; most of the pitchers with higher ERAs than Herbie ERAs were pitchers with few strikeouts.

John Burkett's 1998 season is, in a sense, a fluke. The discrepancy there (2.18 runs) is easily the largest discrepancy between a pitcher's Herbie ERA and his actual ERA among the 3,449 pitchers in the study. Nobody else was over 1.92.

But there are meaningless flukes and there are meaningful flukes. This is a meaningful fluke. Maybe Carlton had some good luck in 1969, but the difference between Carlton and Burkett is not luck, but is, rather, the many facets of performance that we have not encompassed within this measurement. Burkett's actual ERA was always worse than his Herbie ERA, every year he pitched 180 innings except one. Steve Carlton's actual ERA was better than his Herbie ERA every year from 1969 through 1981, although not usually a run better.

Obviously, the main thing we haven't considered yet is strikeouts. Most of the pitchers who had better actual ERAs than Herbie ERAs were power pitchers; most of the pitchers with higher ERAs than Herbie ERAs were pitchers with few strikeouts. Couldn't we adjust Herbie for strikeouts, and come up with a stat that is a better measure of the pitcher's true value?

Well, yes, we could. But we're crossing a line there. In fact, I'm going to draw a line here to indicate that we're crossing a line. I'll see you on the other side.

There are two kinds of invented stats in sabermetrics. There are serious analytic methods, and there are little tools that are fun to play around with but don't really mean much, such as Secondary Average, Game Scores, Season Scores and Frustration Scores for baseball games.

Herbie is just a fun thing to play around with. You can figure it in 20 seconds; you can convert it into an ERA in another 20 seconds. "How do you most accurately predict a pitcher's ERA, based on his strikeouts, walks and home runs allowed?" is a serious sabermetric question. If we were going to take it to that level, we'd have to do a whole bunch of studies and tests and stuff, review the formulas that already exist for that sort of thing, and take seriously the issue of whether the new one is better than the old ones. I'm not really up for that.

Well, OK, here's how you can do that, sort of. Replace Herbie with Herbie-2:

Innings Pitched Times 3, minus strikeouts
Divided by 3
Plus Walks
Plus Hit Batsmen
Plus 4 times Home Runs
Times 9
Divided by Innings Pitched

Now the best Herbie-2 score since 1950 is no longer Maddux, it's Pedro Martinez in 1999.

You can convert Herbie-2 into ERA by this formula:

$$(H2 - 5) * .424 = ERA$$

That formula is more accurate, for predicting ERA, than the Herbie ERA. It's way off for Martinez in 1999 (1.30 vs. 2.07), but on average, it's more accurate.

But not dramatically more accurate. Herbie ERA has an average error, for pitchers pitching 180 innings or more, of 0.47. This formula has an average error of 0.41. I'm sure we could improve the formula more by messing around with the weight of a home run vs. a walk, but that's real work, and I don't foresee a big payoff to it.

You can never be sure what is a serious sabermetric tool and what is just something to mess around with, because many times the things you think you're messing around with turn out to be extremely useful when you're seriously studying something. But we have two Herbies here, one which is very simple but not tremendously accurate at predicting ERA, and one which is a lot more complicated but not tremendously accurate at predicting ERA, either. For my purposes, I'll stick with the simple one.

(Note: The best Herbie scores of all time, plus the best Herbie scores of 2007, are listed on page 241, under the San Diego Padres.)

Toronto Blue Jays

Toronto Blue Jays – 2007
Team Overview

Description		Ranking
Won-Lost Record	83-79	
Place	3rd of 5 in American League East	
Runs Scored	753	17th in the majors
Runs Allowed	699	4th in the majors
Home Runs	165	19th in the majors
Home Runs Allowed	157	11th in the majors
Batting Average	.259	24th in the majors
Batting Average Allowed	.251	4th in the majors
Walks Drawn	533	13th in the majors
Walks Given	479	5th in the majors
OPS For	.746	17th in the majors
OPS Against	.706	3rd in the majors
Stolen Bases	57	27th in the majors
Stolen Bases Allowed	134	28th in the majors

Key Players

Pos	Player	G	AB	R	H	2B	3B	HR	RBI	SB	CS	BB	SO	Avg	OBP	Slg	OPS	WS
C	Gregg Zaun	110	331	43	80	24	1	10	52	0	0	51	55	.242	.341	.411	.752	9
1B	Lyle Overbay	122	425	49	102	30	2	10	44	2	0	47	78	.240	.315	.391	.706	6
2B	Aaron Hill	160	608	87	177	47	2	17	78	4	3	41	102	.291	.333	.459	.792	20
3B	Troy Glaus	115	385	60	101	19	1	20	62	0	1	61	102	.262	.366	.473	.839	14
SS	John McDonald	123	327	32	82	20	2	1	31	7	2	11	48	.251	.279	.333	.612	8
LF	Adam Lind	89	290	34	69	14	0	11	46	1	2	16	65	.238	.278	.400	.678	7
CF	Vernon Wells	149	584	85	143	36	4	16	80	10	4	49	89	.245	.304	.402	.706	15
RF	Alex Rios	161	643	114	191	43	7	24	85	17	4	55	103	.297	.354	.498	.852	22
DH	Frank Thomas	155	531	63	147	30	0	26	95	0	0	81	94	.277	.377	.480	.857	17

Key Pitchers

Pos	Player	G	GS	W	L	Sv	IP	H	R	ER	BB	SO	BR/9	ERA	WS
SP	Roy Halladay	31	31	16	7	0	225.1	232	101	93	48	139	11.30	3.71	16
SP	Shaun Marcum	38	25	12	6	1	159.0	149	76	73	49	122	11.49	4.13	10
SP	Dustin McGowan	27	27	12	10	0	169.2	146	80	77	61	144	11.09	4.08	11
SP	A.J. Burnett	25	25	10	8	0	165.2	131	74	69	66	176	11.35	3.75	11
SP	Jesse Litsch	20	20	7	9	0	111.0	116	56	47	36	50	12.89	3.81	7
CL	Jeremy Accardo	64	0	4	4	30	67.1	51	19	16	24	57	10.29	2.14	14
RP	Scott Downs	81	0	4	2	1	58.0	47	15	14	24	57	11.17	2.17	8
RP	Casey Janssen	70	0	2	3	6	72.2	67	22	19	20	39	11.15	2.35	10

Toronto and San Diego led the majors with seven games with Game Scores above 80.

The same two teams also had the most starts with Game Scores above 70, 26 each.

Toronto Blue Jays – 2007
Performance by Quality of Start

Game Score	#	ERA	W	-	L
80 and above	7	0.57	7	-	0
70 to 79	19	1.15	17	-	2
60 to 69	34	1.98	23	-	11
50 to 59	26	3.82	13	-	13
40 to 49	36	4.62	17	-	19
30 to 39	18	5.84	3	-	15
20 to 29	14	8.25	2	-	12
Below 20	8	9.51	1	-	7

Jeremy Accardo cut his ERA in 2007 from 5.35 to 2.14, in essentially the same number of games and innings.

What do he different?

The splitter. In 2006 he threw the splitter only 3% of the time. In 2007 he made the Sutter Special his primary complement to the fastball, throwing it 16% of the time.

Jeremy Accardo – 2006
Pitch Type Analysis

Overall		
Total Pitches	1210	
Fastball	886	73%
Curveball	1	0%
Changeup	113	9%
Slider	92	8%
Split Finger	34	3%
Cut Fastball	57	5%
Pitchout	1	0%
Not Charted	26	2%

	Vs. RHB		Vs. LHB	
Total Pitches	702		508	
Outs Recorded	125		82	
Fastball	537	76%	349	69%
Curveball	1	0%	0	0%
Changeup	41	6%	72	14%
Slider	70	10%	22	4%
Split Finger	6	1%	28	6%
Cut Fastball	38	5%	19	4%
Pitchout	1	0%	0	0%
Not Charted	8	1%	18	4%

Jeremy Accardo – 2007
Pitch Type Analysis

Overall		
Total Pitches	1081	
Fastball	772	71%
Curveball	1	0%
Changeup	31	3%
Slider	78	7%
Split Finger	172	16%
Cut Fastball	3	0%
Pitchout	3	0%
Not Charted	21	2%

	Vs. RHB		Vs. LHB	
Total Pitches	558		523	
Outs Recorded	93		109	
Fastball	422	76%	350	67%
Curveball	1	0%	0	0%
Changeup	11	2%	20	4%
Slider	60	11%	18	3%
Split Finger	55	10%	117	22%
Cut Fastball	0	0%	3	1%
Pitchout	2	0%	1	0%
Not Charted	7	1%	14	3%

Adam Lind hit 59 ground balls toward right field.
Fifty-eight of them failed to make it through the infield.

Adam Lind – 2007
Hitting Analysis

Batting Left-Handed								1B	2B	3B	HR
Ground Balls to Left	11	Outs	10	Hits	1	Average	.091	Hit Type	1 - 0	- 0	- 0
Ground Balls to Center	32	Outs	22	Hits	10	Average	.313	Hit Type	10 - 0	- 0	- 0
Ground Balls to Right	59	Outs	58	Hits	1	Average	.017	Hit Type	1 - 0	- 0	- 0
Line Drives to Left	12	Outs	6	Hits	6	Average	.500	Hit Type	3 - 3	- 0	- 0
Line Drives to Center	14	Outs	3	Hits	11	Average	.786	Hit Type	11 - 0	- 0	- 0
Line Drives to Right	16	Outs	3	Hits	13	Average	.813	Hit Type	12 - 1	- 0	- 0
Fly Balls to Left	34	Outs	24	Hits	10	Average	.294	Hit Type	3 - 5	- 0	- 2
Fly Balls to Center	30	Outs	21	Hits	9	Average	.310	Hit Type	3 - 4	- 0	- 2
Fly Balls to Right	19	Outs	11	Hits	8	Average	.444	Hit Type	0 - 1	- 0	- 7
Total on Ground Balls	102	Outs	90	Hits	12	Average	.118	Hit Type	12 - 0	- 0	- 0
Total on Line Drives	42	Outs	12	Hits	30	Average	.714	Hit Type	26 - 4	- 0	- 0
Total on Fly Balls	83	Outs	56	Hits	27	Average	.333	Hit Type	6 - 10	- 0	- 11
Total Hit to Left	57	Outs	40	Hits	17	Average	.298	Hit Type	7 - 8	- 0	- 2
Total Hit to Center	76	Outs	46	Hits	30	Average	.400	Hit Type	24 - 4	- 0	- 2
Total Hit to Right	94	Outs	72	Hits	22	Average	.237	Hit Type	13 - 2	- 0	- 7
Bunts	2	Outs	2	Hits	0	Average	.000	Hit Type	0 - 0	- 0	- 0
All Balls in Play	229	Outs	160	Hits	69	Average	.307	Hit Type	44 - 14	- 0	- 11

Maybe We Should Try It Their Way?

90% of major league pitchers will throw the slider at least 1% of the time. However, among those who don't, or who at least don't throw anything that we count as a slider, are Mariano Rivera, Brandon Webb, Brad Penny, Roy Halladay, A.J. Burnett, Ben Sheets, Josh Beckett, Justin Verlander, Erik Bedard, James Shields, Cole Hamels and Tim Wakefield. The overall won-lost record of the ten starting pitchers who throw the slider least often was 127-80.

Roy Halladay – 2007
Pitch Type Analysis

Overall		
Total Pitches	3330	
Fastball	1533	46%
Curveball	712	21%
Changeup	194	6%
Cut Fastball	820	25%
Pitchout	6	0%
Not Charted	65	2%

	Vs. RHB		Vs. LHB	
Total Pitches	1576		1754	
Outs Recorded	314		362	
Fastball	746	47%	787	45%
Curveball	398	25%	314	18%
Changeup	22	1%	172	10%
Cut Fastball	382	24%	438	25%
Pitchout	4	0%	2	0%
Not Charted	24	2%	41	2%

The Blue Jays' #3 hitters drove in only 75 runs, fewest in the majors. They also had the lowest on-base percentage (.326) and slugging percentage (.403) of any team's #3 hitters.

Toronto Blue Jays – 2007
Runs and RBI by Batting Order Position

Pos	Players	Runs	RBI
1	Rios (57g), R. Johnson (49g), Wells (35g)	100	69
2	Overbay (51g), Stairs (29g), Rios (18g)	93	75
3	Rios (71g), Wells (62g)	102	75
4	Thomas (76g),Glaus (48g), Wells (24g)	82	98
5	Thomas (56g), Hill (34g), Glaus (32g)	110	116
6	Hill (42g), Overbay (28g), Glaus (20g)	80	77
7	Hill (73g), Lind (20g), Zaun (19g)	70	88
8	Zaun (45g), Phillips (23g), Clayton (22g)	60	67
9	McDonald (97g), Clayton (22g)	56	54
	Total	753	719

Toronto Blue Jays – 2007
Productivity by Batting Order Position

Pos	Players	Avg	OBP	Slg	OPS
1	Rios (57g), R. Johnson (49g), Wells (35g)	.247	.321	.407	.728
2	Overbay (51g), Stairs (29g), Rios (18g)	.256	.319	.420	.739
3	Rios (71g), Wells (62g)	.258	.326	.403	.729
4	Thomas (76g), Glaus (48g), Wells (24g)	.267	.342	.444	.787
5	Thomas (56g), Hill (34g), Glaus (32g)	.304	.391	.547	.939
6	Hill (42g), Overbay (28g), Glaus (20g)	.263	.334	.445	.780
7	Hill (73g), Lind (20g), Zaun (19g)	.275	.324	.423	.747
8	Zaun (45g), Phillips (23g), Clayton (22g)	.209	.274	.319	.594
9	McDonald (97g), Clayton (22g)	.251	.301	.360	.662
	Total	.259	.327	.419	.746

Vernon Wells – 2007
RBI Analysis

Hits		RBI Hits		RBI Total		Drove In	
Home Runs:	16			RBI on Home Runs:	25	Russ Adams	2
Triples:	4	RBI Triples:	1	RBI on Triples:	1	Howie Clark	2
Doubles:	36	RBI Doubles:	12	RBI on Doubles:	16	Royce Clayton	2
Singles:	87	RBI Singles:	18	RBI on Singles:	24	Sal Fasano	2
				Sacrifice Flies:	6	Troy Glaus	1
		Other RBI: Walks	2			Aaron Hill	3
		Other RBI: Ground Outs	4	Total Other:	8	Reed Johnson	2
						Adam Lind	5
				Total RBI:	80	John McDonald	5
						Lyle Overbay	12
						Jason Phillips	3
						Alex Rios	16
						Ryan Roberts	1
						Jason Smith	1
						Matt Stairs	2
						Curtis Thigpen	2
						Gregg Zaun	3
						His Own Bad Self	16
						Total	80

Historic Fielding Excellence

Aaron Hill had the second highest assist total (560) for a second baseman in the last 77 years. Ryne Sandberg's 571 assists in 1983 topped him, but to find a higher total than Sandberg's and Hill's you have to go all the way back to that household name, Ski Melillo, who recorded 572 assists for the St. Louis Browns in 1930.

Aaron Hill won the Fielding Bible Award for second basemen last year. He led all second basemen in baseball for the second year in a row with a +22 Plus/Minus at second base.

Aaron Hill – 2005-2007
Fielding Bible Basic Data

Second Base										
Year	Team	G	GS	Inn	PO	A	E	DP	Pct	Rng
2005	Tor	22	19	177.2	33	77	1	15	.991	5.57
2006	Tor	112	106	914.1	174	345	7	93	.987	5.11
2007	Tor	160	158	1410.0	244	560	14	114	.983	5.13
Total		294	283	2502.0	451	982	22	222	.985	5.15

Aaron Hill – 2005-2007
Fielding Bible Plus/Minus

Second Base																
			GROUND DP				PLAYS				PLUS/MINUS					
			GIDP				Expected Outs		Outs Made		To His	Straight	To His				
Year	Team	Inn	Opps	GIDP	Pct	Rank	GB	Air	GB	Air	Right	On	Left	GB	Air	Total	Rank
2005	Tor	177.2	34	14	.412		65	12	68	10	0	+1	+2	+3	-2	+1	
2006	Tor	914.1	132	86	.652	2	254	76	282	73	+15	+2	+11	+28	-3	+25	1
2007	Tor	1410.0	193	110	.570	3	458	95	481	94	+7	+9	+7	+23	-1	+22	1
Total		2502.0	359	210	.585	2	777	183	831	177	+22	+12	+20	+54	-6	+48	3

However, Placido Polanco won the American League Gold Glove for a historic season of his own, the first errorless season ever turned in by a regular second baseman. Polanco commited zero errors in 683 chances. The most errorless chances in a season prior to Polanco was Luis Gonzalez with 317 chances playing second base part time for Colorado in 2005.

All in all, we'd rather have Hill with his 560 assists, his +22 and his 14 errors than Polanco's 389 assists, +10 and 0 errors. Hill had 1400 innings to Polanco's 1200, but that doesn't come close to making up for nearly 200 more assists and 12 extra Plus/Minus plays (which factor in the errors).

Looking further at that incredible assist total, there are likely to be other factors besides excellent fielding that come into play to attain such a level. Blue Jays second basemen as a team had an extremely unusual ratio of assists to putouts (568 to 250, or 2.27 to 1). This is by far the highest such ratio in baseball history; only one other team was even 2 to 1, and they were less than 2.01.

This could mean that Hill is playing a long way from second base...he might be playing shallow right a lot, leaving the shortstop to cover second. What does the following data from Baseball Info Solutions suggest?

Team Shifts – 2007

Defense	Shifts
Nationals	44
Devil Rays	41
Rangers	40
Brewers	38
Braves	35
Tigers	35
Blue Jays	29
Cubs	27
Diamondbacks	27
Red Sox	25
Marlins	25
Athletics	25

Note: Number of times a ball was put in play
when the team was playing a shift.

The Blue Jays are seventh on the list of the teams with the most balls put into play against them while they were employing a shift, but not really out of line with other teams. By the way, here are the "shiftiest hitters" in baseball:

Batter Shifts – 2007

Hitter	Shifts
David Ortiz	69
Travis Hafner	66
Barry Bonds	60
Carlos Delgado	56
Jim Thome	56
Ryan Howard	48
Adam Dunn	40
Ken Griffey Jr.	37
Jason Giambi	34
Mark Teixeira	19
Vladimir Guerrero	15

That's a list of the top 11. Vlad Guerrero is number 11 and he's the only right-handed hitter in baseball with a double-digit total of balls he hit into play against the shift.

It appears that the shift isn't a major contributor to the high assist total for Aaron Hill, but here's something that is. It's the number of left-handed hitters that faced the Blue Jays' predominantly right-handed pitching staff in 2007. The Blue Jays were the only team in baseball that faced lefties 50% of the time last year. In fact, this is the fourth highest percentage out of 180 teams in the six years we've been tracking this stat. The highest was the 2004 Red Sox with 52%.

Major league hitters pull grounders twice as often as they go the other way. (Not true of balls hit in the air, by the way, where the ratio is close to even, even leaning towards the opposite field.) Facing a lot of lefties will clearly create more chances for the right side of the infield defense, and that is something that happened to the 2007 Toronto Blue Jays.

The Toronto Blue Jays in 2007 got fewer starts out of their first five starters than any American League team except the Yankees—and yet their starting pitching was the strong point of the team. The Blue Jays' first five starters were Roy Halladay, A.J. Burnett, Gustavo Chacin, Tomo Ohka and Josh Towers. Ohka and Chacin went out early with injuries, and Towers was never effective—but the pitchers who replaced them (Dustin McGowan, Shaun Marcum and Jesse Litsch) were terrific.

Starts Made by First Five Starters

Team	Apr	May	June	July	Aug	Sept	Total
Los Angeles	20	17	17	17	23	21	115
Baltimore	25	18	17	14	16	6	96
Boston	24	26	26	20	24	20	140
Chicago	23	25	28	27	26	21	150
Cleveland	22	24	21	21	24	23	135
Detroit	25	25	20	16	20	16	122
Kansas City	24	19	16	17	18	17	111
Minnesota	25	24	17	16	17	14	113
New York	16	15	13	15	11	11	81
Oakland	23	23	23	19	17	17	122
Seattle	18	23	21	25	28	26	141
Tampa Bay	25	26	17	17	17	14	116
Texas	23	17	19	19	13	13	104
Toronto	25	13	15	10	12	11	86
Arizona	24	23	24	21	23	24	139
Atlanta	25	24	21	17	15	16	118
Chicago	24	22	22	22	22	28	140
Cincinnati	25	27	21	20	15	17	125
Colorado	24	23	26	20	16	15	124
Florida	23	18	18	21	23	15	118
Houston	22	24	28	24	22	11	131
Los Angeles	24	21	20	14	17	15	111
Milwaukee	25	29	22	23	20	18	137
Washington	26	14	8	9	8	16	81
New York	23	22	21	22	23	21	132
Philadelphia	19	17	17	16	18	19	106
Pittsburgh	24	27	22	15	28	22	138
St. Louis	21	21	17	20	22	15	116
San Diego	26	23	21	19	21	23	133
San Francisco	24	23	22	20	20	11	120

Washington Nationals

Washington Nationals – 2007
Team Overview

Description		Ranking
Won-Lost Record	73-89	
Place	4th of 5 in National League East	
Runs Scored	673	30th in the majors
Runs Allowed	783	18th in the majors
Home Runs	123	27th in the majors
Home Runs Allowed	187	26th in the majors
Batting Average	.256	26th in the majors
Batting Average Allowed	.269	17th in the majors
Walks Drawn	524	17th in the majors
Walks Given	580	26th in the majors
OPS For	.715	28th in the majors
OPS Against	.772	20th in the majors
Stolen Bases	69	23rd in the majors
Stolen Bases Allowed	80	7th in the majors

Key Players

Pos	Player	G	AB	R	H	2B	3B	HR	RBI	SB	CS	BB	SO	Avg	OBP	Slg	OPS	WS
C	Brian Schneider	129	408	33	96	21	1	6	54	0	0	56	56	.235	.326	.336	.661	11
1B	Dmitri Young	136	460	57	147	38	1	13	74	0	0	44	74	.320	.378	.491	.869	16
2B	Ronnie Belliard	147	511	57	148	35	1	11	58	3	0	34	72	.290	.332	.427	.759	15
3B	Ryan Zimmerman	162	653	99	174	43	5	24	91	4	1	61	125	.266	.330	.458	.788	20
SS	Felipe Lopez	154	603	70	148	25	6	9	50	24	9	53	109	.245	.308	.352	.659	11
LF	Ryan Church	144	470	57	128	43	1	15	70	3	2	49	107	.272	.349	.464	.813	16
CF	Nook Logan	118	325	39	86	18	4	0	21	23	5	19	86	.265	.304	.345	.649	6
RF	Austin Kearns	161	587	84	156	35	1	16	74	2	2	71	106	.266	.355	.411	.765	20

Key Pitchers

Pos	Player	G	GS	W	L	Sv	IP	H	R	ER	BB	SO	BR/9	ERA	WS
SP	Matt Chico	31	31	7	9	0	167.0	183	96	86	74	94	14.12	4.63	5
SP	Jason Bergmann	21	21	6	6	0	115.1	99	59	57	42	86	11.16	4.45	5
SP	Mike Bacsik	29	20	5	8	0	118.0	141	73	67	29	45	13.42	5.11	2
SP	Shawn Hill	16	16	4	5	0	97.1	86	42	37	25	65	10.73	3.42	6
SP	Tim Redding	15	15	3	6	0	84.0	84	35	34	38	47	13.50	3.64	5
CL	Chad Cordero	76	0	3	3	37	75.0	75	31	28	29	62	12.48	3.36	10
RP	Jon Rauch	88	0	8	4	4	87.1	75	37	35	21	71	9.89	3.61	10
RP	Saul Rivera	85	0	4	6	3	93.0	88	39	38	42	64	12.77	3.68	7

It is easy to pick at the flaws of the 2007 Washington Nationals. They had a .308 on-base percentage from their leadoff men. They were last in the major leagues in runs scored. Their most valuable starting pitcher, Shawn Hill, finished the season with a won-lost record of 4-5. Their cleanup hitter hit 13 homers. Their best position player, Ryan Zimmerman, really only looks kind of good because he had 653 at bats; if you scaled him back to the same number of at bats he would look exactly like Greg Dobbs or Chad Tracy or Frank Catalanotto or Bobby Kielty.

And yet, you have to say this for them: they didn't just lie down and lose. They won 73 games. They flew in from Montreal on a wing and a prayer, no players and no farm system and no money. A lot of people a year ago this spring were talking about the Nationals losing 100 games. The Royals, the Pirates, the Rays have all lost 100 games in recent years with teams that had a lot better core of talent than the Nationals did. 73 wins with this roster was a hell of an accomplishment.

How did they do it? They were very sharp in taking advantage of the available lop-sided talent:

Catcher Brian Schneider (now with the Mets) is a .235 hitter with no power who runs as if he was storing his valuables in his cleats, but he is a good defensive catcher and he was one of a handful of National League regulars who had as many walks (56) as strikeouts.

First Baseman Dmitri Young doesn't get invited to respectable parties because of domestic violence and substance abuse issues, plus he is fat and probably slower than Brian Schneider, but the son of a gun can hit.

Second Baseman Ronnie Belliard is a good hitter for a second baseman and actually a pretty decent defender as well, but he is slow and has a pear-shaped body and was available cheap because of a glut of second basemen on the market.

Shortstop Felipe Lopez is perhaps the prototypical Nationals player. For many years I have wondered what would happen if a team that didn't have a shortstop would just take some marginal third baseman and play him at short. We finally found out. Felipe Lopez is no more a shortstop than he is an aircraft designer, a Chinese diplomat or the president of the Teamsters Union. He never was a shortstop, but he hit very well in 2005 and 2006, which enabled his teams to get by with putting him in the place on the field where the shortstop normally plays. Unfortunately he had a poor year at the plate in 2007 while hitting leadoff, which made him neither a shortstop nor a leadoff man, but he hung in there and did the best he could with it.

Left Fielder Ryan Church (also now with the Mets) hits *almost* well enough to be a major league regular corner outfielder—almost, but not quite. He hits like guys like Jeffrey Hammonds, Olmedo Saenz and David Dellucci, but he was the best the Nationals had so they just kept running him out there and letting him do as much as he could do. At the end of the year they were able to package him with Schneider for a guy (Lastings Milledge) who might actually turn out to be good.

Center Fielder Nook Logan is basically Corey Patterson without the power, but you have to have *somebody* on the team who can play center field, and he can play center field.

The Nationals are not poised to spring on the league like a pride of lions on a wildebeest. They have a lot of work to do, a lot of aging, make-do players filling in around a couple of young lions. But you have to start somewhere, and in the meantime, you have to give the fans something to root for. You can pick on the Nationals because they didn't really have any "whole" players, but their collection of half-players was in its own way very impressive.

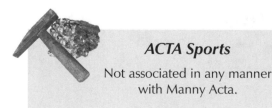

ACTA Sports

Not associated in any manner with Manny Acta.

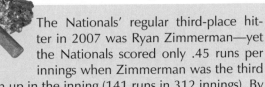

The Nationals' regular third-place hitter in 2007 was Ryan Zimmerman—yet the Nationals scored only .45 runs per innings when Zimmerman was the third man up in the inning (141 runs in 312 innings). By contrast, the Nationals scored

.49 runs per inning when Brian Schneider was the third man up

.64 runs per inning when Dmitri Young was the third man up

.55 runs per inning when Austin Kearns was the third man up

Ryan Zimmerman – 2007
Impact by Position in Inning

Position	Innings	Runs	Runs/Inning	Runs/RBI
Leading Off	133	63	.47	24/6
Batting Second	130	94	.72	26/14
Batting Third	312	141	.45	27/26
Batting Fourth	67	42	.63	7/13
Batting 5th or later	80	165	2.06	15/32

Over the last three years Austin Kearns has hit .188, .167 and .170 in clutch situations.

Austin Kearns
Clutch Hitting

Season	AB	H	2B	3B	HR	RBI	BB	SO	GIDP	Avg	OBP	Slg
2002	46	14	3	0	0	7	6	12	2	.304	.389	.370
2003	25	7	3	0	1	8	5	7	0	.280	.419	.520
2004	15	5	1	0	2	10	1	7	1	.333	.375	.800
2005	32	6	2	0	0	12	4	8	2	.188	.297	.250
2006	54	9	2	1	2	14	3	13	3	.167	.217	.352
2007	47	8	0	0	1	7	9	12	4	.170	.322	.234
Totals	219	49	11	1	6	58	28	59	12	.224	.323	.365

The Washington Nationals were the only team in the major leagues that did not have any spot in their batting order score or drive in 100 runs.

Washington Nationals– 2007
Runs and RBI by Batting Order Position

Pos	Players	Runs	RBI
1	Lopez (103g), Logan (28g)	84	57
2	Belliard (80g), Guzman (28g), Lopez (28g)	84	65
3	Zimmerman (162g)	99	91
4	Young (106g), Church (30g), Kearns (21g)	92	97
5	Kearns (126g), Church (22g)	79	77
6	Church (68g), Pena (22g), Schneider (19g)	71	79
7	Schneider (58g), Belliard (25g), Fick (23g)	60	76
8	Schneider (43g), Logan (38g), Flores (24g)	59	60
9	Chico (30g), Bergmann (21g), Bacsik (18g)	45	44
	Total	673	646

Dmitri Young in 2007 hit .824 on line drives to left field—28 for 34.

Dmitri Young – 2007
Hitting Analysis

Total						1B	2B	3B	HR
Ground Balls to Left	41	Outs 29	Hits 12	Average .293	Hit Type	10	2	0	0
Ground Balls to Center	63	Outs 44	Hits 19	Average .302	Hit Type	19	0	0	0
Ground Balls to Right	62	Outs 52	Hits 10	Average .161	Hit Type	8	2	0	0
Line Drives to Left	34	Outs 6	Hits 28	Average .824	Hit Type	20	8	0	0
Line Drives to Center	25	Outs 6	Hits 19	Average .760	Hit Type	13	6	0	0
Line Drives to Right	25	Outs 8	Hits 17	Average .680	Hit Type	14	3	0	0
Fly Balls to Left	60	Outs 42	Hits 18	Average .305	Hit Type	6	9	0	3
Fly Balls to Center	42	Outs 34	Hits 8	Average .200	Hit Type	3	4	0	1
Fly Balls to Right	36	Outs 20	Hits 16	Average .444	Hit Type	2	4	1	9
Total on Ground Balls	166	Outs 125	Hits 41	Average .247	Hit Type	37	4	0	0
Total on Line Drives	84	Outs 20	Hits 64	Average .762	Hit Type	47	17	0	0
Total on Fly Balls	138	Outs 96	Hits 42	Average .311	Hit Type	11	17	1	13
Total Hit to Left	135	Outs 77	Hits 58	Average .433	Hit Type	36	19	0	3
Total Hit to Center	130	Outs 84	Hits 46	Average .359	Hit Type	35	10	0	1
Total Hit to Right	123	Outs 80	Hits 43	Average .350	Hit Type	24	9	1	9
All Balls in Play	388	Outs 241	Hits 147	Average .382	Hit Type	95	38	1	13

What do you do with a guy like Dmitri Young? Dmitri usually batted cleanup for the 2007 Nationals—not an ideal choice in view of his .320 batting average but fairly limited power. I got to wondering whether the Nationals might be better off to bat him leadoff, since they don't really have a leadoff man, either. Dmitri's extreme lack of speed would make him a very unusual choice to lead off, of course, but it can be convincingly demonstrated that, in reality, speed is much less important in a good leadoff man than a good on-base percentage. Might it work better to lead off with Dmitri?

Apparently not. Look at the charts (below) of Dmitri's impact by position in the batting order. The data seems to leave little doubt that you're better off if Dmitri is the second or third man up in the inning.

Dmitri Young – 2005
Impact by Position in Inning

Position	Innings	Runs	Runs/Inning	Runs/RBI
Leading Off	95	40	.42	15/5
Batting Second	118	56	.47	10/5
Batting Third	128	86	.67	15/12
Batting Fourth	84	74	.88	11/20
Batting 5th or later	84	169	2.01	10/30

Dmitri Young – 2007
Impact by Position in Inning

Position	Innings	Runs	Runs/Inning	Runs/RBI
Leading Off	130	52	.40	18/3
Batting Second	97	51	.53	12/4
Batting Third	100	64	.64	11/14
Batting Fourth	123	93	.76	13/27
Batting 5th or later	58	118	2.03	3/26

Game Scores, invented by the author about twenty years ago, have somehow wormed their way past the guardians and become a sort of standard part of a baseball information set. A Game Score is a way of "scoring" a starting pitcher's performance on a zero-to-a-hundred scale, with the intention being that an average game should be about 50. Mike Webber got interested in what the overall distribution of Game Scores for starting pitchers vs. Wins for teams would look like, and produced the following chart:

Major Leagues – 2007
Performance by Quality of Start

Game Score	#	W	L	Pct.
80 to above	92	86	6	.935
70 to 79	378	308	70	.815
60 to 69	903	651	252	.721
50 to 59	1051	627	424	.597
40 to 49	982	453	529	.461
30 to 39	704	195	509	.277
20 to 29	485	87	398	.179
0 to 20	267	24	243	.090
50 and above	2424	1672	752	.690
Below 50	2438	759	1679	.311

Bell Curve?

Game Score	% of starts
80 to above	2%
70 to 79	8%
60 to 69	19%
50 to 59	22%
40 to 49	20%
30 to 39	14%
20 to 29	10%
0 to 20	5%

To left-handed batters, Nationals' ace Matthew Chico throws his slider seven times as often as his change.

To right-handed batters, he throws the changeup 57% more often than the slider.

Matt Chico – 2007
Pitch Type Analysis

Overall		
Total Pitches	2829	
Fastball	1682	59%
Curveball	132	5%
Changeup	495	17%
Slider	487	17%
Not Charted	33	1%

	Vs. RHB		Vs. LHB	
Total Pitches	2296		533	
Outs Recorded	399		102	
Fastball	1419	62%	263	49%
Curveball	88	4%	44	8%
Changeup	466	20%	29	5%
Slider	296	13%	191	36%
Not Charted	27	1%	6	1%

When It Seems Like Every Team in the League Is Over .500 except Yours

Saul Rivera has thrown nearly 50% more innings against winning teams than against losing teams during his two seasons in the big leagues. He's made the best of it by doing his best work against the stronger clubs – his career ERA against winning teams (2.75) is more than two runs lower than it is against losing teams (4.82).

Saul Rivera
Career Records Against Quality of Opposition

Opponent	G	IP	W	L	SO	BB	ERA
.500 - .599 teams	82	91.2	1	5	65	49	2.75
.400 - .499 teams	57	61.2	6	1	40	25	4.82

Medley

by Bill James

The fifteen or so articles in this book were culled from articles posted in the Bill James Online. There are many other articles there, most of which aren't included here because they're longwinded and boring. The articles here were written by me but were selected for this book by Greg Pierce of ACTA Sports. Greg tried to select articles that were interesting, for obvious reasons, and he tried to select articles that were not too long, because paper is a lot more expensive than electrons. Many of the articles in the online contain long charts listing data for hundreds of players. You can get by with that if you're not buying paper to print it on, but you can't do too much of it in book form.

While selecting these articles, Greg had a "second list" of articles that didn't quite make the cut, and he asked me to write a chapter for the Gold Mine suggesting the direction of these longer and more boring articles. (He was nice enough not to describe them that way, but if you choose the shorter and more interesting articles to publish, what's left?)

The articles published there have accumulated on my computer over the years, a few of them written as much as fifteen years ago. The idea of the Bill James Online is to give me a place to interact with my audience in real time. I haven't had that for quite a number of years, and articles have been building up on me, along with research waiting to be pulled together into reports. The article "Baseball's Best Player", for example, was written in December, 2003, in a context explained in the article's third paragraph:

There are many other articles there, most of which aren't included here because they're longwinded and boring.

Baseball's Best Player

Who is the best player in baseball? I don't mean who had the best year or who is having the best year, but just…who is the best player? Who was the best player in 1972? Who was the best player in 1935?

It is the most basic of baseball debates, the simplest and the most pervasive—and, I suppose because of that, it is a question rarely faced squarely in sabermetrics. It seems too simple to discuss. We are more interested in the shadings of value between Garrett Anderson and Mike Cameron, between Jacques Jones and Juan Pierre, between Quinton McCracken and Bobby Estalella, than in bringing our analytical arms to bear on the fairly obvious.

This question forced its way into my conscious mind as a consequence of the Red Sox' failed efforts, postseason 2003, to secure the very valuable services of Alex Rodriguez. It was routinely written and said, as we went after Alex, that Nomar was a great player too, but A-Rod was the best player in baseball. But is he really? Is A-Rod actually a better player than Barry Bonds? Over what time frame? If you look at the last two years, the last three years, the last four, would you really rather have had A-Rod on the field, rather than Bonds?

This article goes on, through what seem like hundreds of pages but are actually only 32, to establish a multi-year method, based on Win Shares, to determine who the best player in baseball was at the end of any season, and then to chart the results—not only number one but the top five contenders—for each season since 1901. Eventually it reaches the conclusion that A-Rod

1) never was actually the best player in baseball, and
2) probably never would be, either.

The article argues or concludes or calculates, however you want to say it, that the best player in baseball in the years just before 2003 had obviously been Barry Bonds, with A-Rod second, and then gratuitously observes that, looking forward, the mantle of baseball's best player was more likely to pass to Albert Pujols than to A-Rod. Bonds then had *another* sensational year in 2004—that was the year he drew 232 walks and had a .609 on-base percentage, .812 slugging—retaining his title as baseball's best player for one more year. And the gratuitous prediction proved to be true, or at least has proved true so far: the title of baseball's best player, as determined by the method outlined in that article, did pass from Bonds to Pujols, and is retained by Pujols to this day. Post-2007 the top five are:

1. Albert Pujols
2. Alex Rodriguez
3. David Wright
4. Ichiro Suzuki
5. (Tie) Carlos Beltran and David Ortiz

After Pujols the title of baseball's best player seems likely to pass to David Wright. That, however, is drifting into the area covered by another, much shorter article:

Baseball's Best Player
Mirror View

This article is a companion piece to the article, "Baseball's Best Player." Suppose that we reversed the assumptions of that article, and rated players by the same method, but walking *backward in time, rather than forward. What we would then be asking is not "Who had established himself as the best player in baseball in 1930?" but rather, "Looking forward from 1930, who would be the best player in baseball?"*

The question occurs: is one list more legitimate than the other? It is an interesting philosophical question. Time moves in only one direction, which is forward, and thus our view of time looks in only one direction, which is backward. In retrospect, however, we can look backward or forward with equal ease from a point in the past; 1932 is as close to 1935 as it is to 1929. By one method, Jimmie Foxx was never the best player in baseball—but by the other method, he was. So was he or wasn't he?

It seems to me that he was—or, more accurately, that it is difficult to argue logically that he wasn't. Looked at in one way, Lou Gehrig was the best player of the years 1932-1935; looked at in another way, it was Foxx. One is no more accurate than the other.

That's not actually the first three paragraphs of the article; I gave you the first paragraph and then borrowed two paragraphs from later in the piece. Another article that Greg wanted me to give you a little bit of was an article about Bert Blyleven. I think that a version of this article may have been published before somewhere else...not sure where, but probably a few of you have seen it before:

The Bert Blyleven Problem

I. Set Up

A couple of years ago I did a television show which consisted on the air of being yelled at by Alan Dershowitz, which wasn't fun, but off the air included sitting in a room for eight hours with Steve Garvey and Dave Parker and Bill Lee and a couple of other guys, which was a lot of fun. Lee and Parker and Garvey spent an hour or more telling stories about the Nasty Dutchman, many of which I can't repeat.

For years I have been fascinated by the Bert Blyleven problem, and I have long wanted to do a definitive study of the issue. The Bert Blyleven problem, simply stated, is that Blyleven's won-lost record does not jibe with his innings pitched and ERA. Blyleven pitched just short of 5,000 innings in his career, with a 3.31 ERA. Other pitchers with comparable combinations won 300 games, 310, 320. Blyleven didn't.

This shortfall is well known, and Bert Blyleven has been left out of the Hall of Fame because of it. Life isn't always fair. Other pitchers with 280 wins, and some with 220 wins, and some with less, have made the Hall of Fame—and with the same ERA. Alright; life's a bitch.

Bert Blyleven is an intriguing figure because he is the most conspicuous victim of what most of us regard as a malicious fiction. You ask any baseball writer from Blyleven's era why Bert hasn't been bronzed, and the guy will tell you "He wasn't a winner. His team scored 3 runs, he gave up 4. They scored 1, he gave up 2. He had good numbers, but he didn't win the tough games."

Most of us don't believe that this ability to win the close games really exists, and many of us kind of resent Blyleven being discriminated against because he fails a bullshit test. Still, in theory, Bert's detractors could be on to something. Suppose that you have two pitchers. One, whom we will call Ferguson Winner, loses a game 6-0, but wins six others 1-0, 2-1, 3-2, 4-3, 5-4 and 6-5. The other, whom we will call Bert Loser, wins a game 6-0, but loses six others by the same scores (1-0, 2-1, etc.)

The run support for both pitchers is exactly the same: 21 runs in 7 games. Their runs allowed are exactly the same: 21 runs in 7 games. The average is the same; the distribution of the runs is the same. But Ferguson has gone 6-1 and Bert has gone 1-6, because Ferguson has matched his effort to the runs he has to work with. My point is, there could be something there that isn't measured by run support and isn't measured by runs allowed. We'll call it the ability to match.

The article goes on, through eighteen pages of what I must say in all modesty is tedious detail, to examine Blyleven's career record game by game (with the help of Retrosheet), attempting to determine whether there is any validity to the anti-Blylevian argument. The article has eleven sections…here, I'll give you a sentence or two from each section:

II. The Method

Suppose that we form a group of pitchers who are similar to Blyleven in terms of games started, innings pitched and ERA, but different from Blyleven in terms of wins and losses.

III. Flotsam

Before giving you the straight results, let me first report on one rather stunning data point from the study.

When given three runs to work with—not three or more but three exactly—Don Sutton had a career won-lost record of 52-33, and his teams had a won-lost record of 65-51.

When given three runs to work with, Bert Blyleven had a career won-lost record of 29-48, and his teams had a career record of 35-62.

IV. Actual Results of the Study

Blyleven's relatively poor won-lost records are primarily a result of poor offensive support. He was below the group average in terms of his ability to match the effort of the opposing pitcher, and this did cost him a few games over the course of his career—somewhere between 7 and 11 games. But most of the discrepancy is caused by sub-standard offensive support.

V. Data Overkill

The charts following (not shown here; following in the original article) give the number of times that each pitcher in the study was given each number of runs to work with, the pitcher's individual won-lost record and ERA in those games, and the pitcher's team's won-lost record in those games.

VI. A Couple of Methods

I developed a couple of methods to analyze this data, one of which I will report on and one of which I will bury. I developed a method to create what I call an "effective runs allowed rate", or "win based runs allowed rate."

VII. Great Seasons

The best season by any of these pitchers, obviously, was Steve Carlton's 1972 season. I credit Carlton that season with a run-neutral winning percentage of .846, and with an effective runs allowed rate of 2.80. The run-neutral winning percentage is the best of any of these pitchers in any season; the 2.80 effective runs allowed rate is second, behind Don Sutton's 2.77 in 1980.

VIII. Game Scores

Defining a "Cheap Win" as any win in which the pitcher had a Game Score under 50 and a "Tough Loss" as any loss in which the pitcher had a Game Score over 50, Blyleven had 26 Cheap Wins and 109 Tough Losses.

IX. Bullpen Support

There were a couple of issues I didn't get into here, which were bullpen support and runs scored after the pitcher left the game. I didn't get into these because
a) I don't have the technical sophistication to work with box scores that way, and
b) I'm not sure how it should be done anyway.

X. One-Run Games

One-run games have an obvious bearing on this study. Remember the what-if example I gave in part one of this admittedly too long study?

XI. Conclusion

Although Blyleven's critics have made too much of his disappointing won-lost record, there is something there. Blyleven did not do an A+ job of matching his effort to the runs that he had to work with.

However, this probably should not be keeping him out of the Hall of Fame. Blyleven was 344 runs better than an average pitcher. The largest penalty that we could reasonably charge him for failing to match his best games with the games that he had a chance to win would be about 83 runs.

The Blyleven article discusses a very narrow issue, and proposes methodology only so far as is necessary to drill directly toward that issue. The other article starts with a reasonably narrow issue—whether A-Rod can accurately be described as the best player in baseball—and proposes a general method to study the issue. The article below is purely intended to introduce a method—or actually, two methods, one for hitters and one for pitchers—which are of very general use:

Season Scores

Before we get started here, let me ask you a few random questions, and I'll ask you to pull out an Encyclopedia or whatever source you use to evaluate these things. What was the best season of Stan Musial's career? What was the best season of Jerry Remy's career, or Phil Rizzuto's, or Roberto Alomar's, or Kevin Appier's, or Tony Armas', or Rich Aurilia's?

What were the three best seasons by hitters in the 1920s? The 1950s? The 1970s? What were the three best seasons by pitchers in the 1930s? The 1960s? The 1990s?

OK, I have this system for Season Scores. It's hard to explain the need for this system, probably because there isn't any real need for this system; the world is already overrun with unmemorable statistical rating systems, and this is just another one.

Well, it's useful to me, OK? I like it. This came about, sometime in the late 1990s, because I needed a system to quickly and easily identify the best season by a pitcher within a group of seasons. There's no easy reference here. The sort of "technical" evaluation is, perhaps, Runs Saved Against Average, or Wins Above Average, or Win Shares…something like that. But let's take these two seasons:

Pitcher, Season	*G*	*IP*	*W - L*	*Pct.*	*SO*	*BB*	*ERA*
Joe Coleman, 1971	*40*	*280*	*20 - 9*	*.690*	*236*	*96*	*3.15*
Brad Radke, 1996	*35*	*232*	*11 - 16*	*.407*	*148*	*57*	*4.46*

If you adjust for everything you are supposed to adjust for, Radke's season is actually better than Coleman's. The American League ERA was 3.46 in 1971, 4.99 in 1996, so Radke was actually further below the league ERA than Coleman was, either in raw totals or as a percentage. Tiger Stadium in '71 had a Park Run Factor of .91, whereas Minnesota in '96 was 1.08, so if you adjust for that, Radke is actually much better.

That statistics do not always mean what they seem to mean at a glance is a core tenet of sabermetrics, so I'm certainly not denying that. On the other hand, you have to admit: 20-9 with a 3.15 ERA and 236 strikeouts is a hell of a lot better than 11-16 with a 4.46 ERA and 148 strikeouts. Which guy do you want on your fantasy team next year: the guy who goes 20-9 with 236 strikeouts and a 3.15 ERA, or the guy who goes 11-16 with a 4.46 ERA and 148 strikeouts?

There has to be some way to "score" seasons based not exactly on how they are but on how they are independent of context. Not everybody chooses to adjust for everything, you know. If you adjust for everything you can adjust for, Boog Powell was no doubt a better hitter than Jim Bottomley. Nonetheless, Bottomley is in the Hall of Fame, and Powell isn't.

I was very happy to be able to explain that method to my audience (in Bill James Online), because I use that method all the time, but since I had never introduced it to the public I had to "write around" it, which was awkward. It's not something that is naturally done in a book, because it's technical, and very few people actually care. Years ago, in the *Baseball Abstracts*, I would have to spend 40 or 50 pages every book explaining the intricate details of some new statistical system, which I always hated to do because it's impossible to make that entertaining, and most people don't care, anyway; 90% of the audience would be just as happy if you would skip that stuff. Bill James Online allows us to have our cake and eat it, too; we can explain the ugly details of the method in the online, where you can go see it if you really care, but it doesn't jump out front and center like it does in a book.

Speaking of the *Abstracts*, the issue discussed in the study below dates back to those days. This is a six-part article, so, as I did with the Blyleven study, I'll give you a sentence or two from each of the six parts:

Size and Durability

I. Posing the Problem

This article has its origins in a television interview that Joe Morgan gave in September of 1980, when he was playing for the Houston Astros. Morgan had had a very disappointing season, entering September with 6 home runs and a .232 batting average, but he was rallying strongly in September. Asked about this in the TV interview, Morgan said, "I don't think that I've ever had a bad September."

"I think we have finally found Joe's weakness," I wrote in the 1981 Baseball Abstract. "The man has no memory." Checking the record books, I found that Morgan had had... well, quite a number of very bad Septembers indeed. Whether in a pennant race or not, Morgan had slumped in September almost every season of his career before 1980, and I pointed this out with perhaps undue relish. But then I added the words "as one would expect a small player to do." Or something like that...I'm not sure what my exact words were. Anyway, whatever I added was careless, and Larry Taylor called me on it. "I don't know of any actual evidence that small players wear down late in the year," Larry wrote. "Do you?"

OK, fast forward to May of 2007. I'm working for the Red Sox now, and there's a college player that I would like to draft, but we have no scouting report on him. He's not a big guy; he's like 5-10 and 170. We ask the area scout about him, and the scout says, "Yeah, I like him, too, but I was just worried that, with his size, he might get ground down by the long season in the pros."

The time has come to do a real study of this issue.

II. Cutting to the Chase

In short, there is no evidence whatsoever that small players wear down late in the season. A relatively large, careful and systematic study of this issue shows that small players have no more tendency to fade late in the season, on average, than do large players or medium-sized players.

III. The Data

I began by generating a list of the 1000 major league players with the most plate appearances in the years 1957-2006. Using the Complete Baseball Encyclopedia from Lee Sinins, I also listed each player's height and weight. Copying this data into a spreadsheet, I then sorted the players 1 through 1000 in terms of height and then weight, and combined the two into one number, "size". The largest players in the group were Frank Howard, Tony Clark, Frank Thomas and Dave Parker; the smallest were Albie Pearson, Freddie Patek, Joey Cora and Vic Davalillo.

I then chose three groups of players, 50 players in each group:
• the fifty largest players,
• the fifty smallest players, and
• fifty guys right in the middle.

As you no doubt know, listed playing weights for baseball players are less reliable than Tony Soprano's tax returns. In my view, this is not a serious problem for this study. The inaccuracy of listed weights would be a problem for us in this study if it prevented us from making accurate lists of large and small players. But look at the lists. No one who has seen them play would doubt that Mark McGwire, Cecil Fielder, David Ortiz, Boog Powell and Donn Clendenon constitute a list of large baseball players, or that Tim Raines, Joe Morgan, Wayne Tolleson, Omar Vizquel and Luis Polonia are small baseball players. As long as we get a list of large players and a list of small players, there's no problem because that's all we're trying to do with the listed heights and weights.

IV. Late Season/Early Season Playing Time

Just looking casually at the data, you can see that the OPS of the large players declines 32 points between June and September (from .834 to .802), while the OPS of the small players declines by only 11 points (from .699 to .688). This would be enough to cause us immediately to suspect that the proposition that small players fade late in the season is not on solid ground.

V. Performance Patterns

This is a short summary of the players who tended to perform best late in the season and early in the season.

Best Late-Season performer (relative to Overall Performance):

Jerry Browne. Browne, a small second baseman from the 1980s, had a career batting average in April of .214, on-base percentage of .290, slugging percentage of .251—this in 120 games, 400+ at bats. As the season went on, however, he gradually warmed up, incrasing his OPS from .541 in April to .647 in May, .727 in June, .754 in July, and .786 in August. In 155 career games in August Browne hit .307 with 8 homers, 51 RBI.

Best Early-Season performer (relative to Overall Performance):

Henry Rodriguez. Henry Rodriguez was the left-handed hitting outfielder, 6-1, 180 pounds, who came out of nowhere to hit 36 homers, drive in 103 for Montreal in 1995. He was a regular for three years after that, hitting 26-31 homers a year and driving in 83-87 runs a year, but his career was shortened by really awful strikeout/walk ratios.

Rodriguez' career slugging percentage was:

.567 in April (32 homers in 464 at bats)
.542 in May
.451 in June
.468 in July
.457 in August
.386 in September

He also gradually lost playing time, dropping from 642 total at bats in May to 370 in September, not because he was hurt but because he just was not playing well, consistently, late in the year.

VI. Quibbles and Objections

Suppose that the scout who made the remark which triggered this research was a researcher and wanted to defend his position...what could he say?

One could argue that the "small players fading" effect is screened out by the minor leagues. "Yes," he could say, "major league players are not going to fade out because the season is too long for them, but most of the players we sign do not become major league players. Most of them fail short of the major leagues for one reason or another. This is one of the reasons that players never get to the majors."

This could be true; I can't say for certain that it isn't.

Bill James Online allows us to have our cake and eat it, too; we can explain the ugly details of the method in the online, where you can go see it if you really care, but it doesn't jump out front and center like it does in a book.

That's serious sabermetric research, using the tools of social scientists to examine an issue of real consequence to major league teams. The article below, on the other hand, is just kind of kicking back and blowing smoke:

The 100 Greatest Relief Seasons of All Time And the Ten Greatest Relievers

There is no deep thenkin' underlying this article, and I make no claims to the accuracy of my method. I am more or less just messing around with the data, killing a quiet Saturday. But I have this method for scoring seasons—the Season Scores method; I must have introduced it here somewhere.

So I was wondering what the greatest seasons by a reliever were and where Dan Quisenberry would fit into the grand scheme of things, and I thought…well, why don't I pull out the list and see what we have as a starting point for the discussion? Somebody wants to argue that my list isn't right, feel free; I might even agree with you. But this is what the system says:

1. Dick Radatz, 1964 *(16-9, 29 saves, 181 strikeouts and a 2.29 ERA in 79 games, 157 innings. Season score: 312.) Radatz, who was called "The Monster" because at that time the left field wall in Fenway was just called the left field wall, was a 6-foot-6, 265-pound right-hander with an intimidating fastball. There had been hard-throwing relievers before Radatz—notably Ryne Duren—but Radatz may have been the first pitcher to discover what you could do as a reliever if you just threw as hard as you could for an inning or two. They rode him so hard that it seems kind of crazy in retrospect, but it didn't seem to affect him at the time, and logically, it's a little hard to explain how this didn't affect him at the time but ruined his career sometime over the winter. Anyway, he struck out 181 batters, won 16 games and saved 29 others, although he wasn't particularly used in save situations—saves weren't even an official stat then, and "saving games" didn't become the relief pitcher's sole function until more than ten years after the stat became official.*

2. Dennis Eckersley, 1992 *(7-1, 51 saves, 1.91 ERA, 93-11 K/W in 80 innings. Season score: 296.) Eckersley, of course, was the 1992 MVP and Cy Young Award winner, whereas Radatz was 11th in the MVP voting (playing for a bad team) and was not among the three pitchers mentioned in 1964 Cy Young voting. At the same time, it is not immediately apparent that Eckersley was more valuable than Radatz. Radatz pitched twice as many innings, essentially, and wasn't substantially less effective. (Eckersley's ERA was 48% of the league norm, in a pitcher's park; Radatz' was 63% of the norm, in a hitter's park.)*

3. Dick Radatz, 1963 *(66 games, 132 innings, 15-6 with 1.98 ERA, 25 saves. Season Score: 296.)*

4. John (Ducks Unlimited) Wetteland, 1993 *(70 games, 85 innings, 9-3 with 1.37 ERA, 43 saves. Season Score; 286.)*

5. John Hiller, 1973 *(65 games, 124 innings, 10-5 with 1.44 ERA, 38 saves. Season Score: 282.) His 38 saves were a record at the time, and up until 1983. Hiller had a heart attack on the mound in…was it '70 or '71? He was a good pitcher every year from '72 to '76.*

6. Keith Foulke, 2003 *(72 games, 86 innings, 9-1 with 2.08 ERA, 46 Saves. Season Score: 281.)*

7. Eric Gagne, 2002 *(77 games, 82 innings, 4-1 with 1.97 ERA, 52 Saves. Season Score: 279.)*

8. Phil Regan, 1966 *(65 games, 117 innings, 14-1 with 1.62 ERA, 21 Saves. Season Score: 277.) Regan was nicknamed "The Vulture" for picking up wins from departed starting pitchers.*

9. Eric Gagne, 2003 *(77 games, 82 innings, 2-3 with 1.20 ERA, 55 Saves. Season Score: 276.) The Cy Young season among Gagne's three super seasons, 2002-2004. The only pitchers listed more than once among the top 25 are Eckersley (1990 and '92), Radatz ('63-'64) and Gagne (2002 through 2004.)*

10. Jim Kern, 1979 *(71 games, 143 innings, 13-5 with 1.57 ERA, 29 Saves. Season Score: 275.) Kern was really the last closer used in what could be called the Dick Radatz usage pattern.*

By the way, the worst season ever by a reliever, not counting John Rocker's magazine interviews and Jose Mesa's bad dates, was by Dick Welteroth of the Washington Senators in 1949. Welteroth pitched 52 times including two starts, finishing 2-5 with 2 saves and a 7.39 ERA. He struck out 37 hitters and walked 89, also giving up 107 hits in 95 innings—more than two baserunners per inning. Season Score: -89.

The article goes on to list 90 more seasons by relievers, and then to try to derive a list of the greatest career relief pitchers from the list of season's performance. It reaches the conclusion, essentially, that the greatest reliever of all time is either Mariano Rivera or Trevor Hoffman, and between those two it is too close to call.

All of the articles introduced so far are data-driven in one way or another. The article below, however, has no data. It proposes an idea, an approach to a problem involving co-operation by dozens or hundreds of people, but with no data as a starting point. The article is written as a Q & A between me and myself. Crazy people are allowed to do that:

Directly Observed Value
Standing Sabermetrics on its head to see what falls out of its pockets

Alright, I'm assuming that we probably can't do this this year (2008), because we won't have time to organize it before the season starts, but for next year….

What if we converted the MVP argument from an after-the-fact review into a season-long chase? You see what I'm getting at here? The way we do it now, we go to games, we keep stats, we follow the players. When the season is over, or nearly over, we sit down, look at what we have, and try to figure out who the MVP must have been.

What if, instead, we keep track of value as it happens?

How would we do that?

By a system of organized observation.

Aren't statistics just a system of organized observation?

Statistics are a system of organized observation of events. This would be a system of organized observation of value.

Isn't the value in the events?

Events of entirely unlike value are recorded in the statistics as equals. Suppose that the game is 12-1 in the eighth inning, nobody on, a ground ball is hit to the second baseman and he flips to first. This is entered in the statistics as an assist by the second baseman. Suppose that the game is 4-3 in the ninth, men on second and third, the batter hits a rocket toward right but the second baseman knocks it down, scrambles to his feet and gets the out at first. This also is entered in the statistics as an assist by the second baseman. The statistical observation—the "event"—is the same. But the value is different by a margin of a thousand to one.

So you're keeping track of…key defensive plays?

No, I'm proposing that we keep track of value—observed value. Directly observed value.

How do we keep track of directly observed value?

I thought you'd never ask. OK, here's what we do. We have somebody designated to cover every game…hopefully somebody at the game, but in any case somebody very carefully watching the game.

Like an official scorer?

Sort of. Very much like an official scorer, except that he's not official and he's not exactly a scorer.

He's an unofficial non-scorer.

He's an unofficial evaluator, designated by us…designated by the DOV project. We'll call him a scorer, although he's not really keeping score.

And his job is…?

His job is to make an on-the-scene evaluation of each player's contribution to victory, by an organized system of rules designed to ensure fair treatment for every game, every player, and every type of contribution to victory.

In the spring of 2004, after the Red Sox lost the American League pennant because Grady Little failed to notice that Pedro Martinez was lobbing up meatballs, there was a lot of talk about the Curse of the Bambino. It seems quaint, in retrospect, and I've never been happier to see my research rendered irrelevant by the march of events, but anyway, this article was written in March, 2004:

Curses

The majority of the "breaks" went to the Boston team, which thus again profited by the singular "luck" which has followed the Boston teams in World's Series to such good effect.

1919 Reach Guide, page 158
(Reviewing the 1918 World Series)

Premise

I was asked, on air, about the Curse of the Bambino, which is curiously absent from my list of favorite discussion topics. There is no Curse of the Bambino, of course, and I gave what I hoped was a logical response: the Red Sox have not been lucky in World Series play (since 1918), but then, the difference between the two teams—New York 26, Boston 0—is not all luck, nor is it mostly luck. The Yankees have had about 50 seasons since 1920 when they could have won the World Series; the Red Sox have had about five or six. The Red Sox have not been lucky in their five or six chances, yes, but one need not invoke heavy karma to explain the difference.

There are ubiquitous claims and allegations that such and such a team or such and such a manager has/have fallen short of their fair share of post-season success. The Atlanta Braves of the last fifteen years are perceived as having won far fewer championships than they should have won. The Cubs, of course, have a curse of their own, and the Indians claim one as well. Billy Beane's A's regard October as their personal crumple zone.

Whitey Herzog, in You're Missin' a Great Game, wrote that "All my life, I've been good enough to get my teams close. That was true when I was a kid, and it was truer still when I coached and managed. But the strangest things would happen once I got there. You'd have made money betting on Herzog teams over the long haul. But if you'd put your money on some horrible break happening at the last minute, you could've retired early."

The Dodgers of the 1940s and 50s, Da Bums, were in their day the poster boys of season-ending hard luck. The Mariners of the 1990s, the Braves of the 1950s, and the Tigers of the 1960s are among the many teams cited—often by me—as under-achieving in close pennant races or in the post season.

How can all these claims be true? Have the Yankees gotten everybody's luck? Or is it merely that the Yankees have just been that much better than everybody else, that they have won 26 World Championships since the Boston's last one mostly by dumb skill? How can one tell? How can one sort out these competing claims to be Dame Fortune's special whipping boy?

That article has five sections, but in this case I will have to leave you with the questions, since I don't see any way to condense or excerpt the material and make sense of it. The article concludes that the unluckiest teams, in terms of not winning championships that they probably should have won, have been:

1. The Cubs
2. The Giants
3. The Cleveland Indians

Although the Dodgers were equally unlucky if you just count the Brooklyn Dodgers; they've done well since moving to LA, but they were very unlucky in Brooklyn. Greg Pierce probably picked this article for me to tell you about because he's a Cubs fan, but otherwise, we don't talk about that no more.

The article below, the last one that I will introduce for you here, grew out of a chance observation, flipping through old record books:

Don Rush and Bob Cardwell

Bob Rush in 1956 and Don Cardwell in 1965 both finished the season with won-lost records of 13-10, a not particularly notable fact in that there are 67 pitchers in baseball history (through 2006) who finished their season 13-10. Both Rush and Cardwell, however, pitched 240 innings. Each pitcher allowed 101 runs, which in each case included 85 earned runs, giving each of them a 3.19 ERA. Rush struck out 104 and walked 59; Cardwell struck out 107 and walked 59.

Let us say for the sake of argument that these are the two most-similar seasons by pitchers in baseball history, which I don't know that that's true, but we'll debate that later. When you look closely at Rush and Cardwell, you find any number of secondary or incidental similarities.

Back to the time when I first became a baseball fan in 1961, I have always been fascinated by players who had very similar statistics for a season or a career. In the early 1980s I introduced a method to "score" the similarity between any two seasons or two careers. The method isn't important and I don't really remember what it was; what was significant was not the method but the realization that, even though "similarity" is essentially a subjective concept, we could nonetheless define it and measure it, so long as we were willing to accept that our definition and our measurement were somewhat arbitrary.

This article is not about players who are essentially similar or profoundly similar. This is about random matches between pitcher's seasons which look a lot alike:

Tommy Bond, 1877, and Tommy Bond, 1878

Pitcher	G	IP	W	-	L	Pct	H	SO	BB	ERA
1877	58	521.0	40	-	17	.702	530	170	36	2.11
1878	59	532.2	40	-	19	.678	571	182	33	2.06

My similarity score for these two seasons is only 932, as opposed to 980 for Rush and Cardwell, but the differences magnify with the innings, and Bond's consistency is extraordinary for a pitcher pitching 500+ innings.

Although the Dodgers were equally unlucky if you just count the Brooklyn Dodgers; they've done well since moving to LA, but they were very unlucky in Brooklyn.

Bob Caruthers, 1886, and Pete Conway, 1888

Pitcher	G	IP	W - L	Pct	H	SO	BB	ERA
Caruthers	44	387.1	30 - 14	.682	323	166	86	2.32
Conway	45	391.0	30 - 14	.682	315	176	57	2.26

Similarity: 950. Caruthers was 22 years old at the time; Conway, 21. Caruthers also played the outfield that year, and hit .334. Conway didn't play a position that year—he had played some in the outfield earlier in his career—but hit .275 with 3 homers, 23 RBI.

Tiny Bonham, 1940, and Mel Stottlemyre, 1964

Pitcher	G	IP	W - L	Pct	H	SO	BB	ERA
Bonham	12	99.0	9 - 3	.750	83	37	13	1.91
Stottlemyre	13	96.0	9 - 3	.750	77	49	35	2.06

Similarity: 953. Both rookies, both Yankees. Mel Stottlemyre, called up when the Yankees were floundering in August, 1964, arrived just in time to save the Yankees' bacon in 1964. Bonham, called up in August, 1940, got there too late to save the Yankees in 1940.

Joe Dobson, 1947, and Sal Maglie, 1952

Pitcher	G	IP	W - L	Pct	H	SO	BB	ERA
Dobson	33	229.0	18 - 8	.692	203	110	73	2.95
Maglie	35	216.0	18 - 8	.692	199	112	75	2.92

Similarity: 980. Dobson's nickname was "Burrhead". Maglie's was "The Barber".

Johnny Sain, 1947, and Joaquin Andujar, 1985

Pitcher	G	IP	W - L	Pct	H	SO	BB	ERA
Sain	38	266.0	21 - 12	.636	265	132	79	3.52
Andujar	38	269.2	21 - 12	.636	265	112	82	3.40

Similarity: 965. Somehow, it just struck me as funny to pair Joaquin Andujar with anyone named "Sain". You had to know Joaquin to get the joke.

Johnny Podres, 1961, and Cliff Lee, 2005

Pitcher	G	IP	W - L	Pct	H	SO	BB	ERA
Podres	32	183.0	18 - 5	.783	192	124	51	3.74
Lee	32	202.0	18 - 5	.783	194	143	52	3.79

Similarity: 968.

Whitey Ford, 1963, and Frank Viola, 1987

Pitcher	G	IP	W - L	Pct	H	SO	BB	ERA
Ford	38	269.0	24 - 7	.774	240	189	56	2.74
Viola	35	255.1	24 - 7	.774	236	193	54	2.64

Similarity: 967. Both veteran left-handers of exceptional quality. Matches this good are common among pitchers who win 12-15 games, but not common among pitchers of Cy Young quality.

Tom Henke, 1980, and Akinori Otsuka, 2006

Pitcher	G	IP	W - L	Pct	H	SO	BB	ERA	Saves
Henke	61	74.2	2 - 4	.333	58	75	19	2.17	32
Otsuka	63	59.2	2 - 4	.333	53	47	11	2.11	32

Bert Blyleven, 1984, and Roy Halladay, 2002

Pitcher	G	IP	W - L	Pct	H	SO	BB	ERA
Blyleven	33	245.0	19 - 7	.731	204	170	74	2.87
Halladay	34	239.1	19 - 7	.731	223	168	62	2.93

Similarity: 968. Watch out, Roy; they're going to screw you in the Hall of Fame voting.

Oil Can Boyd, 1984, and Kris Benson, 2004

Pitcher	G	IP	W	-	L	Pct	H	SO	BB	ERA
Boyd	29	197.2	12	-	12	.500	207	134	53	4.37
Benson	31	200.1	12	-	12	.500	202	134	61	4.31

Similarity: 980. Think about it. Boyd was a colorful, eccentric character who had a famous emotional melt-down after being left off the All-Star team in 1986. Benson is more famous for his wife's hooters than for his pitching.

Bill Gullickson, 1986, and Tom Browning, 1989

Pitcher	G	IP	W	-	L	Pct	H	SO	BB	ERA
Gullickson	37	244.2	15	-	12	.556	245	121	60	3.38
Browning	37	249.2	15	-	12	.556	241	118	64	3.39

Similarity: 988. The measured similarity of these two seasons (988) is even higher than that of Rush and Cardwell. Gullickson and Browning both pitched for the Reds at the time of these two very-similar seasons. Gullickson had other seasons in which he was 20-9, 14-13, 14-12 and 10-14. Browning had other seasons of 20-9, 14-13, 14-14 and 10-13.

Roger Clemens, 1998, and Johan Santana, 2004

Pitcher	G	IP	W	-	L	Pct	H	SO	BB	ERA
Clemens	33	234.2	20	-	6	.769	169	271	88	2.65
Santana	34	228.0	20	-	6	.769	156	265	54	2.61

Similarity: 946. Perhaps the best-matched Cy Young seasons. (Whitey Ford would have won the American League Cy Young Award in 1963 had there been such an award.) In truth, Clemens and Santana could hardly be less similar as pitchers.

Matt Clement, 2002, and Kerry Wood, 2002

Pitcher	G	IP	W	-	L	Pct	H	SO	BB	ERA
Clement	32	205.0	12	-	11	.522	162	215	85	3.60
Wood	33	213.2	12	-	11	.522	169	217	97	3.66

Similarity: 973. Teammates. Nolan Ryan, 1988, was also very similar.

The original article is just like that, except that it has about a hundred sets of matching seasons rather than 13, and there's a lot of specious pseudo-philosophical rambling about accidental, profound and defining similarities.

The full text of these articles, and many more like them, can be found in the Bill James Online (www.billjamesonline.com). The Gold Mine is intended to be an annual book, publishing annual selections from the best of Bill James Online, although I suppose that how many annuals we will do will depend on how many of you buy the book.

Thanks for reading.

The Gold Mine is intended to be an annual book, publishing annual selections from the best of Bill James Online, although I suppose that how many annuals we will do will depend on how many of you buy the book.